**Disjunctivism**

Selected from EGLI

**MIT Readers in Contemporary Philosophy**

*Persistence: Contemporary Readings*, Sally Haslanger and Roxanne Marie Kurtz, eds. (2006)

*Disjunctivism: Contemporary Readings*, Alex Byrne and Heather Logue, eds. (2009)

# Disjunctivism

**Contemporary Readings**

edited by Alex Byrne and Heather Logue

The MIT Press
Cambridge, Massachusetts
London, England

MIT Press books may be purchased at special quantity discounts for business or sales promotional use. For information, please e-mail special_sales@mitpress.mit.edu or write to Special Sales Department, The MIT Press, 55 Hayward Street, Cambridge, MA 02142.

This book was set in Stone Serif and Stone Sans on 3B2 by Asco Typesetters, Hong Kong, and was printed and bound in the United States of America.

Library of Congress Cataloging-in-Publication Data

Disjunctivism : contemporary readings / edited by Alex Byrne and Heather Logue.
    p.  cm.—(MIT readers in contemporary philosophy)
Includes bibliographical references and index.
ISBN 978-0-262-02655-0 (hardcover : alk. paper)—ISBN 978-0-262-52490-2 (pbk. : alk. paper)
1. Perception (Philosophy). I. Byrne, Alex, 1960–. II. Logue, Heather, 1979–.
B828.45.D56  2009
121'.34—dc22                                            2008027497

10  9  8  7  6  5  4  3  2  1

# Contents

**Introduction**    vii
Alex Byrne and Heather Logue

**1   Visual Experiences**    1
J. M. Hinton

**2   Selections from *Experiences***    13
J. M. Hinton

**3   Perception, Vision, and Causation**    33
Paul Snowdon

**4   The Objects of Perceptual Experience**    49
Paul Snowdon

**5   Selections from "Criteria, Defeasibility, and Knowledge"**    75
John McDowell

**6   The Reality of Appearances**    91
M. G. F. Martin

**7   Arguments from Illusion**    117
Jonathan Dancy

**8   The Idea of Experience**    137
Alan Millar

**9   Selections from *Perception***    153
Howard Robinson

**10   Selections from *The Problem of Perception***    167
A. D. Smith

**11   The Theory of Appearing Defended**    181
Harold Langsam

**12   The Obscure Object of Hallucination   207**
Mark Johnston

**13   The Limits of Self-Awareness   271**
M. G. F. Martin

Bibliography   319
Contributors   327
Index   329

# Introduction

## Alex Byrne and Heather Logue

The philosophy of perception has been undergoing something of a resurgence recently, enlivened by fresh positions and arguments. One central debate concerns the status of perception as intentional or representational (see many of the essays in Crane 1992, Gunther 2003, Gendler and Hawthorne 2006). Another (related) central debate concerns the disjunctive theory of perception, the present topic. This book collects together work on disjunctivism, from its beginnings in the 1960s to a few years ago, that has played a significant role in the development of the theory and its rivals; a comprehensive bibliography follows these selections. We hope this book will be something of a companion volume to *Disjunctivism: Perception, Action, Knowledge* (Haddock and Macpherson 2008b), a collection of new essays on disjunctivism.

## 1 What Is Disjunctivism?

Imagine that you are looking at an ordinary lemon in good light. Your vision is good: you see the lemon, and it looks yellow and ovoid. Now suppose that, unbeknownst to you, some minor deity removes the lemon, while preserving its proximal neural effects. Your brain is in the same local physical states as it was in when the lemon was there: the neurons in your visual cortex, for instance, are firing in the same pattern. After the removal, you do not see the lemon, because the lemon is not around to be seen. Yet—we can all grant—you notice nothing amiss. Questioned after the removal, you claim that you have been looking at the lemon for the last few minutes. In Mark Johnston's terminology ("The Obscure Object of Hallucination": 230, this volume[1]), you have undergone a "subjectively seamless transition" from seeing the lemon to not seeing anything at all—at least, to not seeing any material object.

The minor deity has changed your situation: it has removed the lemon, for one thing. But has the deity changed you mentally, or psychologically? More specifically—assuming that we can help ourselves to the notion of a "visual experience"—has the deity changed the kind of visual experience you are enjoying? There is certainly some temptation to think that the answer is "no." The lemon is a (distal) cause of your experience, not a part of it, and still less an essential part of it. So removing the lemon but keeping the proximal cause constant will not change the nature of the effect, your experience.[2]

But this answer seems highly problematic. When you see the lemon, a certain yellow ovoid object is, as J. J. Valberg puts it, "present in experience" (1992: 4). Intuitively, that object "is right there, available for [you] to pick out or focus on, and refer to demonstratively" (ibid.: 7). Further, that object seems to enter into the nature of the experience itself. "What sort of experience am I now having?," you ask yourself. How can this question be answered, other than by attending to the objects of experience? Your "experience" is apparently not something that can be identified independently of its objects. So you cannot do better than reply: "I am having an experience of *that object.*"

What is that yellow ovoid object that is present in your experience? It is, of course, overwhelmingly natural to take it to be the lemon. But is this right? After the deity has removed the lemon, it is no longer "right there" and "available." If the nature of your experience has not changed, then the very same yellow ovoid object remains present in your experience. Therefore, this object is not the lemon. And since it can hardly be any other "external object," we must join in what, according to the eighteenth-century Scottish philosopher Thomas Reid, has been the overwhelming consensus practically since philosophy began:

All philosophers, from Plato to Mr. Hume, agree in this, That we do not perceive external objects immediately, and that the immediate object of perception must be some image present to the mind. So far there appears to be a unanimity rarely to be found among philosophers on such abstruse points. (1785/1941: 86)

In the terminology of the last century, this is the sense datum theory. Setting aside the question of whether Reid's history is entirely accurate, that theory has certainly been extremely popular.[3] The sense datum theory's star began to fade, however, in the 1940s. (In "Visual Experiences," published in 1967 and reprinted here, J. M. Hinton remarks that the theory is "so out of fashion" [10].) There was no silver bullet that killed the theory off for good—indeed, Howard Robinson, another contributor to this book, is one of the theory's most prominent contemporary defenders. Rather, there was a general air of bafflement at the sense datum theorist's insistence that if you seem to be seeing something yellow and ovoid, then there really is something yellow and ovoid that you are seeing.[4]

One might accuse many of the sense datum theory's opponents of not realizing that their position in fact has radical consequences—and this is where disjunctivism comes in. A few paragraphs back, it was suggested that if the nature of your experience has not changed, then the very same yellow ovoid object remains present in your experience. This conditional claim should be accepted by proponents and opponents of the sense datum theory. Contraposing, if the very same yellow ovoid object does not remain present in your experience, then the nature of your experience has changed. Before the deity removes the lemon, it is present in your experience; after the removal, something else is going on entirely—no physical object is present in your experience, and maybe no object of any sort is. So the pre- and postremoval experiences are radically different. Of course, they can be united verbally: each is an experience as of a yellow ovoid lemon. But the more metaphysically perspicuous characterization is disjunctive: each is either an experience in which the lemon is present, or an experience of a radically different sort.

Let us call the preremoval situation *the good case* and the postremoval situation *the bad case*.[5] Then the basic claim of disjunctivism can be put as follows: the experiences in the good case and the hallucinatory bad cases share no mental core, that is, there is no (experiential) mental kind that characterizes both cases.[6] More exactly, there is no such reasonably specific kind—specific enough, say, not to characterize a situation in which you veridically perceive a green stalk of asparagus, or veridically perceive the same lemon after it has been dyed pink or squashed into a cube. As Hinton, the first explicitly to propose a disjunctivist position, puts the idea in the excerpt from his book *Experiences*: there is no "common element" to the experiences in the good and bad cases (22ff.).[7] Hinton's formulation is echoed with minor variations by other contributors to this volume. In "The Objects of Perceptual Experience," Paul Snowdon characterizes disjunctivism as a view on which "looks-judgements are made true by two types of occurrence: in hallucinations ... by some feature of [an] inner experience, whereas in perception they are made true by some feature of a certain relation to an object, a non-inner experience, (which does not involve such an inner experience)" (56–57).[8] According to M. G. F. Martin in "The Limits of Self-Awareness," the disjunctivist denies that "statements about how things appear to a perceiver ... report a distinctive mental event or state common to these various disjoint situations" (271).[9] And in "The Obscure Object …," Johnston describes the disjunctivist as holding that such an appearance statement "is just shorthand for a disjunctive report, not the description of a kind of mental act common to hallucination and seeing" (214).

According to disjunctivism, the good case and the (hallucinatory) bad case share no mental core. According to what we will call *the Cartesian view*, in both the good case and the bad case you are having exactly the same kind of perceptual experience. A specific version of the Cartesian view has already been mentioned: your experience consists in your awareness of a yellow ovoid sense datum in both cases. Howard Robinson gives a partial defense of this version in the excerpt from his book *Perception*, but the Cartesian view may be developed in other ways. According to intentional versions of the Cartesian view, experiences are individuated by their representational contents, and the experiences in the good and bad cases have exactly the same content: that there is a yellow ovoid object before you, or something similar. This sort of view is discussed in Martin's "The Reality of Appearances" (94–95). In "The Idea of Experience," Alan Millar defends the Cartesian view (in his terminology, "the experientialist picture") while rejecting sense data and remaining tacitly neutral on the issue of intentionalism.[10]

Since there is a halfway house between being completely dissimilar in so-and-so respects and being exactly similar in so-and-so respects, disjunctivism and the Cartesian view do not exhaust the options. According to *the moderate view*, the experiences in the two cases do have a common core, but nonetheless in certain respects differ mentally. Intentional versions of the moderate view agree with intentionalist Cartesianism on the similarities: both experiences represent that there is a yellow ovoid object before you. (This sort of position is defended in Byrne and Logue 2008.) Along related lines, Mark Johnston argues that in both cases you are aware of a certain "sensible profile," "a complex, partly qualitative and partly relational property, which exhausts the way the particular scene before your eyes is if your present experience is veridical" ("The Obscure Object …": 225).

Those are two suggestions for the moderate view's experiential similarities; what about the experiential differences? Here are two obvious candidates: in the good case, but not in the bad case, you see the lemon, and it looks (to you) yellow and ovoid.

A proponent of the Cartesian view will thus deny that seeing the lemon (for instance) is a mental state; or, at least, she will deny that it is a mental state that (partly) constitutes the experience in the good case.[11] Although this is not compulsory, she may insist instead that seeing the lemon is a hybrid state, consisting of an internal mental component caused in such-and-such ways by a nonmental environmental component, the presence of the lemon. (A similar account might be given of the lemon's looking yellow and ovoid.)[12]

So far, we have distinguished the Cartesian view, disjunctivism, and the moderate view. But a note of terminological caution is needed, because our characterization of disjunctivism isn't entirely uncontroversial. Some take it to be (roughly) the view that there are mental differences between the good and bad cases: disjunctivism, on this characterization, is simply the denial of the Cartesian view. For example, Snowdon has recently formulated disjunctivism as follows: "The experience in a perceptual case reaches out to and involves the perceived external objects, not so the experience in other cases" (2005: 136–137). This is compatible with a mental similarity between the good and bad cases: Johnston, for instance, although recognizing a common element, also claims that "[s]eeing goes all the way out to the things seen, the things with which it acquaints the subject" ("The Obscure Object . . .": 229).

In our view, it is a better terminological policy to adopt the narrower use of "disjunctivism"; we will accordingly do so for the rest of this introduction. (For more discussion see Byrne and Logue 2008: 80–81.)

## 2 Distinctions between Disjunctivisms

In the previous section only a hallucinatory bad case was considered, but there are other kinds of bad case. Imagine that the deity instantly replaces the lemon with a blue book, but cleverly distorts the conditions of viewing so that the book looks exactly as the lemon did. Like the earlier example, you undergo a subjectively seamless transition from seeing the lemon to seeing the book; unlike the earlier example, you continue to see a material object; in fact, you see a blue book, although of course you do not realize this. Call this situation the *illusory* bad case.

On any version of disjunctivism, the good case and the hallucinatory bad case have no common mental element. What about the illusory case? Here disjunctivists divide. $V \vee I/H$ *disjunctivism* classifies the illusory and hallucinatory cases together, at least in this sense: neither shares a mental core with the good case. ("V," "I," and "H" stand for, respectively, veridical, illusory, and hallucinatory cases.) $VI \vee H$ *disjunctivism* classifies the illusory case with the good case. On this version of disjunctivism, the good and illusory cases share a mental core.[13]

Harold Langsam is a VI ∨ H disjunctivist, and this version is also discussed in the two papers by Snowdon. According to Langsam, "experiences
themselves are either relations between material objects and minds (if they
are perceptual experiences) or something else (if they are hallucinatory
experiences)" ("The Theory of Appearing Defended": 188). Similarly, according to Snowdon, the contrast is between situations in which "there is
something which looks to [a subject S] to be F)" and hallucinations ("Perception, Vision, and Causation": 41; see also the quotation from "The
Objects . . ." in the previous section).

It might seem obvious that Hinton is a V ∨ I/H disjunctivist, since he
contrasts a veridical perception of a flash of light with an "illusion of a
flash of light" ("Visual Experiences": 1).[14] However, Hinton does not use
the term "illusion" in the now-customary narrow philosophical sense,
which applies only to situations in which an object is perceived.[15] An example of a Hintonesque illusion of a flash of light is "what you get for instance when an electric current is passed through your head in a certain
way by experimental psychologists" (*Experiences*: 22; see also "Visual Experiences": 1), which does not involve seeing anything at all. In standard
philosophical terminology, Hinton is thus contrasting a *veridical* perception of a flash of light with a *hallucination* as of a flash (cf. *Experiences*:
20), which leaves the placement of illusory cases open. But a number of
other passages indicate that he classifies them with hallucinations. For
example, in *Experiences* he gives the following example of a "perception-
illusion disjunction": "Either I see a cobra, looking every inch a cobra and
not looking to me in the least like any kind of non-cobra, or I am having
that illusion" (32, n. 3). It is natural to understand "that illusion" as including a situation in which, owing to an excess of sherry, Hinton's briar pipe
looks to him "every inch a cobra." And in a section of *Experiences* not
reproduced here Hinton writes that he "would say that in the case of a
revolving-beam lighthouse you have an illusion of perceiving a flash of
light" (1973: 118). Hence Hinton's "illusions" apparently comprise (in our
terminology) both illusions and hallucinations.[16]

Martin is a V ∨ I/H disjunctivist. He does not discuss illusory cases in detail, but when he mentions them, he groups them with hallucinatory cases
on the "right-hand side" of the disjunction. "[P]erceptions," he says, "fail
to be the same kind of mental episode as illusions or hallucinations" (2006:
360; see also "The Reality . . .": 95).[17]

There is a second distinction between disjunctivisms, concerning how to
characterize the cases described by the right-hand disjunct (i.e., the halluci-

natory and illusory cases for a V ∨ I/H disjunctivist, or just hallucinations for a VI ∨ H disjunctivist). According to Jonathan Dancy:

> The disjunctive account of perception really says that there are two quite different sorts of oasis-experience, which may none the less be indistinguishable to their owner. The first is the genuine article, and the second, though it is indistinguishable, has nothing in common with the first other than the fact that they are both oasis-experiences. In the standard formulation of the account, misleadingly, this is explicitly the way in which the second disjunct is characterized: we characterize it solely by saying that it is like what it is not. Presumably, however, there may be available a more direct characterization of the second disjunct, and in a totally explicit version of the theory it would indeed be characterized in that better way. The current characterization is just a sort of place-holder, showing what has to be said about the relation between the first and second disjunct. ("Arguments from Illusion": 132)

Dancy is suggesting (on behalf of the disjunctivist) that there is a positive characterization, in terms of specific kinds of mental states or events, of the cases on the right-hand side of the disjunction. We will call this disjunctivist position *positive* disjunctivism. Here is an example: you see the lemon in the good case (with no intervening sense data), and bear some other psychological relation (perhaps "acquaintance" in the sense of Russell 1912) to a yellow ovoid sense datum in the bad case. (See Robinson, *Perception*: 155.) Langsam's proposal is another example: he suggests that hallucinatory experiences consist in "[certain] relations between regions of physical space and minds, the regions of physical space in which the hallucinated objects seem to be" ("The Theory of Appearing ...": 193).[18]

According to Martin, however, the only viable version of disjunctivism is *negative* disjunctivism: there is no such positive characterization of the (hallucinatory) bad case.[19] What, then, is happening when you hallucinate the lemon? Martin defends "a modest or minimal conception" of experience, on which "some event is an experience of a [lemon] just in case it couldn't be told apart through introspection from a veridical perception of [a lemon]" ("The Limits ...": 281). Trivially, the experience in the good case cannot be told apart from a veridical perception of a lemon, since it is such a veridical perception. And it will be agreed on all sides that the experience in the bad case, although not a veridical perception, cannot be distinguished from one by introspection. What is distinctive about Martin's brand of negative disjunctivism is its claim to exhaustively characterize hallucinations in these negative epistemological terms: at a first pass, to hallucinate a lemon is simply to see nothing, and to be in "a situation which is indiscriminable through reflection from a veridical perception of a [lemon]" (284).[20,21] And it is tempting to read Hinton as agreeing (*Experiences*: 29, 32).

These distinctions are between versions of disjunctivism about perceptual experience. But there are other kinds of disjunctivism, principally disjunctivism about action and epistemological disjunctivism (the latter terminology is from Snowdon 2005). As might be expected, these other kinds of disjunctivism closely parallel the original Hintonesque kind: they deny that two kinds of situation have a "common element," and they involve some similar arguments. Disjunctivism about action is discussed by Dancy in "Arguments from Illusion": on one version of the view, an act of trying to flip the switch is not a common element in successfully flipping the switch and trying but failing to flip it. Epistemological disjunctivism is defended by John McDowell in "Criteria ...," and is briefly discussed below.[22]

## 3  Defending Disjunctivism

Some preliminary motivation was given for disjunctivism about perceptual experience in section 1. The lemon, not a sense datum, is present in your experience before the deity intervenes, and this object enters into the nature of the experience itself. Hence, after the lemon is removed, your experience changes. However, given the distinction between disjunctivism and the moderate view, this argument doesn't establish its conclusion, even if we grant that the premises are correct. At best, the argument shows that the good case and hallucinatory bad case differ mentally, but that is consistent with the two cases having a common element.

Four principal arguments for disjunctivism can be found in the papers and book excerpts that follow. But before we outline them, some cautionary remarks are in order about the positions of Snowdon and McDowell.

### 3a  Snowdon and McDowell

In the literature, Hinton, Snowdon, and McDowell are often mentioned as the trinity of senior disjunctivists. This is misleading, because Snowdon has never actually endorsed the view in print, and there is a question mark over McDowell's commitment to it.

Snowdon's main aim in "Perception, Vision ..." and "The Objects ..." is to argue against the "causal theory of perception," as defended by H. P. Grice and others. This may be roughly characterized as the view that (in the visual case) a necessary condition for $S$ to see $o$ is that $o$ cause in $S$ an "inner experience" ("The Objects ...": 51), thought of as something that can be a common element in perception and hallucination. Traditionally, the causal theory was supposed to be a "conceptual truth," knowable from the armchair. Snowdon deploys disjunctivism to argue both that the causal theory is not a conceptual truth and that the causal theory is not obviously true.[23] But he does not conclude or assume that disjunctivism is true: he merely argues that it is neither a conceptual falsehood nor obviously false for other reasons. (See also Snowdon 2005: 137, n. 15.)

Although Snowdon does not endorse disjunctivism, at least it takes center stage in his discussion. McDowell, on the other hand, is arguably not concerned with disjunctivism at all, at least as it is characterized in section 1.

In "Criteria, Defeasibility, and Knowledge" (partially reprinted here), McDowell's chief topic is the epistemology of other minds, especially as Wittgenstein conceived it. The traditional view sets up the problem as one of inferring another's psychology from nonpsychological evidence, namely "a corpus of 'bodily' and 'behavioral' information" (78). Crucially, this evidence is supposed to be shared between "good" cases (where one knows that another person is in pain, say), and the corresponding "bad" cases (for example, where the person is just pretending to be in pain). The skeptic about other minds then argues that such an inference from this common behavioral evidence is shaky at best, and concludes that we never know that others are in pain. McDowell (following, he thinks, Wittgenstein) "reject[s] the assumption that generates the sceptic's problem" (78), namely that one needs to traverse the divide from behavioral evidence to psychological facts. Instead, we can say that (at least sometimes) "the [psychological] fact itself is directly presented to view" (81).

As McDowell notes, the traditional problem of the external world is structurally similar to the traditional problem of other minds. Your evidence in the good case, when you see the lemon and thereby come to know that it is yellow and ovoid, is supposedly the same as your evidence in the bad case—this common evidence presumably concerns "appearances," in some sense.[24] The skeptic about the external world then argues that an inference from the appearances to the presence of a lemon is shaky at best, and concludes that you do not know that there is a lemon before you. More generally, perception never allows you to know what your environment is like. Again, McDowell diagnoses the mistake in the initial setup of the problem. In the good case, the fact that the lemon is yellow is "made manifest" (82) to you: you know it without any "inference from a highest common factor" (83).

So McDowell thinks the good and bad cases are epistemologically very different: your evidence in the good case is much stronger than it is in the hallucinatory bad case. He is thus an epistemological disjunctivist.[25] What is open to dispute is whether he endorses Hintonian disjunctivism—that is, disjunctivism as explained earlier.[26] (Admittedly, McDowell himself draws a comparison with Hinton: see "Criteria ...": 87, n. 13.) In any event, the two positions are not equivalent: in particular, one may agree with McDowell's claim about evidence while also accepting that the good and bad cases are mentally importantly alike. As McDowell himself has recently remarked, "[t]his difference in epistemic significance is of course consistent with all sorts of commonalities between the [good and bad cases]" (2008: 382, n. 7).[27]

## 3b    Disjunctivism as the Default View of Perceptual Experience

Although disjunctivism might seem an outlandish view, Hinton seems to have thought that the onus is on his opponent to show that it is false. After laying down some requirements for a report of experience to concern the elusive "common element," Hinton writes:

If nothing meets all those requirements then there is no such thing as an experience-report of that kind, in one sense or non-sense. I do not see that anything does meet all those requirements. Indeed, my impression or tentative belief, which may of course be entirely mistaken for all that I am by no means the first to hold or to have received it, is that as far as anyone knows or has a right to believe, nothing meets all those requirements. (*Experiences*: 26–27)

He goes on to remark that arguments for the sense datum theory—which, if sound, would establish one kind of common element—are the subject of "widespread scepticism."

In "The Limits ...," Martin elaborates and defends Hinton's position:

When Michael Hinton first introduced the idea, he suggested that the burden of proof or disproof lay with his opponent, that what was needed was to show that our talk of how things look or appear to one to be introduced more than what he later came to call perception-illusion disjunctions.... The aim of this paper is [in part] ... to explain the way in which Hinton was correct in his challenge. Properly understood, the disjunctive approach to perception is the appropriate starting point for any discussion of the nature of perceptual experience. (271–272)

The upshot of Martin's argument is that the nondisjunctivist has to make substantive assumptions about one's epistemic access to one's perceptual experiences, assumptions the disjunctivist does not have to make. Thus, Martin concludes, disjunctivism is the default view of perceptual experience.[28]

### 3c Disjunctivism as Following from the Theory of Appearing

As William Alston explains it, the theory of appearing "takes perceptual consciousness to consist, most basically, in the fact that one or more objects appear to the subject as so-and-so, as round, bulgy, blue, jagged, etc." (1999: 182). In the good case, the lemon appears (as) yellow and ovoid. In the illusory case mentioned earlier, the blue book also appears yellow and ovoid. Since, according to the theory of appearing, "appearing yellow and ovoid" is a genuine respect of mental similarity, the theory of appearing entails that the good case and the illusory case have a common element, and so that V ∨ I/H disjunctivism is false.

On the other hand, assuming (on the face of it correctly) that nothing appears yellow and ovoid to you in the hallucinatory case, the theory of appearing does entail VI ∨ H disjunctivism, since the theory (at least as naturally interpreted) does not recognize any other mental respects in which the hallucinatory and good cases might be similar. As Langsam puts it, "[T]he phenomenal features of hallucinatory experiences cannot be instantiations of relations between material objects and minds, for the only material objects that can enter into these relations are objects of perception, and when a subject is hallucinating, he is not perceiving any material object" ("The Theory of Appearing . . .": 185).[29]

One might block the entailment by denying the assumption, and indeed Alston himself suggests that in hallucinations "what appears to the subject is a particularly vivid mental image" (1999: 191). This sort of position is not disjunctivism as explained here, because it recognizes a common element: an object appears yellow and ovoid in both the good and hallucinatory cases. (Contrast the examples of positive disjunctivism given in section 2, which involve different psychological relations across the good and hallucinatory bad cases.) However, there is something "disjunctive" about the view, because the objects of experience in the (hallucinatory) bad and good cases are supposed to be radically different: a lemon in the good case, and a mental image in the bad case.[30]

### 3d Disjunctivism as Saving Naive Realism

In "The Limits . . . ," Martin characterizes a view he calls "Naive Realism" as follows:

Some of the objects of perception—the concrete individuals, their properties, the events these partake in—are constituents of the experience. No experience like this, no experience of fundamentally the same kind, could have occurred had no appropriate candidate for awareness existed. (273)

Here Martin is talking about veridical experience: so, according to Naive Realism, in the good case the lemon is a constituent of your experience. On Martin's understanding of "constituents," it is supposed to follow that the lemon is an essential constituent of your experience—the experience could not have occurred if the lemon had not existed. And the "fundamental kind" to which your experience belongs is "its most specific kind; it tells what essentially the event or episode is" (Martin 2006: 361).[31]

According to Martin, Naive Realism forms an inconsistent triad with two other claims: the Common Kind Assumption (CKA) and Experiential Naturalism (EN). According to CKA, "whatever [fundamental] kind of mental event occurs when one is veridically perceiving some scene, such as the street scene outside my window, that kind of event can occur whether or not one is perceiving" ("The Limits ...": 273–274; cf. Martin 2006: 357). According to EN, "our sense experiences, like other events or states within the natural world, are subject to the causal order, and in this case are thereby subject just to broadly physical causes (i.e. including neuro-physiological causes and conditions) and psychological causes (if these are disjoint from physical causes)" ("The Limits ...": 273; cf. Martin 2006: 357).

In brief, the argument that Naive Realism, CKA, and EN are jointly inconsistent is this. Let $K$ be the fundamental kind characterizing the experience in the good case, when you see the lemon. By CKA, an experience of kind $K$ could have occurred when hallucinating a lemon. By EN, such a hallucinatory experience can be generated in the complete absence of lemons, "through suitable manipulation of mind and brain" (Martin 2006: 358). Hence an experience of kind $K$ can occur even though the lemon had not existed, and so Naive Realism is false. (See "The Limits ...": 273–275.)

Naive Realism, Martin argues, is "the best articulation of how our experiences strike us as being to introspective reflection on them" ("The Limits ...": 276). So either CKA or EN must be sacrificed, and since EN is entirely unobjectionable, CKA must go.

Note that to deny that the experience in the bad case falls under $K$—the fundamental kind instantiated in the good case—is not yet to embrace disjunctivism. As Martin notes, this is consistent with the experiences in the good and bad cases falling under the same (specific) mental kind $K\dagger$: it is merely ruled out that $K\dagger$ is the fundamental kind instantiated in the good case. The rest of Martin's argument is intended to establish that there is no such kind $K\dagger$—more strongly, that the bad case can only be characterized in "negative epistemological" terms.

Suppose that the experience in the bad case falls under a mental kind $K\dagger$—for example, suppose that the experience involves awareness of yellow ovoid sense data, or of a certain Johnstonian "sensory profile." Since the good case preserves the "same proximate causal conditions" (285) as the bad case, Martin argues (following Robinson: see 285) that the experience in the good case also falls under $K\dagger$.

But Martin thinks that if the Naive Realist were to stop here, she wouldn't be able rebut the charge that the presence of $K\dagger$ in the good case renders the Naive Realist kind $K$ "explanatorily redundant" (279). "It would be a severe limitation on the disjunctivist's commitment to Naïve Realism," he writes, "if the Naïve realist aspects of perception could not themselves shape the contours of the subject's conscious experience" (295).

And negative disjunctivism is Martin's way out: the experience in the bad case does not fall under any such positive mental kind $K\dagger$:

[T]here are certain mental events, at least those hallucinations brought about through causal conditions matching those of veridical perceptions, whose only positive mental characteristics are negative epistemological ones—that they cannot be told apart by the subject from veridical perception. ("The Limits …": 302–303)[32,33]

## 4  Against Disjunctivism

For the most part, objections to disjunctivism fall into two categories: appeals to indistinguishability, and appeals to causal considerations. (The papers by Millar and Johnston add other complaints.) Both kinds of objection are discussed at length in the contributions to this book.

### 4a  Indistinguishability

When the demon removes the lemon, you are unable to detect any change. As Johnston puts it, "[t]ry as you might, you would not notice any difference, however closely you attend to your visual experience" ("The Obscure Object …": 215). In that sense, your preremoval veridical experience is subjectively indistinguishable from your postremoval hallucinatory experience: you are not in a position to tell that the first experience differs mentally from the second (if it does at all).

One objection to disjunctivism stems from the idea, mentioned earlier, that the distinction between appearance and reality collapses in the special case of experience. In "The Reality of Appearances" Martin nicely poses the intuitive threat to disjunctivism as follows:

[I]f something really is an essential aspect of the conscious or phenomenal character of an experience, then what is true of it should be true of any state of mind indistinguishable from it for the subject: for what more can there be to the character of conscious states of mind than a subject can herself discern when she reflects on them? (98)

Millar states an (apparently) similar concern in "The Idea of Experience," although he does not press it.[34] Martin, however, takes the challenge very seriously, and responds to it in some detail, trying to offer a diagnosis of its appeal.

Note that this sort of objection could be cast as an objection to the moderate view as much as disjunctivism; indeed the rhetorical question at the end of the quotation from Martin suggests as much. And Hinton has his opponent ask "But is it not the very same experience?" on the ground that the "illusion is … indistinguishable from the perception" (*Experiences*: 30).

A second objection that applies only to disjunctivism is that an explanation of the indistinguishability between the pre- and postremoval experiences is required, which the disjunctivist is accused of failing to supply. As Johnston puts it:

The Disjunctive View has nothing satisfactory to say in answer to the pressing question: What kinds of things can visual experience be a relation to so that in a transition from a case of [seeing] to a case of [visual hallucination] there need be no difference which the subject can discern? Once the resources are found to address this question, the Disjunctive View will fall by the wayside. ("The Obscure Object …": 216)

This challenge is briefly addressed by Langsam ("The Theory of Appearing …": 187–188) and Dancy ("Arguments from Illusion": 134–135).

The kind of subjective indistinguishability—call it *indistinguishability*$_1$ —characterizing the "subjectively seamless transition" is a relation between two of your experiences. The preremoval experience is indistinguishable$_1$ from the postremoval experience, and Johnston is demanding an explanation of that fact.

Indistinguishability$_1$ is defined in terms of your inability to know a statement of nonidentity: that the preremoval experience is not identical in mental respects to the postremoval experience. Since the proposition that *a* is not identical to *b* in respect *R* is trivially equivalent to the proposition that *b* is not identical to *a* in respect *R*, indistinguishability$_1$ is symmetric. If one is not in a position to know the first proposition, one is not in a position to know the second. So, if the first experience is indistinguishable$_1$ from the second, then the second is indistinguishable$_1$ from the first.[35]

It is important not to confuse this sort of subjective indistinguishability with the notion of indistinguishability Martin uses to explain his version of negative disjunctivism—call it *indistinguishability*$_2$. According to Martin, the experience in the bad case can only be characterized in negative epistemological terms: in particular, the experience cannot be "told apart through introspection from a veridical perception [of a lemon]" ("The Limits ...": 281).

Like indistinguishability$_1$, indistinguishability$_2$ is defined in terms of the inability to know. Unlike indistinguishability$_1$, it is not a relation between experiences, and the relevant unknowable items are not statements of non-identity between two experiences. Instead (as it is put in Martin 2006: 363–364) they are statements to the effect that an "individual experience" is not a certain kind of veridical perception, for instance a veridical perception of a lemon as yellow and ovoid.

One reason why it is important to keep the two notions of indistinguishability separate is that a Cartesian may endorse the slogan that experiences are mentally identical if and only if they are indistinguishable (cf. the principle "(IND)," in Martin's "The Reality of Appearances": 91), a slogan that the disjunctivist must reject. Since identity in mental respects is an equivalence relation on experiences, the relevant notion of indistinguishability must be an equivalence relation on experiences too. A precise rendering of the slogan accordingly requires something like indistinguishability$_1$, not indistinguishability$_2$.[36]

A third indistinguishability-based objection is directed solely to negative disjunctivism, and to Martin's version in particular. Consider Johnston's lowly cane toad, which he uses to press a closely related objection ("The Obscure Object ...": 217). The cane toad, suppose, is hallucinating a stationary light; it is not hallucinating a moving dark spot. The "mind-blind" toad is not in a position to know anything about its experience. A fortiori, it is not in a position to know that its experience is not a veridical perception of a moving dark spot. According to Martin, if an experience is indistinguishable (or, as he often says, "indiscriminable") from a veridical perception of a moving dark spot, then it is an experience of a moving dark spot. So, on Martin's view, it would appear to follow that the toad is having a (hallucinatory) experience of a moving dark spot, which is false.

As Martin says, this sort of objection raises the question of "how exactly the disjunctivist should articulate the way in which indiscriminability is employed in the positive account of the notion of perceptual experience in general" ("The Limits ...": 303), which he addresses at length in that paper and elsewhere.[37]

## 4b  Causal Arguments

We have already briefly seen how causal considerations pose a threat to disjunctivism in our discussion of Martin's argument in section 3d. Martin concedes that if the experience in the hallucinatory bad case falls under a mental kind $K$†, then so does the experience in the good case, because the proximal causes are the same. However, he denies the antecedent, claiming that the bad case only has the negative epistemological property of being indistinguishable$_2$ from a veridical perception of a yellow ovoid lemon.

This sort of causal argument purports to establish that if the experience in the bad case is of kind $K$†, so is the experience in the good case. It is compatible with the argument that the converse fails: the experience in the good case is of a certain kind $K$ that is absent in the bad case. Let us call this *the Bad-to-Good Causal Argument*: it argues from the bad case to a conclusion about the good case.

A. D. Smith, in the selection from his book *The Problem of Perception*, endorses the Bad-to-Good Causal Argument, with a specific candidate for the hallucinatory kind $K$†. Smith argues that if you are aware of a "non-normal object" (a sense datum) in the hallucinatory bad case, then you are aware of such an object in the good case. And if you are aware of a yellow ovoid sense datum in the good case, then (according to Smith) you do not enjoy "immediate awareness" of the lemon, a "normal physical object" (175). Hence, Smith concludes, "[o]nce [non-normal] objects get into your philosophy, Direct Realism is sunk" (178).

Notice that this conclusion need not bother Johnston, who is "a 'Direct' Realist, and a radical one at that" ("The Obscure Object . . .": 208), because although he concedes that there is a common kind $K$†, he denies that it involves awareness of sense data.

If the Bad-to-Good Causal Argument is sound, and the experience in the bad case falls under $K$†, then there is a Hintonesque common element, and disjunctivism is false. However, since this conclusion is consistent with the experience in the good case essentially involving a relation to the lemon, it is consistent with the moderate view.

The *Good-to-Bad* Causal Argument purports to rule out the moderate view, and so establish the Cartesian view. It proceeds in a similar manner but in the other direction, arguing from the good case to a conclusion about the bad case. That is, according to the Good-to-Bad Causal Argument, if the experience in the good case is of kind $K$, so is the experience in the bad case, because the proximal causes are the same. However, the Good-to-Bad direction is considerably more problematic than the reverse. The obvious worry about the Good-to-Bad Causal Argument is that if the experience in the good case is individuated partly in terms of external environmental objects (in particular, the lemon), then a proximal neural state can hardly be sufficient for it. As Johnston puts it, "[t]here is no such 'last' brain state that then causes seeing" ("The Obscure Object . . .": 229). A similar point is made by Langsam, who argues that "the 'same cause, same effect' principle applies only to *intrinsic* changes" ("The Theory of Appearing ...": 190).

The Bad-to-Good Causal Argument is particularly threatening to positive disjunctivism; as we have seen, this is why Martin is a negative disjunctivist. Langsam defends his positive disjunctivism against the argument by proposing an extrinsic account of hallucinations: as quoted earlier, he suggests that they involve "relations between regions of physical space and minds" ("The Theory of Appearing": 193). In effect, he gives the same reply to both directions of the Causal Argument. And the cogency of this reply is apparently endorsed by Johnston, who says that "the Disjunctivist has a quick way with the [Bad-to-Good Argument]," namely to deny "that there is an interesting type of mental act that supervenes just on one's brain state" ("The Obscure Object ...": 214). Indeed, Hinton himself denies it (*Experiences*: 28–30).

Robinson defends the Causal Argument in both directions, thus offering an argument for the Cartesian view. According to Robinson, "[i]t is necessary to give the same account of both hallucinating and perceptual experience when they have the same neural cause" (*Perception*: 153), and he assumes that in a situation like the one involving you, the deity, and the lemon, the "perceptual experience" does have the same (sufficient) neural cause. This assumption, however, is open to the accusation that he is begging the question against his opponents. (For a similar complaint, see Martin, "The Limits ...": 287–288.)[38]

Robinson's argument could be used to establish a form of intentionalist Cartesianism, or the form of Cartesianism favored by Millar. However, Robinson's own version of the Cartesian view is that the experiences in both the good and bad cases are constituted by awareness of sense data, which he argues for elsewhere in the book.[39]

### Notes

1. Throughout this introduction, page references with titles are to this volume; page references with dates are to items listed at the end of this introduction.

2. For the purposes of this introduction we will assume (with many of the contributors to this volume) that talk of "experiences" is reasonably clear. However, as the excerpt from J. M. Hinton's book *Experiences* brings out (see also the last few pages of his "Visual Experiences"), in a more careful treatment this assumption needs to be questioned. See Byrne and Logue 2008: 82–83, Byrne forthcoming.

3. For a brief history of the sense datum theory with especial relevance to the present volume, see Crane 2000.

4. See, for example, Barnes 1944–45: 152–153. Incidentally, the alleged sense datum is more accurately described as yellow and semiovoid, since sense data were typically not supposed to continue out of view.

5. The terminology is borrowed from Williamson 2000, although used somewhat differently.

6. Like the contributors to this volume, we will focus on visual experience, although disjunctivism itself is not so constrained.

7. A. D. Smith (forthcoming) argues that Husserl, the nineteenth-century founder of phenomenology, was a disjunctivist.

8. Note that Snowdon goes a little beyond our official characterization of disjunctivism in offering a specific account of the experience in the good case, as involving "a certain relation to an object"; another example is Campbell 2002a: 134–135. Other disjunctivist views are possible: for instance, one might take the experience in the good case to involve a certain relation to a fact.

9. For a complication in connection with Martin, see note 21 below.

10. Millar 2007 finds more insight in disjunctivism than "The Idea …," although Millar still defends the experientialist picture.

11. On the sense datum version of the Cartesian view, these issues about seeing might not even arise, because it is hard for the sense datum theorist to maintain that we ever see physical objects like lemons (see Barnes 1944–45: 139–140).

12. See Johnston, "The Obscure Object …: 209–213, on the "Conjunctive Analysis of Seeing"; and Jonathan Dancy, "Arguments from Illusion": 117.

13. Cf. Snowdon, "The Objects …": 58.

14. Hinton's choice of "I see a flash" to characterize a veridical perception of a flash (which is clearly his intent) is unfortunate, since one may see what is in fact an *F* even though it looks nothing like an *F* (see Snowdon, "Perception, Vision,…": 41). Hinton fixes this problem in *Experiences* by stipulating that "see" means (in his jargon) *plainly see*. See *Experiences*: 19, 22.

15. For Hinton's discussion of this terminological issue, see 1973: 115–117.

16. This interpretation (which we are only tentatively advancing) might be thought to be at odds with this passage: "the perception-proposition in a perception-illusion disjunction can very well be a proposition about how something looks: one kind of perception-illusion disjunction is exemplified by: 'Either I visually perceive an optical object which looks (a great deal, a little, hardly at all) like a two-dimensional coloured shape, or I am having the illusion of doing so'" (*Experiences*: 24). Here the left-hand disjunct describes cases in which objects are seen and look to be a certain way, regardless of whether or not they are that way. But Hinton's point seems to be

that the alleged "inner experience" (the common element) is not specifiable in terms of an external object's looking a certain way, because the common element is supposed to be present in the hallucinatory case. That is consistent with the experiences in the good and illusory cases having no common element, and so consistent with V ∨ I/H disjunctivism. (See also the following note.)

17. Note that V ∨ I/H disjunctivism does *not* imply that the experiences in the illusory and hallucinatory cases are mentally the same, or even that they share a mental core. The view simply denies that the experience in the good case shares a mental core with the experiences in the illusory and hallucinatory cases. Further, the V ∨ I/H disjunctivist may consistently take *seeing the lemon* to be an experiential mental state, and so a point of overlap between the good and illusory cases. This is not a Hintonesque "common element," however, because it is not specific enough. For instance, one may see the lemon (in good light, etc.) if it has been dyed pink or squashed into a cube (see page ix above).

18. A similar suggestion is briefly canvassed and rejected in Alston 1999: 191. Alston, however, takes the relevant relations to be the same in both cases; we are assuming that Langsam takes the relations to be different. See section 3c below and note 30.

19. Note that Johnston has negative disjunctivism in mind when he claims to have "provided a positive account of hallucination in the face of the denials of the Disjunctivists" ("The Obscure Object ...": 255).

20. This is only a first pass, because one may hallucinate a lemon while seeing other objects.

21. We assume that to be in such a negative epistemological situation is not thereby to be in a specific *mental* state. Martin may think otherwise (see "The Reality ...": 96); this issue is more terminological than substantive.

22. For a version of disjunctivism about action that is closely related to epistemological disjunctivism, see Hornsby 2008.

23. The "causal theory of perception," as Snowdon characterizes it, implies the existence of "inner experiences." That theory should be distinguished from the claim that a necessary condition for S to see o is that o cause S to see it, which has no such implication and which the disjunctivist need not dispute. There is nothing obviously problematic about o's causing S to see it, as Snowdon's own example of marriage ("Perception, Vision, ...": 40) shows: sometimes (indeed, usually), A causes B to be married to him, namely by asking her. (Note that this does not appear to violate Humean strictures about cause and effect being "independent existences": A's proposal might have been turned down.)

Hinton, incidentally, evidently took the causal theory of perception *not* to imply the existence of "inner experiences." Commenting on Snowdon, he remarks that "[i]n my *Experiences* the view I took with reference to Grice was that there is no incompatibility [with disjunctivism], unless the Grice-like view goes out of its way to create one" (1996: 220).

24. A qualification: since the bad case comes after the good case, your evidence will differ with respect to time.

25. For a more precise characterization of epistemological disjunctivism, see Byrne and Logue 2008: 65–68.

26. There is no doubt that McDowell endorses the *moderate* view: see McDowell 1986 and 1994: 191–193.

27. For more discussion of McDowell in this volume, see Snowdon, "The Objects ...": 58, and Dancy, "Arguments from Illusion": 124–125. See also Thau 2004; Snowdon 2005: 139–140; Byrne and Logue 2008: 65–68; Haddock and Macpherson 2008a; Neta 2008; Pritchard 2008; Wright 2008; Millar forthcoming.

28. For discussion of Martin's argument, see Siegel 2004; Byrne and Logue 2008: 73–78.

29. Cf. Chisholm: "It is significant that no philosopher (as far as I know) has suggested that the language of appearing be applied to experiences other than those involved in external perception" (1963: 111). Barnes (1944–45: 163) adopts the theory of appearing as an alternative to the sense datum theory, but gets himself into an uncharacteristic tangle over hallucinations.

30. For the distinction between disjunctive accounts of experience and disjunctive accounts of the objects of experience, see Thau 2004: 194–195. If Alston's "mental images" may be taken to be sense data, then Alston's position is *Austinian disjunctivism*, so-called in Byrne and Logue 2008: 63 because it makes a brief appearance in Austin 1962: 32; Austinian disjunctivism is the "Selective Theory," as Johnston describes it ("The Obscure Object ...": 234). (For Alston's position on the metaphysics of mental images, see Alston 1999: 191–192.)

31. For a different but closely related formulation of Naive Realism see Langsam, "The Theory of Appearing ...": 199–201. Since Langsam is a VI ∨ H disjunctivist, he thinks that in cases of illusion the merely apparent properties of objects are (in Martin's terminology) "constituents of the experience."

32. See "The Limits ...": 299–300 for Martin's explanation of why these negative epistemological features do not render the Naive Realist kind $K$ explanatorily redundant.

33. For other arguments for disjunctivism, see Campbell 2002b: ch. 6; Martin 2002.

34. Millar explains "experiential indistinguishability" in terms of "looks-as-if ascription[s]" (138); given the use to which he puts these ascriptions, namely to help define "a hallucinatory counterpart of [a] perception" (138), Millar's explanation of indistinguishability might not be epistemological.

35. See Williamson 1990: 10–21.

36. That is not to say that indistinguishability$_1$ *is* an equivalence relation on experiences, merely that it is at least a *relation* on experiences. It is usually not taken to be an equivalence relation, on the grounds that it is not transitive. See Martin, "The Reality ...": 92, 106, and "The Limits ...": 303–308; for discussion, see Hawthorne and Kovakovich 2006; Sturgeon 2006.

37. For a brief summary of this and other related objections with references see Byrne and Logue 2008: 74–75, n. 31. See also Siegel 2004, 2008; Hawthorne and Kovakovich 2006; Martin 2006; Sturgeon 2006, 2008.

38. For further discussion of the Causal Argument, see Foster 2000: 23–43.

39. For valuable advice and/or comments on the introduction and/or assistance with the bibliography at the end of this volume, thanks to David Chalmers, Tim Crane, Nina Emery, Fiona Macpherson, Paolo Santorio, and Susanna Siegel.

**References**

Alston, W. P. 1999. Back to the theory of appearing. *Philosophical Perspectives* 13: 181–203.

Austin, J. 1962. *Sense and Sensibilia*. Oxford: Oxford University Press.

Barnes, W. H. F. 1944–45. The myth of sense-data. *Proceedings of the Aristotelian Society* 45: 89–117. Page references are to the reprint in Swartz 1965.

Byrne, A. Forthcoming. Experience and content. *Philosophical Quarterly*.

Byrne, A., and H. Logue. 2008. Either/Or. In *Disjunctivism: Perception, Action, Knowledge*, ed. A. Haddock and F. Macpherson. Oxford: Oxford University Press.

Campbell, J. 2002a. Berkeley's puzzle. In *Conceivability and Possibility*, ed. T. Gendler and J. Hawthorne. Cambridge, Mass.: MIT Press.

Campbell, J. 2002b. *Reference and Consciousness*. Oxford: Oxford University Press.

Chisholm, R. 1963. The theory of appearing. In *Philosophical Analysis*, ed. M. Black. Englewood Cliffs, N.J.: Prentice-Hall.

Crane, T. 2000. The origins of qualia. In *The History of the Mind-Body Problem*, ed. T. Crane and S. Patterson. London: Routledge.

Crane, T. (ed.). 1992. *The Contents of Experience*. Cambridge: Cambridge University Press.

Foster, J. 2000. *The Nature of Perception*. Oxford: Oxford University Press.

Gendler, T., and J. Hawthorne (eds.). 2006. *Perceptual Experience*. Oxford: Oxford University Press.

Gunther, Y. (ed.). 2003. *Essays on Nonconceptual Content*. Cambridge, Mass.: MIT Press.

Haddock, A., and F. Macpherson. 2008a. Introduction: Varieties of disjunctivism. In *Disjunctivism: Perception, Action, Knowledge*, ed. A. Haddock and F. Macpherson. Oxford: Oxford University Press.

Haddock, A., and F. Macpherson (eds.). 2008b. *Disjunctivism: Perception, Action, Knowledge*. Oxford: Oxford University Press.

Hawthorne, J. P., and K. Kovakovich. 2006. Disjunctivism. *Proceedings of the Aristotelian Society Supp. Vol.* 80: 145–183.

Hinton, J. M. 1973. *Experiences: An Inquiry into Some Ambiguities*. Oxford: Oxford University Press.

Hinton, J. M. 1996. Sense-experiences revisited. *Philosophical Investigations* 19: 211–236.

Hornsby, J. 2008. A disjunctivist conception of acting for reasons. In *Disjunctivism: Perception, Action, Knowledge*, ed. A. Haddock and F. Macpherson. Oxford: Oxford University Press.

Martin, M. G. F. 2002. The transparency of experience. *Mind and Language* 17: 376–425.

Martin, M. G. F. 2006. On being alienated. In *Perceptual Experience*, ed. T. Gendler and J. Hawthorne. Oxford: Oxford University Press.

McDowell, J. 1986. Singular thought and the extent of inner space. In *Subject, Thought, and Context*, ed. J. McDowell and P. Pettit. Oxford: Oxford University Press.

McDowell, J. 1994. The content of perceptual experience. *Philosophical Quarterly* 44: 190–205.

McDowell, J. 2008. The disjunctive conception of experience as material for a transcendental argument. In *Disjunctivism: Perception, Action, Knowledge*, ed. A. Haddock and F. Macpherson. Oxford: Oxford University Press.

Millar, A. 2007. What the disjunctivist is right about. *Philosophy and Phenomenological Research* 74: 176–198.

Millar, A. Forthcoming. Disjunctivism and scepticism. In *The Oxford Handbook to Scepticism*, ed. J. Greco. Oxford: Oxford University Press.

Neta, R. 2008. In defense of disjunctivism. In *Disjunctivism: Perception, Action, Knowledge*, ed. A. Haddock and F. Macpherson. Oxford: Oxford University Press.

Pritchard, D. 2008. McDowellian neo-Mooreanism. In *Disjunctivism: Perception, Action, Knowledge*, ed. A. Haddock and F. Macpherson. Oxford: Oxford University Press.

Reid, T. 1785/1941. *Essays on the Intellectual Powers of Man*. Edited by A. D. Woozley. London: Macmillan.

Russell, B. 1912. *The Problems of Philosophy*. London: Williams and Norgate.

Siegel, S. 2004. Indiscriminability and the phenomenal. *Philosophical Studies* 120: 91–112.

Siegel, S. 2008. The epistemic conception of hallucination. In *Disjunctivism: Perception, Action, Knowledge*, ed. A. Haddock and F. Macpherson. Oxford: Oxford University Press.

Smith, A. D. Forthcoming. Husserl and externalism. *Synthese*.

Snowdon, P. F. 2005. The formulation of disjunctivism: A response to Fish. *Proceedings of the Aristotelian Society* 105: 129–141.

Sturgeon, S. 2006. Reflective disjunctivism. *Proceedings of the Aristotelian Society Supp.* Vol. 80: 185–216.

Sturgeon, S. 2008. Disjunctivism about visual experience. In *Disjunctivism: Perception, Action, Knowledge*, ed. A. Haddock and F. Macpherson. Oxford: Oxford University Press.

Thau, M. 2004. What is disjunctivism? *Philosophical Studies* 120: 193–253.

Valberg, J. J. 1992. *The Puzzle of Experience*. Oxford: Oxford University Press.

Williamson, T. 1990. *Identity and Discrimination*. Oxford: Blackwell.

Williamson, T. 2000. *Knowledge and Its Limits*. Oxford: Oxford University Press.

Wright, C. 2008. Comment on John McDowell's "The disjunctive conception of experience as material for a transcendental argument." In *Disjunctivism: Perception, Action, Knowledge*, ed. A. Haddock and F. Macpherson. Oxford: Oxford University Press.

# 1 Visual Experiences

J. M. Hinton

I

One of the things we can say and think is:

(A)  I see a flash of light: actual light, a photic flash.

Another is:

(B)  I have an illusion of a flash of light: I do not see a photic flash, but something is happening that to me is like seeing one.

This is true, for instance, when I am given such an illusion by passing an electric current through my brain.

A third thing we can say and think is:

(A ∨ B)  Either I see a flash of light, or I have an illusion of a flash of light.

Nothing stops us from introducing some sentence as a more compact way of saying this. It might be

(A ∨ B)′  I see a flash, or
           It is to me as if I saw a flash of light, or
           I seem to see a flash of light,

though no doubt these sentences can also be used in other ways.

(A ∨ B) necessarily is true when (A) is true and (B) false, and also when (B) is true and (A) false. It is neutral as between (A) and (B). It is of course false if (A) and (B) are both false.

Other things we can say and think are:

((A))  I am inclined to believe that (A) is true

J. M. Hinton, "Visual Experiences," *Mind* 76: 217–227 (1967). By permission of Oxford University Press.

and

((B))   I am inclined to believe that (B) is true.

   If, however, we were to say

((A ∨ B))   I am inclined to believe that (A ∨ B) is true,

we would make people stare. Surely a man can be in no kind of doubt as to whether that is true? You can of course be in doubt as to whether (A) or (B) is true, but that is different. If someone said ((A ∨ B)), this would raise in people's minds the question whether he was doubtful as to the meaning of some word that he had used.

   (A ∨ B) does not, of course, say what is happening, as distinct from saying non-committally that one of a number of things is happening. This, as distinct from that, is just what it does. It does not give a definite answer to the question "What is happening?" The same, then, is true of (A ∨ B)'.

   Some will wonder whether (A), and perhaps even whether (B), gives an answer to that question either. My main point in this paper is not that they do, but that certain other things do not. In fact, though, I think they do give an answer to it. The idea that they do not, springs partly from the incongruity here of the continuous present in "saying what is happening." A flash is over before you have time to ask what is happening; also the continuous present suggests a process, a series of changes, though I argue below that it need not imply this. You could make the example a series of flashes. Also, or instead, you could put the whole set of statements into the past tense and/or the third person and talk about answering or not answering the question "What happened?" This would set the discussion outside the context of the search for absolute certainty, but not outside the main context in which I mean it to be set: that in which a special kind of event is excogitated from a special kind of relatively incorrigible statement.

   Why not put it all in the past, then? And why not in the third person? A certain immediacy would be lost. Besides, I want to stress the fact that if at time $t$ you did not answer in advance the question "What happened at $t$?" which someone might have asked you after $t$, then you did not at $t$ answer "the question as to what was happening at $t$." Here the continuous past is forced or suggested not by the idea of a process, a series of changes, but merely by the coincidence of the time at which, and the time about which, you answered or failed to answer. Similarly, the continuous present in "What is happening?" need not imply a process, but may just express the coincidence of the time at which, and the time about which, the question is being asked. Other languages would use "What happens?," but in English "What happens now?" means, perversely enough, "What will happen next?" However, if you prefer, instead of saying that (A ∨ B) and (A ∨ B)' do not answer the question "What happeneth?" you can say that they do not answer in advance the question as to what happened.

Where (A) is concerned it should not be forgotten that an actual flash of light, such as can occur unobserved, is a happening: so that even if "(I see) a flash of light" degenerates—as I think it never does—into a mere compliance with the request "Use your eyes and tell me what's going on over there," it still answers the question as to what happens. As for (B), I dare say few will deny that it answers that question, as distinct from the question as to what process, what series of changes, is occurring. It is what we call an answer to, as distinct from a rejection of, that question.

It is, nevertheless, implicitly disjunctive: the illusion of seeing a flash of light is the disjunction of cases that are not, but to the subject are like, seeing a flash of light. Thus (B) does not give a definite as distinct from an implicitly disjunctive answer—does anything?—though it gives a more definite answer than (A ∨ B). A more definite answer than (B) on the side of illusion would be "I am having a phosphene," but there are doubtless many kinds of phosphene. (A "phosphene" is the flash-illusion that you are given by passing an electric current through your brain.)

Similarly, (A) is implicitly disjunctive: some flashes of light are lightning-flashes, others are flashlight signals, and so on. The reality of seeing a flash of light is the disjunction of cases of seeing a flash of light.

Yet there is a good sense in which both (A) and (B) give a definite answer to the question what happened, and in which (A ∨ B) does not; quite apart from the relatively trivial difference between implicit and explicit disjunction. In as much as (A) and (B) come down on the side of reality and of illusion respectively, they have *a fortiori* the following complex property: that of either coming down on one side of that dichotomy, or avoiding this without merely disjoining illusion and reality, and without ambiguity. I am using the word ambiguity as I think it is ordinarily used, to mean what is opaque, obscure, in its sense unclear. As for "merely disjoining illusion and reality," I would think of a report as doing this if there was no difference between the illusion and the event it reported in the case of illusion, and no difference between the reality and the event it reported in the case of veridical perception.

When I speak, in what follows, without qualification of a statement that gives a definite answer in this context to the question as to what happened, I shall mean an answer that has that complex property.

Perhaps someone will say that the question "What happened?" would contextually mean "What happened, an actual flash of light or a flash-illusion?"—and that, solely for this reason, nothing other than (A) or (B) can answer the question. But whatever answer the questioner may expect, he can still be given one that he does not expect if there is one that he does not expect and that is true. We may ask "Flash or false flash?," but if the guarded answer "I'm not saying, but something certainly happened which happens when either of those things happens, namely I psi-ed" can be the truth, then we may get that answer whether we want it or not.

It is, however, a moot point whether there is to be found among the things we can say and think such a thing as

(Q)   I psi—possible wordings: I see a flash, I have a visual experience of a flash—which does give a definite answer to the question "What is happening?" but which is like (A ∨ B) in at least two of the other respects that I have mentioned: necessarily being true if either (A) or (B) are true, and being hard to understand if prefixed by "I am inclined to believe that...."

That there should be such a thing as (Q) is vital to a number of philosophical positions. If there is no such thing as (Q) then there is—of course—no such thing as my psi-ing for the following statements to be about.

(i)   My psi-ing is one and the same event as some happening that is describable in the language of physics and-or physiology including neurophysiology.

(ii)   That is not so, but no doubt there is some such happening from which my psi-ing could have been inferred.

(iii)   When I see a photic flash, a part of what happens is that I psi. This is also a part of what happens when I have an illusion of a flash of light.

(iv)   Seeing a photic flash may be defined as psi-ing due to a photic flash.

I do not at present see how it can be, or could be, shown that there is such a thing as (Q). Consequently I do not see how it can be shown that there is such a thing as my psi-ing for these and other statements to be about; and since one surely should not make statements without being able to show that they are about something, this means that as far as I can see no such statements should be made. Perhaps I just can't see far enough, but I should like to be shown that this is so. If I am short-sighted it is a short-sightedness that afflicts others as well.

That there is, as I think, no such thing as my psi-ing, does not of itself prevent us from making statements that are just like (i) and (ii) above, except that either "my seeing a photic flash" or "my having an illusion of a flash of light" are substituted for "my psi-ing." *Tertium non datur* is the limited moral. Nor does it prevent us from asserting that there is something that happens both when I see a photic flash and when I have an illusion of one; only neither that happening nor any other happening would be my psi-ing. It would be absurd not to posit that happening, but this is no reason to identify it with, or marry it to, a chimaera.

## II

Some will object:

"I can and do say and think 'I see a flash,' using this form of words not to mean (A) or ((A)) or (B) or ((B)) or (A ∨ B), but using it in such a way that what I mean has just the properties required for (Q)."

How can you be so sure of this?

"It is a matter of what I intend by the words I use. I am not afraid of being mistaken about my own intentions."

Does your intention show itself to me in any other way than by this declaration?

"Yes. When I say 'I see a flash' (or 'I am having a flash-type visual experience' or 'I see a flash that is, however, only an intentional object' or 'Flash!' or whatever form of words I use) you can ask me whether I would withdraw this statement if it turned out that there had been no photic flash. I shall say no, and this will establish that I do not mean (A). Then you can ask whether I would withdraw if it turned out that there had been a photic flash, and that I saw it and saw nothing else of any relevance. I shall again say no, and this will make it clear that I did not mean (B) either—"

—For all that this shows, you might have a confused or dishonest intention. You might be using 'I see a flash' ambiguously, intending to let it be thought that you meant (B) or ((B)) if (A) turned out to be false, and to let it be thought that you meant (A) or ((A)) if (B) turned out to be false.

"Well then; suppose I say 'I see a flash' and you tell me, and I accept, that there was no photic flash. I do not, however, withdraw my original statement. This establishes that I did not mean (A) unless I am flatly contradicting myself, and I agree that I did not mean (A). But now you convince me that you were pulling my leg when you said there was no photic flash; in fact there was one and I saw it. Accepting this, I still do not withdraw my original statement. Again assuming that I am not contradicting myself, this establishes that I did not mean (B) either."

It might be interesting to ask how the assumption that you are not contradicting yourself is to be verified. But in any case, even on that assumption, the events described are quite consistent with your having meant $(A \vee B)$.

"I did not mean $(A \vee B)$ because when I said or thought 'I see a flash' I was not hesitating between alternatives, or in any sort of doubt."

To assert a disjunction is not always to hesitate between alternatives, or to be in doubt. It is, essentially, to deny a conjunction: it is to say or think "Not neither p nor q."

"I didn't say or think anything like that either."

Perhaps this establishes that you did not assert a disjunction. It cannot establish that you did not assert something that *means* a disjunction.

"But if my thought was not 'p' then surely I cannot have had a thought that *means* 'p'?"

This makes short work of the business of definition and logical analysis. It leaves nothing standing. By this criterion, "That is a circle" does not mean "That is a locus of points equidistant from a given point" when it is said or thought by someone who does not know this definition.

"I am not prepared to assume that there is such a thing as a definition or analysis of my statement that I see a flash."

You are neither required to assume this nor to assume the opposite, but to refute a suggested analysis.

"I do not understand the notion of definition or analysis as applied to whole statements."

You need at most to understand it as applied to predicates: the suggested analysis is of "I *see a flash*" into "I $A \vee B$" where A-ing is doing what is mentioned in (A) and B-ing is doing what is mentioned in (B).

"On reflection, I do not think I understand the notion of definition or analysis at all."

I have some sympathy with this, but I must remind you that my own contention is not quite that your "I see a flash" means, or analyses into $(A \vee B)$. It is just that you cannot show that it differs from it in the way that (Q) would. That you should show this is surely a reasonable prerequisite for your being allowed to make any statements about your seeing a flash that are like (i) to (iv), above.

"It is widely held to refute an analysis if you can show that there is no contradiction in the supposition that the analysandum is true and the analysans false. But there is in fact no contradiction in the supposition that I see a flash—have the visual experience called seeing a flash—without either seeing a photic flash or having an illusion of one. I can imagine myself having the visual experience in a state of disembodiment; in which state the question whether I saw a photic flash or had an illusion of one would hardly apply."

How many philosophical ways there are of seeing an X in your mind's eye. There is the one where you perform this feat and call it by that name; the one where you do it and call it "noticing the transparency of consciousness," the one where you do it and call it "imagining myself seeing an X while in a disembodied state".... Your imagining a flash proves that you can do this, and it proves nothing else.

"$(A \lor B)$ is something I have a ground for; 'I see a flash' is not. In fact, 'I see a flash' is my ground for $(A \lor B)$."

You do, and you don't, have a ground for $(A \lor B)$. You have a ground for it in the sense that something happens which entirely justifies you in thinking it to be true. What it is that happens, and that justifies you, you need not know. When what happens is that you see a photic flash, you are justified by this, irrespective of whether you know that this is what is happening; and when what happens is that you have an illusion of one, you are justified by this, irrespective of whether you know that this is what is happening. A ground for $(A \lor B)$ in the sense of a proposition that you know to be true and from which you infer $(A \lor B)$, is something you do not have and do not need.

"I do have such a ground, whether I need it or not, and the ground is that I see a flash: that I psi. The ground is $(Q)$."

If $(Q)$ existed, it would be such an unnecessary ground; this is not a proof of $(Q)$'s existence.

"$(A \lor B)$ does not say what the situation asserted by $(A)$—my A-ing—and the situation asserted by $(B)$—my B-ing—have in common. 'I see a flash' does just this: the situations have in common that in both of them I see a flash."

In a way $(A \lor B)$ does say what my A-ing and my B-ing have in common, though my use of the unrelated letters A and B obscures this for the sake of other advantages. It says that my A-ing and my B-ing have in common what an illusion and its reality have in common: these necessarily have in common that one is, what the other merely is like. To keep this fact before us we could use $(A_i)$ instead of $(B)$ and $(A \lor A_i)$ instead of $(A \lor B)$. The disjunction says that there is the illusion or reality of seeing a flash of light.

"But in what respect or respects is the illusion of seeing a flash of light like the reality of seeing a flash of light?"

In more complex cases of this kind, where a reality XYZ is compared with its illusion $XYZ_i$, we can reply that in both cases there is the appearance, *i.e.* the illusion or reality, of X (or of Y, or of Z). In a simple case such as this seems to be, where we are asked what the illusion of X and the reality of X have in common, we can only reply that in both cases there is the appearance, *i.e.* the illusion or reality, of X.

"But what predicates are true both of my seeing a flash of light and of my having that illusion?"

Well, there must be some physiologically describable event phi such that the predicate "when x happens phi happens" is true of both. But of course that is not the sort of predicate you want. You want a predicate whose applicability to what is happening in or to me is made clear to me by the very fact of that thing's happening.

"Yes, and the predicate 'when x happens I see a flash' fills the bill. Both my A-ing and my B-ing have in common that when they occur I see a flash; and my seeing a flash is all that I experience of my A-ing or B-ing as the case may be."

Interpreting this last remark is not child's play. It does not mean that my seeing a flash, my having that visual experience, is something I experience in the sense of undergoing or literally living through it with a contingently accompanying awareness of it, like the awareness one might or might not have of moving on to a rail ferry in a wagon-lit. Nor does it mean that my having the visual experience, my psi-ing, is something that I experience in the sense of having that kind of awareness of it: a fine, and in this context possibly negligible, distinction there. It also does not mean that I experience my psi-ing in the sense of its being to me as if I were psi-ing: that would be nonsensical, perhaps because my psi-ing is its being to me if I saw a flash of light. Furthermore it does not mean that I do *not* experience my seeing a flash of light (as distinct from my psi-ing) in the sense in which we have just this moment said that I do perhaps experience it in the very act of psi-ing. I think it means that it's the same experience whether I'm A-ing or B-ing, an observation I try to deal with later.

Getting back to the matter of common properties. What reason is there to think that my A-ing and my B-ing must have a common property that each wears as it were on its sleeve to me? One way of thinking is that they have such a property in common because they have my psi-ing in common, but then that assumes the point at issue.

"They have in common the property that in both cases it is to me as if I were seeing a flash of light; and I cannot believe that I am just saying 'in both cases it is one case or the other.'"

When in a given case you say "It is to me as if I were seeing a flash of light" you could, of course, mean "I have that illusion"; but then you would not be stating a common property. If you really do not mean "What is happening either is or just is like seeing a flash of light" (= "Either what is, or what just is like, seeing a flash of light is happening") then perhaps you mean something very close to this, namely (R) "I couldn't tell whether this was, or just was like, the seeing a flash of light if I didn't know the circumstances." This may not be the mere disjunction but it does not differ from the mere disjunction in the way in which (Q) would: it does not give a definite answer to the question "What is happening?," since it does not give an answer to that question.

You could truly say, in both cases, (S) "Now, as not before, it could be that I see a flash of light." But *this* notion of possibility does not seem to have a categorical interpretation, like that of logical possibility in terms of non-contradiction. It seems unsuitable to be taken as primitive, and I do not see how it can be explained except as the disjunction of "really, actually I X" (*i.e.* "I X") with "illusorily I X" (*i.e.* I have the illusion of X-ing).

"It could be that I see a flash of light" could mean ((A)), "I am inclined to believe that (A) is true." In the remark "Both when there is A-ing and when there is B-ing, ((A)); in both cases it could be that there is A-ing" the (A)-asserting force of ((A)) would be wiped out by the context, and only the speaker-describing force would remain. But such a speaker-description would not describe a visual experience: this is distinguished by definition from what you may or may not be inclined to believe. (It would be a bad argument to say that being inclined to believe is not an event, for becoming inclined to believe is one. Or rather, "He became inclined to believe that p" tells of an event, though it does not tell of a process. The event of which it tells may or may not be a process; that is quite another matter).

"If A-ing and B-ing did not have a worn-on-the-sleeve property in common, how could you take one for the other?"

If things had to have a common property for you to take one for the other then a dagger, or a flash of light (such as may occur unobserved) would have to have properties in common with a "dagger of the mind" or a "phosphene": a flash you see when an electric current is passed through your brain. Or else it would have to be, strictly speaking, a sense-datum of the one that you took for a sense-datum of the other. Why, if we don't think that, should events have to have properties in common in order to be mistaken for one another? Why should it not just seem as if they had properties in common? Seeing a flash of light and having that illusion seem, but only seem, to have in common the property "when x occurs a flash of light occurs."

"But it is, or can be, the same experience when I see a photic flash and when I have the illusion of such a flash. In both cases the same experience can occur."

It can indeed be the same experience, but this only means that it can "be the same" experientially or subjectively or "qualitatively," *i.e.* that you can be quite unable to tell the difference. It is no more allowable to twist subjectively indistinguishable events into indistinguishable subjective events than to twist subjectively indistinguishable girls into indistinguishable subjective girls.

### III

If it is really as bad as that, why does it not seem so? Why do so many want to do for events, what nobody wants to do for objects? Well, it is pretty obvious that there are not subjective girls. The intermediate idea is, of course, that of the indistinguishable subjective girl-like sense-data. The extreme temptingness of that doctrine—its deep and ramified root-system—is well known. That it should be so out of fashion, and the indistinguishable subjective events so far from being out of fashion, is something I do not understand very well. One or two things occur to me in partial explanation.

In the first place, there must be indistinguishable, or at least closely similar, subjective events; though not at all in the way that the doctrine of visual experiences requires, not ones that I can tell you about. We have touched on this already: it would be absurd not to posit, not to hypothesize, similar goings-on in me when I see a flash of light and when I have that illusion. It is then easy to confuse these posited goings-on with the subjective events that our *esprit faux* prompts us to introduce.

It prompts us strongly when, say, we see a flash of light while reflecting on the fact that there must be something similar going on in us to what goes on when we get a phosphene. "Not only must there be, but there is, and this is it"—is then our thought. "This," however, is whatever it happens to be: if we are in fact seeing a flash of light it is our seeing a flash of light and not something that happens when we see a flash of light; and if we are having an illusion of a flash of light it is our having an illusion of a flash of light and not something that happens when we have such an illusion.

I do not want to deny that seeing is, and involves, a visual experience. Seeing something is an experience, an event of which one is the subject, even if the notion of the subject here is not quite the same as in "the experience of moving on to a rail ferry in a wagon-lit." Seeing an actual X, where an X is an optical object, involves a visual experience in the sense that if you see an actual X then either it is to you as if you saw one, or it is (for some Y) to you as if you saw a Y. This logical entailment of an indefinite statement by a definite one need not be thought of as the involvement of some kind of indefinite event in a definite one. Nor would it be an improvement to make it a definite event that was involved.

I hope that I am getting at some of the rootlets that keep the shattered trunk of "visual experiences" standing, though deeply undermined and pruned of its topmost sense-datum twigs. It is certainly strange that people should readily agree that one must not introduce a private Polly-Ann who is seen whenever Polly or Ann is seen, and yet go on introducing—or at least not extraditing—a private Polly-Ann-sighting that is done whenever Polly or Ann is sighted: a quasi-hallucination, for which one must no more supply an actual object than for a genuine hallucination, but which occurs whenever one has a veridical experience.

Finally: it is perhaps tempting to some to equate illegitimate hypostatization with the introduction of bogus objects, as distinct from events, properties, etc. It is perhaps believed—quite wrongly, I should have thought—that there can be no danger of introducing bogus events, etc., because one is going to extradite all events, etc., anyway. This idea that an "eventity" is only a very little one, is surely mistaken. It may well be that "My A-ing at that time was an actual event" just means "I A-'d then" (to take what I hope is a leaf from P. T. Geach's book) but this does not alter the fact that there is something quite differently and specially bogus about "this" event, the event that I now conclusively find to be occurring, irrespective of whether I'm sitting by the flickering fire or asleep and dreaming. If I went in for being the subject of that event, I should be afraid of your asking me whether it was at all like sitting by the fire.

## 2 Selections from *Experiences*

J. M. Hinton

## I   A VERY GENERAL NOTION, AND SOME SPECIAL ONES

### 1   An Event of Which One Is the Subject: General

"An event of which one is the subject": I can see three components, three requirements, in the idea of "the subject of an event" here. In the first place, whoever is reported as having or having had the experience is the grammatical subject of the event-report, or he can easily be made the grammatical subject. Then he is also still to some extent the test-subject; it seems that the event must not depart too widely from the old, submerged meaning of an experience as an experiment, test, or trial to which something is subjected. The third requirement is one which I will now state in an ambiguous and potentially misleading, though not unnatural, form as a preliminary to analysing what it involves: the grammatical subject and test-subject of the event must also be the conscious subject, or there must be the right sort of consciousness or awareness on his part. Most of Part I is an attempt to say how this third requirement is to be taken in various types of case. The other two requirements do not present so many problems. One of them, the requirement that you be the grammatical subject of the event, just puts a ring round things you "do" or "are" that happen. The other adds "... and that test you in some way." Given that you are human, this is likely to involve you in some sort of consciousness; the requirement of being tested has faded, though that of consciousness has not, or not to the same extent.

Instead of just saying that the grammatical subject did or "did" or "was" or underwent whatever it was, swam the Bosphorus or was ferried across it or whatever, the event-report sometimes says what almost comes to the

J. M. Hinton, *Experiences: An Inquiry into Some Ambiguities* (1973). By permission of Oxford University Press.

same thing, that he "had the experience of" swimming the Bosphorus or being ferried across it. It almost comes to the same thing because when our talk in English about someone's, or the, "experience of" doing this or that has the present sense, as distinct from another sense that I shall come to, the word "of" is like a mere comma. (In some languages, German for instance, it is translated by one.) The experience of swimming the Bosphorus is just the experience, swimming the Bosphorus. What the origin of this queer "of" is, linguists would know. Probably they can tell us why we talk about the island of Mull and the township of Craignure and the virtue of honesty and the sum of one pound and the act of raising your arm, but not the postmistress of Mary Donaldson. What I have to point out is that, just as the island of Mull is not something like the map of Mull; not something other than Mull which is related to Mull in a way indicated by the word "of"; so the experience of being ferried across the Channel, in *this* sense of the phrase, is not something other than being ferried across the Channel. The experience, (of) X-ing, in this sense, is no other event or thing than X-ing, the event of which one is the grammatical subject.— The reason why talk about someone's, or the, "experience, (of) X-ing" only almost, and not quite, comes to the same thing as talk about X-ing is that the characterization of X-ing as an experience may be essential to the sense of the passage; for instance if the question is whether things that come under that characterization always or sometimes come under some other specified characterization or classification.

There is quite a marked resemblance between the common noun, an "experience," and the common noun, an "act." The last of these common nouns is, or could be, used in an indefinite number of different ways on a scale of generality. Most generally of all, as a word for anything at all that you "do" in the sense that you are the grammatical subject of it—you did get born, did grow. If we used "act" in this utterly general way, then even getting cremated or mummified, or posthumously rehabilitated or otherwise revalued, let alone dying, would be an act. A little more restrictively, we might impose the proviso that the subject of the verb be at least alive. Being operated on, even under a general anaesthetic, and even if you died on the table, would be an act then, in contrast to undergoing a literal or figurative post-mortem—but so would weighing eleven stone and knowing this or that. More restrictively again, we could impose the further requirement that the so-called "act" must be a happening. And then we could further impose, in all its unclearness, the proviso that there must be the right sort of consciousness on the part of the subject of the verb, if the happening is to be an "act." I do not see any difference between an act, in this last possible sense, and an experience in the ordinary biographical sense of the word, unless you count the restriction that survives from the old meaning of a test.

Where an experience is just an act in this sense, to experience it is just to "do" it. In other words, to experience X-ing, in this sense, is just to X—provided that X-ing is a happening, provided that there is the right sort of consciousness on your part, whatever that may mean, and subject to the further restriction just mentioned that survives from the old meaning.

I do not want to stress this last restriction too strongly, that the experience must be something like a test or trial through which the subject passes—to which he, she, or it is subjected. In some cases this requirement is imposed in a very attenuated form if at all, and we can lift it completely if we are so inclined. Still, a loose and altered connection with that old meaning of a test may help to explain why we do not colloquially call just anything and everything that we literally live through as conscious subjects an experience. The connection is altered; not only because the "experiencing" used to be the testing and not the being tested, but because from being an occurrence whose "event" in the old sense, outcome, establishes whether or not the thing tested has certain qualities, an experience may now by extension have become alternatively something whose mere occurrence, or whose tautologous outcome, establishes that he, she, or it has them—or even merely something that has a characteristic result, such as the giving of a report. The experience of passing through the streets of a foreign city may fail to establish more than that one has some part of the wealth and leisure of a globe-trotter, and may result only in one's boring others. Yet perhaps it also tests whether one can make something of what one sees, and perhaps this fact is thrown into the background only because the outcome of the test is so often thought by others to be negative. The connection is loose; it can always be tightened. Sean O'Faolain writes, looking back,[1] that the revolutionary period in Ireland which he had come out of when he wrote his first successful short story was too filled with dreams and ideals and a sense of dedication to be what he would now call an experience "in the meaning of things perceived, remembered and understood." The basic idea, here, is that of things and times lived through; a more general idea than that of an event of which one is the subject, and one with which I shall not be directly concerned. In other words the verb, here, is "to live through" in a broad sense, broader than that of "doing," while alive, something which is a happening. Within that broader general idea, the reference to "things perceived" shows a shift towards a meaning of "to experience" ...; a meaning more like "witness," "behold," or "perceive" than "do" or "undergo." Yet these last two ideas are very much alive in the context, and to the extent that they are, the stress is on a test or trial of the mind's power to remember and understand the things done or undergone.

No doubt it has something to do with the older meaning of a test that suggestions of passivity, belied by that example and many others, and of something out of the ordinary, even of something rather unpleasant, cling at times to the noun an "experience." However, these are associations merely, and not requirements; we speak of the gratifying experience of clearing six foot two in the high jump, and of humdrum, everyday experiences too.

There remains to be investigated the requirement that there must be the right sort of consciousness on the part of the grammatical subject of the event, or in other words that he must be the conscious subject of the event. What does this mean?

## 2   Things That You Can Experience, But That Can Also Happen to You without Your Experiencing Them

*We characteristically require the grammatical subject of an event to be in some sense its conscious subject, before we are happy to call the event one of his experiences in the ordinary biographical sense of the word. But what, more exactly, does this requirement involve when the event is of the sort mentioned in this section's title? The answer suggested is that, in this type of case, we normally require the subject to have a certain special kind of awareness of the event itself. This awareness, which need not be simultaneous with the event, can take many forms within certain limits. It need not amount to knowledge that the event in question is occurring or has occurred, nor is such knowledge sufficient.*

Let us take cases in which the grammatical subject of the event might not have been the conscious subject of it, because there might not have been the right sort of consciousness or awareness on his part. And then the event would not have counted as one of his "experiences." Only that is putting it too strongly; the requirement of the right sort of consciousness is only *more or less* built into the ordinary biographical notion of an experience in this type of case—and in a more or less stringent form.

For instance, suppose a young man tells you that when he and his friend Peter were conscripts, sent to suppress revolution in a distant former colony, and were taken prisoner, Peter had the experience of being operated on, in a field hospital of the revolutionaries, for the removal of six bullets. Your informant's using the word "experience" may lead you to assume that they were not able to give Peter a general anaesthetic, but only a local or regional one, or only rice wine, or nothing at all. However, you may be inclined to let the word "experience" pass even if you are told that Peter did have a general anaesthetic and was completely unconscious throughout the operation—no simultaneous relevant awareness, presumably. But what if your informant goes on to add that Peter now remembers nothing at all about the entire period of his captivity? You may still be willing to call the operation one of Peter's experiences. This is partly because you will naturally assume that when Peter came to, after the operation, he realized or was told what had happened—though of course he has now forgotten this. But what if you are told that, for some peculiar reason, when Peter came to, he did not know he had been operated on, and was led to believe that his wounds had been caused by falling on stakes of sharpened bamboo in a man-trap? Even now, you may still be prepared to call the operation one of Peter's experiences, perhaps because his now-forgotten former awareness of his wounds before and after the operation counts, for you, as the right sort of consciousness on his part. His awareness of his wounds was, after all, relevant to the operation although Peter did not know that it was.

Let us now exchange the case for one in which we can more easily suppose the subject to have no consciousness, whether before, during, or after the event, that is at all relevant to what he undergoes. The convalescent Peter is sound asleep on the ground in a clearing when he is gently turned over by some tame animal that can smell the palm leaves or hay he is lying on. The friend who now tells you of the incident is sure that Peter knew nothing about it at the time and knows nothing about it now. There was no sign of its disturbing his sleep, nor did he later tell of a dream that could be connected with what happened. Yet your narrator, who believes Peter to have had no kind of awareness at any time that was at all relevant to the animal's turning him over, still says that Peter had the "experience" of being turned over by the animal. His is, in virtue of his belief, an unconventional use of the word. Nevertheless, someone might so use the word, not just as a momentary aberration but regularly; making it cover any event you literally lived through as the grammatical subject, and altogether suspending the requirement of consciousness, whatever this requirement is exactly. We could countenance such a use; partly, perhaps, because we lack some such noun as an "undergoing" for what the happening was if it was not an experience.

In point of fact we sometimes countenance a use in which not even the requirement that the grammatical subject and test-subject be a living thing, let alone any requirement of consciousness, is involved; when we are told that a bullet, or the fuselage of an aircraft, or the hull of a ship, experiences such and such testing stresses under such and such conditions. Since this is just a matter of refraining from imposing a proviso or restriction, it is not strictly speaking an analogy; or at any rate not quite in the way in which it is an analogy to talk about a malicious deck-chair. . . .

What I have just said contrasts with the view that seeing is in no sense an experience; a view to which Ryle appeared to commit himself in *Dilemmas*. But I take Ryle to have been saying that seeing is not an 'experience' in a redefined philosophical-psychological usage, for whose existence he, Ryle, is not responsible. In this special usage there is a contrast between an "experience" and an achievement, whereas if we avoid special dictions there is no contrast between an experience and an achievement. Winning a game of chess against a much better player may be one of my more memorable experiences, and so may seeing a flash of light if my doing so saved my life. In the ordinary and literary use of the common noun "an experience," an event of which one is the subject, there is no inescapable implication that an experience is a process, a series of changes; or an episode, something of which one is a spectator; or a *stretch* of, as distinct from a momentary happening in, one's life history; or something that one was "engaged in"; or something that has "a beginning, a middle, and an end"; or a passive business; or anything at all like that.

But in order to get to closer grips with the matter of awareness of seeing, let me make what I believe to be a familiar, though not self-explanatory, distinction between two meanings of "see X"; (1) the meaning exemplified by "see a cobra, in the general sense of seeing something which is, in point of fact, a cobra" and (2) a narrower meaning exemplified by "not only see what is in point of fact a cobra, but also see a cobra as distinct from only (just, merely) seeing what is in point of fact a cobra." There is a natural parallel with, for instance, "try to pick up a cobra, I mean try to pick up something which is in fact a cobra" and "try to pick up a cobra; I mean try to do that, as distinct from only or just trying to pick up what is in fact a cobra." In this case the difference lies in whether one knows that it is a cobra; the case of seeing is similar to this extent, that seeing what is in point of fact a cobra, while knowing it to be a cobra, is *sufficient* even if not necessary for "seeing a cobra" in the narrower sense.

I must make it clear, by the way, that I shall be concerned with "seeing what is in fact X" only to the extent that such a phrase clarifies some established non-theoretical usage of "see X" (same X as in the first expression). Not when "see what is in fact X" is used where no such usage of "see X" (same X as in the first expression) exists. For instance, I shall not be concerned with the sense in which a man who sees a table sees what is in fact a set of ultramicroscopic, i.e. invisible, particles, since this is not, neither is anything else, a case in which we would ordinarily speak of someone as seeing a set of invisible particles. The distinction I am making between "see $X$, see what is $X$" and "see $X$, as distinct from only seeing what is $X$," is a distinction between and within ordinary uses of "see $X$" (same $X$)—it does not go beyond these.

I was saying that it is clear that seeing a cobra, in the sense of seeing what is in fact a cobra, does not logically entail seeming to see a cobra in any sense. But what about seeing a cobra in the second and narrower of those two senses, call it "properly" seeing one? Does this entail seeming to see a cobra? If we were to say so, we should be using the notion of "seeming to see," or ostensible visual perception, more broadly even than the broad and vague notion of the relevant visual appearance's being present or being presented. For someone who sees what is a cobra, looking to him then and there exactly like a root, but who happens to know for certain that it is a cobra, may if you like be said to see a cobra, as distinct from just or merely seeing what is in fact one. Now we are not here interested in any sense of "seem to see" or "ostensibly visually perceive" which is broader than the vague notion of a visual appearance of the relevant sort's being presented. We therefore shall not say that "properly" seeing an $X$ entails seeming to do so.

What if we simply leave out of consideration all those cases (of seeing $X$ in the "proper" sense) in which what is seen does not look like $X$ to the one who sees it, as well as all cases in which, while it does look like $X$ to him, it also looks to him to a non-negligible extent like something different?[2] Do the remaining cases, those in which, as we say, the unambiguous testimony of his visual sense is of $X$, yield a sense of "see $X$" which entails seeming to see $X$ (same $X$)? It is plausible to say yes, *plainly* seeing $X$, in this sense, entails seeming to see $X$ (same $X$). I defer ... the question as to what truth exactly there is in this reply. I think there is truth in it. It is worth stressing a couple of things about what has just been marked out as "plainly seeing": first, that plainly seeing $X$ is a special case of seeing what is in fact $X$; second, that plainly seeing $X$ does not entail taking what you see to be $X$. This last point is true because I may see what is in fact a cobra, not looking to any extent worth mentioning like anything but a cobra, in my sitting-room and yet, on the assumption that English sitting-rooms do not have cobras in them, take it to be a toy or a spoof. Here I plainly see, but to revive an old word I do not "apperceive," a cobra because I do not realize what it is, do not correctly identify what I see as a cobra. When a man both apperceives $X$ and plainly sees $X$, unlike the man who apperceives a cobra looking exactly like a root, then it might be said that he "strongly" visually apperceives $X$....

## 5 A Contrast

Apart from any interest which such a philosophico-lexical study may have in itself, the main point of Part I has been to make a contrast between the ordinary biographical notion of an experience and the special philosophical notion of one, to which we shall come....

## II A VERY SPECIAL NOTION

### IIa Perception-Illusion Disjunctions (1)

*By way of what is seen as an essential, and so to speak contiguous, preliminary to the investigation in IIb of the relevant, very special, philosophical notion of an experience, IIa concerns itself with a type of proposition to which IIc returns, called perception-illusion disjunctions. These are first roughly defined in Section 6. In Section 7 certain propositions of this kind are assumed to be true in a hypothetical case, and some of their properties are set forth....*

### 6 Perception-Illusion Disjunctions: General

Even if few things are certain, it is certain that there are what I will call perception-illusion disjunctions: sentences or statements like "Macbeth perceives a dagger or is having that illusion," which you can compose by adding words like "... or $x$ is having that illusion" to a sentence which says that a particular person, $x$, perceives a thing of some particular kind. Words like "... or $x$ is having some different illusion" are to be counted as *un*like "... or $x$ is having that illusion": a perception-illusion disjunction mentions the illusion of the very perception it mentions. This does not mean that no perception-illusion disjunction is or would be true when, for instance, it is true that "Macbeth perceives a dagger or is having the illusion of perceiving Banquo." But this sentence or statement is not what I am calling a perception-illusion disjunction.

It is perhaps surprising that perception-illusion disjunctions are not more often deliberately placed in the centre of the picture, in the philosophy of perception. Philosophers do quite often introduce the notion of an experience-report as that of a statement, or even *the* statement, which is true both when you perceive a given thing and when you have the illusion of doing so. This makes it sound as if they had in mind a perception-illusion disjunction. In a high proportion of cases, however, one has only to ask them whether they do, to find that they do not. They did not express their whole thought. They had in mind a suppositious kind of statement which has the property they mentioned, but which also has other properties. I believe that they often have in mind something that "answers the question as to what is happening to the subject," in a sense which I will pick out.... But this in itself, apart from not being invariably required, would never be enough. In IIb (Section 10) I am going to set forth some requirements which the sort of statement they have in mind might have to satisfy in a particular hypothetical case, defined as one in which certain perception-illusion disjunctions are true: I will describe the hypothetical case in Section 7....

## 7   Some Descriptions That Apply to Certain Perception-Illusion Disjunctions

I will use "$D^*$" as a name for the following statement, which we will assume someone to make truly—perhaps by pressing a button which he has been told to press if and when the statement is true.

$D^*$   "I see a flash of light of a certain sort or I am having the perfect illusion of seeing one of that sort."

Solely in virtue of its containing the words "... of a certain sort ... of that sort" in the way it does, $D^*$ is what I shall call a "pointed" perception-illusion disjunction; "pointedness" is indicated by the asterisk. Contrast the "blunt" perception-illusion disjunction,

$D$   "I see a flash of light or I am having the perfect illusion of doing so."

A more specific, yet "blunt," perception-illusion is

$D^b$   "I see a flash of bluish-white light or I am having the perfect illusion of seeing one."

This, as well as $D^*$, is to be true *ex hypothesi* of the person who states $D^*$, but we do not assume him to state $D^b$....

There is to be no difference at all between $D^*$ and

"I am having the perfect illusion of seeing a flash of light of a certain sort or I perceive a flash of light of that sort."

So, if you like, $D^*$ is really

$D^*$   "Of at least one sort of flash of light it is true either that I see, or that I am having the perfect illusion of seeing, a flash of light of that sort."

Perhaps this is true or false under just the same conditions as $D$; perhaps not. In any case, it goes against the grain to say that it means just the same as $D$. Obviously $D^*$ does not mean the same as $D^b$. The fact that $D^b$ is true may be what has given our speaker his incentive to state $D^*$, but this does not mean that in stating this he states something which means the same as $D^b$.... What you "say" or "state," at least as I am here and now using these verbs, is a matter of the meaning of the conventional sign you use, not of what you have in mind. It is a little, though in the first person not very, like the fact that if I say "At least one Australian is of Chinese origin," having in mind a certain colleague who, however, in point of fact is of Korean origin, then what I say or state is true all the same if at least one Australian is indeed of Chinese origin.

The illusion, and it might be the perfect illusion, of (seeing) a flash of light is—$I$ say—what you get for instance when an electric current is passed through your head in a certain way by experimental psychologists. *They* call it giving you a "phosphene," etymologically a light-appearance. No light is involved....

**7 (i)** $D^*$ and $D^b$... logically entail that the subject is at least tempted to believe that he visually perceives a flash of light. For if $D^*$ or $D^b$ is true, and if it is not a case of perfect illusion, which entails the temptation... then it is a case of seeing a flash of light. But I rule that "seeing," "visually perceiving," and "perceiving," in all these statements, have the sense we called "plainly seeing." And if you plainly see $X$ then you are at least tempted to believe that you do. For you are at least so tempted when, as we say, the unambiguous testimony of your senses is to the effect that there is $X$ in your environment. Your plainly seeing $X$ is one of the things this saying can relate to; your being perfectly illuded that you plainly see $X$ is another.[3]

**7 (ii)** $D^*$ [is a] proposition that can be worded, without doing much violence to language, in one of such ways as "In a neutral sense, it is/seems/ appears to me a little/rather/very much/exactly as if I saw a flash of light." Or simply as "I see a flash of light," used in the relatively incorrigible sense of neutral appearance; any perception-sentence can be used exceptionally in this weakened sense by making it, for the moment, equivalent to a pointed perception-illusion disjunction....

## IIb   The Common Element in Perception and Illusion

*The relevant philosophical notion is first, in Section 9, identified in a rough way in relation to the relevant hypothetical case. Next, in Section 10, requirements are*

*laid down for what is called an R-statement; this, if there were such a thing,*
*would be a hard-core example of a report of an "experience" in the problematic*
*conception or misconception. A weaker set of requirements for an "experience"-*
*report or E-report is then extracted. It is maintained that, as far as anyone knows*
*or has the right to believe, there is no such thing as an E-report, let alone an R-*
*statement. In Section 11 the idea is dismissed that there are events which would*
*be reported by E-reports if there were such reports but which, in the absence of*
*these, cannot be reported at all....*

## 9 The Common Element: General

We now come to the special, philosophical notion of an experience, which
it is the main purpose of this essay to reconsider, though not to rehabili-
tate. It was referred to, in the opening paragraphs of the book, as involving
a form of the following general idea: that a visual experience is "inner"
independently of the extent to which it is given meaning by the subject's
experience of life. There is truth in this general idea, if only because one's
individuality is not a function of experience alone. Inherited as well as
acquired differences, together with the essential interminability of an account of the meaning which a given object or change that affected his eye
had for a given human being, make the supposition that two people have
given exactly the same total meaning to such a stimulus always unverifi-
able, and often easily falsified.

The relevant philosophical notion, however, is a form of the general idea
that the experience had by each of two people would still be "inner,"
however many tests or observations, of a kind that might have revealed
a difference in the giving of meaning, failed to do so; and not at all because the next test or observation might have revealed such a difference.
We can say that there is truth in this general idea, too. Take for instance
the...experience, (of) visually perceiving a flash of light. (Light, that
which affects photographic plates and causes photosynthesis, a photic
flash.) Visually perceiving a flash of light is "inner," quite apart from any
differences in the giving of meaning that might be detected, in at least two
senses: something literally inner, an electrical or electrochemical process
occurring in the central nervous system, is a *sine qua non* for its occurrence;
and others depend upon the sentient subject's behaviour, or his reports
of one sort or another, in order to be as sure as they can be that it has
occurred. There is, by the way, no special kind of report that we need. A
perception-claim will do though we do not need it; so will a mistaken
illusion-report in the right circumstances, and so will a perception-illusion
disjunction.

However, the relevant philosophical notion is not the notion of a kind of perception, in the objective sense in which we are using the word. So it is not, in this present context, the notion of perceiving a flash of light, nor is it the notion of perceiving some optical object that looks like a flash of light—if there is such an optical object. This last point ought perhaps to be stressed. In the main-line notion of an inner experience which we are selecting for scrutiny, there is a gap between one's report of such an experience and any proposition as to how some external object, event, or process looks; a gap exactly as wide as the gap between such an experience-report and *any* sort of proposition about the "external world." Connectedly, by the way, the perception-proposition in a perception-illusion disjunction can very well be a proposition about how something looks; one kind of perception-illusion disjunction is exemplified by: "Either I visually perceive an optical object which looks (a great deal, a little, hardly at all) like a two-dimensional coloured shape, or I am having the illusion of doing so."

The relevant philosophical notion is also not the notion of a kind of illusion. So it is not, in this present context, the notion of getting the illusion—under which heading I include the total hallucination...—of a flash of light. An experience of the relevant sort is supposed to occur both when you perceive a flash of light and when you have the illusion of seeing one.

We can almost, but not quite, add that the kind of experience which is supposed to occur then is supposed not to occur on any other kind of occasion. Not quite, because in one sub-conception which could be further subdivided, that kind of experience might occur without there being either the perception or the illusion. Still, the experience is *most naturally* assumed to occur only when, as we say or used to say, one's visual sense is giving testimony of a flash of light. So it is roughly though not exactly correct to say that—as applied to our case—the relevant notion is of a kind of experience common *and peculiar* to the perception and the illusion of a flash of light. (Obviously, the relevant kind of experience is supposed to be divisible into indefinitely many kinds.)

The notion is not the only one which can be expressed by the phrase "the common element in the perception and the illusion of a flash of light." It is, perhaps, the most general notion which this phrase can express and which is not merely truistic. Someone who thinks in the relevant way, and who says that the common element in perceiving and having the illusion of a flash of light would be an example of the sort of experience he has in mind, does not mean to be saying *merely* that perceiving a flash of light is an event which belongs to some wider class to which the illusion also belongs, so that the common element is "the occurrence of an event of that class." On the other hand he may not—though equally he may—want to say that there would be a *difference* between someone's perceiving a flash of light on a given occasion and the relevant particular experience, or that there would be a difference between someone's having the illusion on a given occasion and the relevant particular experience.

It is because he may not want to say that there is or would be a difference, that I had to speak carefully, and say that the notion of having the experience is neither the notion of perceiving something nor the notion of having a certain illusion; instead of saying that the posited experience is neither a perception nor an illusion. Positing the experience is not the same as positing a perception or positing an illusion; it is other than those posits, and other than the posit that "one or other of those things has occurred," but not, necessarily, the posit of something other than those things.

If the philosopher who advances the notion thinks that "there is a difference," then he may or may not think that the common element is common to the two "acts," the perceiving and the being illuded. He may think it precedes the acts.

After these general remarks about the relevant controversial conception I will try to get to closer grips with it by articulating the question as to whether there is indeed an "experience," in the relevant sense or nonsense, in the hypothetical case which was constructed in Section 7. But first the question will be, whether there is such a thing as a *report* of such an experience.

## 10   Experience-reports

**10 (i)   *R*-statements**  Is there, can one compose, such a thing as an *R*-statement: a statement that meets all the following requirements, from R.1 to r.x?

R.1   The statement must be one that we can assume, suppose to be true in our hypothetical case in which $D^b$ is true; without the new supposition's being, in this context, either problematic or extraneous. By an extraneous supposition, here, I mean one which is no more strongly suggested as a possibility by the assumption $D^b$ than by some completely different assumption. (For example, the supposition that the subject experiences "*déja vu.*")

R.2   The statement must be one that can without absurdity be supposed, in our hypothetical case, to "answer the question as to what happened to the subject"...Moreover, it must be one that can be supposed to identify, state exactly the what-it-is of, the event by whose occurrence the subject was at least tempted to believe that he perceived a flash of light. (I assume this takes care of "extraneousness," but the point is that I shall be talking about subsets of these requirements as well as about the whole lot.) As a brief way of expressing R.2, I will sometimes say that it requires the statement to have "the desired kind of precision"—it is less my duty to be invariably exact about precision and exactitude than it is (as Austin indicated) the duty of one who espouses the problematic conception of an experience.

R.3   The statement must be one which it would seem incongruous...for the speaker to preface by "I am inclined to believe that...."

R.4   ...the statement must speak of, declare the occurrence of, an "act" or "doing" in the broadest auxiliary sense, which is moreover an event of which $x$ is the grammatical subject, and of which furthermore we naturally, albeit ambiguously, say that it "could not occur without being an experience," or "could not occur without there being the right sort of consciousness in the case for it to be an experience"....

R.5   The statement must be such that the subject, $x$, can satisfy himself that it meets requirement R.2; moreover, he must be able to do so without relying on any undischarged assumption about the physical.

The rest of the requirements that will be mentioned may well be, and I should have thought they were, corollaries of those five; I will lay them down in case they are not all corollaries: (r.vi) The statement is not allowed to be a physiological one, nor (r.vii) is it allowed to be a non-specific statement whose truth would follow from a physiological fact. It cannot (r.viii) in any natural or normal sense of the words be an idea or hypothesis or conjecture or theory or thesis when asserted by the one to whom it relates. He, if he states it, states a fact; or at any rate he does not put forward an idea as distinct, for instance, from stating a fact. He speaks very much as he finds, not at all as he fancies. (r.ix) The statement must neither be nor entail a perception-proposition where "perception" has the full, objective sense—in this class I include all statements about how an object looks—and (r.x) it must neither be nor entail an illusion-proposition.

Those requirements collectively, R.1 to r.x, are intended to capture or recapture a certain elusive, fairly broad yet problematic, conception of "a visual experience-report relevant to the case of a bluish-white flash of light." If nothing meets all those requirements then there is no such thing as an experience-report of that kind, in one sense or non-sense. I do not see that anything does meet all those requirements. Indeed my impression or tentative belief, which may of course be entirely mistaken for all that I am by no means the first to hold or to have received it, is that as far as anyone knows or has the right to believe, nothing meets all those requirements.

This declaration may seem pointless, and even a breach of the ethics or manners of disputation. Is it not too much like declaring with a judicial air that one is not convinced by the other party's arguments? The criticism might be fair if, today, familiar arguments were generally held to establish that there are statements which meet all those requirements. In effect this is how things used to be. For it was widely held that the existence of such things as visual sense-data, sensa or sensibilia, conceived as actual or possible objects of a kind of vision, or at least as having qualities such as bluish-whiteness which are normally thought of as being detected by sight, or if not as having such qualities then as containing things that have them, could be established by familiar arguments. These would indirectly establish that there were statements about such entities. These statements would include some that met all those above-mentioned requirements, R.1 to r.x, which relate to the case of a bluish-white flash of light.

The present philosophical and psychological situation is one of widespread scepticism about such arguments and such entities, among which I hope we may include the "visual field" if this is something that sense-data are found in, as well as the transparent stream of consciousness in which round red patches floated like red cells in the plasma. Yet unless I am quite mistaken it is now often believed, and more often taken for granted than argued, that there are statements which meet all those requirements without being about such entities. Visual sense-data and things like that are discredited; we tend to talk nowadays about "statements about visual experiences," meaning for instance statements that meet all those requirements. Of course I do not mean that everyone speaks or thinks in this way. . . .

**10 (ii) *E*-reports** In order to broaden the question, I will introduce the notion of an "*E*-report." If there were such a thing as an *R*-statement, then it would be an *E*-report, but there might be an *E*-report which was not an *R*-statement. An *E*-report need satisfy only two requirements. It must meet R.1, the requirement of being something we can suppose to be true in the context. Moreover it must fit a description which . . . we held to be unsuited to a perception-illusion disjunction—the description, "report of an experience which is or would be the same, whether the subject's case is/were one of perception or one of illusion." This tag must be not just applicable in some tongue-in-cheek way, but seriously worth applying to the statement in the present philosophical context. Within the suppositious class of *E*-reports I would distinguish, as "precise *E*-reports," any which met R.2, the requirement of the desired kind of precision.

I do not see that there are any *E*-reports, precise or not. For the rest of this section let us consider some arguments or trains of thought which might be held to show that there are.

### 10 (ii) (A)   The Argument from Science

*Some trains of thought, which appear to justify the belief that there are E-reports, and which appear to be based on Science, turn out to be based on dubious and arbitrary general metaphysical beliefs about objects of reference and about effects of causes. Others are genuinely based on Science, but do not terminate in the conclusion that there are E-reports. Others again are rather based on Science Fiction.*

With more than a little plausibility one can say in a general way that, if the elusive controversial doctrine of "experiences" were to prove sound after all, this would be because it had proved after all to be a genuine product of creative science. And one can, without any difficulty, find in scientific writings passages about "sensations" or "experiences" which may appear to endorse, more particularly, the doctrine that there occur reportable events whose reports would be *E*-reports.

Some of these passages, however, present a stronger appearance of doing this than others. The appearance is not all that strong when a physiologist, after giving a careful, accurate account of certain electrical and electro-chemical changes in the eye–brain system that are normally initiated by light striking the retinas, merely tops off this account by adding that there next occurs an event of an entirely different, not physiologically describable, kind called a sensation or experience, with which he is not professionally concerned. His talk of one's "then, and only then—after the relevant changes have occurred in the relevant structures—getting the sensation or experience of a flash" might merely mean that then, and only then, one visually perceives a flash of light or has the illusion of doing so, according to the character of the initial stimulus.

However, what I have just said gives rise to an objection. The impulse reaches certain specified structures, and then—what? My continuation was, "—and then, one perceives a flash of light or has the illusion of doing so, as the case may be, according to the nature of the initial stimulus." But it is natural to make some such retort as this, that what then happens cannot depend on the initial stimulus; what happens next must be the same, whether the initial stimulus was light striking the retina, or an electric current passing from an electrode through the retina, or whatever it was. Well, and indeed it would be strange if, given a certain type of impulse reaching certain structures, what happened next there, or in adjacent structures, was different according to the nature of the remoter cause, the initial stimulus; the mechanically "observable" effect of the given proximate cause taking after its grandfather, so to speak. But this is not the only possibility which the person who makes that retort means to exclude. He means, that the immediately following event which the subject can explicitly and truly report must be the same. This is true in the sense that the subject can, no matter what the stimulus was, truly make the same event-report, the report that he sees a flash; which we are not, by this fact, prevented from interpreting as the report that he perceives a flash of light or has the illusion of doing so. But the objector wants to say: "Not only can the subject thereupon truly make the same event-report irrespective of the initial stimulus; but also the *event*, which he can truly and explicitly report, is then the same." Hence we have a linguistic distinction; do we have a difference?

The feeling that there is a difference may persist; let us reconsider the objection. It is based on the principle, "Same cause, same effect." It is fair to point out that the assumption of there being the same (proximate) cause, in the case of a perception and its perfect illusion, tends to be derived from an application of the converse principle, "Same effect, same cause," where the premiss, that we indeed have here the "same effect," is intended in a sense that assumes the point as issue. Nevertheless, let us suppose for the sake of argument that the condition, that *for all one can tell from what happens one perceives a flash of light,* is the invariable consequent of some neural condition which could in principle be exactly specified. To use the sort of language that comes naturally; the consequent condition must, we are liable to feel, be a definite, identifiable type of event, which is what it is in itself, though there may of course be a rule or convention to call it "perception of a flash of light" if its remoter antecedents are of one kind, and to call it "illusion of a flash of light" if they are of another kind. It cannot, we may feel, be something that is not identifiable more precisely, without knowledge of its ancestry, than as "perception or illusion of a flash of light." It must be "this" specific and well-identified type of event, whichever of those two descriptions it may fall under in virtue of its relation to other things, not just "this" generic type of event, perception or illusion of a flash, whichever of those species it may belong to in virtue of its antecedents. That is the idea we tend to have, but is it well founded?

One thing it may be based on is the further idea that, otherwise, we should not know what we were talking about—and indeed should not be talking about anything, really—when we said that *it*, the event which the subject can expressly report when the relevant impulse reaches the relevant structures, is the perception or illusion of a flash of light, according to the character of the initial stimulus. That we could not answer the question, "What do you mean; what are you referring to? *What* is the perception or illusion of a flash of light according to the antecedent circumstances? What is it, that is the perception or the illusion according to the circumstances?" It is clear that when we think like this, we are not disposed to accept, as a sufficient condition for one's knowing what one is talking about, the mere availability of a substantive or substantival phrase to sustain the pronominal reference. For this could easily be arranged. We could introduce the phrase "the flash-experience," simply to mean "the flash-perception or flash-illusion, as the case may be." It is no good doing that, if we are back where we started as soon as an explanation of the meaning of the substantival phrase is asked for—so we are liable to feel. When this is how we feel, then it turns out that our idea that the effect must be "a definite something" is based on an idea about what meaningful speech and thought involve. An idea which, laudably enough, tries to get through and beyond conventional grammar and sees as too permissive its standards for knowing what one is talking about....

... When you look at it, what reason is there to say that the pronoun "it," in "it is perception or illusion, according to the circumstances," *must* grammatically refer to something other than "the perception or illusion"? None.

True, there is the feeling that if not everything, then at any rate every *effect*, must be what you might call "narrowly identifiable"; meaning that one can state the what-it-is of it, to a degree of exactitude which satisfies normal human interest in the matter, without having to know what its proximate, let alone more remote, cause is. But what is the feeling based on? Surely it is based only on the tautologous fact that an effect is always narrowly identifiable where, as in a purely physiological case for instance, public procedures enable us narrowly to identify it. Here they do not, and it does not follow that private procedures do. I need not assert that they do not. The point at present is merely that a universal principle of the narrow identifiability of effects does not, in view of its basis, compel our assent and oblige us to attribute a narrowly identifying character to whatever procedures issue in the recording of a "private" effect....

**10 (ii) (B)**  ... But is it not the very same experience, when one sees a flash of light and when one has the perfect illusion of doing so? Well; the perfect or indistinguishable illusion is, to the subject, from itself alone, indistinguishable from the perception. And you can dress up this tautology as

"The perfect illusion is experientially, subjectively the same as the perception," and this in turn as "The perfect illusion is the same experience as the perception." However, the relation underlying this growth of verbiage is non-symmetrical, unlike identity. From the fact that "you could not tell this from the real thing," it does not follow that you could not tell the real thing from this; the real thing may occur only under a condition which is not present to the memory in the case of the simulacrum, and which issues in decision. Though it does not follow it may nevertheless be true that, given the perception, you could not "then and there" tell it from the perfect illusion; if "then" is defined narrowly enough. Even when this is true, it does not follow that on each occasion something occurs the report of which would be an *E*-report; your premiss is merely that the perception and the illusion cannot, under certain conditions, be told apart by the subject himself.

Some people feel that you must have a ground for a perception-illusion disjunction. Why? Are they unprepared for a contingent disjunction to be assertible without a ground? If so, they have perhaps forgotten that their suppositious *E*-report could itself be formulated as a disjunction unless there are absolutely simple propositions. Moreover, even if it were to be shown that the now widely rejected doctrine of absolutely simple propositions was wrongly rejected, it would still be necessary for the objector to show that none but absolutely simple propositions can be both contingent, and assertible without a ground. This idea certainly *looks* like a mere confusion between what makes a thing true and what makes a thing known. A disjunction cannot be true otherwise than by one of its disjuncts being true, but of course this does not mean—nor is it true—that a disjunction cannot be known otherwise than by one of its disjuncts being known. If this were true, then a perception-illusion disjunction could never take the agnostic suffix, "... I don't know which," and the philosophy of "experiences" could not get started. . . .

## 11 Something about Which Nothing Can Be Said

If there is no reason to think that there are *E*-reports, then is there any reason to think that there occur events which would be explicitly reported by *E*-reports if there were any *E*-reports to report them, but which in the absence of *E*-reports cannot be reported or described at all? It does not seem to me that any of the trains of thought we have considered, as possibly leading to a belief in the existence of *E*-reports, can be adapted so as to become good arguments for this rather strange idea. . . . it is hardly the sort of idea one can accept without a reason. Its acceptance seems unwarranted. Yet it is not easy to see what else but this idea can be intended by philosophers who say that we cannot describe our sensations. They do not mean that I cannot describe the sensation which I do describe, quite well, as "the queer tickling sensation you get all up your spine when you are a fourteen-year-old boy and the attractive art mistress looks over your shoulder." Nor do they mean that we cannot make perception-claims and illusion-reports, or assert perception-illusion disjunctions....

## Appendix

. . .

**B.** I wrote...about the indistinguishability of perfect illusion *from* perception—from, rather than "and." I think that what I wrote implies, but it does not clearly state, my answer to the question how perfect illusion should be conceived. A perfect, or as we say the perfect, illusion of a given perception or other reality should be thought of as follows. It is an illusion of that reality, such that if you are involved in the illusion then you cannot tell, simply by being involved in it, that it is not that reality. It should not be defined as an illusion of such a sort that, if you are involved in that reality, then you can by no means tell that you are not involved in an illusion of that sort! The result of defining perfect illusion in this second way would be that no one, who held it to be certain at a given time that he was involved in a specified reality, could admit that there ever occurred such an illusion. And a "perfect" perception-illusion disjunction would be rather a strange thing if "perfect" illusion were taken in this way....

### Notes

1. *Stories of Sean O'Faolain*, Penguin Books, 1970.

2. Here the relevant use of "look" is one in which you (just) say how some optical object looks to you, without intending any guess or estimate as to the object's nature or properties.

3. [Text taken from Part IIc: "It is obvious that, in a perception-illusion disjunction whose disjunct of perception is in terms of seeing, seeing plainly is sometimes meant. One can have occasion to say or think, 'Either I see a cobra, looking every inch a cobra and not looking to me in the least like any kind of non-cobra, or I am having that illusion.' This is as much as to say in our sense, 'Either I plainly see a cobra, or I am having that illusion.' Which in turn is as much as to say in our sense, 'Either I plainly see that there is a cobra before me, or I am having that illusion.' ..."—Eds.]

## 3 Perception, Vision, and Causation

It is believed by some that reflection on many of our psychological notions reveals that they can be instantiated by an object only if some sort of causal condition is fulfilled. Notions to which it has been supposed this applies include those of remembering, knowing, acting for a reason and perception.[1] I wish here to discuss the application of such a view to this last case, an application which is, I think, often believed to be more or less obviously correct, or at least to be as obviously correct as it ever is.[2] Although the present discussion is primarily of causal theories of perception (or more accurately, of one case of perception, namely vision), some elements in it may be relevant to the assessment, or understanding, of causal theories for some other psychological notions. The reason this may be so is that the principal argument used to support a causal theory of perception of this sort exhibits a similar form to arguments used to support some causal theories elsewhere and involved in any consideration of how strongly causal theories of perception are supported is the task of getting clear about the force of arguments with that structure.

I

I want to begin by characterising the causalist viewpoint—a viewpoint first propounded by Grice, and endorsed and added to in an impressive tradition, containing Strawson, Pears and Peacocke (and, of course, many others).[3] In contrast to this assenting tradition, there has also been a

Meeting of the Aristotelian Society held at 5/7 Tavistock Place, W.C.1 on Wednesday, May 27, 1981 at 6:30 p.m.
Paul Snowdon, "Perception, Vision, and Causation," *Proceedings of the Aristotelian Society* 81: 175–192. Reprinted by courtesy of the Editor of the Aristotelian Society: © 1981.

dissenting one, but the points raised in it have seemed to most people not strong enough to threaten the causal theory.[4]

The view is defined by three claims. I shall specify them for the visual case, rather than for the more general case of perception itself.

The first claim is this; it is necessarily true that if a subject ($S$) sees a public object ($O$) then $O$ causally affects $S$. I shall call this the causal thesis. Different theorists may (and do) disagree about how to explain the required relation of causal dependence and may (and do) differ about quite what sort of objects the claim should be formulated for. I want to ignore these variations.

The causal claim says nothing about what effect $O$ must have on $S$. The second claim fills that gap and asserts: (II) $O$ must produce in $S$ a state reportable in a sentence beginning "It looks to $S$ as if ...," where those words are interpreted both phenomenologically (rather than as ascribing, say, a tentative judgement by $S$) and, in Quine's terms, notionally rather than relationally. I shall call this the effect thesis, and refer to the alleged effects as looks-states (or $L$-states).

The third thesis amounts to a comment on the status of the other two. It says (III) theses (I) and (II) represent requirements of our ordinary concept, or notion, of vision. It is thus asserting, notably, that the causal thesis is, in some sense, a conceptual truth. I shall call this the conceptual thesis.[5]

It is, of course, very hard to say precisely what the conceptual thesis is claiming, but it seems reasonable to suggest that part of what is involved in a truth's being a conceptual one is that it is supportable (but not necessarily only supportable) in a distinctive way. And at least part of what is distinctive about the way is that there is a restriction on the data to which appeal can be made in the supporting argument. A somewhat rough way of specifying the restriction is that the data must be relatively immediately acknowledgeable by any person, whatever their education, who can count as having the concept in question. The aim of the restriction is to exclude any facts of which we can become aware only in the context of certain activities (for example, carrying out experiments, or becoming acquainted with the results of experiments, or reading psychological textbooks) which need not be indulged in by just anyone who has the concept. It has to be asked, therefore, whether any good argument satisfying this constraint exists for the causal thesis.

Now, that the causal thesis is true is something which most educated people would accept, and it is fair to suppose that its truth is a matter of relatively common knowledge. In this it resembles, say, the claim that the earth goes round the sun, or the claim that there has been evolution. It should, though, be clear that its having this status is no ground for accepting that the conceptual thesis is correct. For it is obvious that, despite there being widespread acquaintance with the conclusion, the fundamental justification of the causal thesis may rely on data outside the restricted class.

Theses I to III constitute the theory the support and correctness of which I wish to assess, but, of course, there is another claim, which anyone subscribing to this position would accept. It is that it is not sufficient for a subject to see an item that the item relate to the subject in accordance with the requirements of the first two theses. The problem then is to isolate the further conditions which will rule out deviant ways in which an object can fulfil the earlier two. Contributions to the assenting tradition, as I have called it, are mainly attempts to refute earlier purported solutions, combined with suggestions as to better ones.

The theory which has been specified is a causal theory of vision. There are, of course, structurally parallel theories about the other actual senses, but there is also a parallel thesis about perception itself, which is, probably, the one which is most often explicitly endorsed. There is, though, a reason for concentrating on the more specific visual claim, namely that it is possible thereby to avoid discussing a lacuna in the standard argument for the more general thesis. Thus the usual (although not invariable) procedure is to provide an argument for (say) the visual thesis, but to draw as a further immediate consequence the general thesis about perception. However, the more specific claim does not entail the general conclusion and something needs to be said in support of the move.

## II

The main argument for the described position which was originally propounded by H. P. Grice, I shall consider in the next section. But before taking that up, there are some recent remarks of Professor Strawson which are, I think, aimed at providing support for the causal and conceptual thesis (at least, I shall interpret then that way) and on which I wish very briefly to comment.

Strawson says this:

The idea of the presence of the thing as accounting for, or being responsible for, our perceptual awareness of it is implicit in the pre-theoretical scheme from the very start. For we think of perception as a way, ... of informing ourselves about the world of independently existing things: we assume, that is to say, the general reliability of our perceptual experiences; and that assumption is the same as the assumption of a general causal dependence of our perceptual experiences on the independently existing things we take them to be of. The thought of my fleeting perception as a perception of a continuously and independently existing thing implicitly contains the thought that if the thing had not been there, I should not even have seemed to perceive it. It really should be obvious that with the distinction between independently existing objects and perceptual awareness of objects we already have the general notion of causal dependence of the latter on the former, even if this is not a matter to which we give much reflective attention in our pre-theoretical days.[6]

Now this is a very suggestive but also a very concise passage, in which it seems possible to detect three, no doubt intended to be interlocking, considerations. The first is as follows. Perception (of objects) is thought to be a way of acquiring information about the world. This amounts to (or at least involves) the assumption that experiences which are perceptual are, in general, reliable. This assumption is the same as the belief that if an experience is perceptual of object $O$ it is causally dependent on that object.

To assess this we need to explain what the assumption of the reliability of perceptual experience is supposed to be. One plausible way to view it is this: we treat experiences which we take to be perceptual as reliable in the sense that how it seems in these experiences to us to be is, by and large (in general), the way our environment actually is. If that, however, is the correct interpretation then it seems wrong to suppose that the reliability assumption is equivalent to the causal claim. In the first place, the mere assumption that if an experience is perceptual then it is causally dependent on the object it is a perception of, does not have as a consequence that appearances in these cases are even more or less accurate. This point, though, is unimportant, since all that is needed by the line of thought is that the reliability assumption requires the causal one, not that there is an equivalence. There is, however, no logical requirement here, since this sort of reliability could be present, if, say, our perceptions and the states of the world were joint effects of some other cause which produced the match. The reply is possible that it is excessively rigid to interpret "requires" as "entails," but it needs then to be explained what kind of transition between the assumptions is involved. There is, I think, a reason for doubting that any transition of a sufficiently interesting sort can be made here. Thus, we can re-express the reliability assumption (on the present interpretation, and limiting it to vision for convenience) as follows; if our experience is a case of an object $O$ looking certain ways to us (that is, is visually perceptual of object $O$) then (by and large) $O$ is how $O$ looks. In so far as a causal assumption is implicit in this claim it would be that how an object looks is causally dependent on (amongst other things) how the object otherwise is. To unearth this causal assumption, though, is not to unearth a commitment to the causal thesis, for what if anything has been revealed is the assumption that when an object is seen, its being seen a certain way (that is, how it looks) causally depends on the nature of the object, which amounts in no way to the view that what it is for the object to be seen (a certain way) is for it to affect the viewer. An analogy is this; it is one thing to admit that whether *A* is heavier than *B* is, in part, causally determined by (say) *A*'s previous history, another to hold that *A*'s being heavier than *B* is a matter of *A* (or *A*'s previous history) having an effect on *B*.

The second consideration in favour of the theory is the claim that to think of someone as perceiving an object implies that if the item perceived had not been there then the subject would not have even seemed to perceive it. To avoid triviality here we must treat "seem to perceive it" as equivalent to "seem to perceive something of its character." Now, taken that way, it does not seem that this claim is unrestrictedly true. There are two sorts of counter example (which I shall specify for the visual case). The first is where a subject sees an object in an environment which would have appeared the same to him even if that object had not been present in it. For example, a man can see a coin immediately behind which is an identical coin, removal of the front coin would not alter the scene. The second is when a subject sees an object in circumstances which would have given him an hallucination of just such an object if the item had not been present. For example, a man can see a clock the noise from which is the only thing preventing a drug he has already taken from giving him the hallucination of a clock. Suppose, however, that the counterfactual is true. The belief that it implies the causal thesis relies on the assumption that the claim "If *S* sees *O* at *t* then if *O* had not been present things would have seemed a different way to *S*" implies "If *S* sees *O* at *t* then (the presence of) *O* causally accounts for how it seems to *S*," an assumption which would be correct if the consequent of the first of these conditionals (itself a conditional) entailed the consequent of the second (a causal claim). It is unobvious that there is any such entailment, for the first consequent merely records a dependence of one fact on another, and there can, surely, be dependencies where the relation is not causal dependence. (An example would be; if I had not parked on those yellow lines I would not have broken the law.) The causal thesis is not, therefore, an immediate implication of the remark under discussion.

Finally, it is true that we draw a distinction between (say) sighting an object and the object sighted, and that means that for there to be a sighting more must obtain than presence of the object, but it is not obvious that this extra is the object's having an effect on the sighter.

The causal thesis remains, therefore, to be supported, and I want next to determine how good the main argument is.

## III

The main argument[7] relies on the acceptance of something implied by (but not implying) the looks-thesis, namely, the claim that if $S$ sees $O$ then $S$ is in an $L$-state. This is, surely, highly plausible, and not something I wish to question.[8] The argument also assumes that if $S$ sees $O$ then $O$ exists. (Rather than calling that an assumption we might say—the theory just deals with sightings of actual objects.)

The argument itself (sometimes expressed with extreme brevity) has three stages. The first consists in the presentation of certain interesting possible cases of visual experience. The second consists in judging of these that they are cases where certain, what we might call, candidate objects involved are not seen. The third stage is simply an inference to the correctness of the causal thesis.

Now, the following are examples of the sort which are given. (a) Lady Macbeth has the hallucination that there is blood on her hands, there in fact being none. Her nurse then smears on some blood. (b) A man is facing a pillar of a certain character and it looks to him as if there is in front of him an object of that character. However between him and the pillar is a mirror in which is reflected another pillar. (c) A man is facing a clock, it looks to him as if there is a clock, but his experience is the result of a scientist's direct simulation of his cortex in a way which would have yielded experience of that character even if there had been no clock.

The intention is to specify possible cases fulfilling three conditions. First, the two basic necessary requirements for an object-sighting are met. Second, they are cases where there is no sighting of the "candidate" object. Third, there is an absence of any sort of causal dependence of the looks-state on that object.

Now, it is dubious that the descriptions of the cases necessitate the fulfilment of the last two features. For example, to consider the second requirement and case (a), it may be that smearing blood on Lady Macbeth stops the hallucination and enables her to see the blood. Again, considering the third requirement, and (b), it may be that the pillar behind the mirror is depressing a light-switch which controls the illumination of the reflected pillar. However, it seems clear that there are possible cases matching the descriptions and fulfilling these features, and it is very natural to interpret the description of the examples as introducing cases of this sort. When taken this way, I shall call them $U$-cases ("$U$" for unseen).

If, then, we allow such cases are possible, we must agree that it is not enough for a subject to see an object that the object be present and it looks as if there is an object of that character present. That much is established, but it is not conclusively established that the causal thesis is correct. All we have is the claim that there are possible cases where (i) $S$ is in an $L$-state appropriate to seeing $O$, (ii) $O$ is in his environment, (iii) the $L$-state is not causally dependent on $O$; and (iv) $O$ is not seen. That such cases are possible does not entail that there are no cases where $S$ and $O$ are so related as to fulfil (i) to (iii) but in which $O$ is seen by $S$.

If there is no entailment, how should we think of the move from accepting that in the described cases the object is not seen to accepting the causal thesis? We should, I want to propose, view it as a suggested inference to the best explanation. The issue raised is; why, in $U$-cases, are the mentioned objects not sighted? The causal theorist is suggesting that they are not sightings because of the lack of causal connexion. It is a plausible suggestion because the absence of such a causal connexion is a prominent element in the cases, and there is no other obvious explanation.

A question that arises at this point is where this interpretation leaves the conceptual thesis. Plainly, if the argument given is to be, not only a good reason for accepting the causal thesis, but, as well, a reason of a sort which licenses the conceptual thesis as a gloss on the status of its conclusion, then, in line with the elucidation of that gloss proposed earlier, the "data" it relies on should be acknowledgable by (more or less) anyone who has mastered the concept (of vision). The data in our case consists of the supposed facts reported in the judgments about the specified examples to the effect that they are not cases of (appropriate) vision. Now, it seems that these facts are of the right sort, for they are ones which are recognised by people who have no specialist information about vision at all. Hence, if the argument is a good one the conceptual thesis is warranted.

Now treating the argument in the way suggested leaves the causal thesis with the status of an attractive explanatory hypothesis. It would seem incautious, though, to be confident of its correctness without giving some consideration to other hypotheses, of which we can, I think envisage two sorts. The first sort of alternative which we might call non-radical, stays fairly close to the causal theory in structure, in that it allows that it makes sense to regard the looks-state as something causally produced by the seen object, but it claims that, nonetheless, we can best explain why the $U$-cases are not cases of vision by adding to our theory of vision an extra condition (or set of conditions) which requires less than the full causal connexion proposed by the causalist.

There is no argument demonstrating that this strategy is in principle wrong, but it is hard to see how it can work. If different $U$-cases are explained by different features, then (i) a sense, which it is hard to resist, that there is a unified explanation is not satisfied, and (ii) there will be a suspicion that either the various features do not cover all U-cases or they do but at the cost of turning out to be equivalent to the causalist's explanation. If, in contrast, there is a single, non-causal but non-radical, explanation, what is it? The reason I do not wish to pursue this idea further is really that there is what I call a radical alternative which has the advantage that it can, at least, be specified and developed.

## IV

To introduce the radical idea, in the form in which I shall develop it, consider this line of thought which bears some formal resemblance to the main argument. Its aim is to support a theory of what it is for A to be married to B. We agree, surely, that if A is married to B then A is a spouse. But it is clear that A could be a spouse and B also be around when A became a spouse without A being married to B. For example, suppose that when A became a spouse the ceremony at which it happened was one to which B's presence was completely irrelevant. It would have gone ahead exactly as it did whether B had been there or not. However, this case suggests something else that is needed: not only must A be a spouse, with B around when A became a spouse, but B's presence must have been causally relevant to A's becoming a spouse. Of course, this is still not sufficient, since the residing clergyman (or what have you) also fulfils this condition. So we might consider adding that for A to be married to B is for B to be causally relevant to A's being a spouse in the way in which ... etc.

There is, of course, the analogue of the non-radical reply even here; "it is rather strong to require causal dependence, let us, instead, rule out certain ways for B to be involved."

Plainly both the argument and this reply lack plausibility. But why? A shot at explaining why this theory moves in the wrong direction, an explanation having two stages, is as follows; (i) the best theory we could offer of what it is to be a spouse is simply that it is to be married to someone or other; (ii) so, replacing in the original theory the notion of being a spouse by its explanation, we see that the original is trying to add conditions to the requirement that A be married to someone, which guarantee that A is married to B. But this is absurd, in that if we could explain what must apply to someone in order to be married to A, all we need to do to explain what it is for B to be married to A is to say that the someone to whom those conditions apply is B. Now, the more radical non-causalist response to the main argument is to allege that to draw a causal conclusion on its basis is similarly absurd.

We have, so far, then, an analogy and a general suggestion, and what is needed is a specific proposal to carry out the general suggestion. Pursuing the analogy, what is needed is a suggested theory about the supposed effect-end in the causal theory which renders its treatment in the causal theory, as the effect, absurd.

Such a suggestion can be extracted from J. M. Hinton's article (*Mind*, 1967) "Visual Experiences" [this volume, chapter 1]. Hinton's idea is that the best theory for the state of affairs reported by "I seem to see a flash of light" (or "I seem to see an *F*") is that it is a case of either my seeing a flash of light or my having the illusion of a flash of light (or my seeing an *F* or my having the illusion of an *F*). The claim, then, is that the best theory of seeming to see is disjunctive. For our purposes, the suggestion becomes that a theory of the same structure and content applies to the state of affairs reported by "It looks to *S* as if there is . . ."

But this suggestion as it stands is mistaken, for far from being the best theory, the explaining disjunction is not even coextensive with the state it is offered as explaining. There are at least two sorts of counter examples. (i) The disjunction is true if *S* sees an *F*. But *S* might see an *F* which does not look like an *F*, in which case it might well not look to *S* as if there is an *F*. For example, *S* might be seeing a rabbit which had been shaved and painted to look like a cat. (ii) It seems we can have illusions which are not visual—e.g. auditory or tactile ones. Consider a kind of thing—say an explosion—which is both sightable and can be felt. Then *S* might be having the illusion of such a thing in virtue of how it feels to him. It would not follow that it looked to him as if there was an explosion. Hinton's example—of a flash of light—masks the second difficulty, in that it is only sensible to treat an illusion of it as visual.

We can avoid these objections by offering the following revised disjunction:

it looks to *S* as if there is an *F*; (there is something which looks to *S* to be *F*) ∨ (it is to *S* as if there is something which looks to him (*S*) to be *F*).

Let us assume that it is correct. Now, if we make this assumption it seems that the visual case does resemble the spouse-example. Thus, we replace the supposed effect, by what it is best explained to be. We are given, that is, that there is some way (*F*) such that either something looks that way to *S* or it is to *S* as if something looked that way. How can we add to this to guarantee that *O* is seen? The answer, surely, is that *O* is seen so long as it is overall a case of something's looking F to S, rather than its being to S as if something looked that way, and O is the something that looks that way. But for O to be that something is not for O to bring about the separate state of affairs of something's looking F, it is, evidently, simply for O to be the something; i.e. for O to look that way.

On the assumption that this theory is correct, we can provide an alternative explanation for the status of the U-cases. This explanation relies on the claim that an object is seen only if it looks some way to the subject and on noticing that we are given in the description of the U-cases information which makes it likely that the cases are not ones where the specified objects look some way. The information is precisely that what *actually* went on *would have gone on* whether the objects were present or not. But if that is true they could not have been cases in which the objects were looking some way to the subject, since that could not have obtained in the absence of the object.[9]

A comment that it would be natural to make at this stage is that if the discussion so far is tenable, the main argument is rejectable if a disjunctive theory is correct, but little has been said as to quite what a disjunctive theory is claiming, and even less as to precisely what a non-disjunctive account would be. The request in this comment for further elucidation is totally reasonable, but difficult to respond to adequately.

The phrase so far used to explain the disjunctive approach has been that the disjunct gives "the best theory." Something like this is needed because even someone who accepts the picture involved in the causal theory could agree that the claim resulting from a bi-conditional between "it looks to S as if ..." and the disjunction expresses a truth, hence the contrasting (disjunctive) theory cannot be identified as the requirement that such a bi-conditional be true. Further, I see no help, in an account of the dispute, in saying that for the disjunctive theorist the disjunct *"gives the meaning"* of "It looks to S as if ..." whereas for the causalist it does not, since the fairly superficial factors which might make a remark about meaning appropriate in the case of the phrase "is a spouse," are not present in our case. Without these factors, such a remark fails to illuminate what is in dispute.

But we are able to add vividness to the contrast by expressing it this way. The non-disjunctive theorist espouses a picture in which there is in all cases a single sort of state of affairs whose obtaining makes "looks"-ascriptions true. This sort of state of affairs is common to such diverse cases as seeing a cricket ball and having an after-image with one's eyes shut tight. This obtaining of such states is intrinsically independent of the arrayed objects surrounding a subject, but will, so long as it is suitably produced by them, constitute a sighting of them. If it is not suitably caused it is not a sighting.

The disjunctive picture divides what makes looks ascriptions true into two classes. In cases where there is no sighting they are made true by a state of affairs intrinsically independent of surrounding objects; but in cases of sightings the truth-conferring state of affairs involves the surrounding objects.

It is this picture, rather than the claim that the *actual* formula given to express the disjunctive theory adequately does so, which constitutes the core-idea, on the basis of which radical alternative explanation can be given.

## V

If the present suggestion is correct, the next question to settle is whether a disjunctive theory is correct. If it is, then the main argument fails and the theory it is supposed to support is incorrect; if it is not, it is still possible that the non-radical rejection of the argument is the right response, but it cannot be said that the structure of the causalist theory is absurd.

It is, of course, impossible to settle this question now, but what I want to do instead is to propose a sketchy line of thought which relies on claims which seem intuitively plausible and which favours the disjunctive approach. In this line of thought an important role is initially played by demonstrative judgements—i.e. those expressible in the words "that is an F."

Let us suppose that the visual scene you are scanning contains only what appears or looks to be a single feint light. If you hold, there and then, that you can actually see a real feint light-bulb, you will also hold of the thing which looks to be a feint light that it (that thing) is a light bulb. You will hold a judgement that you could express to yourself in the words "That is a light bulb." We can put the same point this way; if you are in doubt as to whether the judgement expressed by "that is a light bulb" is correct, then, in these circumstances, you will, also, be in doubt as to whether you are seeing a light bulb.

It is tempting to generalise this by saying; if S holds that he can see an F then he must accept that there is a certain item of which he is correct in demonstratively identifying it as an F. This would be a mistake since the direct tie between the self-ascribed perceptual claim and the demonstrative identification present in the first case derives from its extremely simple character. Thus it is consistent and possible for me to hold in a case where there are three distinct objects apparently seen that I can see Boycott's bat even though I am not prepared to make of any of them the identification of it as the bat, simply because I do not know which it is. Still, it is evident in this sort of case that if I do not hold a disjunction of identificatory judgements correct, I will not hold that I see the bat.

So far, the tie between demonstratives and judgements about seeing has been presented in terms of a tie between perceptual judgements about yourself that you would make and demonstrative identifications you would make. But surely the tie is more general and, as a first shot, we might express it this way:

(S) (O)   (If S sees O and O is an F then there is some object to which S is so related that if he were to demonstratively identify it as an F the judgement would be correct.)

Now, we can add to this, I suggest, a further principle which we are inclined to hold; let us restrict ourselves to the visual case; consider a scene that you can see and the public objects in it; now we can imagine a list of all the true identificatory demonstrative judgements you could have there and then made of the elements in the public scene. The second principle claims that if you encounter such a scene and are not at that time having after-images, a partial hallucination or undergoing any experiences of that sort, then the previously specified set of true identificatory demonstrative judgements contains all the true demonstrative judgements you could there and then have made on the basis of your current *visual* experience. The best support for this is contained in the challenge; try to specify an extra demonstrative judgement.

Holding this in mind, we can return to the contrast between the disjunctive and non-disjunctive theories of looks-states. This time I want to concentrate on the non-disjunctive picture (theory) and to link it with the preceding claims.

The picture of perception it involves can be explained as follows; when we have an after-image (say) there is an L-state produced in a certain way, a way which rules out its being a perception of an object. Further what we are talking about when we speak of the image itself is, as it were, an element in the visual impression (or L-state) in this case. When we see (say) a feint light there is also such a state produced, but this time it is produced by the feint light, which is therefore, not in the same way an element in it. However the sort of element produced in both types of case is the same; that the instance of the sort in the first case is an after-image whereas the instance in the second is not, is due entirely to the difference in how the

elements are produced. It seems to be carried by this that the subject is related in the same way in both cases to the elements in the impression
(= the effect).

I want now to assume that we can make (true and false) demonstrative-
type judgements about what I am calling the elements in the L-state. To
recognise that this is plausible (though not, I hope, certain) consider the
following case. It looks to you as if there is a feint light before you. You
are not, however, sure whether you are seeing a feint light or having an
after-image. Now you might pose the question thus; what is that—an
after-image or a feint light? In fact you are having an image and you persuade yourself that you are; the question then receives the answer; *that* is
an after-image. Prima facie, this is a (true) instance of the kind of demonstrative judgement which I am assuming can be made.

Consider next, a related but different example. S is in fact seeing a feint
light. Initially he believes (wrongly) that he is having an after-image.
Granting the previous assumption, we can ascribe to him the demonstrative judgement—that is an after-image—supposed true by him of what it
is he takes to be the image. However, he subsequently realises he is not
having an after-image but rather seeing a feint light; he comes to hold of
that that it is a feint light. The problem to be faced is; what relation obtains
between his initial, incorrect, demonstrative judgement and his subsequent
one?

Now, on the present picture (and given our assumption) there are two
possible erroneous judgements the man might have been making at the beginning. Either he judged of what was the feint light that it was an after-
image or he judged of an element in the impression (produced in fact by
the feint light) that it was an after-image. The latter demonstrative judgement was also of course erroneous. But the new demonstrative judgement
as well, on this picture, has two possible interpretations. Either he is judging (correctly) of what is the feint light that it is a feint light; or (incor-
rectly) of an element in the L-state that it is a feint light. He should, on
this picture, be able, however, to make a new and correct demonstrative
judgement about the elements in the L-state; viz. that it (that) is an element of an L-state produced by a feint light in a certain way. So there are
two possible truth-accruing changes S could make in his demonstrative
judgements. He could move from "that is an after-image" to "that is a feint
light," where his demonstrative picks out the feint light; or he could move
from "that is an after-image" to "that is an element in an L-state caused
in a certain way by a feint light" given that he was identifying an element in the impression. But it seems plain, now, that this is incompatible

with the second principle which most of us accept, for it requires the existence of true identificatory judgements outside the class the principle claims are exhaustive. This theory as to what the effect in perception is, allied to our assumption about the permissibility of demonstrative judgements, is committed to the possibility of a "language-game" which cannot be played.

So, to sustain the picture of the effect as a common visual element whose presence constitutes the truth of a looks-claim, it seems we must either (i) modify the assumption that demonstrative judgements are possible of "elements" in "impressions" or (ii) abandon the principle. Two modifications of the first assumption seem possible. The first tries to accommodate the case which made the initial assumption plausible, by claiming (i) where the visual effect is produced in a way that means it is not a case of perception, demonstrative judgements can be made about its elements, but (ii) where it is produced in a perception-making way, demonstrative identifications are not possible in respect of its elements but only in respect of the influencing object. Now, this may be a correct result, but it is impossible, I think, for this picture to explain why it is correct. For, why should ancestry affect identifiability? The second modification is more radical; (i) no elements in the $L$-state can be demonstratively identified, only objects, so to speak, in the world can be so identified; (ii) a subject who when actually having an after-image thinks he is seeing a feint light and thinks to himself "that is a feint light" really makes no mistaken judgement with those words at all; his mistake is to suppose that he has made a judgement; (iii) a person seeing a light but believing that he is having an after-image may be allowed to make a demonstrative judgement to the effect that that is an after-image, but, of course, it can only be corrected in one way. I leave undecided whether such a view is acceptable.

However, even if it is, a difficulty still remains. For if we cannot demonstratively identify elements in impressions, there are certain psychological attitudes we can have towards the visual states which we are, in some sense, aware of when we have after-images. We can be interested by, concentrate on, be distracted by, scrutinize and attempt to describe them. Now, on the present interpretation of the causal theory with $L$-states as visual effects it is committed to there being in cases of vision features of this sort (though distinctly brought about). This seems to amount to supposing that in ordinary cases of vision we can have the cited psychological attitudes to features quite distinct from the object which produces them (i.e. the object seen). But, this is not at all obviously true; certainly it is not a supposition we are commonly inclined to make.[10]

## VI

There is nothing in the previous discussion which amounts to a disproof of the causalist viewpoint (that is, of the conjunction of theses I to III). If the disjunctive account of looks-states is correct, then thesis II is incorrect, hence the overall position also is. Even if the disjunctive theory is not acceptable, and theses I and II are admissible, the overall position may still be wrong if the refutation of the disjunctive theory involves considerations external to those permitted by the conceptual thesis. (So an assertion of the disjunctive theory is not needed for a rejection of the present causalist view). However, what I hope to have made some sort of case for is not so much a rejection of the causalist viewpoint as non-acceptance of it.

The issue of the proper attitude to the overall position should be sharply distinguished from the issue of the proper attitude to the causal thesis (thesis I). There are, I think, good empirical reasons for believing that to see an object is for it to have, in a certain sort of way, a certain sort of effect. Thus, (i) it seems physically necessary for $S$ to see $O$ that $O$ have an effect on $S$, and we can either think of the affecting as a de facto necessary condition for another relation's obtaining (viz. seeing) or treat the seeing *as* the affecting. The parsimonious naturalist will incline to the latter. (ii) There are things about us (for example, certain capacities for avoiding, if we want to, or hitting, if we want to, objects) which we hold vision explains; I assume that these capacities can, in fact, also be traced to the ways in which the objects affect us. This seems to support an identity and with it thesis I. If this is correct, the question that emerges is; given thesis I is true, why does it matter that there is no proof of it which licenses its status as a "conceptual" truth? But that, like much else, I propose to leave hanging in the air.

### Notes

1. See Martin and Deutscher, "Remembering," *Philosophical Review* (1966), Goldman, "A Causal Theory of Knowing," *Journal of Philosophy* (1967), Davidson, "Actions, Reasons, and Causes," *Journal of Philosophy* (1963) and Grice, "The Causal Theory of Perception," *Aristotelian Society, Supp. Vol. 35* (1961), reprinted in Warnock, *The Philosophy of Perception* (Oxford, 1967). Hereafter, page references to Grice's article will be to the reprint.

2. David Wiggins, for example, talks of "the finality of Grice's argument about perception," "Freedom, Knowledge, Belief and Causality" in G. N. A. Vesey (ed.), *Knowledge and Necessity* (1970), p. 137. P. F. Strawson describes the view as "obvious," "Perception and its Objects," in G. F. Macdonald (ed.), *Perception and Identity* (1979), p. 51.

3. See P. F. Strawson, "Causation in Perception" in *Freedom and Resentment* (1974), D. F. Pears, "The Causal Conditions of Perception," *Synthese 33* (1976), and Christopher Peacocke, *Holistic Explanation* (1979).

4. The "dissenting tradition" includes A. R. White, "The Causal Theory of Perception," *Aristotelian Society, Supp. Vol. 35* (1961), Jenny Teichmann, "Perception and Causation," *Proceedings of the Aristotelian Society, LXXI* (1970–1971), Jaegwon Kim, "Perception and Reference without Causality," *Journal of Philosophy* (1977), and (perhaps), Michael Dummett, "Common Sense and Physics," pp. 35–36, in G. F. Macdonald (ed.), *op. cit.*

5. Grice describes himself as "characterising the ordinary notion of perceiving," in Grice *op. cit.* p. 105. Strawson talks of "the general idea" of "causal dependence" being "implicit" in "the concept of perception," in "Causation in Perception," p. 83.

6. Strawson, "Perception and its Objects," p. 51.

7. For expositions see Grice *op. cit.* pp. 103–4, Strawson, "Causation in Perception," p. 83, Wiggins *op. cit.* p. 137.

8. It should be clear that the claim I am here accepting just means; if $S$ sees $O$ then it is true to say of $S$ that it looks to him to be some way. The talk of $L$-states is merely abbreviatory of that. I am not, as will emerge, granting the ontological picture the causalist has in mind when formulating it this way (i.e. in terms of states).

9. It may be objected, "you are still left with an unexplained distinction between an object's looking $F$ to $S$ and it merely being to $S$ as if something looks $F$ to him, and you have not shown that the best account of this is not a causal theory for the former." These remarks are true, but that the alternative explanation to the normal one relies on distinctions for which no explanation is provided does not discredit it as an explanation. How could it avoid this feature? Since it remains a possible explanation, its role in the present argument is not affected. So if the best account of the distinction involves a causal theory of the relational disjunct, another argument than the main one is needed.

10. I intend the argument here as a challenge to supporters of the causal theory to explain where it goes wrong, rather than as a serious attempt to show they have gone wrong. There are three lines of reply available; (i) to agree that in ordinary perception we cannot have the cited attitudes to anything but the perceived objects, but to deny the claim that in (for example) after-imaging there are "elements" we can have the attitudes to; (ii) to agree that we can have such attitudes in cases like after-imagings, but to claim we also have them to "elements" distinct from the perceived objects in perceptual cases; (iii) to agree that there is a prima facie puzzle about what we are able to attend to but to allege that our inability in the ordinary perception case does not show that there is no common visual element shared by it and (say) after-imaging. I have said nothing to block any of these options.

# 4 The Objects of Perceptual Experience

## Paul Snowdon

It is hardly surprising that not all philosophers who count as studying perception are doing exactly the same sort of thing. Some are trying to provide an informative account, at that highly general level characteristic of philosophy, of the ingredients in the perceptual process. Sometimes the account they accept suggests to them that certain central, commonsensical judgements are incorrect.[1] The study of perception has certainly inspired a revisionary tradition. With others, of course, there is no thought that the correct account of perception necessitates revisions of, as opposed to additions to, our beliefs. However, it has also seemed worthwhile to many philosophers, certainly recently, to try to give, what are called, analyses of our perceptual concepts. The present paper pursues an issue in that part of the theory of perception.[2] The concepts the analysis of which I want to consider are those of seeing an (external) object and of perceiving an (external) object. I shall say a little about perceiving, but talk mainly about seeing. My aim is not to provide full and definitive analyses of these concepts but, rather, to make a case for thinking that the dominant causal analyses are wrong, and to sketch the directions of an alternative account.

It needs to be emphasised at the beginning that the topic is analysis of the *concepts* of perceiving and seeing. Despite a goal of conceptual analysis (amongst other things) having been adopted by the vast majority of recent so-called analytical philosophers, it remains unclear exactly what constraints are imposed by it. But one thing about conceptual analysis that is obvious, I think, and which I shall assume without argument is that it is wrong to incorporate as an element in the analysis of a concept C any condition F which can be revealed as a necessary and essential condition for the correct application of C only by arguments relying on what are,

Paul Snowdon, "The Objects of Perceptual Experience," *Proceedings of the Aristotelian Society Supp. Vol.* 64: 121–150. Reprinted by courtesy of the Editor of the Aristotelian Society: © 1990.

broadly, empirical considerations.[3] It would, therefore, be a serious mistake to think that, if there is a good but empirically based argument of a traditional philosophical sort, or a good but empirically based argument of a scientific sort, which shows, say, that vision, or perception, requires a certain element, then we are entitled, for such reasons, to mention that element in the analysis of the concept. Unless this is explicitly recognised it is likely to remain for most people quite inconceivable how a non-causal analysis could be correct.

I do not propose to say much more about analysis at this stage, but I do want to make three remarks about it which have some bearing on the present case. (1) An analysis needs to be based on, and to make sense of, the judgemental tendencies shared by all people who count as having the concept in question; there is no entitlement to go beyond what can be shown on that basis. (2) With a concept, like that of perception (or vision), which has been of great interest to philosophers, and which has, in particular, elicited quite a lot of scepticism about some ordinary judgements containing it, we should hope, I think, that an analysis of it would help to explain why people have thought that grounds of a certain kind threaten the normal application of the concept. To do this requires analysing it in a way which both leaves room for the thought that its current (or common-sensical) application is wrong, and explains to some degree why certain considerations (the ones that have seemed to have weight) might be grounds for endorsing the thought for which room has been left.[4] (3) In treating the analytical issue at a certain amount of length I am not committing myself to the claim that the only proper business of philosophy in relation to perception (or to the mind generally) is conceptual analysis.

I

### The Causal Theory and Its Alternatives

There is an approach to the analysis of the concept of seeing which, although it has not received unanimous assent, deserves to be described as the orthodox view. It combines a positive and a negative claim. An initial statement of the positive claim is:

(1)   it is a conceptual requirement that, necessarily, if P (a subject) sees O (an object) then O is causally responsible for an experience (call it E) undergone by (or had by) P.

I shall call this the Causal Theory of Vision and shall adopt CTV as the abbreviation of it (and CTP as an abbreviation for the more general Causal Theory of Perception).

The negative thesis is:

(2)   it is not sufficient for P to see O that O be causally responsible for an experience E undergone by P.

There is no doubt that (2) is true. Indeed arguments in support of (1) often cite examples which clearly confirm (2). It tends to be thought, though, that (1), if not quite as obviously true as (2), is at least fairly obviously correct.

The task facing anyone who accepts (1) and (2) is then to specify further conditions which can be added to (1) and which will eventually yield a total set of conditions which are also sufficient. This research programme has produced many interesting suggestions but little agreement.

What alternatives are there to (1) (with its associated research programme)? This is a hard question to answer at this stage in the development of the argument, but it is important to try in order to convey a sense of the structure of the debate. Thesis (1) uses a notion of experience, and it can be asked: what conception of experience does it incorporate? Experiences are thought of as events which happen to a subject, and on one conception the events which are the subject's experience must happen within the subject. According to this view, experiences are amongst the events, the intrinsic natures of which are independent of anything outside the subject. Let us call this the conception of experience as inner, and read (1) as involving it. There are, then, I think, three main alternatives to (1). On the first alternative it is agreed that it is a conceptual truth that if P sees O then P must undergo an inner experience E, but it is not necessary that O cause E for O to be seen. A non-causal relation between O and E can be enough. On the second alternative we can provide something amounting to a conceptual demonstration that if the most that can be said about O's relation to P is that O is causing an inner experience E in P, in certain ways, etc., then P cannot be seeing O. Seeing, that is, requires something that cannot be generated by a causal relation between an inner experience and O. We can treat this as a thesis which is, in effect, accepted by people who endorse arguments to the conclusion that we do not really see external objects, which are based on the empirically grounded thought that our actual contact with objects is at most a matter of them causing experiences in us. The third alternative denies a thesis of this sort as well as that of (1). This version counts the concept of seeing as innocent of both sorts of causal requirements. This will, of course, be the view of anyone who wishes to be both a non-causalist and not revisionary about our judgements about what we perceive, if some such empirically based thought is accepted.

How are the second and third alternatives possible? The answer is that there is another conception of experience available, according to which it is quite possible for elements (objects or states of affairs) external to the subject to be ingredients of an experience. If there are experiences with this character, their intrinsic nature is not independent of the subject's environment. (I shall, of course, be saying a little more about these conceptions.) Let us call this the conception of non-inner experience. On the second alternative I have mentioned, (1) is rejected because it is supposed that it is a conceptual requirement for a sighting of O by P that P have a non-inner experience (involving O). According to the third alternative there are no arguments of a conceptual kind which sustain (1), but also there are no arguments of a conceptual kind which show that sightings require non-inner experiences. In so far as an analysis is possible it must remain neutral on that, which means not accepting (1). These are, as far as I can see, the positions between which we must choose. In the present paper a case is made for saying that either the second or third alternative is correct, but it is left open which.

A suggestion that is likely to be made at this point is that if (1) is interpreted as using an inner-experience concept then the description of alternatives is accurate, but it is possible to hold that (1) is true even when it is read as using a non-inner-experience concept. It would follow that we are not entitled to reject (1) simply because it is objectionable (assuming that it is) when the term "experience" is read one way.

On this suggestion I wish to make four comments. (i) I see no incoherence in it. It may be that it is a necessary truth about a non-inner experience involving O that it be causally produced by O. (ii) It is, I think, a radically different theory from the sort propounded in the tradition of argument about perception and causation initiated by Grice, with which I am concerned. It is clear that they conceived of the effect end as something which does not involve the sighted object O. They thought of their account as decomposing perception into its (causally related) subcomponents. The present suggestion does not decompose perception of objects into sub-components, but views it as essentially tied to a certain sort of cause. (iii) It, therefore, needs to be argued for in a different way from the standard causal theory. For the proponent of such a theory cannot suppose that we can, for the purpose of any argument, envisage perception as involving a self-standing component which would not be an experience of O unless it were suitably caused. That is precisely what the standard argument does do. (iv) There is, in my opinion, no strongly persuasive argument of this sort.

I propose, therefore, to read (1) as it is interpreted (according to me) in the dominant tradition.

Having given some account of the issue, I want to argue that (1) is not as well supported as is usually thought and to locate more precisely the central question which arises in this area. There is a rather simple argument (or line of thought) that has persuaded people of the truth of CTV. I shall try to show that no reliance can be placed on it.

## II

### The Simple Argument

The identification of the central difficulty in the argument is made easier if there is a specimen expression of it with which to deal. I shall use the exposition given by David Pears.[5] I hope that the passage reveals both how simple the argument is, and also how it is taken as more or less obvious, on the basis of the simple argument, that CTV is correct.

Pears says:

There are two questions which will serve to introduce the topic. Both are questions about the meaning of the verb "perceive" ...
(Q1) Does the statement, that a person P sees an object, O, by having a visual experience, E, entail that O caused E in P? ...
These questions are not too difficult ...
The first of the two questions can be answered quickly. The suggested entailment does hold because, if O did not cause E in P, then P could not have seen O by having E. This can be verified by the following example. P is a traveller in the desert, and he hallucinated an oasis with his eyes closed, so that there can be no doubt that E is not caused by anything beyond his eyelids. However, there is a real oasis, O, in front of him and E matches it perfectly feature by feature. But P cannot be seeing O because, though the match is perfect, it is entirely coincidental.[6]

The simple thought here is that the fact that the desert traveller does not see O shows that CTV is correct. The desert traveller case is, of course, simply a representative example; the literature contains lots of other examples. What unites them is that they are all cases where a putative percipient P has an experience E which matches an object O in P's environment, but where O has no effect on P and where it is agreed that P does not see O. I shall call these cases U-cases. Pears is really claiming that the verdict in U-cases shows that CTV is correct.

We can begin our comments on this passage by noticing that a highly significant assumption is made in the way the question (Q1) is posed. It is, in effect, assumed in (Q1) that the statement

(2)   P sees O (at T),

entails that

(3)   there is a visual experience E in P (at T).

If this is assumed then it can be agreed that the example shows that an E which matches an O in the environment might well not be a sighting of O. It would then be plausible to conjecture (though it would not immediately follow) that what more is needed at least includes a causal dependence of E on O. By what right is this assumption made?

The first reply that might be made to this question is that we all surely agree that if P sees O then P has a visual experience. Seeing is, we would all say, a sort of experience. Let us grant this claim, which we might call the Experiential Truism. What is not obvious, though, is whether the truism licenses us to think in the way that is being assumed in the question to be correct. Putting it aphoristically, the truism says that seeing is a form of experience, whereas the assumption is that seeing involves an experience. The force of "involves" is this: there is, when P sees O, an occurrence in P which is an experience and which is quite separate from O. It is not accurate to say that it is being assumed that the actual experience E could have happened without O being there; the assumption is though that E is, in its intrinsic nature, as a type of inner occurrence, possibly exactly the same as an experience E* which could have happened in the absence of O (or any seen external object at all).[7] It now becomes obvious, I think, that the import of the Experiential Truism, that seeing is an experience, is nowhere near as strong as the assumption made in the posing of question (Q1).

The answer, that I just tried to undermine, to the question about the legitimacy of the assumption, agreed that in posing question (Q1) an assumption is being made, but tried to defend the assumption as one which it is obviously correct to make. A different response would be to deny that question (Q1) involves any disputable assumption. Now, as question (Q1) actually stands, this would be implausible. However the question can be reformulated:

(Q1*)   Does the statement that P saw O entail that there is a visual experience E in P caused by O?

This reformulated question does not presuppose that there is an entailment from (2) to (3), but it becomes hard now to think that the examples appealed to in the simple argument enable us to give a quick answer to it. Having dropped that presupposition in question (Q1), the example must reveal to us, somehow, both that vision involves a visual experience in the significant sense and that it must be an effect of the seen object. What, one might wonder, is there about the simple story which can achieve both these tasks?

If it is agreed that the Experiential Truism does not support the claim that is being disputed, then there is another obvious way to give it support. It will be said: if we accept the possibility of total hallucination, and it is obvious that we do accept this possibility, then we must accept that hallucinations involve experiences which are separate from any external object, and so are inner experiences in the subject. This, I think, is correct. What there seems no obvious reason for believing is that in simply going along with the judgements about U-cases that we all make we are committed to holding that experiences of this inner type are elements in ordinary, non-hallucinatory, perceptual experiences.

It would be natural to try to reject the difficulty I am claiming there is in supposing that the example supports an answer to question (Q1*), by making the following reply. The difficulty is supposed to be that there is nothing in the examples which makes it reasonable to require that visual perception involves an experience of the basic sort which is agreed to be present in hallucinations. Another way of putting this difficulty is that there is nothing in the example which mandates us to think that there is a visual non-world-involving experience common to both hallucinations and perceptions. However, this is not really a question which an account of our language and concepts can leave open; we all acknowledge that there is a kind of claim true of both which must, therefore, be reporting just such a common visual element. These are claims about how it looks to the subject. An example would be: it looks to P as if there is an oasis in front of him.

The initial reply to this argument is clear. That "looks" sentences are true in hallucinations and in perceptions, and are not ambiguous, does not entail that they are made true by (or are true in virtue of) exactly the same kind of occurrence in both cases. Nothing said so far has ruled out thinking of them as having disjunctive fulfilment conditions. This remark needs some preliminary clarification. The sort of disjunctive theory I have in mind says this. The claim that it looks to P as if R (e.g. there is an oasis in front of him) should be treated as being true in virtue of two distinct sorts of states of affairs: either there is an object which looks to be an oasis to P (this is the case where an object is seen), or it is to P as if there is something of that sort happening (P is hallucinating an oasis). It is allowed, according to this, that the two cases which are described in the same way—or which ground the same description—might be of a quite different nature.[8]

I conjecture, then, that a large part of the explanation for its being thought that the simple argument of the sort propounded by Pears (or arguments of its kind) strongly support CTV lies in its being taken as obvious that vision must involve an experiential occurrence, in the subject, of the type also present in hallucinations. If that is taken as obvious then CTV does seem a reasonable conclusion from the example, because it provides an admirable explanation as to why the case is not a sighting. But this is taken as obvious in part because the possibility of a disjunctive theory is simply overlooked. I suggest therefore that once that possibility has emerged the simple types of argument can no longer be regarded as the basis for strong support for CTV.

One thing I am trying to establish is the weak claim that the simple argument has, as it stands, no force. It is not yet being claimed that the disjunctive theory is correct, nor even that its denial is not a conceptual truth. The claim is merely that its emergence means that the simple argument needs supplementation if it is to be used in support of CTV. The other thing that I have been trying to do is to indicate what the central issue is: namely, what type of experience are we entitled to regard as required for the occurrence of perception (or vision), simply to do justice to the concept we all possess?

I want now to consider two problems, one of which has been, and the other of which might be, felt to be difficulties in the direction of the present argument.

## III

### The Role of the Disjunctive Thesis

My aim so far has been to undermine an argument for a thesis about the concept of vision. In criticising the argument I have appealed to the possibility of what is known as the disjunctive theory of appearance. It is, at this point, important to understand how limited, in the criticism of the Simple Argument, is the commitment to the disjunctive theory. This is important because one sort of criticism of the approach seems to me to overestimate the role of the disjunctive thesis in this argument.

For the moment I shall take it that the disjunctive theory about looks-judgements states that:

(4)   looks-judgements are made true by two types of occurrence: in hallucinations they are made true by some feature of a (non-object-involving) inner experience, whereas in perceptions they are made true by some fea-

ture of a certain relation to an object, a non-inner experience, (which does not involve such an inner experience).

Now, (4) will be opposed by anyone who thinks that there is good evidence that vision involves an experiential occurrence of the same sort as that involved in hallucination. There are indeed well-known arguments, of which in my opinion no final assessment has been reached, which purport to show this. But the only version of such arguments which are at all persuasive or worth taking seriously, it seems to me, are those which appeal to scientifically established facts about perceptual and hallucinatory processes. If this claim is true, then we see that it would be quite wrong for someone who denies (4) to think that he needs to oppose the use of the possibility of a disjunctive analysis in the present discussion. The rejection of the simple argument does not require the truth of (4), and hence is immune to attack on the basis of the claim that (4) is false. Rather, all it requires is this:

(5)   It is not a conceptual truth that (4) is false.

It therefore needs to be recognised that the importance, in the philosophy of perception, of the idea of a disjunctive theory is not restricted to the claim that (4) is true. I hope that the distinction between (4) and (5) constitutes a reply to comments in the spirit of the following one made by Howard Robinson. He says: "The disjunctive theory has achieved something of a vogue, but its two most recent exponents, Snowdon and McDowell, ignore the difficulties posed for the theory by allowing that perception and hallucination might have the same immediate cause."[9] It is clear that the kind of difficulty Robinson is thinking of is one based on empirical claims about the processes involved in the two sorts of case, perception and hallucination. Such a difficulty does require a reply by a proponent of (4), but it is not a difficulty confronting (5).

The clarification I have just made shows, I hope, how to avoid one supposed problem. But I think that talk of disjunctive theories (of appearance or experience) stands in considerable need of further clarification. In particular there are, it seems to me, three dimensions (as well as the one just pointed out) along which expositions of disjunctive theories of perception vary. There are (a) variations in the disjuncts which are chosen to figure in the theory, (b) variations in the claim which is made about the disjunctions, and (c) variations in the sort of importance they are supposed to have, that is to say, variations in views about the sorts of issues to which they are relevant.

Under (a), we should notice these differences. In one account (that embodied in the present discussion), the disjuncts are perception and hallucinations. Into the perception disjunct would go both accurate and inaccurate perceptions. The other accounts form a disjunction between accurate perception on the one side and, on the other, all non-accurate cases. These are the disjunctions to which Hinton himself and McDowell have attended.[10] But there is a difference between them: Hinton's non-illusion disjunct is specified as a case of object perception, e.g. P (plainly) sees a flash of light—whereas McDowell's non-illusion disjunct is a case of a fact making itself perceptually manifest. In general though there is an enormous difference between object-perception and fact-perception.

(b) Having drawn attention to differences between the disjunctions, what is being said? What theoretical claim is being made about them? This is not easy to answer. It tends to be thought that we have a disjunctive theory of appearances, but what is that? It is too weak to say simply—if it appears to P that Q then it is either one case or the other—because no-one would want to deny it. It seems, on the other hand, too strong to say—if it appears to P as if Q then it is either one or the other and there is nothing at all in common between the cases. This is too strong in the sense that it cannot be true. If we allow that each disjunct reports an event, then the disjuncts have that in common. Further, it cannot be the point to compare appearance-judgements with the disjunctive concepts prominent in recent philosophy, namely, the totally artificial notions devised by Goodman and Kripke. No-one can want to say that it is mere artifice to apply the same description to both cases. It seems to me, therefore, that one alternative is to treat the disjunctive theory as the claim that a certain non-disjunctive theory is wrong. On this alternative it is saying: when it looks to P as if Q, there is no uniform experience present which makes it true, but, rather, it can either be a case of ... or a case of.... Given this understanding, we can use the notion of appearance (of a certain character) to specify a disjunct, since the aim is not to provide a disjunctive and reductive account of appearances. However, an alternative purpose, present in Hinton, is to provide just such a reductive account. Given this aim, an appearance concept cannot figure in a disjunct.

(c) The third contrast is that sometimes, as with McDowell, the disjunctive idea is taken as of significance for epistemology, whereas its present interest is for an account of perception, or at least perceptual concepts.

I want to leave clarification at this point, with two remarks. First, such differences do not necessarily represent theories between which we have to choose. Second, it is vital to recognise the variety behind talk of disjunctive theories. From my point of view the task is to explore how far we can articulate a disjunctive conception suitable for the present issue, (i.e. something like (5)).

## IV

### A Problem for This Disjunctive Idea

The previous classification might have shown how a supposed criticism of a disjunctive thesis is irrelevant to its application here, but a rather more general doubt might now be felt. This general doubt can be expressed thus: if we take seriously such disjunctive theses (about concepts) then lots of philosophical analyses are brought to a standstill at a very early stage, and that would be an intolerable result. This general doubt starts from noting a structural similarity between lots of concepts. Thus let $\langle I(x) \rangle$ stand proxy for an interesting psychological or epistemological concept true of x. There is another notion $\langle C(x) \rangle$ which has this feature: $I(x)$ entails $C(x)$. There is also a further property, call it $E(x)$, which also entails $C(x)$. $E(x)$ and $I(x)$ are contraries. Now, this is the position of many concepts for which causal analyses are suggested, and the tendency is to treat $C(x)$ as a common element shared by each of $I(x)$ and $E(x)$ and which will (or at least can) figure as the effect end in a causal analysis of I, thereby revealing the difference between I and E to be a causal difference.

Let me note three cases sharing this structure. The first one is the case we are considering. If P is seeing an object, it follows that it looks to P as if something is the case; but if P is hallucinating then that also looks to be the case. The standard causal theory thinks that it is entitled to talk of looks-states and to regard them as a common visual element suitably caused when seeing occurs. A second case is that of occurrently remembering an occurrence which the subject underwent or witnessed, e.g. remembering going to London. This requires what has been called a re-presenting of an apparent occurrence, which is also required if there is to be something called an imagining of such a trip. The representing is then taken as a common element which amounts to a remembering only if suitably caused.[11] Finally, take the case of knowledge. Let us allow that knowing that Q entails believing that Q. But equally its merely being P's opinion that Q entails that P believes it. Belief is then taken as a common element to which further causal conditions can be added to make it qualify as knowledge.[12]

In fact it is not simply causal theories which rely on these as common elements; it is also an assumption of other approaches which locate the difference between the concepts they are comparing in the presence of certain non-causal conditions linked to the common element.

Having noted the pattern and some cases, it seems to me that the worry is this. If we can block a decompositional causal theory of the concept of seeing by invoking the disjunctive account, cannot we make the same manoeuvre in other cases? Maybe there is no experience in common between remembering and imagining; maybe there is no state in common between knowledge and opinion. There is of course a form of words true in both cases, but why not treat it disjunctively? Finally, if we cannot rule this out (as a conceptual error), then it seems we will have no determinate way of building an analysis up from what has been agreed, no grounds at all for building in causal requirements.

There are steps in the expression of this problem which no doubt need more attention. I want, however, to treat that doubt in a serious way and to consider how to respond to it. It seems to me that there is one thing which this line of thought cannot do, and that is to ground an a priori ban on taking disjunctive analyses seriously. It cannot ground such a ban, for there can be disjunctive concepts. We can introduce them explicitly. It cannot therefore be acceptable to rule out in advance the admissibility of natural disjunctive concepts. This means that, in itself, the worry cannot be treated as giving a reason for being suspicious of the present application of a disjunctive account.

The viewpoint I wish to propose on this problem builds on that remark. The spirit in which the problem is raised is that of believing that a theory or approach which might have these consequences for analysis when generalised is eo ipso suspect. The assumption, that is, is that there is here a problem for someone taking disjunctive accounts seriously. Rather, it seems to me, the possibility of a disjunctive approach should be regarded as a problem for those who think that a decompositional analysis of these concepts is possible. They need to explain why such a disjunctive possibility does not block the programme. Further, if they cannot explain that then it would not be absurd to hold that a lot of current conceptual analyses have overestimated the amount of purely conceptually ascertainable structure in our concepts. That is, it is in no way a *reductio* of the idea if it should have this consequence. On this conception there really is no threat in the air. The question is: can proponents of causal analyses say something which is legitimately conceptual and which blocks a disjunctive strategy?

If the direction in which I have tried to push this problem is acceptable then this question needs an answer. I wish to say a little about one of the cases, that of memory.

What is there to prevent someone from suggesting that the re-pre-sentation when it is a case of genuine memory is one sort of thing and when it is a case of imagination is another sort of thing? This would be the analogue for memory of the disjunctive theory of perceptual appear-ance. We can bring against this the ubiquity of the talk of memory images; that is a form of talk in which the representation seems to be characterized as involving (or being) the same sort of thing, viz. an image, as in the imag-ination case. This leads to the following characterisation of memory: it is a feature of our general pre-scientific, completely ordinary attitude to recall-ing that it involves an image. It is, therefore, quite permissible to present an analysis of the concept in which such occurrences are treated as requir-ing a distinct sort of cause. It would be in this case a quite unnatural move to invoke a disjunctive account of the re-presentation feature.

Now it has to be conceded that it is not entirely clear that this legitimizes invoking a common re-presenting element in the analysis of memory.[13] However there is one thing that I can add. Why is it relatively obvious that there is a common sort of re-presenting? Here is one conjecture. It might be that this is obvious to us because we have the same sort of control over memory images (or the experiences in memory) as we do over the experiences in imagination (imagination images). Our relation to the experiences of memory reveals it to involve a joint experience with imagination.

The conclusion, a rather interim one, is that there are things that can be said to block the disjunctive theory at least in the case of memory. What I have said though is, I must admit, speculative.

## V

### Against the Causal Theory

So far I have attempted to undermine the claim that a fairly simple argu-ment will support CTV. I want, in this section, to present an argument against CTV and then to assess its strength. The argument contains basi-cally two premises. The first premise is the claim that when we see an item there is nothing in the occurrence which is both manifest to us and can count as an effect induced by, and hence separate from, the item seen. The second premise is that if this is so then it is quite implausible to claim that the concept we have all mastered and which applies to such occurrences (the concept of seeing) is a causal concept with a separable experience required as the effect end. I shall try to give a brief elucidation and defence of the two premises.

The most direct way to support the first premise is to invite someone to consider this. Take a typical case of vision, say one where you are seeing a book in front of you. Now, the book is the object of sight. According to CTV, its being the object consists in its producing an experience in you. Now, the experience is a separate event in the subject, separate, that is, from the object. In that case, to find it we need to ignore the object and to locate an effect of it. However, it seems quite impossible to find or locate or direct one's attention on anything in this normal, standard case of seeing, other than the book. What else is there? It seems to me, therefore, that there is nothing manifest in perception which can count as the effect of the perceived object.

This claim is in line with a thought traditionally expressed in the words "experience is invisible or translucent." That is, we, as it were, look straight through the experience to the object; there is nothing to the experience, from our point of view, other than the aspects of the object it acquaints us with. It is also, I believe, in line with an account sketched by Gareth Evans about the route to knowledge of how the world appears to us. Evans says that a subject can gain knowledge of what he calls that subject's "informational states" in this way:

> he goes through exactly the same procedures as he would go through if he were trying to make a judgement about how it is at this place now, but excluding any knowledge he has of an extraneous kind. . . . Now he may prefix the result with the operator "It seems to me as though . . . ." This is a way of producing in himself, and giving expression to, a cognitive state whose content is systematically dependent upon the content of the informational state. . . . But in no way has the state become an object to him. . . . What this means is there is no informational state which stands to the internal state as that internal state stands to the world.[14]

Why, we might ask, should Evans adopt this approach to the self-ascription of appearances? The answer, I believe, is that in perception there is nothing to latch on to other than the world; in particular, there is no such thing as a state produced in us, and which is manifestly distinct from the world, to which we can attend. This, I have been claiming, is precisely how perceptual experience strikes us.

That concludes my initial presentation of support for the first premise. What of the second? To support the second premise is not easy, since it is, in effect, a generalisation about causal concepts, and it can hardly be claimed that we have a clear enough understanding of the extent of such concepts to ground such a generalisation. However, to give it some support, we can note that, in general, with concepts that will be acknowledged to be causal, there is a manifest effect end involved in their instantiation.

Consider the notion of one object drying another. It is hardly deniable that this relation obtains only if the first object is causing the second to be drier than it was. In this case the second object's getting drier is a manifest effect end. It is manifest in the sense that anyone who understands what it is for one object to dry another will understand the notion of one object getting drier and this understanding will play a role in the generation of judgements about one object drying another. For example, if there is a dispute as to whether a certain action with a towel is drying an object, anyone is disposed to count it as relevant, and worth getting evidence about, whether the object is getting drier.

Now, where there is this manifest potential effect we can sensibly treat another notion as amounting to the notion of one item producing, in a suitable way, that effect. Where, however, there is no such manifest potential effect within an overall occurrence it is hard to see how our basic understanding of the notion of that type of occurrence can have a causal structure.

Neither premise has the status of the absolutely obvious and some remarks of Professor Strawson seem to me to be relevant to a consideration of the first one. Strawson says:

We are philosophically accustomed—it is a Humean legacy—to think of the simplest and most obvious kind of causal relation as holding between types of item such that items of both types are observable or experienceable.... Since we obviously cannot distinguish the observation of a physical object from the experience of observing it—for they are the same thing—we shall then be lead to conclude that the idea of a causal dependence of perceptual experience on the perceived object cannot be even an implicit part of our pre-theoretical scheme....

But the difficulty is spurious. By directing our attention to causal relations between objects of perception, we have simply been led to overlook the special character of perception itself. Of course, the requirement holds for causal relations between distinct objects of perception, but not for the relation between perception and its objects. When x is a physical object and y is a perception of x, then x is observed and y is enjoyed.[15]

The question we need to consider is whether this passage contains anything which can undermine our first premise. The central thought in the passage should be agreed to. If we think of perception as a causal process, our relation to the effect end in it will not be the same as it is to those items which, by causing the effects in us, are being observed by us. As Strawson puts it, we observe the items which are causes, but enjoy the occurrences which are their effects. However, it is not correct to conclude from this that we cannot observe the effect ends also; it may be that as well as enjoying a certain effect of an object x (and thereby observing x) the effects we are enjoying can themselves produce further effects whereby they are themselves in some sense observed. It is an important question whether the effects in us of objects can in this way become objects of observation. In the discussion by Evans, I think, the view is taken that they cannot. However, the tradition which talks of introspection as inner perception is precisely committed to this possibility. The unobservability of the effect end in perception (if it is unobservable) is not, therefore, accounted for by noting the distinction between observing and enjoying. We should, though, be led by Strawson's remark to acknowledge the possibility of unobservable inner effects. Now, it would be a mistake to conclude that it was not obvious to someone that there was a certain unobservable effect simply because it was not obvious through observation that it was present. And, I take it, it would be in the spirit of Strawson's remarks to allege that the support I offered for the premise we are currently considering involved such a mistake. I think it must be allowed that this allegation is close to the truth. The support for the premise consisted entirely in pointing out that there is no observable effect end in perception; but it does not follow that there is no manifest effect end. However, it needs to be asked, just why is it manifest? What makes it manifest that the type of occurrence we call percep-tion involves an effect in us of the object perceived? What remains of my argument is that it shows that the most obvious and standard ground for supposing this is not present in the experience of vision. What else is there about perception which might ground the view that it involves an effect?

It seems to me that Strawson's remarks mean that the first premise can-not be counted as obviously true; but it remains quite unclear how the sup-posed causal structure is manifest to the concept grasper, given that it is not by being an observable effect end. We have to agree, then, that the sim-ple argument against the causal theory is not decisive; it remains, though, that the initial argument contains two premises which are not obviously wrong, and by doing so, it highlights the burdens on a proponent of CTV.

## VI

### An Alternative Account

We need, if the considerations I have given are to yield something which approaches a convincing case against CTV, to indicate what an alternative account of the concept of vision would be. In fact, we might regard what has been indicated so far as one constraint on an acceptable analysis. The analysis should not explicitly require that the relation of seeing an object involves the object's producing an internal experience in the subject. To limit the range of theories further we must lay down more requirements, and that involves considering issues about vision and perception which are standardly treated as arising in the task of adding to the causal requirement to give a more nearly sufficient analysis of sight.

Before making some tentative remarks in this direction I want to point out that many proposals that have been made with the intention of supplementing a causal theory can be made and assessed without embedding them in a causal theory. For example, Grice suggested that it is essential to seeing that it involved the perceived object affecting the percipient in a certain way: his idea was that what this way in fact is could only be determined by empirical investigation, but that it has been fixed as the way present in certain sorts of cases, for example, as Grice puts it, "when I look at my hand in a good light ... (and so on)." In effect Grice anticipated the theory of natural kinds later propounded by Kripke and Putnam.[16] Now Grice linked his proposal to the notion of perceiving. Thus he says, "for an object to be perceived by X, it is sufficient that...." It seems, however, much more dubious to treat perception as a natural kind notion than it is to treat the notion of seeing that way. We have the strong conviction that it is possible for there to be perceptual mechanisms which rely on physical properties quite unlike those around us as earth-bound animals. It can hardly be that we have restricted the range of application of the notion of perception to forms of causal processes which we have encountered, whatever they might be. It seems more plausible to view perception as a functionally definable relation; roughly, a relation is perceptual just in case it confers upon its subject certain cognitive capacities. I do not think we can in a similar way make the idea that seeing is essentially a natural sort of process appear so dubious.

However, and this is my point, we can make the same sort of suggestion as Grice's without an explicit causal requirement, by proposing that seeing an item is standing to it in that sort of relation, whatever it is, in which I stand to my hand in normal conditions when I face it with my eyes open. That relation is in fact one of the hands affecting me in a certain way. The idea that it is appropriate to treat seeing as a natural relation is, therefore, quite independent of CTV. While refusing to go along with CTV we can still consider proposals of this sort, which normally emerge in its context.

A second example which illustrates the same point is Strawson's account of the concept of perception.[17] He endorses the CTV but attempts to provide sufficient conditions (or, more nearly sufficient conditions) by suggesting that:

implicit in the naive concept of perception ... are restrictions of a different kind. ...
The naive concept of perception ... includes that of a perspective or "view." ... Thus,
as regards range, we have the tautology that, however large the visible things, if
removed far enough away, it will be out of sight ...[18]

Now, whatever the merits of Strawson's strategy it is quite independent of
the thesis that perception is causal. We could say that it is implicit in the
concept of seeing that a subject cannot see an object at absolutely any distance. So the claim that there are such conceptual requirements can be de-
tached from any link with CTV.

This is, I think, worth pointing out for the following reason. The causal
theory is held in the esteem it is partly because it seems to be the agreed
and necessary starting point for practically all interesting proposals about
our perceptual notions. It improves the propsects for a non-causal view to
realise that this is quite wrong.

I am going to try to formulate an analysis which is not causal, but I think
that the reverse of the above point applies to this attempt. The positive elements it offers and some of the constraints it is intended to satisfy are independent of the rejection of CTV. So, anyone who is out of sympathy with
the argument so far can consider these suggestions on their own merits.

I want to suggest that an account should be consistent with the following claims. (1) It is not an explicit requirement that seeing is a causal relation going from object to subject. This I have been trying to support. (2)
Seeing is, as a matter of fact, a causal relation. That is, the complex causal
process is not an accompaniment of seeing but precisely is the seeing. It
follows that we want an account which in some way enables us to make
and validate such a discovery. (3) There is nothing impossible about artificial substitutes for some of the natural components involved in the processes. So a subject could still see if his natural eyes were replaced by
artificial organs having the same role. However, it seems that the precise
means employed need not be the same as those exhibited by the natural
organ. That is, neither the internal objects involved in the subject's seeing,
nor the precise types of internal processes which are involved, need be the
same as those which are actually involved. There is no evidence of any
clear limitation to this in the notion we have. There are two reasons for
saying this: (a) there just is a general preparedness to allow that we might
preserve a person's sight by replacing defective natural organs (etc.) by
physically rather different artificial ones; (b) in assigning vision to animals
in general there is no propensity to check on internal similarities between
them and us. If (3) is accepted, then, it seems to me that it blocks a straightforward natural kind type analysis of seeing.

(4) We do, I think, understand the revisionary conclusion that we do not really perceive external objects, even though they are there. That is, we do understand someone who claims that we have quite misidentified the objects of perception. This is another reason why we cannot treat seeing as whatever the relation is in which I stand to my hand when ... etc. The notion has extra content which it is in principle possible should not be fulfilled by our actual relation to the world.

(5) There is a further feature of seeing which I want to mention as a constraint. That is, that our account of seeing objects should be consistent with, and preferably should make some sense of, an entailment pattern between perceptual sentences pointed out by Colin McGinn.[19] It is that if P sees Y, and Y is a part of Z, then P sees Z. Here is an illustration of that: suppose I have a treasure chest which I ask you to bury so that it is totally hidden from sight. If, when I look, I can still see a very small part of it, I can still say that I can see the chest.

(6) I have said that it is a truism that seeing is experiential; if so, we should want our analysis to require that.

If it is allowed that (1) to (6) are correct, is there an account consistent with them? The account I wish to suggest as fulfilling (1) to (6) basically attaches one intuitive idea to a large gap. The intuition is that to be in perceptual contact with an object is to be so related to it that you could, all other aspects of your mind being suitably developed and attending, entertain demonstrative thoughts about the object. The gap is that I shall make no attempt to explain what is involved in the distinctively visual realisation of this relation.

Thus, we have: for P to see O is for P to stand to it in that experiential relation R which (i) is distinctively visual and (ii) is such that its obtaining means that O can be an object of demonstrative thought by P, given that P is suitably cognitively endowed and attending.

This is a rough proposal and it is not obvious that it meets my requirements, but I want to make a few comments to reveal the thinking behind it. The notion of a form of contact enabling demonstrative thought to occur is included for three reasons. (a) It is the candidate for the component in the notion of perception which validates (4). To be doubtful that we really perceive external objects (allowing that they are there) is to be doubtful that our contact with them enables us to grasp them in thought demonstratively. (b) It is also intended to allow prosthetic devices into the procedure. They are allowed because they do not disturb those aspects of the relation which make it one grounding demonstrative thought. (c) It is included also because it seems to me to be plausible to claim that our notions of perception are linked to it in some way. Thus we would all agree that in perceiving, objects are presented to us. The best elucidation or amplification of this would seem to be that presentation is simply a relation which enables a distinctive kind of thought to occur.

Here is a linked intuition about how the concept of vision enters our conceptual scheme. The child first acquires an understanding of certain relatively observational categories, for example, cat, drink, table (etc.). In effect, we make something like demonstrative judgements of perceptually encountered items that are of these sorts. The concept of vision is then mastered as the concept of that subject-world relation (whatever it is) which enables himself (and others) to make such judgements. I have wanted my account to be faithful to this intuitive conception of how the concept emerges.

Let me, also, link clause (ii) of the proposal to requirement (5). Fulfilment of (5) falls out of this because it is a feature of demonstrative thought that to be in a position to demonstrate a part of Z one is in a position to demonstrate Z. Thus, if I can think "This (street) is the main street of Calais," then I can also think "This (town) is Calais," and I can also think "This (country) is France," and also "This (continent) is Europe." So the account seems to satisfy (5).

There is one consequence that needs acknowledging; it is that our theory of basic demonstrative judgements should not have them contain, or presuppose mastery of, the concepts of perception or vision. The order of conceptual dependence is the other way. Of course, this is quite consistent with our explaining certain aspects of our demonstrative thought capacities on the basis of the nature of our perceptual faculties. So the truth, if it is a truth, that demonstrative capacities are explicable in terms of perception, does not contradict our analytic thesis. The constraint is on the account of the content of our most basic demonstrative thoughts.

I want to finish this section with a few observations on the role of demonstrative thought in the analysis.

(i) With a proposal like this the best one can do is to provide some motivation for it and then to see how well it withstands criticisms. I have claimed that it is both a plausible way to spell out certain intuitions about perception, and also that its inclusion fulfills certain other desiderata. I do not have the space to consider all the difficulties likely to be raised, but must here content myself with a few clarifications.

(ii) The intention is not that unsophisticated possessors of the concept of vision must themselves have the concept of demonstrative thought. It is, rather, that they must have the concepts exercised in demonstrative thought and that in their judgements about seeing objects they will respect the link expressed in the analysis. Thus, they will not, when looking at something both say "That is Excalibur" and also judge "I cannot see Excalibur."

(iii) It is not an implication of the analysis that all sighted creatures are capable of demonstrative thought. Obviously, animals and infants are not, but they can see. The assumption in the analysis is that such creatures stand to outer objects, in virtue of seeing them, in a way which needs only the addition of further cognitive capacities (and attention) to yield the possibility of demonstrative thought.

(iv) It would be in the spirit of this approach to claim that the concept of seeing is a primitive concept. When Strawson said this about the concept of a person he meant that the concept could not be analysed as requiring that a person be decomposable into different parts of different types. I mean something similar. We cannot decompose what is *a priori* required for seeing into a series of separate elements. Of course, this is not to oppose the decomposability of the phenomenon.

(v) It would be an objection to the analysis as it stands if it could be shown that there are more conditions that an object O must fulfill than being perceived by S for S to be able, given suitable cognitive endowment, to frame a demonstrative thought about O. Now, it can be said that for O to be capable of being thought about demonstratively by P, O must stand out from its surrounding, be presented as, in some sense, a distinct element. It might also be thought that O need not stand out to be perceived. Thus P can see the left half of a completely uniform wall, without that half standing out. However, there is, I believe, no contrast here between demonstrability and perceivability. Simply in virtue of seeing the wall, including the left half, P is in a position to think demonstratively about that half. He is in a position to think "That half is the same colour as that (other) half." The claim that a significant condition for demonstrative thought is fulfilled by perception is not equivalent to the claim that such a demonstrative thought is likely to be elicited in the actual circumstances.

(vi) A final difficulty that the analysis faces is that certain non-perceptual relations to objects also enable us to frame demonstrative thoughts about those objects. For example, memory of an incident enables us to demonstratively think about it. I have space for only two remarks about this problem. First, the analysis can be defended by finding features, not to be specified using the notion of perception, which distinguish the different sorts of demonstratives. The memory case can be distinguished by the demonstratives grounded on it being essentially dependent ones. That is, a subject at $t$ can frame a memory-based demonstrative thought about an incident at $t-n$, only if at $t-n$ (or thereabouts) he was in another relation to the incident which enabled him to think demonstratively about it. We can then say that the perceptual relation essentially enables non-dependent demonstrative thought contact with items. It remains to be seen whether the same sort of strategy works for other cases. Further, it may be that analyses of these other cognitive relations should utilise their distinctive role in grounding demonstrative thought.

## VII

### Vision and Function

I have sketched an elucidation of the notion of vision which, if correct, would ground some of the claims which I have said are plausible. I want, finally, to consider whether the account leaves out an essential element. That element has recently been alleged to be involved by Martin Davies.[20] Davies says: "... for an experience to be perceptual it should be produced by a mechanism which has a certain (teleological) function." Davies expresses his theory within the context of a causal analysis, but it seems to me that it would be quite possible to incorporate the core of the proposal into a non-causal analysis: thus one could simply say that in order to see an object one must stand to it in a relation which itself is sustained by an organ (or system) which has a certain teleological function.

Now, it would be natural, if one thinks that this is on the right track, to attempt to specify what the teleological function in question must be. However, we can, I think, consider the proposal without having the function identified. That is, we can ask whether there is any evidence that we would want to withhold application of the concept of seeing from cases where it cannot be said to be sustained by something having a teleological function. If there are no grounds for withholding the application of the notion then we can, it seems, dismiss the proposal without considering in detail what the suggested essential function is. I shall discuss Davies's proposal without either explaining why he thinks that it is plausible or providing any alternative treatment of the cases he felt it helps with.

The question of the plausibility of this proposal turns on what condition is imported by the idea of something's having a teleological function. Davies says:

it is relatively uncontroversial that something like this is correct. (i) It is sufficient for a mechanism to have F-ing as its function that it was selected for the F-ing; the selection might ⟨be⟩ by (a) the natural selection of the evolutionary process or (b) the intentional selection of the design process. (ii) However much of the notion of the function may be extended from this notion of design function, it is not a sufficient condition for a mechanism to have F-ing as its function that it happens (to operate as a totality in such a way as) to F.[21]

Now, it is not made explicit in these two remarks what is necessary for a mechanism to count as having a teleological function: rather two sorts of sufficient conditions are endorsed, and one putative sufficient condition is rejected. This means that it is hard to test the suggestion. However, I want to argue that it is difficult to accept what seem to be some of the implications of it.

The first move I want to make is to argue that intentional design function, that is, Davies's (b), has to be regarded as irrelevant to the concept of vision. That is to say, in so far as any notion of function can be implicated in the concept of vision, it must be biological function. Thus, intentional function can only come in where we are concerned with a perceptual process involving artificial devices. Now, it seems to me that whether such a process is perceptual cannot depend on the intentions of the artificer of the device. If we suppose it could then the following situation would make sense. X makes and intends to make an artificial eye for P which he implants, and which does its job. Y intends to blind P* and so makes exactly the same sort of device and replaces P*'s eyes with the device. We are to imagine that Y is an extremely incompetent designer. When P wakes up he rejoices that he can see. When P* wakes up he rejoices that Y's plot has failed. At this point Y says: "Bad luck, you are not really seeing because the device in you does not have the appropriate function." This comment would hardly make P* think that he did not see, nor, surely, should it.

I draw from reflection on this dialogue the conclusion that intentional function is quite beside the point. Whether a creature, in which there are artificial components in the visual process, can see in no way depends on the intentions of the person who artificed the components. I think, therefore, that the interesting question is whether the concept of vision is a concept linked to the notion of biological function. What I wish to make a case for is the answer that it is not, given that biological function is understood, or explained, in the way Davies explains it.[22] When biological function F is ascribed to an organ (or mechanism) it is standard, as Davies does, to treat that as claiming of it that it was selected for that function. Now, that seems to require the claim that the type of organism containing the mechanism does so in virtue of the organ's standardly doing F. Such a claim can be true only after the life of the organism has permitted the forces of natural selection to at least try to deselect that mechanism. In which case biological function can only apply to an organ which has passed an evolutionary test. However, it seems that the first creature which happened to mutate light sensitive organs (etc.) was able to see. Hence, it is in no way a requirement for seeing that a naturally selected mechanism is at work at all.

That was my first claim. The argument which I used is similar in point to a kind of example that is often produced in debates about the biological nature of psychology, namely, the example of an unevolved animal replica (sometimes known as a swampman). Would it not see? I think the present example is more clear cut because it cannot be dismissed as mere science fiction.

Here is another case. If for a mechanism to have a biological function F it must be selected because it achieves F, then it seems perfectly possible that a faculty which emerged might get deselected. In that case it would not acquire a function. Why could not a perceptual mechanism emerge which confers on its possessor a positive disadvantage? It therefore does not get selected. Was it not still a perceptual faculty?

It, therefore, follows that if the notion of teleological function retains its ties with the sort of sources Davies links it to, it is very implausible to insist that the organ of vision requires such a function. Standing back, it seems that both sources for the notion of function require processes or entities outside the entity containing the mechanism. Now, I think it is not a requirement for seeing that a creature can see only if it is connected in some way to external entities conferring purposes on its organs or mechanisms. Rather, it seems to be an intuitively plausible principle about vision that if P can see in virtue of instantiating physical properties P1 ... Pn, then any creature instantiating them would also see. It is irrelevant to its capacity whether the elements have teleological functions, that is, whether they are related in the right way to other cases.

The proposal we are considering seems to have counter-intuitive implications; and, in considering it we have formulated a basic principle which is both plausible and which the account I have given seems to sustain. I conclude that it is not a mistake to have left out reference to teleological function.[23]

## VIII

### Conclusion

I have tried to draw out the consequences of three features of perception. The first is that in perception there is no inner experience manifest to the subject. This, I have claimed, counts against CTV. The second is that perceiving, when it is attached to the right cognitive capacities, crucially enables a certain kind of thought contact to be established with elements in the perceiver's environment. This is utilised in the positive account of the concept of perception. The third, and least important, is, putting it rather crudely, that perceiving is the achievement of an individual in relation to its environment. This counts against linking the notion to biology.

## Notes

1. Hume is a clear example. See his *Enquiry Concerning Human Understanding* (Oxford, 1975), sec. 12, Pt. I, esp. pp. 151–152. Very often such philosophers label their opponents "naive realists." The idea is surely, not merely that the view is philosophically naive, but that it is the view of the naive, that is to say, the ordinary man.

2. This paper continues the development, with some differences, of a position which I tried to argue for in an earlier paper. See "Perception, Vision and Causation," in *Proceedings of the Aristotelian Society* 81, (1980–81), pp. 175–192, reprinted in (ed.) J. Dancy, *Perceptual Knowledge* (Oxford, 1988), pp. 192–208 [this volume, chapter 2].

3. There are some who deny this assumption, and who are prepared to say that the analysis of concepts can utilise what I am calling empirically based claims. The question faced by proponents of this position is whether it is possible to describe an activity which is, by their lights, legitimate (not objectionable) and which explicitly excludes reliance on what would be standardly regarded as empirical considerations. If they think that this is possible then it is fair, I think, to describe them as merely taking the name—"analysing concepts"—from one thing and giving it to another. If they think that it is not possible then, whatever the merits of their view, and the consequences of accepting it, they are merely disguising from themselves the extent of their disagreement with standard practice by using the old name.

4. This is one way in which, in a final theory, there should be an integration between conceptual and non-conceptual claims.

5. See D. F. Pears, "The Causal Theory of Perception," *Synthese*, 33, (1976), pp. 41–74.

6. See D. F. Pears, *op. cit.* p. 42. I have altered the numbering in the original passage in an insignificant way.

7. I use this somewhat indirect specification of the conception of experience as inner to ensure that the conception does not conflict with the doctrine, which is popular and indeed reasonable, that the actual causal origins of an event are essential properties of that event. It follows, and we should be clear about it, that to affirm of a particular experience that necessarily it could not have happened without a certain external object, is not the same as saying that the experience is not an inner occurrence.

8. This currently influential idea of a disjunctive account is due to Michael Hinton. See his book *Experiences* (Oxford, 1973) [excerpted in this volume, chapter 2].

9. See Howard Robinson, "The Argument for Berkeleyan Idealism," in (eds.) John Foster and Howard Robinson, *Essays on Berkeley* (Oxford, 1985), p. 174.

10. See John McDowell, "Criteria, Defeasibility, and Knowledge," in (ed.) J. Dancy *op. cit.* pp. 209–219 [excerpted in this volume, chapter 5].

11. See C. B. Martin and M. Deutscher, "Remembering," *Philosophical Review*, 1967.

12. See A. Goldman, "A Causal Theory of Knowing," *Journal of Philosophy*, 1967.

13. At this point we encounter problems with our understanding of the enterprise of conceptual analysis well beyond the scope of what I can discuss in this paper.

14. See G. Evans, *Varieties of Reference* (Oxford, 1982), pp. 227–228.

15. See P. F. Strawson, "Perception and Its Objects" in (ed.) G. MacDonald, *Perception and Identity* (MacMillan, London, 1979), p. 52.

16. Recognising that Grice's theory is an anticipation of these ideas helps to acquit it of the charge of circularity.

17. See P. F. Strawson, "Causation in Perception" in *Freedom and Resentment* (Methuen, London, 1974), pp. 66–84.

18. See Strawson *op. cit.*, p. 79.

19. See C. McGinn, *The Character of Mind* (Oxford, 1982), p. 41.

20. See M. Davies, "Function in Perception," *Australasian Journal of Philosophy*, vol. 61, no. 4, 1983, pp. 409–426.

21. See Davies *op. cit.*, pp. 421–422.

22. I do not believe that this argument represents the only problem for this suggestion.

23. I wish to thank Michael Martin, David Owens, and Bill Child for discussions and writings which have been very stimulating, and Katherine Snowdon for real help in producing this paper.

# 5 Selections from "Criteria, Defeasibility, and Knowledge"

John McDowell

... In Wittgenstein's view, clearly, there are criteria in behaviour for the ascription of "inner" states and goings-on (see *Philosophical Investigations* (*PI*), §§269, 344, 580). Commentators often take it to be obvious that he must mean a defeasible kind of evidence; if it is not obvious straight off, the possibility of pretence is thought to make it so.[1] But really it is not obvious at all.

Consider a representative passage in which Wittgenstein uses the notion of a criterion for something "internal." *PI* §377 contains this:

... What is the criterion for the redness of an image? For me, when it is someone else's image: what he says and does.

I think that amounts to this: when one knows that someone else has a red image, one can—sometimes at least—correctly answer the question "How do you know?," or "How can you tell?," by saying "By what he says and does." In order to accommodate the distinction between criteria and symptoms, we should add that inability or refusal to accept the adequacy of the answer would betray, not ignorance of a theory, but non-participation in a "convention"; but with that proviso, my paraphrase seems accurate and complete. It is an extra—something dictated, I believe, by an epistemological presupposition not expressed in the text—to suppose that "what he says and does" must advert to a condition that one might ascertain to be satisfied by someone independently of knowing that he has a red image: a condition someone might satisfy even though he has no red image, so that it constitutes at best defeasible evidence that he has one.

Commentators often take it that the possibility of pretence shows that criteria are defeasible.[2] This requires the assumption that in a successful

John McDowell, "Criteria, Defeasibility, and Knowledge." © The British Academy 1983. Reproduced by permission from *Proceedings of the British Academy* 68; 1982.

deception one brings it about that criteria for something "internal" are sat-isfied, although the ascription for which they are criteria would be false. But is the assumption obligatory? Here is a possible alternative; in pretend-ing, one causes it to *appear* that criteria for something "internal" are satis-fied (that is, one causes it to appear that someone else could know, by what one says and does, that one is in, say, some "inner" state); but the criteria are not really satisfied (that is, the knowledge is not really available). The satisfaction of a criterion, we might say, constitutes a fully adequate answer to "How do you know?"—in a sense in which an answer cannot be fully adequate if it can be really available to someone who lacks the knowledge in question. (Of course we cannot rule out its *seeming* to be available.)

In the traditional approach to the epistemology of other minds, the con-cept of pretence plays a role analogous to the role of the concept of illusion in the traditional approach to the epistemology of the "external" world. So it is not surprising to find that, just as the possibility of pretence is often thought to show the defeasibility of criteria for "inner" states of affairs, so the possibility of illusion is often thought to show the defeasibility of crite-ria for "external" states of affairs. At *PI* §354 Wittgenstein writes:

The fluctuation in grammar between criteria and symptoms makes it look as if there were nothing at all but symptoms. We say, for example: "Experience teaches that there is rain when the barometer falls, but it also teaches that there is rain when we have certain sensations of wet and cold, or such-and-such visual impressions." In de-fence of this one says that these sense-impressions can deceive us. But here one fails to reflect that the fact that the false appearance is precisely one of rain is founded on a definition.

Commentators often take this to imply that when our sense deceive us, criteria for rain are satisfied, although no rain is falling.[3] But when the passage says is surely just this: for things, say, to look a certain way to us is, as a matter of "definition" (or "convention," *PI* §355), for it to look to us as though it is raining; it would be a mistake to suppose that the "sense-impressions" yield the judgement that it is raining merely symptomatically—that arriving at the judgement is mediated by an empir-ical theory. That is quite compatible with this thought, which would be parallel to what I suggested about pretence: when our "sense-impressions" deceive us, the fact is not that criteria for rain are satisfied but that they *appear* to be satisfied.

An inclination to protest should have been mounting for some time. The temptation is to say: "There must be something in common between the cases you are proposing to describe as involving the *actual* satisfaction of criteria and the cases you are proposing to describe as involving the *apparent* satisfaction of criteria. That is why it is possible to mistake the latter for the former. And it must surely be this common something on which we base the judgements we make in both sorts of case. The distinction between your cases of actual satisfaction of criteria (so called) and your cases of only apparent satisfaction of criteria (so called) is not a distinction we can draw independently of the correctness or otherwise of the problematic claims themselves. So it is not a distinction by which we could guide ourselves in the practice of making or withholding such claims. What we need for that purpose is a basis for the claims that we can assure ourselves of possessing before we go on to evaluate the credentials of the claims themselves. That restricts us to what is definitely ascertainable anyway, whether the case in question is one of (in your terms) actual satisfaction of criteria or merely apparent satisfaction of criteria. In the case of judgements about the "inner" states and goings-on of others, what conforms to the restriction is psychologically neutral information about their behaviour and bodily states.[4] So that must surely be what Wittgenstein meant by 'criteria.'"

It is difficult not to sympathize with this protest, although I believe it is essential to see one's way to resisting the epistemological outlook that it expresses. I shall return to that in the last section of this essay; the important point now is how the protest exposes a background against which the reading of Wittgenstein that I am questioning seems inescapable. The protest is, in effect, an application of what has been called "the Argument from Illusion," and its upshot is to locate us in the predicament envisaged by a traditional scepticism about other minds, and by the traditional ways of trying to meet that scepticism. The predicament is as follows. Judgements about other minds are, as a class, epistemologically problematic. Judgements about "behaviour" and "bodily" characteristics are, as a class, not epistemologically problematic; or at any rate, if they are, it is because of a different epistemological problem, which can be taken for these purposes to have been separately dealt with. The challenge is to explain how our unproblematic intake of "behavioural" and "bodily" information can adequately warrant our problematic judgements about other minds. . . .

With this epistemological framework in place, it is undeniable that the warrants for our judgements about other minds yield, at best, defeasible support for them. We could not establish anything more robust than that, if what we need is a certainty immune to what supposedly makes psychological judgements about others, in general, epistemologically problematic. So if we take Wittgenstein to be operating within this framework, we are compelled into the interpretation of him that I am questioning. According to this view, the sceptic is right to insist that our best warrant for a psychological judgement about another person is defeasible evidence constituted by his "behaviour" and "bodily" circumstances. The sceptic complains that the adequacy of the warrant must depend on a correlation whose obtaining could only be a matter of contingent fact, although we are in no position to confirm it empirically; and Wittgenstein's distinctive contribution, on this reading, is to maintain that at least in some cases the relevant correlations are a matter of "convention," and hence stand in no need of empirical support.

To an unprejudiced view, I think it should seem quite implausible that there is anything but contingency in the correlations of whose contingency the sceptic complains.[5] And I argued in the first section of this essay that it is quite unclear, anyway, how the appeal to "convention" could yield a response to scepticism, in the face of the avowed defeasibility of the supposedly "conventional" evidence. In fact I believe this reading profoundly misrepresents Wittgenstein's response to scepticism about other minds. What Wittgenstein does is not to propose an alteration of detail within the sceptic's position, but to reject the assumption that generates the sceptic's problem.[6]

The sceptic's picture involves a corpus of "bodily" and "behavioural" information, unproblematically available to us in a pictured cognitive predicament in which we are holding in suspense all attributions of psychological properties to others. One way of approaching Wittgenstein's response is to remark that such a picture is attainable only by displacing the concept of a *human being* from its focal position in an account of our experience of our fellows, and replacing it with a philosophically generated concept of a *human body*.[7] Human bodies, conceived as merely material objects, form the subject matter of the supposed unproblematically available information. The idea is that they may subsequently turn out to be, in some more or less mysterious way, points of occupancy for psychological properties as well; this would be represented as a regaining of the concept of a human being. In these terms, Wittgenstein's response to the sceptic is to restore the concept of a human being to its proper place, not as something laboriously reconstituted, out of the fragments to which the sceptic reduces it, by a subtle epistemological and metaphysical construction, but as a seamless whole of whose unity we ought not to have allowed ourselves to lose sight in the first place.[8]

Such a response might appropriately be described as urging a different view of the "conventions" or "grammar" of our thought and speech about others. But it is a misconception to suppose the appeal to "convention" is meant to cement our concept of a human being together along the fault-line that the sceptic takes himself to detect. It is not a matter of postulating a non-contingent relation between some of what the sceptic takes to be given in our experience of others, on the one hand, and our psychological judgements about them, on the other. Rather, what Wittgenstein does is to reject the sceptic's conception of what is given.[9]

I have suggested that to say a criterion is satisfied would be simply to say the associated knowledge is available in the relevant way: by adverting to what someone says or does, or to how things look, without having one's epistemic standing reinforced, beyond what that yields, by possession of an empirical theory. That implies an indefeasible connection between the actual, as opposed to apparent, satisfaction of a criterion and the associated knowledge. But it would be a confusion to take it that I am postulating a special, indefeasible kind of evidence, if evidence for a claim is understood—naturally enough—as something one's possession of which one can assure oneself of independently of the claim itself. It is precisely the insistence on something of this sort that dictates the idea that criteria are defeasible. Rather, I think we should understand criteria to be, in the first instance, ways of telling how things are, of the sort specified by "On the basis of what he says and does" or "By how things look"; and we should take it that knowledge that a criterion for a claim is actually satisfied—if we allow ourselves to speak in those terms as well—would be an exercise of the very capacity we speak of when we say that one can tell, on the basis of such-and-such criteria, whether things are as the claim would represent them as being. This flouts an idea we are prone to find natural, that a basis for a judgement must be something on which we have a firmer cognitive purchase than we do on the judgement itself; but although the idea can seem natural, it is an illusion to suppose it is compulsory.

The possibility of such a position is liable to be obscured from us by a certain tempting line of argument. On any question about the world independent of oneself to which one can ascertain the answer by, say, looking, the way things look can be deceptive; it can look to one exactly as if things were a certain way when they are not. (This can be so even if, for whatever reason, one is not inclined to believe that things are that way.[10] I shall speak of cases as deceptive when, if one were to believe that things are as they appear, one would be misled, without implying that one is actually misled.) It follows that any capacity to tell by looking how things are in the world independent of oneself can at best be fallible. According to the tempting argument, something else follows as well; the argument is that since there can be deceptive cases experientially indistinguishable from non-deceptive cases, one's experiential intake—what one embraces within the scope of one's consciousness—must be the same in both kinds of case. In a deceptive case, one's experiential intake must *ex hypothesi* fall short of the fact itself, in the sense of being consistent with there being no such fact. So that must be true, according to the argument, in a non-deceptive case too. One's capacity is a capacity to tell by looking: that is, on the basis of experiential intake. And even when this capacity does yield knowledge, we have to conceive the basis as a *highest common factor* of what is available to experience in the deceptive and the non-deceptive cases alike, and hence as something that is at best a defeasible ground for the knowledge, though available with a certainty independent of whatever might put the knowledge in doubt.

This is the line of thought that I described as an application of the Argument from Illusion. I want now to describe and comment on a way of resisting it.

We might formulate the temptation that is to be resisted as follows. Let the fallible capacity in question be a capacity to tell by experience whether such-and-such is the case. In a deceptive case, what is embraced within the scope of experience is an appearance that such-and-such is the case, falling short of the fact: a *mere* appearance. So what is experienced in a non-deceptive case is a mere appearance too. The upshot is that even in the non-deceptive cases we have to picture something that falls short of the fact ascertained, at best defeasibly connected with it, as interposing itself between the experiencing subject and the fact itself.[11]

But suppose we say—not at all unnaturally—that an appearance that such-and-such is the case can be *either* a mere appearance *or* the fact that such-and-such is the case making itself perceptually manifest to someone.[12] As before, the object of experience in the deceptive cases is a mere appearance. But we are not to accept that in the non-deceptive cases too the object of experience is a mere appearance, and hence something that falls short of the fact itself. On the contrary, the appearance that is presented to one in those cases is a matter of the fact itself being disclosed to the experiencer. So appearances are no longer conceived as in general intervening between the experiencing subject and the world.[13]

... The idea of a fact being disclosed to experience is in itself purely negative; it rejects the thesis that what is accessible to experience falls short of the fact in the sense I explained, namely, that of being consistent with there being no such fact. In the most straightforward application of the idea, the thought would indeed be...that the fact itself is directly presented to view, so that it is true in a stronger sense that the object of experience does not fall short of the fact. But a less straightforward application of the idea is possible also, and seems appropriate in at least some cases of knowledge that someone else is in an "inner" state, on the basis of experience of what he says and does. Here we might think of what is directly available to experience in some such terms as "his giving expression to his being in that 'inner' state"; this is something that, while not itself actually being the "inner" state of affairs in question, nevertheless does not fall short of it in the sense I explained....

In *PI* §354—which I quoted earlier—Wittgenstein seems concerned to insist that the appearances he draws attention to, in order to discourage the thought that there is "nothing at all but symptoms" for rain, are appearances that it is raining. If there is a general thesis about criteria applied here, it will be on these lines: one acquires criterial knowledge by confrontation with appearances whose content is, or includes, the content of the knowledge acquired. (This would fit both the sorts of case I have just distinguished: obviously so in the straightforward sort, and in the less straightforward sort we can say that an appearance that someone is giving expression to an "inner" state is an appearance that he is in that "inner" state.)

This thesis about match in content might promise a neat justification for denying that criterial knowledge is inferential. The content of inferential knowledge, one might suggest, is generated by a transformation of the content of some data, whereas here the content of the knowledge is simply presented in the data.[14] But this does not establish the coherence of a position in which criteria are conceived as objects of experience on the "highest common factor" model, but the accusation that criteria function as *proxies* can be rejected. If the object of experience is in general a mere appearance, as the "highest common factor" model makes it, then it is not clear how, by appealing to the idea that it has the content of the knowledge one acquires by confrontation with it, we could save ourselves from having to picture it as getting in the way between the subject and the world. Indeed, it is arguable that the "highest common factor" model undermines the very idea of an appearance having as its content that things are thus and so in the world "beyond" appearances (as we would have to put it).

This has a bearing on my query...as to whether the blankly external obtaining of a fact can make sense of the idea that someone experiencing a "criterion" might know that things were thus and so. Suppose someone is presented with an appearance that it is raining. It seems unproblematic that if his experience is in a suitable way the upshot of the fact that it is raining, then the fact itself can make it the case that he knows that it is raining. But that seems unproblematic precisely because the content of the appearance is the content of the knowledge. And it is arguable that we find that match in content intelligible only because we do *not* conceive the objects of such experiences as in general falling short of the meteorological facts. That is: such experiences can present us with the appearance that it is raining only because when we have them as the upshot (in a suitable way) of the fact that it is raining, the fact itself is their object; so that its obtaining is not, after all, blankly external.[15] If that is right, the "highest common factor" conception of experience is not entitled to the idea that makes the case unproblematic. It would be wrong to suppose that the "highest common factor" conception can capture, in its own terms, the intuition I express when I say that the fact itself can be manifest to experience—doing so by saying that that is how it is when, for instance, experiences as of its raining are in a suitable way the upshot of the fact that it is raining. That captures the intuition all right; but—with "experiences as of its raining"—not in terms available to someone who starts by insisting that the object of experience is the highest common factor, and so falls short of the fact itself.

The "highest common factor" conception has attractions for us that cannot be undone just by describing an alternative, even with the recommendation that the alternative can cause a sea of philosophy to subside. The most obvious attraction is the phenomenological argument: the occurrence of deceptive cases experientially indistinguishable from non-deceptive cases. But this is easily accommodated by the essentially disjunctive conception of appearances that constitutes the alternative. The alternative conception can allow what is given to experience in the two sorts of case to be the same *in so far as* it is an appearance that things are thus and so; that leaves it open that whereas in one kind of case what is given to experience is a mere appearance, in the other it is the fact itself made manifest. So the phenomenological argument is inconclusive.

A more deep-seated temptation towards the "highest common factor" conception might find expression like this: *"Ex hypothesi* a mere appearance can be indistinguishable from what you describe as a fact made manifest. So in a given case one cannot tell for certain whether what confronts one is one or the other of those. How, then, can there be a difference in what is given to experience, in any sense that could matter to epistemology?" One could hardly countenance the idea of having a fact made manifest within the reach of one's experience, without supposing that that would make knowledge of the fact available to one.[16] This protest might reflect the conviction that such epistemic entitlement ought to be something one could display for oneself, as it were from within; the idea being that that would require a non-question-begging demonstration from a neutrally available starting-point, such as would be constituted by the highest common factor.[17]

There is something gripping about the "internalism" that is expressed here. The root idea is that one's epistemic standing on some question cannot intelligibly be constituted, even in part, by matters blankly external to how it is with one subjectively. For how could such matters be other than beyond one's ken? And how could matters beyond one's ken make any difference to one's epistemic standing?[18] ... But the disjunctive conception of appearances shows a way to detach this "internalist" intuition from the requirement of non-question-begging demonstration. When someone has a fact made manifest to him, the obtaining of the fact contributes to his epistemic standing on the question. But the obtaining of the fact is precisely not blankly external to his subjectivity, as it would be if the truth about that were exhausted by the highest common factor.[19]

However, if that reflection disarms one epistemological foundation for the "highest common factor" conception, there are other forces that tend to hold it in place.[20]

Suppose we assume that one can come to know that someone else is in some "inner" state by adverting to what he says and does. Empirical investigation of the cues that impinge on one's sense-organs on such an occasion would yield a specification of the information received by them; the same information could be available in a deceptive case as well. That limited informational intake must be processed, in the nervous system, into the information about the person's "inner" state that comes to be at one's disposal; and a description of the information-processing would look like a description of an inference from a highest common factor. Now there is a familiar temptation, here and at the analogous point in reflection about perceptual knowledge of the environment in general, to suppose that one's epistemic standing with respect to the upshot of the process is constituted by the availability to one's senses of the highest common factor, together with the cogency of the supposed inference.

When one succumbs to this temptation, one's first thought is typically to ground the cogency of the inference on a theory. But the conception of theory as extending one's cognitive reach beyond the confines of experience requires that the theory in question be attainable on the basis of the experience in question. It is not enough that the experience would confirm the theory; the theory must involve no concept the formation of which could not intelligibly be attributed to a creature whose experiential intake was limited in the way envisaged. And when we try to conceive knowledge of the "inner" states of others on the basis of what they do and say, or perceptual knowledge of the environment in general, on this model, that condition seems not to be met.[21]

Keeping the highest common factor in the picture, we might try to register that thought by grounding the cogency of the inferences on "grammar" rather than theory; this would yield something like the conception of criteria that I have questioned. But we have been given no idea of how to arrive at specifications of the content of the supposed "grammatically" certified warrants, apart from straightforward empirical investigation of what impinges on someone's senses on occasions when we are independently prepared to believe he has the knowledge in question. The truth is that, for all their similarity to inferences, those processings of information are not transitions within what Wilfrid Sellars has called "the logical space of reasons,"[22] as they would need to be in order to be capable of being constitutive of one's title to knowledge. Acquiring mastery of the relevant tracts of language is not, as acquiring a theory can be, learning to extend one's cognitive reach beyond some previous limits by traversing pathways in a newly mastered region of the "space of reasons." It is better conceived as part of being initiated into the "space of reasons" itself.[23]

I want to end by mentioning a source for the attraction of the "highest common factor" conception that lies, I think, as deep as any. If we adopt the disjunctive conception of appearances, we have to take seriously the idea of an unmediated openness of the experiencing subject to "external" reality, whereas the "highest common factor" conception allows us to picture an interface between them. Taking the epistemology of other minds on its own, we can locate the highest common factor at the facing surfaces of other human bodies. But when we come to consider perceptual knowledge about bodies in general, the "highest common factor" conception drives what is given to experience inward, until it can be aligned with goings-on at our own sensory surfaces. This promises to permit us a satisfying conception of an interface at which the "inner" and the "outer" make contact. The idea that there is an interface can seem compulsory; and the disjunctive conception of appearances flouts that intuition—twice over, in its view of knowledge of others' "inner" states.[24]

No doubt there are many influences that conspire to give this picture of the "inner" and the "outer" its hold on us. The one I want to mention is that we are prone to try to extend an *objectifying* mode of conceiving reality to human beings. In an objectifying view of reality, behaviour considered in itself cannot be expressive or significant; human behaviour no more than, say, the behaviour of the planets.[25] If human behaviour is expressive, that fact resides not in the nature of the behaviour, as it were on the surface, but in its being the outwardly observable effect of mental states and goings-on. So the mind retreats behind the surface, and the idea that the mental is "internal" acquires a quasi-literal construal, as in Descartes, or even a literal one, as in the idea that mental states are "in the head."[26]

Modern adherents of this picture do not usually take themselves to be enmeshed in the problems of traditional epistemology. But objectifying human behaviour leads inexorably to the traditional problem of other minds. And it is hard to see how the pictured interface can fail to be epistemologically problematic in the outward direction too; the inward retreat of the mind undermines the idea of a direct openness to the world, and thereby poses the traditional problems of knowledge about "external" reality in general. Without the "highest common factor" conception of experience, we can leave the interface out of the picture, and the traditional problems lapse. Traditional epistemology is widely felt to be unsatisfying; I think this is a symptom of the error in the "highest common factor" conception, and, more generally, of the misguidedness of an objectifying conception of the human.

### Notes

1. For versions of this line of interpretation, see Anthony Kenny, "Criterion," p. 260; P. M. S. Hacker, *Insight and Illusion*, pp. 289–290; John T. E. Richardson, *The Grammar of Justification*, pp. 114, 116–117; Gordon Baker, "Criteria: A New Foundation for Semantics." ...

2. The supposed obviousness of this connection allows commentators to cite, as evidence that criteria are defeasible, passages that show at most that Wittgenstein is not unaware that pretence occurs. Note, e.g., Hacker's citation (p. 289) of *PI* §§249–250, as showing that criteria for pain may be satisfied in the absence of pain. In fact the point of those passages is not the vulnerability to pretence, in general, of our judgements that others are in pain, but the *invulnerability* to pretence, in particular, of judgements "connected with the primitive, the natural, expressions of the sensation" and made about someone who has not yet learned "the names of sensations" (*PI* §244).

3. So Hacker, pp. 289–293; Kenny, p. 260; Crispin Wright, "Anti-Realist Semantics: The Role of *Criteria*," p. 227; James Bogen, "Wittgenstein and Skepticism," p. 370.

4. Psychologically neutral information: once the appeal to pretence has done its work—that of introducing the idea of cases that are experientially indistinguishable from cases in which one can tell by what someone says and does that he is in some specified "inner" state, though in these cases he is not—it is quietly dropped. We are not meant to arrive at the idea of behavioural and bodily evidence that would *indefeasibly* warrant the judgement that someone is, so to speak, at least feigning the "inner" state. It is a nice question, on which I shall not pause, how the epistemological motivation for passing over this position should best be characterized. In the case of the "criterial" view, there is a semantical motivation as well; it is plausible that such evidence could not be specified except in terms of the concept of the "inner" state itself, and this conflicts with the idea that criteria should figure in the explanation of the associated concepts. See Wright, "Anti-Realist Semantics: The Role of *Criteria*," p. 231.

5. See the splendid recanting "Postscript" to Rogers Albritton, "On Wittgenstein's Use of the Term 'Criterion.'" (Such regularities are not "conventions" but the "very general facts of nature" on which "conventions" rest: *PI* II.xi, compare §142.)

6. Without going into even as much detail as I shall about the case of other minds in particular, there is already ground for suspicion of this reading in the way it attracts the label "foundationalist"—something that is surely quite uncharacteristic of Wittgenstein's approach to epistemological questions.

7. This is the key thought of John W. Cook's admirable "Human Beings," to which I am heavily indebted in this section. (One tempting route to the substituted notion is the idea that we can cleanly abstract, from the pre-philosophical conception of a human being, the mental aspect, conceived as something each of us can focus his thoughts on for himself in introspection, independently of locating it in the context of our embodied life. This putatively self-standing conception of the mental is the target of the complex Wittgensteinian polemic known as the Private Language Argument. If this were the only route to the sceptic's conception of what is given in our experience of others, the wrongness of attributing that conception to Wittgenstein would be very straightforwardly obvious; see Cook. But I think the situation is more complex; see ... below.)

8. I intend this to echo P. F. Strawson's thesis (*Individuals*, chap. 3) that the concept of a person is primitive. Strawson's use of the notion of "logically adequate criteria" for ascriptions of psychological properties to others has often been subjected to what I believe to be a misunderstanding, analogous to the misunderstanding (as I believe it is) of Wittgenstein that I am considering.

9. Note that seeing behaviour as a possibly feigned expression of an "inner" state, or as a human act or response that one does not understand, is not seeing it in the way the sceptic requires. See *PI* §420; and compare n. 4 above.

10. On the "belief-independence" of the content of perception, see Gareth Evans, *The Varieties of Reference*, p. 123.

11. The argument effects a transition from sheer fallibility (which might be registered in a "Pyrrhonian" scepticism) to a "veil of ideas" scepticism. For the distinction, see Richard Rorty, *Philosophy and the Mirror of Nature*, p. 94, n. 8, and pp. 139ff.

12. In classical Greek, "... *phainetai sophos ōn* [word for word: he appears wise being] means *he is manifestly wise*, and *phainetai sophos einai* [word for word: he appears wise to be], *he seems to be wise ...*": William W. Goodwin, *A Greek Grammar*, p. 342.

13. See the discussion of a "disjunctive" account of "looks" statements in Paul Snowdon, "Perception, Vision, and Causation" [this volume, chapter 3]; and, more generally, J. M. Hinton, *Experiences* [excerpted in this volume, chapter 2]—a work that I regret I did not know until this essay was virtually completed, although I expect this section grew out of an unconscious recollection of Hinton's articles "Experiences" and "Visual Experiences" [this volume, chapter 1].

14. However, this idea is not available to Wright, in view of his insistence that grasp of criteria should not presuppose possession of the associated concepts; see "Anti-Realist Semantics: The Role of *Criteria*," p. 231.

15. This fits the first of the two sorts of case that I distinguished above; something similar, though more complex, could be said about a case of the second sort.

16. This is to be distinguished from actually conferring the knowledge on one. Suppose someone has been misled into thinking his senses are out of order; we might then hesitate to say he possesses the knowledge that his senses (in fact functioning perfectly) make available to him. But for some purposes the notion of being in a position to know something is more interesting than the notion of actually knowing it. (It is a different matter if one's senses are actually out of order, though their operations are sometimes unaffected; in such a case, an experience subjectively indistinguishable from that of being confronted with a tomato, even if it results from confrontation with a tomato, need not count as experiencing the presence of a tomato. Another case in which it may not count as that is one in which there are a lot of tomato façades about, indistinguishable from tomatoes when viewed from the front: compare Alvin Goldman, "Discrimination and Perceptual Knowledge." One counts as experiencing the fact making itself manifest only in the exercise of a capacity—which is of course fallible—to *tell* how things are.)

17. The hankering for independently ascertainable foundations is familiar in epistemology. Its implications converge with those of a Dummett-inspired thesis in the philosophy of language: namely, that the states of affairs at which linguistic competence primarily engages with extra-linguistic reality, so to speak, must be effectively decidable (or fall under some suitable generalization of that concept). See Baker, "Defeasibility and Meaning," pp. 50–51. For criteria as decidable, see Wright, "Anti-Realist Semantics: The Role of *Criteria*," p. 230.

18. See, e.g., Laurence Bonjour, "Externalist Theories of Empirical Knowledge."

19. The disjunctive conception of appearances makes room for a conception of experiential knowledge that conforms to Robert Nozick's account of "internalism," at p. 281 of *Philosophical Explanations*; but without requiring, as he implies any "internalist" position must, a reduction of "external" facts to mental facts.

20. Nozick must be a case in point. The way he draws the boundary between "internal" and "external" must reflect something like the "highest common factor" conception; and in his case that conception cannot be sustained by the "internalist" intuition that I have just tried to disarm.

21. To the point here is Wittgenstein's polemic against the idea that "from one's own case" one can so much as form the idea of someone else having, say, feelings. On the case of perception in general, see P. F. Strawson, "Perception and its Objects."

22. "Empiricism and the Philosophy of Mind," p. 299.

23. These remarks are extremely sketchy. Here are two supplementations. First: when we allow a theory to extend someone's cognitive reach, we do not need to find him infallible in the region of logical space that the theory opens up to him; so we do not need to commit ourselves to the idea that the theory, together with the content of experience, must *entail* the content of the putative knowledge. Second: the rejection of the inferential model that I am urging does not turn on mere phenomenology (the absence of conscious inferences). Theory can partly ground a claim to knowledge even in cases in which it is not consciously brought to bear; as with a scientist who (as we naturally say) learns to see the movements of imperceptible particles in some apparatus.

24. Am I suggesting that the disjunctive conception of appearances precludes the idea that experience mediates between subject and world? It depends on what you mean by "mediate." If experience is conceived in terms of openness to the world, it will not be appropriate to picture it as an interface. (I am sceptical whether a conception of experience as anything but an interface is available within the dominant contemporary philosophy of mind.)

25. See Charles Taylor, *Hegel*, pp. 3–11.

26. This movement of thought can find support in the idea that the mental is conceptually captured by introspective ostensive definition. (That idea is perhaps naturally understood as a response to the obliteration of the notion of intrinsically expressive behaviour.) But some versions of the position are not notably introspectionist. (See n. 7 above.)

**Bibliography**

Albritton, Rogers. On Wittgenstein's use of the term "criterion." In George Pitcher, ed., *Wittgenstein: The Philosophical Investigations* (Macmillan, London, 1968).

Baker, Gordon. Criteria: A new foundation for semantics. *Ratio* 16 (1974).

———. Defeasibility and meaning. In P. M. S. Hacker and J. Raz, eds., *Law, Morality, and Society* (Clarendon Press, Oxford, 1973).

Bogen, James. Wittgenstein and skepticism. *Philosophical Review* 83 (1974).

Bonjour, Laurence. Externalist theories of empirical knowledge. *Midwest Studies in Philosophy* 5 (1980).

Cook, John W. Human beings. In Peter Winch, ed., *Studies in the Philosophy of Wittgenstein* (Routledge and Kegan Paul, London, 1969).

Evans, Gareth. *The Varieties of Reference* (Clarendon Press, Oxford, 1982).

Goldman, Alvin. Discrimination and perceptual knowledge. *Journal of Philosophy* 73 (1976).

Goodwin, William W. *A Greek Grammar* (Macmillan, London, 1894).

Hacker, P. M. S. *Insight and Illusion* (Clarendon Press, Oxford, 1972).

Hinton, J. M. Experiences. *Philosophical Quarterly* 17 (1967).

———. *Experiences* (Clarendon Press, Oxford, 1973).

———. Visual experiences. *Mind* 76 (1967).

Kenny, Anthony. Criterion. In Paul Edwards, ed., *The Encyclopaedia of Philosophy*, vol. 2 (Macmillan and Free Press, New York, 1967).

Nozick, Robert. *Philosophical Explanations* (Harvard University Press, Cambridge, Mass., 1981).

Richardson, John T. E. *The Grammar of Justification* (Brighton, Sussex University Press, 1976).

Rorty, Richard. *Philosophy and the Mirror of Nature* (Princeton University Press, Princeton, 1979).

Sellars, Wilfrid. Empiricism and the philosophy of mind. In Herbert Feigl and Michael Scriven, eds., *Minnesota Studies in the Philosophy of Science*, vol. 1 (University of Minnesota Press, Minneapolis, 1956).

Snowdon, Paul. Perception, vision, and causation. *Proceedings of the Aristotelian Society* 81 (1980–81).

Strawson, P. F. *Individuals* (Methuen, London, 1959).

———. Perception and its objects. In G. F. Macdonald, ed., *Perception and Identity* (Macmillan, London, 1979).

Taylor, Charles. *Hegel* (Cambridge University Press, Cambridge, 1975).

———. Theories of meaning. In Taylor, *Human Agency and Language: Philosophical Papers 1* (Cambridge University Press, Cambridge, 1985).

Wittgenstein, Ludwig. *Philosophical Investigations*. Trans. G. E. M. Anscombe (Blackwell, Oxford, 1953).

Wright, Crispin. Anti-realist semantics: The role of *Criteria*. In Godfrey Vesey, ed., *Idealism Past and Present* (Cambridge University Press, Cambridge, 1982).

# 6  The Reality of Appearances

## M. G. F. Martin

Many philosophers find the following principle compelling: (IND) If two perceptual experiences are indistinguishable for the subject of them then the two experiences are of the same conscious character.

Accepting this principle constrains the kind of account one can give of perceptual experience. I am interested in a view of perception which is committed to the rejection of (IND), a view which I shall label, *naïve realism*. Rejection of the principle is associated in particular with so-called "disjunctive theories of perception."[1] These views claim that it is simply mistaken to suppose that there need be anything more in common across veridical perceptions and delusive experience, other than the fact that all of these states of mind may be indistinguishable for the subject who has them, in some or all respects. When we talk of appearance in general, on the disjunctive view, we should take this to mean no more than *either* that one has a genuine perception of some thing, *or* that one is deluded in some respect, and it is to one as if one had such a perception. Naïve realism, as I present the position, is committed to a form of disjunctivism, as we shall see. So, in this paper, I shall be concerned with the question of what a naïve realist ought to say in response to a defender of (IND).

In general, it is a sound methodological principle to assume that two things which can't be told apart are relevantly similar until one finds reason to overturn that assumption. The naïve realist will be someone who thinks that just such reason can be found for distinguishing between veridical perceptions and illusory or hallucinatory ones. But the support for (IND) goes beyond the endorsement of just such a methodological rule: many philosophers seem to find it inconceivable that appearances, or conscious states could be other in their nature than to fit with (IND). They will

M. G. F. Martin, "The Reality of Appearances," in *Thought and Ontology*, ed. M. Sainsbury, Milan: FrancoAngeli (1997). Reprinted by permission.

suppose that there is something incoherent about the naïve realist's denial of (IND).

As we shall see, they are wrong to suppose that the denial of (IND) is incoherent. The threat of incoherence arises only where someone supposes that if there is any sense in which two things are indistinguishable, then they must seem the same, and that this holds even for the sense in which to have a certain phenomenal experience is for things to seem a certain way to you. But whatever our attitude to (IND) itself, we need to mark a distinction between how things seem epistemically, and how things seem phenomenally. Among many reasons that one can give for that distinction, the firmest is the problem of the non-transitivity of discrimination: two colour samples may seem the same as each other, when compared as a pair, but only one may match a third sample. In order to avoid inconsistency, the sense in which the experiences of the colour samples in the initial case seem the same can only relate to the epistemic sense of seeming.[2]

However, even if the rejection of (IND) is not incoherent, it would be a mistake to ignore the kind of strong intuitive support that it has. Even if one has an otherwise compelling argument to show that one should endorse a view of appearances inconsistent with (IND), it is not clear that the correct response to this argument is to reject (IND), rather than reject some premiss in the argument to the conclusion inconsistent with (IND). In order to defend the rejection of (IND) we need first to have a better understanding of the kind of grounding that it can have. This is the task I undertake in this paper.

The claim has a long history within so-called arguments from illusion as the basis of generalising some claim from an agreed instance of illusion to all perception. H. H. Price, for example, took what he called "the Phenomenological Argument" to be the more significant form of argument from illusion, in contrast to the "Causal Argument" which looks to the causes of our perceptions.[3]

As often as philosophers have explicitly appealed to the thought that where there is subjective indistinguishability there must be sameness of consciousness, other philosophers have rejected the move. Austin, for example, dismisses the appeal in *Sense and Sensibilia*.[4] Frank Jackson, in what is otherwise a rare defence of sense-data in recent philosophy, rejects the appeal to indistinguishability.[5] However, as I shall argue later, such dismissals of the assumption themselves miss the force underlying (IND).

The paper divides into three sections: in the first part I explain why a naïve realist needs to endorse a disjunctive theory of appearance, and what aspect of a common element approach it needs to reject. In the second part of the paper, I diagnose how a common element view may be argued for on the basis of subjective indistinguishability. In the final part of the paper, I suggest an underlying motivation for that argument, and hence a diagnosis that the naïve realist can offer of the obstinate intuitions that support the argument.

## Naïve Realism, Disjunction and Common Elements

1. "Naïve realism," as I shall use the term, is a theory of what the nature of veridical perception is; I bracket here a concern with whether there are in fact any actual examples of veridical perception. For any conscious state of mind there is something that it is like for the subject to be in that state; each such state of mind contributes to the character of one's stream of consciousness. What it contributes, the "what-it-is-like" properties of that state, we may call the conscious character of that state and in the case of perceptual experiences, I shall use interchangeably the term "phenomenal character." According to naïve realism, the actual objects of perception, the external things such as trees, tables and rainbows, which one can perceive, and the properties which they can manifest to one when perceived, partly constitute one's conscious experience, and hence determine the phenomenal character of one's experience. This talk of constitution and determination should be taken literally; and a consequence of it is that one could not be having the very experience one has, were the objects perceived not to exist, or were they to lack the features they are perceived to have. Furthermore, it is of the essence of such states of mind that they are partly constituted by such objects, and their phenomenal characters are determined by those objects and their qualities. So one could not have such a type of state of mind were one not perceiving some object and correctly perceiving it to have the features it manifests itself as having.

Such a theory of appearance is put forward on the grounds that it gives an accurate description of how the subject's situation strikes her when consciously perceiving. For example, at present I can see the Genoa lighthouse. Focusing on the tower, I can note its distinctive shape and colouring; turning my attention inward, and reflecting on the character of my looking at the tower, I can note that the tower does not disappear from the centre of my attention. The tower is not replaced by some surrogate, whose existence is merely internal to my mind, nor are its various apparent properties, its shape and colours, replaced by some merely subjective qualities. So my perceiving is not only a way of providing me with information about an external world, when my attention and interest is directed towards action and the world; in its very conscious and so subjective character, the experience seems literally to include the world.

This naïve realism can be contrasted with two broad alternative approaches to experience. According to a *subjectivist* tradition, most commonly put forward in the form of a sense-datum theory of experience, one's experience is constituted by an awareness of entities whose existence and nature is dependent on that awareness, and the phenomenal character of that experience is just determined by those entities and their qualities. When I look at the tower, and reflect on my experience, there is within my experience some surrogate for the tower with qualities that correspond to those that I am informed that the tower has. Few philosophers now endorse such subjectivism, particularly in the pure form which seeks to explain all aspects of the phenomenal character of experience by appeal to such subjective entities and their qualities.[6]

Naïve realism should also be contrasted with another approach which has become more dominant in discussion of perception recently, the *intentional* approach to perception. This view will agree with the naïve realist that, when we attend to our experiences of the world, we find the external objects of perception and their manifest qualities. But the view will deny that these objects are constituents of the experience, or that their actual natures determine the phenomenal character of experience. Rather, this view assimilates the case of perceptual experience to that of judgement or belief. We should think of experience as having some form of representational content, which admits of correctness or incorrectness. That content is specified by reference to the objects and their qualities which would be present were the content correct, but it is the representational content and not the objects represented which determines the phenomenal character of experience. In effect, the intentional approach agrees with the naïve realist about what is "before the mind," namely the external objects of perception, but it disagrees with it about the manner in which the objects of perception are before the mind. The naïve realist thinks of this relationally: the objects are part of the relational state of affairs which comprises perceptual experience. The intentional theorist denies this relational character. Experience is rather quasi-relational: it has a character such that it is as if the objects of perception are before the mind, but they are not required to be so in order for one to be in this state.[7]

This should make clear quite why the argument from illusion is such a threat to the naïve realist, as here defined. If I am merely hallucinating the lighthouse—for example, if I am taking part in an experiment which involves the stimulation of my visual cortex—then there need be no such appropriate object in existence for it to be a part of my experience. So the naïve realist account of perceptual experience cannot be correct for the case of hallucinatory experience, and more generally cannot be directly applied to any case of delusive experience, such as illusions where one does perceive an external object, but misperceives it as other than it really is. If we suppose that such cases involve the same type of mental state, perceptual experience, as veridical perception, then that will directly contradict the naïve realist account even of those cases. We can see both subjectivist and intentional theories as shaped by the need to accommodate the possibility of illusions or hallucinations. For the subjectivist, the mind-dependent surrogates for the objects of perception are guaranteed to exist whenever one is brought to have the appropriate experience, so there is no risk that an experience might occur without its candidate constituents. For the intentional theory, objects and their qualities can be before the mind in a way which does not require their actual existence, they merely need to be represented by the state of mind, and hence it should be possible to have an experience of the sort which, when one is veridically perceiving is the presentation of certain external objects, even when no such appropriate objects exist.

A naïve realist may instead respond to the challenge by denying the claim that experience is a common element among veridical perception, illusion and hallucination. Here, for example, is John McDowell recommending just such a move:

> ... an appearance that such-and-such is the case can be *either* a mere appearance *or* the fact [made] manifest to someone ... the object of experience in the deceptive cases is a mere appearance. But we are not to accept that in the non-deceptive cases too the object of experience is a mere appearance, and hence something that falls short of the fact itself ... appearances are no longer conceived as ... intervening between the experiencing subject and the world.[8]

Although the naïve realist is forced to admit that his account of experience will not apply directly to the case of illusion or hallucination, he will insist that these are just different cases from veridical perception, and so do not bear on the correctness of his view concerning them. But what exactly is the naïve realist forced to claim here when he denies that experience is a common element?

2. The disjunctive claim itself should be viewed as something which is strictly neutral between views which assume that experience is a common element and those which deny it.[9] Our starting point is the thought that

one can be in states of mind which make true claims that it seems to the perceiver as if there is a tree before her, or it looks to her as if there is such a tree, when she is not perceiving a tree, and may be perceiving nothing at all. Such claims will be true in the situations explicitly marked out by the disjuncts of the disjunctivist's claim: when it looks to S as if there is a tree before her, then either

(P)   There is a tree before her which looks to S to be so

or

(D)   It is to S merely as if this was so.

For a common element view these disjuncts capture the relevant situations in which S will be having a visual experience of a tree, so they should accept the truth of the claim. The disagreement between the views comes rather at the point when we try to say more than just this. If one accepts that experience is a common element, one will suppose that the disjunction is true because there is some state which is present in both cases. This is something that the disjunctivist wishes to deny, but what exactly is being denied here?

Clearly the disjunction is intended as an exclusive disjunction: so one might think of it, from the disjunctivist's point of view, as indicating two radically different types of states of affair. There is the one in which "the fact [is] made manifest" to the perceiver, and the situation in which the perceiver has a "mere appearance." These two radically different situations are yoked together in a report of how things seem to the subject through their indistinguishability, and that is what is expressed by the disjunction.

However, as Timothy Williamson has recently pointed out in a discussion of knowledge, this is perhaps not the best way of viewing the disjunctivist's intention.[10] For, if the delusive disjunct is to be a distinctive state of affairs, then we need to ask what distinguishes it from the situation described by the disjunction, where we are indifferent to the differences between the disjunctions? Here, it should be noted that the naïve realist has no general positive account of delusive experience.[11] Rather, the intent is to avoid having to apply to such states of mind the same account as that to be offered of veridical perception: at best, then, these states of affairs are gathered together as forming a mental kind through being indistinguishable from the parallel cases of veridical perception. But, of course, mere indistinguishability will not be sufficient to single out mere appearances as forming a distinctive class: for veridical perceptions are simply, in virtue of identity, indistinguishable from veridical perceptions, so all seemings and not just mere appearances meet the indistinguishability criterion.

If we cannot find a property distinctive of all mere appearances which makes them so, then it would seem as if there is no distinctive class of mere appearances, but rather a contrast between appearance, which is present whether one is perceiving or not, and veridical perception. This seems to leave us with appearance, equivalent to mere appearance, as a common element after all.

Williamson suggests that in the case of knowledge, what is important to stress is what is peculiar to the case of knowledge, and to resist the thought that the common element, in this case belief, forms a significant part of one's state of knowing. When we look to the explanatory role of the two states, according to him, knowing will play a distinctive role separate from, and more fundamental than, the one ascribed to belief. So the mere fact that there is some state in common between cases of genuine knowledge and cases of mere opinion, does not show that all that is true of the mental state in cases of knowing must also be true in a corresponding case of mere opinion.[12]

For some of the purposes that disjunctive theories of appearance have been put to, Williamson's suggestion is an apt one. For example, Paul Snowdon puts forward a form of the disjunctive theory to undermine a strategy of argument used to support the causal theory of perception; for that argument what matters is whether perceptions of objects can be factored into an internal component, the perceptual experience, and some further condition which makes the difference between genuine perception of an object and mere matching hallucination.[13] But, the move would be an unhappy one for the purposes of the naïve realist. Williamson's suggestion is consistent with (but does not strictly demand) a view on which the subjective component of one's mental life, all aspects of what it is like for one to be as one is, are comprised of the common states, beliefs and appearances, while the states present in only certain cases, knowledge or perception, while of explanatory importance in other realms, play no role in determining conscious life.

Clearly this would be inconsistent with the aim of naïve realism. This seeks to give an account of phenomenal consciousness, and hence the disjunctive account is intended to have a direct bearing on one's account of what it is like for the subject to be perceiving. In contrast to Williamson's suggestion, therefore, the naïve realist form of disjunctivism needs to deny that appearance, in the sense of a common element, has any autonomous status within one's mental economy (in contrast to Williamson's example of belief, which arguably does have just such a status). That is to say, according to the disjunctivist, the case of veridical perception has a fundamental explanatory role with respect to explaining what it is like for one to perceive and also for what it is like merely to have an indistinguishable illusion or hallucination. In such states being indistinguishable for the subject from veridical perception, their conscious character will strike a perceiver the same way if she reflects on it as will a conscious perception. So it will seem to her as if she in the situation of consciously perceiving. Even in the case of conscious perceiving, it will seem to the perceiver as if she is in such a situation. But in that situation the explanation of how things seem to her will coincide with how they are—we can appeal to the fact that the situation is indistinguishable from perceiving, but since it is a case of perceiving there is no need to do so. By contrast, in any case of perfect illusion or hallucination, we can explain its character by reference to the case of veridical perception, and we cannot give an explanation of what it is like except by implicit reference to the kind of veridical perception from which it is indistinguishable.[14]

This puts us in the position to state more exactly what the naïve realist needs to deny, and where the intuitive pull of indistinguishability presses home. The naïve realist need not deny that there is a common mental state to perceiving and perceptual delusion, which state can be picked out by appeal to subjective indistinguishability, for it will be consistent with this, that any such state picked out will have a nature which is unavoidably explained by reference to a non-common element, that is it will be explained by reference to some case of veridical perception.

On the other hand, we can also state more clearly the threat from subjective indistinguishability. That challenge is just that, if something really is an essential aspect of the conscious or phenomenal character of an experience, then what is true of it should be true of any state of mind indistinguishable from it for the subject: for what more can there be to the character of conscious states of mind than a subject can herself discern when she reflects upon them?

## Discrimination and Phenomenal Content

3. How then would an appeal to subjective indistinguishability show that there can be no more to conscious experience than what is common among veridical perception, illusion and hallucination? Indiscriminability and sameness of mental state interact in a complex way, and the strands

of argument need to be distinguished. We need to take into account both a subject's powers of discrimination with respect to the objects she perceives, and separately her powers of discrimination among her own mental states. A failure to separate these two questions, I suggest, underlies some arguments for indistinguishability as a criterion of sameness of mental state, and some over-swift dismissals of the claim.

To have the power of discrimination is to be able to tell whether two things are the same or different. We can discriminate properties or qualities, as when I can tell whether the vase is red or blue, and we can discriminate individuals, I can tell that the person on my left is distinct from the person on my right. Such capacities are tied to relevant circumstances of application, and we can also tie them to methods of discrimination: so we can talk, for example, of whether two objects are observationally discriminable by a subject, restricting ourselves to a concern with whether the subject can tell two things apart just by the use of her senses, without relying on any background information she may otherwise have.

Discrimination is a form of knowledge: if one does discriminate two things then one knows that they are different. So, like all knowledge, discriminatory knowledge is subject to tests of reliability, and hence as symptoms of this we are liable to test whether someone can really discriminate two things dependent on certain counterfactual situations, and not merely by relying on what is actually the case.[15]

We can discriminate among objects and properties in the world and among mental states and their properties within our own minds. Both forms of discrimination are relevant to the question before us now. For, one may claim that at least for some mental states, a subject's powers of discrimination among objects and properties in the world determine identity conditions for the mental states which embody those powers of discrimination.

With respect to perceptual states of mind, this thought is closely associated with the idea that there are observational concepts, and that the phenomenal content of perceptual experience is properly expressed only by such concepts. On an intentional theory of perception, we can take this talk of content in the technical sense of observational content; but that will not apply to either subjectivism or naïve realism. The intuitive idea here does not need to be restricted to the intentional theory, and we can talk here more broadly in the sense of content of consciousness: the thought is that the phenomenal character of experience is constrained by the discriminatory powers a subject has in virtue of their powers of perception.[16]

With this constraint in place, we may suppose that a subject can only experience things as a certain way to the extent that she can discriminate them from other things or from other states of affairs. Consider a familiar example, someone who is red/green colour blind cannot discriminate samples of red things from samples of green. Because they cannot discriminate solely by how the surface looks, whether a sample is red or green, we should suppose that their experiences do not have the content that a sample is red, nor a content that a sample is green; at best such experiences would have a content which is indifferent between these two colours. Note that it would not change things were we to suppose that the colour-blind perceiver lives in an area which lacks all red objects, so that the only samples he ever encounters are green; it would still be true that were he to encounter a red object then he would not be able to tell that it was distinct with respect to colour from any of the green objects in his environment.[17]

This is an example of discrimination of properties, and the corresponding link to the phenomenal character of experience. How does the link fare when we look to discrimination of individuals? Some of our ways of thinking of objects are purely demonstrative, relying on chance encounter, other ways of thinking of objects involve being able to re-identify the object at different times and hence to recognise it on further encounters. An answer to the question needs to address both of these ways of discriminating individuals.

With respect to the latter, there is some plausibility to the thought that we do not recognise an object purely through our phenomenal encounter with it. Were I to encounter an exact double of my mother, then that double would look the same to me as my mother would have done in that situation, and hence I would have been inclined to take the double to be my mother. This should not seem a surprising conclusion: in general we keep track of objects not only through their appearance, but also with some grasp of their passage through space and time relative to ourselves. That latter type of knowledge which helps ground recognition is itself not purely experiential, so we should expect that where we restrict ourselves to phenomenal discrimination, recognition drops out of the picture.[18]

Things are different where we consider mere demonstration. In general, a subject is able to demonstrate an object or feature in her environment where that object is made salient for her, that is where she can focus her attention on it as an object. Now one's ability to do this does not depend on any ability which is directed at one particular object, being sensitive to its history, as a recognitional capacity may require; rather it is of the form of a general ability to pick out whatever can be made salient to one on an occasion. So if we wish to test whether someone has that capacity, we need to consider counterfactual situations in which the object is still present, in order to see whether even in those situations, the subject can single the object out. For example, if the photon from the fifteenth sheet of paper in a densely packed ream prompts the thought, "That sheet contains sheer nonsense," we can consider whether I have genuinely singled out the fifteenth sheet of paper purely perceptually, by considering counterfactual situations in which I am prompted to the same thought but the relevant cause is the fourteenth or sixteenth sheet. We may also consider counterfactual situations containing objects other than the one the perceiver is actually singling out, in order to determine whether the perceiver can exercise the same general capacity with respect to them; that is, we are interested in whether I can single out whatever is the fifteenth sheet, and not really whether I can single out this sheet from any other sheet which might also have happened to have that position in the ream. Since the capacity in question is not tied to a particular object, there would seem to be no requirement that the subject should be able to tell when a different object is being singled out.

If this is right, then no argument which simply appeals to the subject's powers of discrimination in relation to the external world could show that individuals cannot figure within the phenomenal character of experience. Nevertheless some philosophers have certainly asserted that this is so. For example, both Colin McGinn and Martin Davies have attempted to push this line of argument. McGinn claims:

... when we are describing the content of an experience we should not make singular reference to the object of the experience ... In fact it seems right to uphold a stronger thesis about experiential content: that an accurate description of the phenomenological content of experience will employ only *general* terms to specify how the experience represents the world.[19]

McGinn's and Davies's reasons for this are much the same. Davies gives the following reason:

... in the case of perceptual content, it is plausible that if two objects are genuinely indistinguishable for a subject, then a perceptual experience of the one has the same content as a perceptual experience of the other. The source of this plausibility is the thought that the perceptual content of experience is a phenomenal notion: perceptual content is a matter of how the world *seems* to the experiencer ... If perceptual content is, in this sense, "phenomenological content" ... then, where there is no phenomenological difference for the subject, there is no difference in content.[20]

But this is simply a *non sequitur*. First, if we consider the link between powers of discrimination and content, all will agree that for the qualities that either object has, the perceiver is unable to discriminate them, and the experience will have the same content. With respect to the particular objects themselves, the subject will be able to discriminate each if she is able to single each out from among the objects in her environment. *Ex hypothesi* she can do that as well, so powers of discrimination would again ground the assignment of a content relative to the particular object perceived. So it seems as if we can grant all of McGinn's and Davies's assumptions, yet simply deny their conclusion.[21]

One might respond on McGinn and Davies's behalf that no mention has yet been made of the subject's powers to discriminate among her own mental states, and that this may supply the needed additional premiss. It is doubtful that any additional force will be added here: we should at the level of mental states be able to make the same distinction between discrimination of properties and discrimination of particulars. With respect to properties of the mental states, both sides will agree that the experiences are of the same type: with respect to the qualities of the objects perceived, both experiences present the objects as having the same qualities. McGinn and Davies in addition want to say that both experiences are the same in being general in character, presenting the claim that some object has the qualities in question. But their target need not deny that the experiences are the same with respect to their object: both experiences are experiences of particulars. There is, of course, a difference between the two experiences considered as particulars, as datable occurrences: the one experience is an experience of one particular, one apple say; while the other experience is an experience of another particular, another apple. But there is no reason to suppose that the subject should fail in the task of singling out her current perceptual experience from other experiences she has had in the past, and other mental states she currently enjoys. So, even at the level of discrimination among mental states, McGinn and Davies would appear to lack grounds for claiming that their target needs to separate powers of discrimination and contents of experience.

I suggest that it is a recognition of the failure of the McGinn-Davies strategy which underpins some blunt dismissals of the claim that subjective indistinguishability requires sameness of consciousness. Consider, for example, J. L. Austin's rejection of this kind of argument:

But if we are prepared to admit that there may be, even that there are, *some* cases in which "delusive and veridical perceptions" really are indistinguishable, does this admission require us to drag in, or even let in sense-data? No. For even if we were to make the prior admission (which we have so far found no reason to make) that in the "abnormal" cases we perceive sense-data, we should not be obliged to extend this admission to the "normal" cases too. For why on earth should it *not* be the case that, in some few instances, perceiving one sort of thing is exactly like perceiving another?[22]

This dismissal of the problem is disingenuous, it has application on only one conception of hallucinatory experience, and only where the argument under attack trades on the reasoning of the sort discussed above. The picture Austin has in mind is what Price calls "the Selective Theory."[23] When we perceive the external world we stand in some kind of relation to objects such as tables, chairs, and mirror images; when we hallucinate, we stand in a similar relation to unusual objects, sense-data. On this view, although tables and table sense-data have different ontological statuses, the one existing independent of our awareness of it, the other being dependent on that awareness, they share the same manifest qualities. So our powers of discriminating observable properties of objects will classify the two entities, the table and table sense-datum, together, with the metaphysical difference between them being assumed to be imperceptible.

Austin's dismissal will be right if those who use the argument can be made to accept this model of hallucinatory experience, and if their argument appeals to no more than the link between our discriminatory powers over the objects of experience and the phenomenal character of that experience. But, Austin's picture of hallucinatory experience will not even fit most subjectivist accounts of hallucinatory experience, and has no application to any form of intentional theory.

For, to avoid Ryle's familiar charge that there is a "sense-datum fallacy" and a "homunculus fallacy," a subjectivist had better not construe awareness of sense-data as simply on a par with the naïve conception of how we are aware of external objects.[24] It is not as if sense-data are there anyway, waiting for the subject to alight on and exploit her capacities for singling an object out. The subjectivist supposes that at least for the case of hallucinatory experiences, bringing about the experience is sufficient to bring about the relevant entities and instances of qualities which correspond to the phenomenal character of the experience. So it would be arbitrary here to claim that the differences between how the naïve realist conceives of veridical perception and how the sense-datum theorist supposes at least hallucinatory experience to be is a difference merely in the objects of those states of mind: the states of mind themselves would seem to have to be of a radically different nature. That suggests that the challenge of indiscriminability is better raised at the level of discrimination among radically different types of mental state. And Austin is not prepared to engage with the challenge at that level.

4. Although the common element view cannot appeal directly to the link between powers of discrimination and the content of experiential states in order to establish the subjective indistinguishability claim, it may seek to find a parallel between the example of first-order discriminations of features of the world and our higher-order discriminations of our own mental states, and then use that to ground the claim that subjectively indistinguishable states of mind should be treated the same.

Suppose, then, that we stand to our own phenomenal states as we stand to objects and their features in the world. Then, on the assumption that the content of the mental state by which we discriminate objects has its content fixed via our powers of discrimination, we should assume that where two mental states cannot be told apart in kind, that mental state has a content which is indifferent to the differences between those mental states. Since we cannot tell apart veridical perception and hallucination, the putative state of being aware of these states would present the two states as the same, and corresponding to this the states in question would have in common the properties presented to the subject in that state of inner awareness. But, as with external objects, there would be no inconsistency here in supposing that each state had other properties which were not in common, but which were not presented as such through states of inner awareness.

Now, almost all philosophers will agree that the supposition we have just made is itself mere fancy, for one of the most notable features of our own self-awareness is that there does not seem to be a distinctive event of awareness which stands between our judgements and their subject matter in the case of conscious self-ascription as there is in the case of experience of the external world. With experience of the external world, we allow for the possibility that someone is put in the position to make a discrimination but does not make it—one may have experience that something is of a certain character without thereby attending to that matter and forming the corresponding judgement. And as the discussion above highlighted, we also allow for the possibility that our experiences may be misleading, and in coming to suspect that, a subject can withhold judgement on a matter, despite her experience. There seems to be no analogue of these for the case of self-ascription of conscious states. Note that that isn't yet to claim that we need be infallible in our conscious self-ascriptions of phenomenal states: what is being denied is that there is a distinctive state of mind, inner experience, from which one can stand back, and leave oneself undecided as to whether one really has the experience that it presents one as having.

Given that, we cannot suppose that a subject's powers of discrimination with respect to her own conscious mental states are reflected in the content of some distinct mental state from the subject matter of her self-ascriptive judgements. If they are to be reflected in the content of any mental states at all, it will have to be in the content of the experiences that the judgements are about.

The parallel with outer observation would then amount to this: our actual discriminations of the observable properties in our environment are the judgements we make; our powers of discrimination are reflected in the contents of the sensory states we are in which prompt those actual discriminations. Our actual discriminations of our own mental states would be the self-ascriptive judgements that we make; our powers of discrimination would be reflected in the conscious character of our phenomenal states. If this parallel holds, then it will follow that there can be no aspect of the phenomenal character of perceptual experience which does not meet the subjective indistinguishability criterion.

### Reflective Knowledge and the Loss of the World

5. The naïve realist must reject any such line of argument: a subject's failure in the case of hallucination to tell that apart from some veridical perception should not be taken as the subject's ability to discern the common conscious properties of both states of mind. A rejection of the subjective indistinguishability thesis will be satisfying only where one can both explain the mistake in the argument in support of it while also explaining away the intuitive force of it.

There are two points at which one might strike: first, one might complain that the model of self-ascription of conscious experience takes over too much of an observational model of self-awareness, and that such a model is objectionable; second, one might point out that the view tacitly assumes some form of transparency of mental states, or infallibility since the subject's powers of discrimination are simply taken to reflect the genuine sameness and difference among her conscious states.[25] There is some justice to both of these complaints, I shall suggest, but on the face of them neither complaint will be sufficient to show that the opponent has made a mistake in their reasoning or assumptions, while at the same time explaining the continuing force of the intuitions in support of the argument.

For it is not entirely clear what an observational model of self-awareness should amount to, once we deny that there are states of inner awareness distinct from the conscious states one is aware of. Correspondingly, it is less than obvious either that there should be a mistake in adopting such an observational model, or that there is some deep motivation for endorsing one. So, the demand for transparency of the mind may seem a better candidate for locating the deep mistake. But here too, there is some difficulty in explaining exactly what the demanded transparency should amount to. If it is the demand that a subject should have determinate knowledge of her conscious experiences, then the demand for transparency is stronger than need be supplied by the above argument. For example, the demand would not be satisfied by certain standard approaches to phenomenal qualities.

Notoriously, distinct qualities may fail to be discriminated by a subject: a sample A of one colour, may not be distinguishable by sight when compared solely with sample B; and sample B may not be distinguishable when pair-wise compared with sample C; while A and C may be easily distinguished when pair-wise compared. Goodman's solution to the problem is to define identity of qualia in terms of matching: qualia are identical just in case they match all and only the same samples.[26] A variant on Goodman is suggested by Williamson, when he suggested that qualia are identical when it is not the case that there is some situation in which they can be discriminated: the mere fact that there is some situation in which two qualia cannot be discriminated does not show that there is no such situation.[27]

On either of Goodman's or Williamson's proposals, a subject may be unable to determine whether succeeding experiences have the same phenomenal character. Nevertheless, consistent with this, one can hold that the phenomenal character of the experience is determined by (or at least coincident with) the subject's powers of discrimination. There seems to be an intuitive sense in which Goodman's and Williamson's suggestions do still hold on to the intuitive appeal of assimilating identity of conscious state to subjective indistinguishability. So, if that appeal is underpinned by some assumption of the transparency of conscious states, the transparency in question must require less than fully determinate knowledge.

I think that we can sharpen both objections by combining them. To do this, we need first to look away from the case of perceptual experience, to that of conscious thought. It is tempting to think of one's conscious thoughts as involving a certain element of self-intimation. If I pose the question to myself whether I am thinking, and if so what it is that I am thinking, then it seems that, just by posing the question I should be able to settle it. This first-person authority over thoughts is itself the focus of much contemporary discussion.

Although the claimed aspects of first-person authority with respect to conscious thought has been disputed, I suggest naïve realists do not have to dispute it: they can accept that it not only seems to us that we have such reflective knowledge of our conscious thoughts, but that really we do. One might then suggest that lying behind the above argument for the common element thesis is the assumption that the reflective properties of conscious thought carry over equally to the case of conscious experience.

One way of making this vivid is to look to the Cartesian thought experiments for external world scepticism. Cartesian sceptical hypotheses such as lucid dreaming and malign demons generalise cases of delusive experience: perfect hallucinations. Given the manner in which Descartes treats dreaming, a lucid dream may as well be an example of extended hallucination, while the malign demon would appear capable of sustaining a life-time's worth of hallucination, while apparently capable of bringing about other deceptions as well (for example, concerning mathematics). Although there is no one particular way of spelling out the sceptic's challenge, one strand in it is relevant to our current concerns. For, Descartes does seem to assume that even in the face of the sceptical hypotheses, there is no real challenge to our knowledge of our own thoughts. If we raise the question whether we are thinking, and if so what we are thinking, then we are in a position to settle the question just by reflection. The sceptical hypotheses seem to have a hold because it seems as if we cannot in the same way settle the question whether we are in such a situation or not, just by reflection.

Now we can ask, which side of the divide does perceptual experience fall? Do we suppose that when asked what perceptual experience one is having, one can settle this simply by reflection or not? Naïve realism, at least, is committed to claiming that, if we cannot settle by reflection whether we are in the sceptical situation or not, then we cannot settle by reflection what sort of perceptual experience we are having. For on that view, we have one kind of perceptual experience only when we are veridically perceiving, and another state when we suffer a hallucination, albeit one indistinguishable for us from the first kind. Indeed, in order to maintain a positive answer to this, it will appear as if we must claim that perceptual experience is indeed a common element between perception and hallucination; for then, even if we cannot determine just by reflection whether we are perceiving or hallucinating, we can at least determine which kind of state of mind we are in, since it can occur in either situation.[28] Note that such reflective knowledge of one's experiences would be consistent with Goodman's and Williamson's account of qualia and phenomenal qualities. For although even if in my actual position I cannot determine whether two experiences are of the same character, there will be some possible circumstance in which I could have done so simply by reflection: even though I cannot always determine the character of my experience, what I need to determine its character is not something which lies beyond possible reflection.

6. One issue which this raises which would take us far beyond our current concerns is the need for an explanation of why our conscious thoughts do possess the reflective knowledge property. Someone might suppose that they can do so only if we adopt something like the above model of our powers of discrimination among our mental states. That would make it seem natural that the relevant property should spread to all conscious states and not just our thoughts.

But the relevant assumption can and should be challenged. For what it overlooks are features of self-ascription of conscious states which are peculiar to the case of thoughts: namely the guarantee that the content of the lower-order thought is replicated in the higher-order thought; and the kind of identification and endorsement of the thought ascribed which the self-ascription of conscious thoughts typically has.[29] These features of self-ascription would suggest that an account purely in terms of powers of discrimination among one's thoughts could not be the whole picture.[30] Yet it is just these features of self-ascription which are lacking in the case of self-ascription of conscious experiences. When one judges of how things seem to one, such a judgement can precisely embody a certain kind of distance from one's experience in a way that contrasts markedly with the self-ascription of belief.

Nevertheless, even if it wouldn't simply follow from the correct account of self-ascription of conscious states that we should have to possess reflective knowledge of our own experiences, that would not stop it being a desirable feature of our experiences, and hence a respectable motivation for endorsing (IND). Here I suggest that the naïve realist can point out that the desire for reflective knowledge of one's experiences really cannot be satisfied whether we accept the argument from subjective indistinguishability or not. For, if the naïve realist is right to claim that her account of perceptual appearances is the only adequate description of how our experiences strike us, then the alternatives to this approach, some form of intentional theory or subjectivist view, will be giving an account of experience which does not accord with how it initially strikes us—the correct account will be, in J. L. Mackie's term, an "error theory"[31] of perception, which distinguishes between how it seems to us we are perceptually related to the world, and how we are in fact related to the world. Even if philosophical reasoning can reveal to us that experience is not as it first strikes us, reflection on the character of experience alone cannot show us that.

So, the naïve realist can claim that either we simply resist the desire for reflective knowledge of our perceptual experiences, and take at least veridical perceptions at face value, while admitting that delusive experience if it occurs is surd; or, we endorse the desire, accept the subjective indistinguishability argument and are led to endorse a theory of appearance at odds with how things strike us. Adopting either horn will leave us with the desire unsatisfied and no such unsatisfiable desire can be a good reason to endorse the strategy of argument which leads to the common element thesis.[32]

Indeed, I suggest that this diagnosis will help us to explain the following passage from Barry Stroud's discussion of scepticism:

> What *can* we know in such a predicament? We can perhaps know what sensory experiences we are having, or how things seem to us to be.... We are in a sense imprisoned within those representations, at least with respect to our knowledge....
>
> This can seem to leave us in the position of finding a barrier between ourselves and the world around us. There would then be a veil of sensory experiences or sensory objects which we could not penetrate but which would be no reliable guide to the world beyond the veil.[33]

Stroud here suggests that if we give in to Cartesian scepticism, and accept that we merely have knowledge of our own conscious states of mind, then the sensory states of which we have knowledge will seem to be a barrier between us and the world of which we desire knowledge. But Stroud's line of argument here is obscure. Why should my mere lack of knowledge of the reliability of some putative source of knowledge show that would-be source to be some barrier between me and the object of knowledge? Suppose, for example, that I have a document which is either a piece of fiction or a historical record, but I cannot determine which: as frustrated as I may be by my lack of knowledge, this surely does not lead me to view the document as a barrier between me and the historical matters of fact. Indeed, it can seem to me as if the document, if in fact it is a record does reveal the past to me; it is just than I cannot tell that that is so. Nothing Stroud says indicates why we should not view sensory experience in the same light.

The naïve realist can explain why we might feel such a sense of barrier. In order for us to have reflective knowledge of our sensory states in the face of the sceptical challenge, our experiences would have to have a nature very different from that which we pre-theoretically suppose them to have. In that case, such experiences could not be giving us the kind of cognitive contact with the external world that previously we supposed them to provide.

This is to suggest, in effect, that the sceptical threat from a veil of perception does not arise simply from the Cartesian sceptical challenge. Rather it arises from the challenge that Hume puts forward most explicitly in the *First Enquiry* when he claims that there is a form of "consequent" scepticism which challenges the authority of our senses to provide us with knowledge about the world, and then argues that the "common and universal opinion of all men" concerning the objects of perception can be shown to be false by the "slightest philosophy."[34]

On the picture suggested here, there are in fact two steps to the sceptical threat: first, one may feel attracted, in the face of the Cartesian sceptical challenge, to endorse (IND) and hence the common element view of experience. Once one does that, assuming that the naïve realist is correct as a view of common sense, one is then driven to a view of perception which is inconsistent with common sense, and that may then undermine the claims of the senses to provide one with knowledge of the world, engendering a further sceptical challenge to that knowledge.[35]

Finally, this suggests an explanation of the recalcitrance of the intuitions in favour of (IND). If the naïve realist is right to claim that our experience seems to be the way that the theory claims, then if we really did have reflective knowledge of our experience, and experience was as the naïve realist says, we would have a direct answer to the initial sceptical challenge, and the apparent contrast between our knowledge of our thoughts and our knowledge of the world would be undermined. Of course, this motivation is no better than the simple demand for reflective knowledge of experience itself, for in securing sceptic-free knowledge of our experiences we would do so only at the cost of denying the relevant feature of experience. But the false attractions of this move would be dispelled only by a satisfactory dissolution of the sceptical challenge itself. So the intuitive support for the subjective indistinguishability argument does not so much reflect the self-evidence of the common element view of appearances, as reflect the intractability of certain sceptical problems.[36]

**Notes**

1. A disjunctive theory of appearance was first put forward by J. M. Hinton (1973) [excerpted in this volume, chapter 2] and by P. F. Snowdon (1980–81) [this volume,

chapter 3]. John McDowell developed a variant of this, see McDowell (1982) [excerpted in this volume, chapter 5]. Snowdon's and McDowell's rather different theories have been discussed together in W. Child (1994), pp. 143–164.

2. We shall return to the issue of indiscriminable but distinct qualities below. For other reasons to insist on a contrast between "epistemic" seeming and "phenomenal" seeming, see F. Jackson (1977), ch. 2, and F. Dretske (1995), chs. 1, 3 and 5.

3. See H. H. Price (1932), pp. 27–53.

4. J. L. Austin (1962), lecture V.

5. F. Jackson (1977), pp. 110–111.

6. For defence of such subjectivism see, F. Jackson (1977); J. Foster (1986), ch. 2 sec. X; M. Perkins (1983); H. Robinson (1994).

7. Early examples of this approach in recent Anglophone philosophy can be found in G. E. M. Anscombe (1962); D. M. Armstrong (1968), ch. 10; more recent defences of the approach can be found in J. Searle (1983); G. Harman, "The Intrinsic Quality of Experience," *Philosophical Perspectives*, 4; M. Tye (1992); T. Burge (1993); F. Dretske (1995). Note that as I use the term, an intentional theory of perception supposes that experiences admit of correctness or incorrectness. Some philosophers (e.g. John Mc-Dowell) who deny this would still call experience "intentional," appealing to the idea that something is given to the mind in experience, even if it cannot be other than how it is given.

8. J. McDowell (1982), p. 211 [this volume, p. 95].

9. This is made clear in J. M. Hinton (1973), when he claims, "Even if few things are certain, it is certain that there are what I will call perception-illusion disjunctions ..." (p. 37), [this volume, p. 20]. Cf. also A. Millar (1996), at p. 75 [this volume, p. 137].

10. T. Williamson (1995), at pp. 560–562.

11. Indeed, the naïve realist ought to resist any attempt to give such a general account, for reasons that go beyond our present discussion. Briefly, we should accept that the proximate causes of a veridical perception are the same as those which can bring about an hallucination: if such causes are sufficient to bring about a certain type of mental state, hallucination, then they should suffice even in the case of veridical perception, so whatever occurs when one hallucinates will also occur when one perceives. The naïve realist can block this by denying that there is any general kind of mental state for which those immediate causes are sufficient.

12. The same suggestion is endorsed by Jonathan Dancy (1995) [this volume, chapter 7].

13. See P. F. Snowdon (1980–81) [this volume, chapter 3]; I do not claim here that Snowdon intends to restrict his application of the theory in this way. The last section

of his paper suggests otherwise as does P. F. Snowdon (1990) [this volume, chapter 4].

14. This is to reject Dancy's suggestion that "there may be available a more direct characterization of the second disjunct, and in a totally explicit version of the theory it would indeed be characterized in that better way" (J. Dancy 1995, p. 436) [this volume, p. 132]. On the view offered here, one can only characterise the delusive case relationally, by what it is indistinguishable from.

15. See T. Williamson (1990), ch. 1.

16. For two recent accounts of observational concepts see C. Peacocke (1983), ch. 4, and C. Peacocke (1986), ch. 1; and J. Fodor, "Observation Reconsidered," reprinted in J. Fodor (1990). I do not mean to endorse the constraint imposed in the text, but just to show that even given this constraint, certain things do not follow. Peacocke is an example of someone who rejects the constraint, as indeed is Dretske in F. Dretske (1995).

17. Here I am abstracting away from any concern with context-sensitivity which are the relevant counter factual situations to contrast the actual case with.

18. See P. F. Strawson (1959); G. Evans, ed. J. McDowell (1982), ch. 8. Again, I do not mean here actually to endorse the constraint—it is a matter of some dispute whether recognitional capacities can "colour" the character of experience; and the issue is closely related to that of the experience of non-observational kinds.

19. C. McGinn (1982), p. 39.

20. M. Davies (1992), pp. 21–45, pp. 25–26.

21. Note though, given the disjunctivist conception of hallucinatory experience, such experiences will lack particular content in contrast to perceptions—an hallucination of an apple will be indistinguishable from both of the twin apples, and since, by the hypothesis above only indistinguishability can fix the character of purely delusive experience, no particular can figure in the positive characterisation of the illusion.

22. J. L. Austin (1962), p. 52. Compare also F. Jackson (1977), p. 110.

23. H. H. Price (1932), pp. 41–51.

24. G. Ryle (1949), ch. 6.

25. Cf. John McDowell (1986), pp. 137–168: "We need something more contentious: a picture of subjectivity as a region of reality whose layout is transparent—accessible through and through—to the capacity for knowledge" (p. 149).

26. See N. Goodman (1977), pp. 196–200.

27. See T. Williamson (1990), ch. 5 and especially pp. 82–87 for a comparison with and criticism of Goodman.

28. Does this show that the common element thesis must hold for conscious thought also, if we are to have reflective knowledge of it? I would argue not, which itself throws up the question why experience and thought should be treated differently; that is an issue which unfortunately lies beyond the bounds of the current discussion.

29. Cf. C. Peacocke, "Conscious Attitudes, Attention and Self-Knowledge," in C. Wright, B. Smith, C. Macdonald, eds., *Knowing Our Own Minds*; for exceptions among conscious thoughts see M. Martin, "An Eye Directed Outward" in the same volume.

30. Indeed, one might object that to suppose that it would, would be to accept a quasi-observational model of self-knowledge. Compare the issue here with Tyler Burge's discussion of the failings of an observational model of self-knowledge in T. Burge (1996), pp. 108–110.

31. See J. L. Mackie (1975), ch. 2.

32. Note that this response is open only to someone like the naïve realist who supposes that some positive conception of experience can be given, and ascribed to common sense. Someone who endorses a disjunctive view of appearances, but refuses to say more about what is distinctive of the perceiving disjunct, has no grounds to show that if (IND) holds one still lacks reflective knowledge of one's experiences.

33. B. Stroud (1984), pp. 32–33.

34. D. Hume (1975), pp. 150–152.

35. So I would reject McDowell's suggestions in "Singular Thought and the Extent of Inner Space," that the "Cartesian" conception of subjectivity brings with it the consequence that there is "darkness within." There are two points here to make: even if one resists endorsing (IND) in the face of the sceptical challenge, that is not yet to answer the sceptical challenge—endorsement of naïve realism concerning perception is not itself an answer to Cartesian scepticism. Secondly, one generates Hume's scepticism concerning the senses only if one can show, antecedent to any sceptical threat, that we do have some commitment to naïve realism, or some other such theory of perception which is inconsistent with (IND).

36. This paper was first presented at a conference, "Thought and Ontology," in Genoa, November 1995; later versions were read to philosophy societies in Keele and Stirling. I am grateful to those audiences their for helpful comments, and to Scott Sturgeon and Jonathan Dancy for useful questions and discussion of these topics. The paper was written with the support of a British Academy Research Leave Award.

## References

G. E. M. Anscombe. 1962. The intentionality of sensation. In R. Butler (ed.), *Analytical Philosophy*. Blackwell, Oxford.

D. M. Armstrong. 1968. *A Materialist Theory of the Mind*. Routledge, London.

J. L. Austin. 1962. *Sense and Sensibilia*. Clarendon Press, Oxford.

T. Burge. 1993. Vision and intentional content. In R. van Gulick, E. LePore (eds.), *John Searle and His Critics*. Blackwell, Oxford.

———. 1996. Our entitlement to self-knowledge. *Proceedings of the Aristotelian Society*, 96: 91–116.

W. Child. 1994. *Causality, Interpretation and the Mind*. Clarendon Press, Oxford.

J. Dancy. 1995. Arguments from illusion. *Philosophical Quarterly*, 45: 421–438.

M. Davies. 1992. Perceptual content and local supervenience. *Proceedings of the Aristotelian Society*, 92.

F. Dretske. 1995. *Naturalizing the Mind*. MIT Press, Cambridge, Mass.

G. Evans, J. McDowell. 1982. *The Varieties of Reference*. Oxford University Press, Oxford.

J. Fodor. 1983. *Sense and Content*. Clarendon Press, Oxford.

J. Foster. 1990. *A Theory of Content and Other Essays*. MIT Press, Cambridge, Mass.

N. Goodman. 1977. *The Structure of Appearance*, 3rd ed. Reidel, Dordrecht.

G. Harman. 1990. The intrinsic quality of experience. *Philosophical Perspectives*, 4.

J. M. Hinton. 1973. *Experiences*. Clarendon Press, Oxford.

D. Hume. 1975. *Enquiry Concerning Human Understanding*, 3rd ed. Ed. by L. A. Selby-Bigge. Clarendon Press, Oxford.

F. Jackson. 1977. *Perception*. Cambridge University Press, Cambridge.

J. McDowell. 1982. Criteria, defeasibility and knowledge. *Proceedings of the British Academy*.

———. 1986. Singular thought and the extent of inner space. In P. Pettit, J. McDowell (eds.), *Subject, Thought and Content*, pp. 137–168. Clarendon Press, Oxford.

C. McGinn. 1982. *The Character of Mind*. Oxford University Press, Oxford.

J. L. Mackie. 1975. *Problems from Locke*. Clarendon Press, Oxford.

M. Martin. 1997. An eye directed outward: Reply to Peacocke. In C. Wright, B. Smith, C. Macdonald (eds.), *Knowing Our Own Minds*. Clarendon Press, Oxford.

A. Millar. 1996. The idea of experience. *Proceedings of the Aristotelian Society*, 96: 75–90.

C. Peacocke. 1983. *Sense and Content*. Clarendon Press, Oxford.

———. 1986. *Thoughts: An Essay on Content*. Blackwell, Oxford.

———. 1997. Conscious attitudes, attention and self-knowledge. In C. Wright, B. Smith, C. Macdonald (eds.), *Knowing Our Own Minds*. Clarendon Press, Oxford.

M. Perkins. 1983. *Sensing the World*. Hackett, Indianapolis.

H. H. Price. 1932. *Perception*. Methuen, London.

H. Robinson. 1994. *Perception*. Routledge, London.

G. Ryle. 1949. *The Concept of Mind*. Methuen, London.

J. Searle. 1983. *Intentionality*. Cambridge University Press, Cambridge.

P. F. Snowdon. 1980–81. Perception, vision and causation. *Proceedings of the Aristotelian Society*.

———. 1990. Perception and its objects. *Proceedings of the Aristotelian Society*, supplementary volume.

P. F. Strawson. 1959. *Individuals*. Methuen, London.

B. Stroud. 1984. *The Significance of Philosophical Scepticism*. Clarendon Press, Oxford.

M. Tye. 1992. Visual qualia and visual content. In T. Crane (ed.), *The Contents of Experience*. Cambridge University Press, Cambridge.

T. Williamson. 1990. *Identity and Discrimination*. Blackwell, Oxford.

———. 1995. Is knowing a state of mind? *Mind*, 104: 533–565.

# 7 Arguments from Illusion

Jonathan Dancy

We all know about the argument from illusion. In this paper I suggest, with several examples, that *the* argument from illusion is just one example of a style or form of argument which recurs in many other places in philosophy, with effects which according to one's point of view are either very damaging or distinctly enlightening.

I start with a version of *the* argument from illusion. A state which is one of genuine awareness of a world may be indistinguishable from one which is a mere appearance. One cannot tell from the phenomenology of one's awareness which it is—an illusion or awareness of an external reality. The argument from illusion urges us to conclude from this that real perceptual awareness is a combination of two elements. The first element is that which genuine perception and illusion have in common: we could call this appearance. (If what we are dealing with is an illusion, it is a *mere* appearance.) The second element is the extra bit that perception has over and above the appearance. A theory of the following sort is tempting: an appearance is genuine perception when it is caused by an external object which it sufficiently resembles. Causal theories like this are theories about what one has to add to appearance to get perception.

It would be a mistake to suppose that causal theories are all forms of representative realism, that is, theories that analyse a perceptual state as a combination of act of awareness and inner object of awareness. Adverbial theories of the nature of a perceptual state are (or at least can be) equally causal. At issue between adverbial and representative theories is the nature of the state caused in us by the object when we are perceiving it. The adverbial theory describes this state adverbially, as, e.g., "my being appeared to redly"; the representative theory describes it as an awareness of an inner

Jonathan Dancy, "Arguments from Illusion," *Philosophical Quarterly* 45: 421–438 (1995). Reprinted by permission of Blackwell Publishing.

object or percept of a certain sort. Both agree that there is a basic state in common between cases of illusion and cases of genuine perceptual awareness, which is the real conclusion of the argument from illusion.

In fact, however, many of those who accept causal theories of perception make no use of the argument from illusion. The classic instance is Frank Jackson, who rests his case for a representative theory more or less entirely on quite different considerations, those designed to support the act/object analysis of a perceptual state.[1] My own view is that this form of argument is far better, whatever the merits of the theory which it supports. The point here, however, is that Jackson agrees that the argument from illusion is of dubious force. It *proves* nothing. All allow that genuine perceptual experiences are or may be phenomenally indistinguishable (to the perceiver at the relevant time) from illusory or hallucinatory experience. A non-causal theorist is forced to say, therefore, that two states which are completely indistinguishable to their owner in their general nature are in fact very different. The first, the successful case, is not to be understood as consisting of what is present in the unsuccessful case *plus* something else (the outer thing). There is no common element at all. And this certainly seems awkward. The phenomenal similarity between the two states (i.e., the fact that the person concerned cannot tell them apart) appears as a reason for avoiding any analysis of them that makes them radically different in nature. So the causal theorist concludes that the best analysis is to suppose that both states share a common element, but only one has an external object. Since the existence and nature of the external object are *not intrinsic* to the nature of the perceptual state of the perceiver, the phenomenal similarity between the states does not prevent us from saying that one is graced by an external object when the other is not.

So no party to the debate supposes that the argument from illusion is conclusive. It is still possible to suppose that the two states do differ thus fundamentally, despite their phenomenal similarities; the argument from illusion merely acts as a reminder that there is at best something awkward about this, and that it would be more attractive to avoid it. But the appeal to the deliverances of introspection is not generally allowed to be conclusive elsewhere, and there seems to be nothing special about the present case to warrant any more respectful attitude to introspection here. So the awkwardness is to be admitted, without being allowed to be decisive.

This weak conclusion is one with which I do not yet want to quarrel. Among my suggestions will be, however, that in other areas of philosophy arguments from illusion have been wrongly taken to be conclusive. I now offer five further examples.

## First Example: Acting and Trying

I quote from a recent book on the philosophy of action:

The same event of trying occurs both when we fail and when we succeed in bringing about the act-neutral event [of one's body moving, say]. This presence of trying is concealed by the fact that we generally succeed, so that we reserve the word "trying" only for those cases where we failed or where failure was foreseeable. But since failure is always a possibility, we also try when we succeed.[2]

The author here is reporting an argument of Brian O'Shaughnessy, who himself announces it[3] as a version of the argument from illusion. To check this, we can read it through again, substituting "appearance" for "trying" and "perceiving an external object" for "bringing about the act-neutral event." One might still doubt this self-description, however. For there is here no claim that the event of trying and failing is always indistinguishable to the agent (at the relevant time, etc.) from the event of trying and succeeding. How could there be? Nothing is more different than trying to jump over the river and succeeding, and trying and failing. So how can there be any argument from indistinguishability here? Doubts continue when we read later in O'Shaughnessy's book that he actually uses two arguments, an argument from error and another from illusion. What is the difference between an argument from error and an argument from illusion? These names are not well defined in the philosophical profession. Without distorting O'Shaughnessy's position, we can say that both start from cases where we make mistakes, but that arguments from illusion are distinctive in that they focus on cases of indistinguishability. (I would prefer to reserve the name "argument from error" for *sceptical* arguments that appeal to indistinguishability.)

O'Shaughnessy's argument from error makes no use of considerations of indistinguishability. It asks us to consider a case where a man contracts to perform an easy but very important action such as throwing a switch to stop a bomb from going off. He does perform this action, but immediately a team of conjurers, psychological experimenters and master technicians, all in the employ of some Philosopher King (improbable though such staffing levels may appear these days), persuade him with unimpeachably rational arguments that he did not perform it. What is he to say to those who upbraid him for failing to throw the switch? There is one thing he can certainly say, according to O'Shaughnessy, and that is "At least I tried to do it." Since the conditions for his saying this are effectively perfect, he knows that he tried to do it. This shows that he did try to do it. It is also true that he did it. And since this scenario could be played for any action, we can conclude that all cases of success are cases of trying. As Moya said in the quotation above, "since failure is always a possibility, we also try when we succeed."

This argument is not an argument from illusion. It does not claim that some case of trying or of having tried is indistinguishable from one of succeeding or having succeeded. The poor dupe believes that he tried and did not succeed. But O'Shaughnessy distinguishes between this argument from mistake and a different argument which asks us to consider a case where a man's arm is hidden behind a screen so that he cannot tell whether he has succeeded in raising it. Suppose that his arm is so paralysed that, when he thinks he is raising it, in fact it remains immobile. What would he say on being confronted with this stark reality? (Suppose again that it is very important to all that he should succeed, so as to stop the bomb going off.) He could and should say "I tried to raise it." But now we have a genuine argument from indistinguishability. The action of trying to raise one's arm and failing is indistinguishable to the agent at the time from the quite different action of trying and succeeding. O'Shaughnessy concludes (p. 266):

Then since all these ... items [willing, awareness of trying, seeming to succeed] can obtain independently of the occurrence of [the arm moving], and the internal situation was indistinguishable from that which normally obtains, these must be further psychological ingredients of the normal successful voluntary act situation.

My own view here is that the former argument, from error, reduces to the latter one from illusion. Suppose that just when you had, so far as you could tell, succeeded in ringing the bell (for instance), a crowd of philosophers turned up who convinced you that you did not ring the bell after all. What are you to think? Would you think that you had anyway tried to ring it? My own view is that you would reasonably doubt this as well, on the grounds that if you had tried you would have succeeded. What is more, surely the proper excuse in this peculiar case is not "I tried to do it" but "I thought I had done it." The latter seems to me a lot nearer the truth than the former. If the former is in place at all, this must be because there is a suggestion that if one thinks that one succeeded and discovers that one did not, one must suppose that one at least tried. But this will itself depend on the claim that, to the agent whose faith in his grasp on external reality has been shaken, an action of trying and failing is indistinguishable from an action of succeeding. I learn that the latter did not happen, and so I suppose that the former, which is indistinguishable to me now, must have been what happened. But why should this establish that when I succeed I also try, let alone that trying is a distinct *element* in succeeding? Take some other case in which we cannot distinguish *A* from *B* and learn to our surprise that we did not do *A*. If we then conclude that we must have done *B*, this does nothing to establish that doing *B* is an element or ingredient in doing *A*, nor even just that when I do *A* I also do *B*. Suppose, for example, that I have a toggle switch which, when pressed, either locks or unlocks my briefcase; it reverses the existing state of the lock, whatever that was. It is only by using extraneous information that I know whether by pressing it I am locking or unlocking the briefcase. Suppose further that, having pressed the switch to open the case, I find to my surprise that instead of unlocking it, I have locked it. This should do nothing to persuade me that locking it is an ingredient in unlocking it, nor even that when I unlock it I also lock it. It seems then that the only use of indistinguishability that will serve O'Shaughnessy's purposes is the one in the argument from illusion. The argument from error adds nothing.

So it seems that there is an indistinguishability argument here after all, despite initial appearances. It is not the argument that successful actions are commonly indistinguishable to the agent from unsuccessful ones, but that if agents are restricted entirely to their own "internal" resources, they cannot draw the distinction in a given case, and that this "proves" that trying is an ingredient in succeeding.

Before moving on, I want to pause to draw two distinctions that have gradually emerged in the discussion of trying.

The first distinction is between the claim that trying is an ingredient in acting, and the claim that when one acts one also tries.[4] Arguments from illusion, as I am presenting the matter, promote the latter conclusion by promoting the former. Hence rebuttals of the argument from illusion can aim either to deny the former (leaving the latter undetermined for the while) or to deny the latter and thereby the former. I shall call the first sort of response anti-conjunctivism, and the second the incompatibility thesis. Both responses can of course be discussed and evaluated on grounds other than any thoughts of indistinguishability; but arguments based on indistinguishability are my official concern here.

The second distinction is between those arguments from illusion that announce that *all* *A*-cases are indistinguishable from *B*-cases and that therefore *A* is an element in *B*, and those that only hold that *some* *A*-cases are indistinguishable from *B*-cases. In my view it is only because of their association with sceptical arguments (with which we are not here concerned at all) that arguments from illusion have so often been presented as if they needed the stronger claim. In fact, what I am calling "the argument from illusion" in this paper is a structural argument in the philosophy of mind, and it is sufficient for this argument to get going that it find some cases (a reasonable range, no doubt) of indistinguishability. These distinctions will play a role in what follows, because they help us to map various moves and responses against each other. I now turn to my second example.

### Second Example: Facts vs. Beliefs as Reasons/Motives

Here I have no nice neat quotation, but I think that the sort of argument I am after is perfectly familiar anyway. Can a fact be anyone's reason for action? Here is an argument that our reasons are always beliefs and never facts. Suppose that Owen claims that his reason for investing in a company is that the stock is undervalued, and let us suppose that he is right—the stock is undervalued. We know, however, that he would have invested even if the stock had not been undervalued. What was required for him to invest was not that the stock *be* undervalued, but that he should have *thought* it was undervalued. So Owen's real reason for investing lay not in the (purported) fact that the stock is undervalued, but in his belief that it is undervalued. And this argument can be repeated for every case. It follows that no fact can be a reason, for an agent would have had the same reason for action even if that fact had not obtained.[5] The same argument will work for reasons for belief rather than for action. Since one would have believed even if what one takes to be fact had not been fact, one's reasons must lie not in the facts themselves but in one's beliefs about the facts. The facts themselves cannot be reasons.

Though I think that this argument is familiar, I do not think that it is clear. To make it clearer, let us compare a version which talks about reasons for belief with one which talks about causes. The causal version says that facts are not causes of action because one would have acted in the same way in their absence, given the same beliefs. Is this a version of an argument from illusion, or is it a simple appeal to some principle of causal reasoning? The relevant principle in this case would be that $A$ is not a cause of $B$ if $B$ would have happened even if $A$ had not happened. But that principle is not at issue in the present case. We have three players: belief, fact and action. The argument we are considering has it that the fact is not a cause of the action because the action would have taken place in the absence of the fact. But to get the action without the fact we would still need the belief, and sometimes the belief would not have been present in the absence of the fact either. (If it had not been true that I have two hands, I would not have believed that I have two hands.) So the admission that with the belief but without the fact we would still have had the action does nothing to show that *in this case* the fact does not cause the action. To show that, we would have to show that without the fact there would still have been belief, which will not always be true.

A better causal argument has the opposite conclusion, that the belief always plays some role in the causal story, since without belief there is no action. In a suitably weak sense we can allow this, because in discussing the argument from illusion we are not trying to avoid the conclusion that when one acts in the light of a fact one also believes and acts because of that belief. We are officially only disputing the conclusion that the latter is an *ingredient* in the former. This leaves it open to us to select our own story about how fact and belief are actually related in a successful case. We might for instance say that the belief is an *enabling* condition—something whose presence makes it possible for the fact to cause the action, but which is not itself a part of the causal story proper. This would give us two possible causal routes to the action, the first where the cause is the fact (always, of course, mediated by the belief) and the second where the cause is the belief. Notice that though we of course hold that no one example is an instance of both of these at once, we do allow that an action caused by a fact is one where the fact is believed, and where the belief is relevant to the causal story. There is no incompatibility claim here.

Even if this causal argument is a good one, I do not think it is a version of the argument from illusion, because it says nothing about indistinguishability. Nor can I see how to adapt it so as to include thoughts about indistinguishability in any significant way. Such thoughts only appear in a version of the argument which focuses on reasons rather than causes. Here we may say that believers cannot distinguish between the situation in which they believe falsely and that in which they believe truly. If their beliefs are false, they still have sufficient reason to act. The truth of their beliefs should not therefore be conceived as changing anything in that respect, and so can only be taken to be an added ingredient.

This approach is much more like the perceptual case, and it has the proper conclusion for an argument from illusion, namely that there is a common ingredient to cases of success and failure. It attempts to drive us from what we want to say in a case of error or defect (mere appearance, in the perceptual case, or mistake about the facts in the other) to what we say about a case where there is no error or defect. As such an argument, it can be resisted. The principle on which it relies is that a successful case must be some sort of function of an unsuccessful case, and there is no general reason in advance to believe anything of the sort. We should be stubborn

here as elsewhere and hold that a fact can be a reason for action as for belief, even if we would still act or believe even if the facts were not as we take
them to be. What this would mean is that where we are mistaken we do
not have the reasons for our actions and beliefs that we take ourselves to
have.

Note that it is common for both my first examples to be taken as conclusive. O'Shaughnessy takes his example to provide a proof, and many suppose that facts are unable to motivate or be reasons on the sort of grounds
I have suggested, as if there can be no two views on the matter.

## Third Example: Knowledge and Justified Belief

The next two examples are from epistemology. The first concerns the view
that belief is an element in knowledge. We might argue that knowledge
and mere justified belief are indistinguishable to the cognizer. Therefore
knowledge must consist of justified belief plus something else, and the
extra bit must be evidence-transcendent. Truth, being an evidence-
transcendent property, is a good candidate for this role; but whatever our
choice for that role we have already established that belief is an element in
knowledge.

This is another version of the argument from illusion. As such it is not
conclusive. It only uncovers a difficulty. This difficulty is the familiar one
of giving entirely different analyses of two states which are experientially
indistinguishable. Perception is phenomenally indistinguishable from
mere appearance, and similarly knowledge is phenomenally indistinguishable from mere justified belief. This fact is *some* reason for giving similar
analyses of the two states, but hardly conclusive reason. We are not *forced*
into the position recommended, that of supposing that there is a common
element to mere justified belief and genuine knowledge. We can be stubborn. We can give an entirely distinct account of knowledge, as a state in
which a fact makes itself manifest to us, not by causing in us some appearance or proxy for itself, but simply by being transparently present to the
mind. In genuine knowledge, the mind is open to the world, and when it
grasps the world the world (or the relevant aspect of it) enters the mind. In
this vein John McDowell offers us a different conception of knowledge, as a
sort of transparent openness to the world.[6] Any state of this sort is quite
different from an opaque state founded on reasons other than the fact
believed. So knowledge is not to be thought of as a state reached by adding
conditions on to something which in its own right is inherently unreliable.
Indeed, if we are in the business of adding conditions so as to make things

better we can tell that we are not talking about knowledge at all. A state reached by piling on extra helpful thoughts, such as that human cognitive systems are truth-effective, will only be a better form of the opaque state, never the transparent state which is knowledge. Knowledge does not need this sort of support. It is already perfect in its own right.

We should be careful to distinguish this position from the stronger claim that knowledge is not a form of belief at all. This incompatibility claim goes further than McDowell needs or wants to go. We may, for all that has yet been shown, continue to think of the opaque state and the transparent state as distinct forms of belief, forms which are, on occasion at least, indistinguishable to their owner. One characteristic of knowledge as McDowell conceives it is that it is infallible, in the sense that if one is in such a state there is no possibility that the world should not be the way one conceives it as being. With the opaque state, no matter how clever, there will always be this possibility; but any state which can exist without the world being as that state presents it as being will not be knowledge of McDowell's sort.

### Fourth Example: The Internalism/Externalism Distinction

This example follows on from my second example. It is not merely the case that if the facts were not as we take them to be we would still believe and act in the same way. It is also commonly held that in doing so our beliefs and actions would be justified. Justification is a normative status, and no complaint can be levelled against us for holding beliefs that are supported by the other beliefs we hold. For by our lights we are doing as well as we possibly could. There is no constraint or requirement which we are capable of recognizing when it applies and capable of meeting when it does, but which we have here failed to meet. Our position is indistinguishable to us from one in which we are in perfect epistemic shape. So no complaint can be raised against us. Our side of the story ("internally," as it were) is faultless. We deserve epistemic praise, of the sort normally handed out by calling our epistemic behaviour rational or reasonable, and our belief justified. But if we are justified in a belief merely because it is well supported by other beliefs we hold, it follows that what justifies is not the facts, but one's beliefs about the facts. For our belief is justified even if the necessary facts are absent; so the only possible candidate justifiers are our other beliefs. It seems that the facts themselves make no contribution to justification beyond that already made by the beliefs.

Suppose, however, that we feel (for whatever reason) that this form of internalism is too restrictive. We want to say that even when internal justification of this sort is fully present, something more is added if certain facts can be established, for instance that the epistemic methods being used are in fact reliable rather than merely (reasonably?) believed to be reliable. An internalist can allow this move in the interests of flexibility, but is likely to say that what is added by these externalist considerations is not more of the same thing as we had at first. Even if the facts do add something, what they add is essentially *independent* of what has already been established, namely that as cognitive agents we are irreproachable in a case like this.

Let us call this the independence thesis. It is the result of an argument from illusion. The independence thesis here has a perfect mirror in the theory of perception. The perceiver's (believer's) side of the story is one that can be told without reference to what lies beyond the perceiver's (believer's) ken, and it follows from this that such things as success-conditions must be placed elsewhere by the theory, in a separate story which is independent of but can be added to what we have established so far. This is the place where we see specification of causal conditions in many currently popular theories of perception—and of justification. What this means is that we do best to start from a perceiver who is in error (reasonable error will probably be the most helpful since it introduces the fewest complications). This is the best starting point because it ensures that we do not confuse elements which are properly part of the perceiver-story with elements which are not. Then perceivers who are not in error are people of whom essentially the same sort of story can be told, as far as their side of the whole goes. Surely the pattern here is exactly the same as the one we have been seeing in the theory of justification. And the reply to it will be the same both times. There is no independent reason to start one's analysis of a cognitive state (whether perceptual or not) from an example of such a state which is in error and then to attempt to build on that one's account of the case where there is no mistake.

There are two aspects of this reply that are worth stressing. The first is that it makes the distinctive move of holding that epistemology is best done by starting from the best cases, those in which there is no mistake, and working back from that. The second is that it rejects a basic Cartesian theme underlying the argument from illusion, namely the distinction between what is internal to agents and hence cognitively available to them, and what is external to agents and so must be placed elsewhere in the analysis. The latter facts are logically independent of the former ones, and this makes possible the view that the agent's mental health (which includes the question whether the agent's beliefs are justified) is to be established in ways that make no appeal to the world external to the agent. This move in the philosophy of mind is a straight expression of Cartesianism and its conception of the self-contained and autonomous individual. It is what drives the sense that our analysis must start from a case of mistake rather than a case of success. So the second aspect underlies the first one. It is one thing, however, to say that the independence thesis has a dubious provenance (i.e., that it is based on a form of argument which I take to be dubious), and another to suggest that it is false. But there are reasons for holding it false. We might agree that we make no complaint about the sort of believers I have been discussing, the kind who perform perfectly by their own lights, even where those lights lead them astray in ways which they are unable to rectify. But does this necessarily mean that their position could not be improved, so that any conceivable improvement must be attributed to some other aspect of the story? I do not see why we should allow this. In my view there is at least one respect in which their position could still have been better than it was, namely that they could actually have had the reasons they thought they had. They do not have those reasons because the facts that would have been their reasons do not obtain. So the believers here are not in the best imaginable cognitive position.

## Fifth Example: The Act/Agent Distinction

The very same moves, *mutatis mutandis*, are the ones which generate a significant distinction between act and agent in moral theory. There is an independence thesis here, driven by the thought that all that we can require of moral agents is that they act as best they may by their own lights. This thesis can, I think, allow that the way they have come by those lights makes a difference. An agent whose position, moral or epistemic, has been formed in ways of which some epistemic or moral complaint can be made is not someone whose conscientiousness *from then on* is a full defence. An indifference to relevant and available information, an insensitivity to counter-evidence and the opinions of others, slovenliness in the gathering and marshalling of reasons—these and other similar faults undermine any attempt to justify agents as having "done as well as they could by their own lights." But where no such complaint can be made, it is said, no *further* complaint is in place when an agent does an action which a perfectly informed and sensitive agent would not have done. It is this thought that drives the act/agent distinction in its traditional form in ethics. The act is something that could have been improved upon; the agent could not. The agent's side of the story (the "internal" story) is independent of any features of the act in any case of discrepancy.

Against this view we can say, first, that it is another version of the argument from illusion. Second, we can doubt the conclusion as before. Rewriting a preceding section, we might agree that we make no complaint about the sort of agent I have been discussing, those who perform perfectly by their own lights, even where led astray by those lights in ways which they are unable to rectify. But does this necessarily mean that their position could not be improved, so that any conceivable improvement must be attributed to some other aspect of the story? I do not see why we should allow this. In my view there is at least one respect in which their position could still have been better than it was, namely that they could actually have had the reasons they thought they had. They do not have those reasons because the facts that would have been their reasons do not obtain. So the agents here are not in the best imaginable moral position.

But is it not true that we make no complaint about such "blamelessly benighted" agents? And does this not force us to accept that, once the satisfactoriness of the agent has been established, every further advance must be ascribed to something else, the action? My response to this sort of pressure is to suggest that we are being offered too few choices. It is as if our moral vocabulary contained only one word of approval and one of disapproval, and we are asked what we think of a blamelessly benighted agent. We clearly cannot apply the term of opprobrium, and so we apply the term of approval. But we in fact have a wide variety of ways in which to think of agents, and a wide variety of terms in which to do it. Surely the best approach is just to say that we think of agents who do not have the reasons they reasonably take themselves to have in precisely that way. People in this position do not deserve the reproach they would have done had their conception of what they were doing been different, and equally, had they been doing the action they took themselves to be doing, they would have deserved the highest praise, perhaps. As things are, however, they merit sympathetic understanding and encouragement, rather than straight reproach or moral abuse on the one hand, or blanket approval on the other.

This suggestion, that we are being offered too few choices, has been made before, but not in this area. J. L. Austin argued against A. J. Ayer's use of the argument from illusion that it only appeared sound if one worked within an unnecessarily restricted vocabulary.[7] In aesthetics he argued that we should sometimes turn our attention to the dainty and the dumpy. I presume that this was not only because these concepts are interesting in their own right. The suggestion is rather that we shall not understand the role of the *thinnest* predicates unless we come to see how they relate to the thicker predicates that underpin them.[8] To try to work with the thinnest predicates alone is a cause not only of a limited but of a distorted view.

## The Five Examples Compared

In this section I draw out some similarities between the six cases I have discussed. Most of the material for this section has already appeared along the way.

The point I want to stress is that the argument from illusion, wherever it appears, has what we might call a "constitutive" conclusion: it encourages us to discover a more complex constitution in something (state, process, object) than we might have expected. This is more obvious in some examples than in others. We see it operating clearly in the idea of the complex constitution of a veridical perceptual state, of a successful action and of knowledge. In each of these examples the idea of a common ingredient is an idea about the constitution of a successful case, which sees the successful as the unsuccessful *plus* something independent. But essentially the same point can be made about my other three examples. It is the independence thesis that is the crucial link. In the motivation case, the idea was that the truth of the relevant beliefs is incidental to the motivation generated by those beliefs. The extra bit present in the successful case is independent of what is imported from the unsuccessful one. In the act/agent case, again, the idea was that we should start from the conception of the unfortunate agent, see that as a common element which is entirely independent of the features distinctive of the successful case, and so see the structure of the situation assessed in terms of the structure of assessment. Assessment of the agent is completed *before* we turn our attention to the question whether things actually are as the agent takes them to be. Hence the action is constructed as the bearer of any properties beyond those borne by the agent. Since these matters are structural, they are constitutive.

The same is true of the internalism/externalism case. It might seem that we have turned with this example from questions of constitution to questions of assessment, or of evaluation, which may rest on constitutive matters, without being themselves constitutive. I do not accept this. The point in the discussion of internalism and externalism at which we reached the role of the argument from illusion, supposedly, was the one where the independence thesis appeared. This thesis asserted that what the facts may add to assessment is essentially independent of what has already been established, namely the agent's own perspective on events. In my view what this means is that the structure of assessment and the structure of the situation assessed should match each other. In the situation assessed, the question whether things are in fact as the agent takes them to be is, according to the argument from illusion, quite independent of the prior question of how the agent takes them to be. The role in assessment played by answers to the former question must therefore be independent of and secondary to that played by answers to the latter question. These are structural matters, and this is enough for me to think of them as constitutive.

### Responses to the Argument from Illusion

If the argument from illusion has a constitutive conclusion, responses to it will reject that structure or constitution. Instead of seeing the relevant situation as a conjunction of two independent elements, they will give a different account of the matter. Two such non-conjunctive accounts have already been mentioned along the way. The first was the incompatibility thesis, more plausible in some areas than in others. We saw an instance of this in the claim that when one acts, one does not try to act. Another instance would be the idea that knowledge is not a form of belief at all. The second arose in McDowell's claim that though knowledge is a *form* of belief, belief is not an element in knowledge. We could express this in the language of determinates and determinables: belief is a determinable of which knowledge is one determinate. (There may be other models than the determinate/determinable one, but I shall not consider any such here.)

As well as these two non-conjunctive accounts, however, there is also what has come to be known as the disjunctive approach—normally, the disjunctive conception of experience, since that is its home concern.[9] I want to end by considering the relation between these various forms of non-conjunctivism. Disjunctivists offer a disjunctive account of, for instance, its looking to S as if there is an oasis before him, as:

*either*   (1)   there is an oasis manifesting itself to S
*or*       (2)   it is for S as if there is an oasis manifesting itself to S.

The second disjunct can be read simply as "(2) it is for S as if (1)." Let us, therefore, invent similar accounts of trying and of belief:

S tries to V iff:
*either*   (1)   S Vs/S succeeds in V-ing
*or*       (2)   it is for S as if (1).

But this is peculiar. Trying is not the same as its seeming to one that one is succeeding. A similar attempt at a disjunctive conception of belief might be:

S believes that *p* iff:
*either*   (1)   S knows that *p*/the fact that *p* is manifest to S
*or*       (2)   it is for S as if (1).

This is clearly wrong, and for similar reasons. Believing in the sense of (2) is not always indistinguishable from knowing. What is happening here?

One thing that has gone wrong is that we have restricted the disjunctive conception to two disjuncts. This was wrong even in the home case, the perceptual one. For after all, there are plenty of experiences that are easily distinguishable from perceivings, and the provision of only two disjuncts denies this. The disjunctive conception of experience should really be:

S has an experience of O before him iff:

*either* (1)   O manifests itself to S

*or*     (2)   it is for S as if (1)

*or*     (3)   S has a recognizable O-illusion.

What we are now in a position to see is that the standard formulation of the disjunctive conception is rather peculiar. What it was really trying to say was that there are two sorts of experience (we could call them an outer experience and an inner experience) which are indistinguishable from each other. It was no part of disjunctivism to say that *all* inner experiences are indistinguishable from outer experiences—only that some are. So we should allow the existence of experiences of a third sort. What is more, that the experiences of the second sort are indistinguishable from those of the first, the thought captured by the phrase "(2) it is for S as if (1)," is a sort of comment on them rather than a positive description of their nature. The indistinguishability of experiences of types (1) and (2) should be a contingent matter, not a matter of definition.

So what does the new disjunctivism amount to, from this perspective? It amounts to the assertion that there are broadly two types of experience, which we can call manifestings and non-manifestings, and that some of the latter are indistinguishable (to their owners, at the relevant time, etc.) from the former. We are told virtually nothing about the natures of these different types of experiences.

What sort of an answer, then, does disjunctivism offer to the argument from illusion? In what way does it go at all beyond what I have already offered, in my description of what is required if one wants to reject the argument from illusion? I do not think it goes any further at all. It just repackages the idea that those who reject the argument from illusion in the perceptual case are bound to say that there can be two states of mind which are indistinguishable to their owner though neither is an ingredient in the other. It makes no move *beyond* this at all. The disjunctive conception, then, does not amount to more than a structured way of expressing opposition to the argument from illusion.

But in that case two questions arise. The first is how there can be *other* ways of expressing that opposition. The second is whether we can actually write suitable disjunctive conceptions for my other examples. After all, the ones we sketched for trying and believing were clearly unworkable. If disjunctivism merely expresses the *form* of opposition to the argument from illusion, and if I am right in claiming that there is an argument from illusion at work in each of my examples, there should be disjunctive conceptions available in each case. Let us deal with this second worry first.

What was wrong with our first attempts at disjunctive conceptions of trying and acting was that we illegitimately took aspects of the perceptual case and imported them into the general structure required of a disjunctive analysis.[10] The disjunctive account of perception really says there are two quite different sorts of oasis-experience, which may none the less be indistinguishable to their owner. The first is the genuine article, and the second, though it is indistinguishable, has nothing in common with the first other than the fact that they are both oasis-experiences. In the standard formulation of the account, misleadingly, this is explicitly the way in which the second disjunct is characterized: we characterize it solely by saying that it is like what it is not. Presumably, however, there may be available a more direct characterization of the second disjunct, and in a totally explicit version of the theory it would indeed be characterized in that better way. The current characterization is just a sort of place-holder, showing what has to be said about the relation between first and second disjunct.

Suppose, then, that we try disjunctive conceptions of the following quite different forms (there is no reason why all disjunctive accounts should be of exactly the same form), first for trying:

*S* tries to do *V* iff:

*either*   *S* does *V*

*or*      *S* does something with the intention of thereby doing *V*.

The account of belief will probably be more like the account of perception:

*S* believes that *p* iff:

*either*   *S* knows that *p*

*or*      *S* takes it with reason that *p*

*or*      *S* has a blind faith that *p*.

These accounts, though they do allow that when we know, we also believe, and when we act, we also try, do *not* allow that the latter is a *component* in the former (that (2) is a *component* in (1)). So they are genuine alternatives to the approach which the argument from illusion is trying to promote.

Even though when one acts one also tries, acting is not to be understood as trying *plus* anything. Similarly, knowing is not to be understood as believing *plus* something else. There is no *conjunctive* account of knowing or of acting derivable here. Knowing and acting are determinates of the determinables believing and trying respectively.

A notable difference between these and earlier attempts is that we have abandoned any attempt to inscribe the primacy of the successful case in our formulations. This might be thought a defect. Seeking to establish the primacy of the successful case was a leading motivation for adopting the disjunctive conception. So should not the primacy of the successful case be retained in any subsequent reformulation? The argument from illusion is an attempt to establish the opposite primacy, that of the unsuccessful, after all, and one purpose of disjunctivism was to block that attempt.

But those with this purpose were surely confused. They ran together two things which should be kept separate: that each disjunct is, at least on occasion, indistinguishable from the other; and that the successful case enjoys a certain priority. They ran them together by giving the original account of the two disjuncts given in my text, where the second disjunct can only be understood in terms of the first, since it reads "(2) it is for S as if (1)." (In different terms, they captured the indistinguishability of seeing and seeming to see in an asymmetric way that leans towards the first.) That this was tendentious is shown by two considerations. First, we can see in the case of belief and knowledge that there need be no suggestion that the worse case be only understood in terms of the better one. "Opinion," whatever it may be, need not be defined in terms of knowledge, and those who think otherwise will have to do more than show the possibility of a disjunctive conception of belief. Second, even in the home, perceptual, case, the contrast between seeing and seeming to see is tendentious: it encapsulates the priority of seeing in a way for which there is as yet no justification. For although we may be persuaded to read the disjunctive conception as holding that there are two states, a better one and a worse one which is indistinguishable from the better one, we could equally well have read things the other way around, saying that there are two states, a worse one and a better one which is indistinguishable from the worse one. Here the apparent primacy of the better state has vanished, leaving only its preferability, which was never in doubt. Calling the worse state "seeming to see" expressed that primacy, but was inessential to the main purpose of responding to the argument from illusion.

Let us take it, then, that these new disjunctive conceptions are satisfactory. Our other question was whether disjunctivism is *the* form of opposition to the argument from illusion, or whether there are indeed other forms. Earlier I suggested that there are three forms: the disjunctive approach, a determinate/determinable approach, and the incompatibility thesis. But now I think that, with our improved understanding of the disjunctive approach, there is no further difference between it and the determinate/determinable one. The incompatibility thesis is the odd one out: this does go beyond anything required to rebut the argument from illusion. One would move from the disjunctive approach to the incompatibility thesis if one took knowledge, say, to be of a completely different *sort* from belief. To the extent that one sees knowledge, as McDowell does, as a sort of transparent openness to the world, and mere belief as an opaque, closed state, to that extent the more or less metaphysical difference between the two sorts of state may prevent one from seeing knowledge as a special case of belief, with the concept of belief ranging from knowledge at one end to blind faith or mere hunch at the other. But this move is separate from anything required to dispel the argument from illusion, and requires a separate motivation.

## Conclusion

What conclusions do I wish to draw, then? There is a weaker one and a stronger one. The weaker, which I have been stressing along the way, is that no use of an argument from illusion should be taken to be conclusive. In the parent case, in the theory of perception, claims of conclusiveness have been long abandoned. In the other cases, however, the relevant arguments are largely held to be conclusive. I think that this is a mistake, and that comparative investigation of different versions of the argument can cure us of it.

Associated with this is the idea that arguments from illusion stem from defective Cartesian presumptions about the independence of the mental. I have certainly not shown this in the present paper. I have only suggested that it is a ground for treating such arguments with suspicion.

There is, however, a stronger conclusion available. In the first section of the paper I effectively accepted that because veridical and illusory appearance are indistinguishable, it is awkward to deny a common-ingredient account of appearance. But now we can see that the determinate/determinable version of the disjunctive approach offers a *competing* explanation of the indistinguishability. That these states are both oasis-experiences is the basis of an explanation of why the owner cannot tell them apart. There are other obvious cases where the fact that two states are determinates of the same determinable explains the respect in which they are similar: two different colours, say red and green, are similar in respect of being colours, and this is a real, not a merely nominal similarity.[11] That they are both colours captures the respect in which they are similar without explaining that similarity in terms of any common ingredient. In the same way we can offer an explanation of the similarities between different disjuncts in other cases—between acting and "merely trying," as it were—by pointing to their common determinable. We can thus offer to explain the indistinguishability without alluding to a common ingredient. If this is so, then the greater plausibility of the common-ingredient model vanishes, and with it the idea that it is awkward even in the parent case to admit the indistinguishability of perception and illusion without allowing a common element.[12]

## Notes

1. F. Jackson, *Perception* (Cambridge UP, 1977).

2. Carlos J. Moya, *The Philosophy of Action* (Cambridge: Polity Press, 1990), p. 22.

3. B. O'Shaughnessy, *The Will* (Cambridge UP, 1980), vol. II, p. 93.

4. I owe my recognition of the importance of this distinction to Tim Williamson.

5. For an expression of the argument I am trying to characterize, see Bernard Williams' claim that the difference between true and false cannot affect the form of the appropriate explanation, in his "Internal and External Reasons," reprinted in his *Moral Luck* (Cambridge UP, 1981), p. 102.

6. See his "Criteria, Defeasibility and Knowledge," in J. Dancy (ed.), *Perceptual Knowledge* (Oxford UP, 1988), pp. 209–219 [excerpted in this volume, chapter 5].

7. Thanks to David McNaughton for this thought.

8. The thick/thin distinction, originally owed to David Wiggins, appears to some effect in Bernard Williams, *Ethics and the Limits of Philosophy* (London: Fontana, 1985), chs. 8–9. Thick properties are so called because they have more empirical content than thin ones do. The thinnest properties in ethics are those of goodness, rightness, badness and wrongness. One knows less about the action if one knows that it has one of these properties than one knows if one knows it to have some thicker property, e.g., courage.

9. See McDowell, *op. cit.*, and Paul Snowdon, "Perception, Vision and Causation," also in J. Dancy (ed.), *Perceptual Knowledge* (Oxford UP, 1988), pp. 192–208 [this volume, chapter 3].

10. I owe this idea to Bernard Williams; the previous, wrong, approach was the one I originally took.

11. This point is Tim Williamson's.

12. I am very grateful to David McNaughton, Jennifer Hornsby and Paul Snowdon for comments on earlier versions of this paper, and especially to Timothy Williamson for his reply to it, read at the Oxford Philosophical Society, which largely reshaped my understanding of the area.

# 8 The Idea of Experience

Alan Millar

It is widely held that there is a sense of "It looks to you as if an F is there" on which it may look to you as if an F is there irrespective of whether you are actually perceiving (in this case seeing) an F or merely hallucinating an F. This view is not in dispute within the dialectic which I address. What is in dispute is *the experientialist picture* which has it that what makes it the case that, in the relevant sense, it looks to you as if, say, a tree is there is your having an experience which you might have in perceiving a tree, but which could be had by someone who is totally hallucinating. Suppose that on some occasion on which it looks to you as if a tree is there you in fact see a tree. There is a *hallucinatory counterpart* of this perception, a (possible) case in which there is a subject such that every looks-as-if ascription true of you is true of this subject and vice versa. According to the experientialist the subject of a genuine perception and the subject of a hallucinatory counterpart of such a perception will have in common a certain psychological state, an experience of a certain type the having of which does not necessarily depend on the presence of the object perceived in the perceptual case.

Many philosophers accept the experientialist picture.[1] It is the starting point for recent work on the nature of experiences and their role in our mental life.[2] There are, however, philosophers who resist the very idea of experience which the experientialist picture articulates. In this paper I pay particular attention to those who are attracted by what has come to be known as the disjunctive conception of experience. Originally suggested by J. M. Hinton, the disjunctive conception has received sympathetic

Meeting of the Aristotelian Society, held in the Senior Common Room, Birkbeck College, London, on Monday, 11th December, 1995 at 8:15 p.m.

Alan Millar, "The Idea of Experience," *Proceedings of the Aristotelian Society* 97: 75–90. Reprinted by courtesy of the Editor of the Aristotelian Society: © 1996.

attention in writings of Paul Snowdon and John McDowell.[3] Snowdon and McDowell agree with the experientialist in holding that it is true both of a subject who sees an F and of a subject who hallucinates an F that it looks to the subject as if an F is there. However, they have a distinctive view of what it is for it to look to you as if an F is there. In the version provided in Snowdon 1980/81 the claim that it looks to you as if an F is there is to be understood in such a way that it is made true *either* by there being something before you which looks to you to be an F *or* by its merely being for you as if there is something before you which looks to you to be an F. This version is troublesome in that its second disjunct employs the notion of its being for a subject as if something is so. In the visual case this comes perilously close to the notion which it is the aim of the account to clarify, that of its looking to one as if something is so. I shall not make heavy weather of this since there is available an alternative, and perhaps more readily comprehensible, formulation according to which the claim that it looks to you as if an F is there is made true either by your seeing something which looks to you to be an F or by its merely seeming to you that you see something which looks to you to be an F. There are yet other versions, but on all versions a disjunctive truth condition is supplied so that "It looks to you as if an F is there" is made true by one or other of the disjuncts, and we are not to suppose that there is an experience such that you must have that experience if either disjunct is true. The disjunctivist is not debarred from deploying a notion of an experience. It is in line with the disjunctive conception to acknowledge that there are experiences of seeing an F and experiences of seeming to see an F. What the disjunctivist rejects is the common element thesis—the claim, integral to the experientialist picture, that every case of your actually seeing an F and its hallucinatory counterpart have in common one and the same visual experience.

The issue comes down to whether there is a logical gap between (a) "It looks to you as if an F is there" and (b) "You have an experience of a sort which you might have in perceiving or hallucinating an F." The experientialist thinks that (a) entails (b) and the disjunctivist denies this. It should be noted that both the experientialist and the disjunctivist can accommodate the idea that perceptions and their hallucinatory counterparts are experientially indistinguishable at least to the extent that any looks-as-if ascription true of a subject in respect of a perception would be true of a subject undergoing the hallucinatory counterpart of that perception, and vice versa. From the experientialist's point of view it is puzzling to acknowledge such experiential indistinguishability and yet baulk at conceding that one and the same psychological state, a visual experience, is had in the two cases.

As the experientialist views matters the very idea of an experience is such that if A has an experience E and B has an experience E', and being in E is experientially indistinguishable from being in E', then E and E' are the same experience. However, this general principle does not yield a decisive objection against the disjunctivist since it is, I suppose, open to disjunctivists to reject the principle.

William Child represents the position which contrasts with disjunctivism as incorporating the claim that "[t]he concept of an experience is basic; we make sense of vision and hallucination by extension from this basic unit" (Child 1992, p. 299). By contrast, on Child's account,

The disjunctive conception reverses that order of explanation. What is fundamental is the idea of a state of affairs in which the subject sees something; that idea is explained in terms only of the subject and the world, without reference to any inner entity ... (Child 1992, p. 300)

This reads more into the position of the opponent of the disjunctive conception than need be there. The experientialist position, as I have set it out, does not entail that our ordinary everyday concept of perception is to be explained in terms of the experientialist concept of an experience. The experientialist may acknowledge that the concept of an experience emerges from reflection on the possibility that there could be hallucinations which are experientially indistinguishable from perceptions.

In this paper I argue that defenders of the disjunctive conception misunderstand the experientialist picture. My principal aim is to remove the misunderstandings.[4] What I shall have to say will fall short of establishing that the disjunctive conception is false, but I am inclined to think that once the misunderstandings are cleared there is little to be said for it.

## II

In this section I show that McDowell and Snowdon both impute to the experientialist the view that experiences are, or essentially involve, appearances which interpose between the subject and the (external) world and that both relate the problems they find in the experientialist picture to such a view.

In the course of a discussion of these matters McDowell outlines a "tempting argument" which defenders of the disjunctive conception wish to resist. It goes as follows:

On any question about the world independent of oneself to which one can ascertain the answer by, say, looking, the way things look can be deceptive: it can look to one exactly as if things were a certain way when they are not.... It follows that any capacity to tell by looking how things are in the world independent of oneself can at best be fallible. According to the tempting argument, something else follows as well: the argument is that since there can be deceptive cases experientially indistinguishable from non-deceptive cases, one's experiential intake—what one embraces within the scope of one's consciousness—must be the same in both kinds of case. In a deceptive case, one's experiential intake must *ex hypothesi* fall short of the fact itself, in the sense of being consistent with there being no such fact. So that must be true, according to the argument, in a non-deceptive case too. One's capacity is a capacity to tell by looking: that is, on the basis of experiential intake. And even when this capacity does yield knowledge, we have to conceive the basis as a *highest common factor* of what is available to experience in the deceptive and the non-deceptive case alike, and hence as something that is at best a defeasible ground for the knowledge, though available with a certainty independent of whatever might put the knowledge in doubt. (1982, p. 471 [this volume, pp. 79–80])

Central to the tempting argument, McDowell suggests, is the idea that in both deceptive and non-deceptive cases "what is embraced within the scope of experience is an appearance that such-and-such is the case, falling short of the fact: a mere appearance." Further, he suggests, the appearance is conceived as "interposing itself between the experiencing subject and the fact itself" (1982, p. 472 [this volume, p. 80]). McDowell deploys a version of the disjunctive conception to show us how we can resist this picture.

[S]uppose we say—not at all unnaturally—that an appearance that such-and-such is the case can be *either* a mere appearance *or* the fact that such-and-such is the case making itself perceptually manifest to someone. As before, the object of experience in the deceptive cases is a mere appearance. But we are not to accept that in the non-deceptive cases too the object of experience is a mere appearance, and hence something that falls short of the fact itself. On the contrary, we are to insist that the appearance that is presented to one in those cases is a matter of the fact itself being disclosed to the experiencer. So appearances are no longer conceived as in general intervening between the experiencing subject and the world. (1982, p. 472 [this volume, p. 80])

Note that McDowell does not take issue with the view that deceptive cases may be experientially indistinguishable from non-deceptive cases. His worry is directed at the idea that appearances interpose themselves between ourselves and the world. The key considerations here seem to be (i) that the availability of the disjunctive conception undermines the arguments on behalf of this idea, and (ii) if the idea were correct—if appearances interpose—then it becomes impossible to see how we can ever obtain the knowledge of the world which we naturally take ourselves to have. (ii) is developed by McDowell in his later paper (McDowell 1986) in which the idea just mentioned is set within the context of a broader Cartesian picture of the mind. The Cartesian picture, as McDowell sees it, has it that appearances are objects in an inner reality "whose layout is transparent" (1986, p. 149) and thus "infallibly accessible." An implication of the picture is that while our knowledge of the inner realm is unproblematic our knowledge of the outer realm—the external world—is put in doubt. For if we do know about the outer realm it can only be via our knowledge of the inner realm. But then "subjectivity is confined to a tract of reality whose layout would be exactly as it is however things stood outside it, and the common-sense notion of a vantage point on the external world is now fundamentally problematic" (1986, p. 151). On this picture we would need to find reason to believe that appearances are correlated with objects in the outer realm and it is hard to see that such a reason could be available.[5]

McDowell's general approach, then, is to show how we can plausibly resist the Cartesian picture. The disjunctive conception is central to the approach and is taken to gain support from the very fact that it helps to avoid the picture and the epistemological predicament in which it is supposed to place us. From this standpoint what is wrong with the experientialist picture is that it conceives of experiences as being or involving appearances which interpose between subjects and the (external) world and thus plunges us into an epistemological predicament from which there is no escape but which we could and should have avoided.

Snowdon's discussions of the disjunctive conception are less explicitly preoccupied with the broad epistemological themes explored by McDowell, and he makes no explicit play with the term "appearance." But there are hints in his writings that he takes the experientialist picture to be committed to, or at least quite naturally to lead to, the first idea just isolated—that appearances interpose between subjects and the (external) world. In Snowdon 1990 he argues against a causal theory of perception which assumes the experientialist picture on the grounds that "when we see an item there is nothing in the occurrence which is both manifest to us and can count as an effect induced by, and hence separate from, the item seen" (1990, p. 136 [this volume, p. 61]). Why does Snowdon think that this bears on the type of causal theory in question? The answer, I take it, is that he assumes that the theory relies on the experientialist picture and interprets that picture in such a way that the experiences which it supposes to be common to perceptions and their hallucinatory counterparts are conceived as objects of which we are aware in ordinary perception. They are thus conceived as interposing appearances as in McDowell's discussions. This, I think, helps to make Snowdon's objection clear: The view that we have access to such appearances in ordinary perception distorts the phenomenology. No such objects are manifest in ordinary perception.

Like McDowell and Snowdon I do not believe that in ordinary perception appearances interpose between the subject and the external world.[6] But nor do I believe that the experientialist picture commits us to such a view.[7] It will help to clarify my position if we compare the experientialist picture with sense-datum theory. Sense-data are conceived to be what we directly perceive when we have sensory experiences. A familiar argument, the argument from hallucination, serves to explain the role which they are supposed to play. The argument starts off from the consideration that it is possible that two people have exactly the same sensory experience—to both it looks, say, as if a dagger is there and in all other respects the experiences are the same—yet one is perceiving a dagger and the other is merely hallucinating a dagger. From this basic consideration, which is shared by the experientialist picture, it is inferred that there is some sense in which the perceiver of a dagger and the hallucinator of a dagger perceive the same thing. The hallucinator, of course, does not in the ordinary sense perceive a dagger, since either no dagger is there or the relevant experience is not causally dependent on there being a dagger there. So it cannot be that both the perceiver and the hallucinator perceive a dagger. It is at this point that the distinction between direct and indirect perception is introduced. The perceiver and the hallucinator *directly* see the same thing, a dagger-type sense-datum. Only the perceiver perceives the dagger in the ordinary sense of "perceives," but such perception is always indirect, being mediated by the direct perception of a dagger-type sense-datum.

A familiar problem for the argument from hallucination is that there seems to be no pressing reason to hold that the perceiver and the hallucinator of a dagger *in any sense* see the same thing. That there is a common element between perceiving a dagger and hallucinating a dagger is certainly no such reason. The common element, on the unadorned experientialist picture (unadorned, that is, by sense-datum considerations) is the having of a visual experience such that it looks to the subject as if a dagger is there, but such an experience is not an object of perception nor are its features objects of perception. The experience, rather, is something the having of which would, if certain other conditions were satisfied, count as perceiving a dagger. However, it is not itself a thing perceived and this is the main lesson to be drawn from the comparison of the unadorned experientialist picture with sense-datum theory. Though the experientialist picture is compatible with sense-datum theory, the picture does not without further ado compel us to posit common objects of perception for ordinary perceptions and their hallucinatory counterparts.

Similar considerations apply to arguments for sense-data which appeal to the variability of experiences with changing points of view on an object. Whereas the argument from hallucination goes from sameness of experience to sameness of object of perception, the argument from variable experience goes from difference in experience to difference in object of perception. Defenders of the experientialist picture see no compelling reason to make either move.[8] It is surprising, therefore, that neither McDowell nor Snowdon considers the possibility that the picture is not committed to the existence of sense-datum-like entities.

## III

To make headway against the disjunctivist it is not enough to point out that experientialists may resist familiar arguments for sense-data and do not in general hold that experiences are, or involve, sense-data considered as objects of perception or awareness. There has to be a way of thinking about experiences, within the experientialist picture, which obviates the need for interposing appearances. On the view which I favour, its looking to you as if a dagger is there is a matter of your having a visual experience of the sort which a dagger would, in suitable conditions of light, produce in a normal, suitably placed, orientated and attentive observer whose sense of sight is functioning properly.[9] Such a view has no obvious commitment to interposing appearances. However, Howard Robinson (1990, pp. 161ff.) has argued that it fails adequately to characterise the experiences in question, because it does not supply an account of the respects in which experiences must be like an experience which a dagger would produce, in the stipulated conditions, to count as being an experience such that it looks as if a dagger is there. Robinson's view at this point, I take it, is that the relevant respect is that the subject is aware of something dagger-like. He thinks that we need some positive account of the apparent object, given that in the hallucinatory case the dagger-like thing is not a dagger. A somewhat similar problem is expressed by J. J. Valberg (1992, pp. 75ff.) in terms of a demand for an account of what grounds "the fact of appearance," for example, its looking to one as if a book is there. Valberg seeks to make the demand seem pressing by imagining a case in which, because of a childhood trauma, whenever you see a book things go blurred in your field of vision. Suppose that on some occasion when you are *not* looking at a book things go blurred. Valberg suggests that it would, in that case, be for you as if a book is present, yet we don't want to say that the sense in which that is true captures how your visual experience would be if you were in some ordinary situation straightforwardly looking at a book. The upshot, Valberg thinks, is that, in the relevant sense, it looks to you as if a book is there because of the presence of a certain object which you can pick out in your experience. The idea is that it is only by reference to an apparent object that we can spell out the respect in which an experience must be like one obtained in appropriate circumstances by looking at a book to count as being such that it looks to the subject as if a book is there. If we drop all mention of an apparent object we deprive ourselves of the means to provide an adequate specification of the character of the experience.

Robinson and Valberg articulate the intuition that in a perfectly clear sense, which no deflationary philosophising can get around, an ordinary visual experience involves your being aware of certain things—this thing (mentally pointing towards, as it seems, a book), that thing (mentally pointing towards, as it seems, a cup). Given the possibility of hallucination, these things cannot be physical objects. This, of course, is just the outlook which Snowdon and McDowell wish to resist. It should be resisted and can be without undermining the experientialist picture.

The trouble with the view in question is that it needs to be shown that the mental pointing to which it is committed is anything other than an illusion.[10] Suppose that I affect to refer to the supposed apparent objects saying, *this* object is book-like and *that* object is cup-like. How is my audience supposed to interpret what I say? If my remark is intelligible the audience ought to be able to report what I say. But they cannot do so in the usual way by saying, with appropriate gestures, "He is saying that *this* object is book-like and *that* object is cup-like." What gestures would be appropriate and how could they indicate the objects in question? Now it is not always the case that the reporter of a demonstrative utterance is in a position to make demonstrative reference to the objects referred to demonstratively by that utterance. (If the report concerns an utterance made in the past the objects picked out by that utterance may no longer be present.) In the present case it might seem that the audience could report my utterance by saying, "He was having a visual experience at the time and said, "This object is book-like and that object is cup-like" mentally pointing towards things which were then within his experience." The problem remains that this report does nothing to convey which objects were referred to since the objects supposedly in question are not ones of a sort which are available to anyone other than me, the subject of the experience.

What of the challenge made by Robinson and Valberg to give an account of respects in which an experience must be like one produced, under the right conditions, by a book to count as being such that it looks as if a book is there? The challenge may be expressed in this way. We are told that a certain visual experience is the type produced under certain conditions by a book and so we are owed some account of which type that is. Here too, it seems to me, we are subject to an illusion.[11] It is true that if you describe a person as the sort who has ten varieties of extra virgin olive oil in their kitchen you ought to be in a position to spell out in a direct way (without using a reference-fixing phrase) the characteristics which define the sort. But why should we suppose that this is so in all cases? If I describe a pain as the sort you get in your arm when your funny-bone is struck sharply, those who have had such a pain will know exactly which kind of pain I mean. That is to say, they will know just how it feels. I do not owe and could not give a specification of the state *which is both direct and just as specific*. I can say that it involves a sharp pain shooting right up to one's fingers, but that would not suffice to convey the distinctive feel of the pain since other pains might satisfy the same description. It is a characteristic of sensations and sensory experiences that there are no direct ways of describing what they are like which are as specific as the ways which describe them in terms of common causes or accompanying circumstances.[12]

## IV

There is a line of thought which is independent of the arguments considered so far and which concludes that experiences, on the experientialist picture, would have to be intermediaries between subjects and the external world. This draws on a consideration, not so far made explicit, which would be widely accepted by defenders of the experientialist picture, namely, that sensory experiences are, or are closely akin to, sensations like pain. This being so, it might be argued that states of this sort are necessarily objects of which we are aware and as such cannot fail to intervene between subjects and their world. (In so far as we are aware of them, the thought would go, we are not, or not directly, aware of objects in the world.) At this point Snowdon's phenomenological objection, already referred to, looms again: "when we see an item there is nothing in the occurrence which is both manifest to us and can count as an effect induced by, and hence separate from, the item seen." If this is right there are no objects of awareness in ordinary perception of the sort to which the experientialist seems to be committed in virtue of thinking of sensory experiences as being sensation-like.[13]

Peter Smith has responded to Snowdon's remark as follows:

Let's agree that experiences are not themselves *perceptually manifest* in any good sense. Our causal theorist can still maintain that the existence of such end effects in the process of perception makes itself manifest in other ways—for these end effects are themselves the initial causes of further upshots.... Seeing, other things being right, *causes* believing. That being so, our causal theorist will say, what more natural than the supposition that seeing, overall, is a causal process starting with the seen object and yielding an intervening state (the visual experiencing) which can in turn generate the further causal upshot of believing? (Smith 1990/91, p. 193)

What indeed? Smith seems to me to be right to challenge the assumption that sensory experiences would have to be *perceptually* manifest. But if sensory experiences are indeed akin to pains and other sensations then more needs to be said to address the puzzle generated by the assumption that it is in the nature of experiences, sensory or otherwise, that subjects should be aware of them. If sensory experiences are not perceptably manifest then how are we aware of them?

First, it is important to appreciate that there is a significant difference between the kind of awareness involved in being visually aware of a dagger, a tree or anything else, and the kind of awareness involved in being aware that one has a sensory experience or a pain. Being visually aware of a dagger is just visually perceiving the dagger. Being aware of having an experience is a matter of noticing that one has the experience, in a sense of "noticing" which involves believing that one has the experience. Snowdon suggests, in effect, that if we had experiences, as conceived on the experientialist picture, then we ought to be visually aware of them in ordinary perception. I am suggesting that this is just false. We can be aware of our visual experiences in the sense that we can be aware that we have them. This is a matter of noticing that it looks to us as if thus and so. It is not a matter of visually perceiving the visual experience.

This last point does not take us as far as we need to go. The puzzle we are addressing turns on the thought that it is in the nature of experiences, sensory or otherwise, that we are aware of having them *so long as we have them*. If this were indeed how things stood then the experientialist would still have a problem, for it is hardly plausible that we are, in the relevant sense, aware of having visual experiences so long as we have them. But it is not how things stand.

Consider pains. It is surely true that to have a pain is to feel a pain. But what is it to be aware of having a pain? The natural way to interpret such talk is in terms of noticing in the sense used earlier. Noticing, in this sense, is a sophisticated business requiring a grasp of concepts and thus an ability to deploy them competently. It seems implausible to suppose that to have a pain one must have such abilities. For one thing it would seem that a creature could be subject to pain yet not have the ability to deploy the relevant concepts. For another, we can and do make sense of having pains which we do not notice that we have. On a long walk you get blisters in your feet which make walking painful. You may be distracted from the pain by a particularly absorbing conversation. Does it follow that during that period your feet ceased to be painful? They might have, in which case once you attend again to their condition you would notice that they are no longer painful. But they need not have. You may have continued to walk carefully and at any point, had you been asked about the condition of your feet, you would have responded by saying, "They are painful" or words to that effect. If the pain had gone you would not have responded in this way when the question arose. It is wrong to take the mere feeling of a pain to be a matter of being aware of having it, if being aware of having it is noticing that you have it. Feeling pain is manifest in all sorts of ways other than through being noticed. Analogous reflections apply to experiences generally, including visual experiences. When you have a visual experience such that it looks to you as if a cup of coffee is on a table in front of you it need not be the case that you are then aware in the relevant sense of having such an experience even if you have the relevant concepts. After all, you are likely to be absorbed by what you are looking at.[14]

There remains an important link between experiences and awareness. It is that experiences are states which those who have the appropriate conceptual skills can become aware that they have in a non-perceptual way simply by directing their thoughts to how they are being affected in, or via, some region of their body. In the case of pains, itches, tickles and the like, the relevance of bodily location is obvious. Though we do not think of visual experiences as being in our eyes or auditory experiences as being in our ears it is plausible that it is constitutive of our notion of such experiences that they are typically obtained via, respectively, our eyes and our ears. Visual experiences are experiences of the sort which objects produce through their effects on our eyes and auditory experiences are experiences of the sort which sounds produce through their effects on our ears.

In conclusion, then, I have argued that the experientialist picture is not committed to thinking of experiences as involving, or themselves being, appearances which interpose themselves between subjects and their world and so is not undermined by objections which assume that it is so committed. I have also drawn attention to the importance of distinguishing between different kinds of awareness in getting clear about these matters.[15]

## Notes

1. See, for example, Grice 1961, Strawson 1974, Pears 1976, Peacocke 1979, 1983, McGinn 1982, Searle 1983, Millar 1991(a).

2. See, for example, Peacocke 1983, 1992, Millar 1991(a), Crane 1992.

3. Hinton 1973 [excerpted in this volume, chapter 2], Snowdon 1980/81 [this volume, chapter 3], 1990 [this volume, chapter 4], McDowell 1982 [excerpted in this volume, chapter 5], 1986. Snowdon 1980/81 and McDowell 1982 have been reprinted in Dancy 1988. The general ideas in this dissenting tradition are taken seriously in Travis 1991 and Child 1992.

4. I find in discussion that the misunderstandings are widespread among philosophers who have no particular liking for the disjunctive conception.

5. Compare Child 1992, p. 303.

6. In one respect McDowell seems to me to be overcharitable towards the view he opposes. For reasons which are implicit in what follows I do not myself think that even in total hallucinations, or other deceptive experiences, appearances interpose between the subject and the world.

7. The question might be raised whether McDowell should be interpreted as opposing the experientialist picture as such rather than a version of it which has interposing appearances. I take the fact that McDowell faces us with a choice between the disjunctive conception and the experientialist picture on the problematic version to be evidence that he does not envisage the possibility of a version of the picture which is not thus problematic.

8. This would be true, I think, of all of the authors cited in note 1. Dagfinn Føllesdal has drawn my attention to the fact that Husserl was concerned to provide an account of perception, in the spirit of experientialism, which avoids positing interposing objects. See his review of Husserl's ideas in Føllesdal 1974, especially, pp. 378 and 381ff.

9. Compare the typology proposed in Millar 1991(a) and 1991(b), according to which the experience in question would be called dagger-type. The ramifications of such a typology are explored at some length in Millar 1991(a). Here I incorporate a requirement that the observer should be normal. Normality has to do with the reactions of the subject to the occurrence of an experience. We lose a grip on the idea that it looks to a subject as if a large obstacle is in front of her if we allow that the

subject might be disposed to behave in ways suitable for colliding with an object so placed, despite having no desire to collide and no cognitive malfunction.

10. Here I am in broad agreement with the scepticism on this matter expressed in Snowdon 1980/81, section V [this volume, pp. 43–46].

11. This theme is addressed in Millar 1991(b).

12. It might be pointed out that there are ways of describing experiences other than in terms of its looking to the subject as if such and such. One might give a specification of the sensational properties of the experience, as in Peacocke 1983, or of the scenario content of the experience, as in Peacocke 1992. These are alternative ways of saying what the experience is like. It is not clear to me that they introduce special levels of phenomenal properties not in principal capturable by the use of "looks as if" locutions with very detailed content clauses. In any case these alternative modes of characterising experiences rely on our having a grasp of experiential features which would be produced by such and such circumstances. This is overtly so in the case of ascriptions of sensational properties and I am inclined to think that it is also so for ascriptions of scenario content. Scenario contents are, roughly, spatial types, ways in which the space around a subject might be filled. The representational content of an experience is given by the spatial type which would be instantiated in the real world if the content were correct. While this tells us what the content of an experience is it does not tell us what it is for the experience to have that content. (Similarly one might give an account of the meaning of a sentence, say by representing its logical form, without explaining what makes the sentence the bearer of that meaning.) I suspect that for a visual experience to have a given scenario content is just for it to be the case that the experience is such as would be produced under appropriate conditions if the scene before the subject instantiated the scenario content.

13. Compare McCulloch 1993. McCulloch endorses the anti-Cartesian themes in McDowell and, like McDowell, takes experiences as conceived on the experientialist picture to be objects of awareness. If what I have said so far is right he is wrong to take experiences in this way. But he also hints at a line of objection to the effect that if they are not objects of awareness they are not anything. See his footnote 8, p. 48.

14. The foregoing considerations complement those in Dretske's excellent paper, Dretske 1993, in which he argues at length that an experience can be conscious even if the subject is not conscious of having it. I had just such a distinction in mind, though with little in the way of argumentative backing, in Millar 1991(a), pp. 11 and 50ff.

15. This paper was brought near to completion during a two-month period as Visiting Research Fellow in Philosophy in the Department of Philosophy at the University of Western Australia (UWA). I am grateful to UWA and the Carnegie Trust for

funding relating to that visit, and to staff in the Department of Philosophy at UWA for discussion of the issues. I also thank audiences who heard versions of the paper at the following universities: Stirling, Glasgow, Queen's University (Belfast), Trinity College (Dublin), Murdoch, New England, La Trobe, UWA, Cambridge, Durham and Oslo.

## References

Child, William. 1992. Vision and experience. *Philosophical Quarterly* 42: 297–315.

Crane, Tim (ed.). 1992. *The Contents of Experience*. Cambridge: Cambridge University Press.

Dancy, Jonathan (ed.). 1998. *Perceptual Knowledge*. Oxford: Oxford University Press.

Dretske, Fred. 1993. Conscious experience. *Mind* 102: 264–283.

Føllesdal, Dagfinn. 1974. Phenomenology. In Edward C. Carterette and Morton P. Friedman (eds.), *Handbook of Perception, Volume I: Historical and Philosophical Roots of Perception*, pp. 378–386. New York and London: Academic Press.

Grice, H. P. 1961. The causal theory of perception. *Proceedings of the Aristotelian Society*, Supplementary Volume 35: 121–152.

Hinton, J. M. 1973. *Experiences*. Oxford: Clarendon Press.

McCulloch, Gregory. 1993. The very idea of the phenomenological. *Proceedings of the Aristotelian Society* 93: 39–57.

McDowell, John. 1982. Criteria, defeasibility and knowledge. *Proceedings of the British Academy* 68: 455–479.

McDowell, John. 1986. Singular thought and the extent of inner space. In Philip Pettit and John McDowell (eds.), *Subject, Thought and Context*, pp. 137–168. Oxford: Clarendon Press.

McGinn, Colin. 1982. *The Character of Mind*. Oxford: Oxford University Press.

Millar, Alan. 1991(a). *Reasons and Experience*. Oxford: Clarendon Press.

Millar, Alan. 1991(b). Concepts, experience and inference. *Mind* 100: 495–505.

Peacocke, Christopher. 1979. *Holistic Explanation*. Oxford: Clarendon Press.

Peacocke, Christopher. 1983. *Sense and Content*. Oxford: Clarendon Press.

Peacocke, Christopher. 1992. *A Study of Concepts*. Cambridge, MA: MIT Press.

Pears, D. F. 1976. The causal conditions of perception. *Synthese* 33: 25–46.

Robinson, Howard. 1990. The objects of perceptual experience. *Proceedings of the Aristotelian Society*, Supplementary Volume 64: 151–166.

Searle, John. 1983. *Intentionality*. Cambridge: Cambridge University Press.

Smith, Peter. 1990/91. On "The objects of perceptual experience." *Proceedings of the Aristotelian Society* 91: 190–196.

Snowdon, Paul. 1980/81. Perception, vision and causation. *Proceedings of the Aristotelian Society* 81: 175–192.

Snowdon, Paul. 1990. The objects of perceptual experience. *Proceedings of the Aristotelian Society*, Supplementary Volume 64: 121–150.

Strawson, P. F. 1974. Causation and perception. In Strawson's *Freedom and Resentment*, pp. 66–84. London: Methuen.

Travis, Charles. 1991. Annals of analysis: Critical notice of H. P. Grice, *Studies in the Way of Words*. *Mind* 100: 237–264.

Valberg, J. J. 1992. *The Puzzle of Experience*. Oxford: Clarendon Press.

# 9 Selections from *Perception*

Howard Robinson

## The Revised—and Successful—Causal Argument for Sense-data

### 1 The Argument Stated

The revised causal argument is a combination of the original causal argument [discussed in chapter III of *Perception*] and the argument from hallucination.[1] It can be stated in the following way.

It is clearly true that

1. It is theoretically possible by activating some brain process which is involved in a particular type of perception to cause an hallucination which exactly resembles that perception in its subjective character.
2. It is necessary to give the same account of both hallucinating and perceptual experience when they have the same neural cause. Thus, it is not, for example, plausible to say that the hallucinatory experience involves a mental image or sense-datum, but that the perception does not, if the two have the same proximate—that is, neural—cause.

These two propositions together entail that perceptual processes in the brain produce some object of awareness which cannot be identified with any feature of the external world—that is, they produce a sense-datum.

Proposition (1) claims that there is some state of a subject's brain which is sufficient for their having a particular type of experience. For example, suppose that they face a brown table stood against a green wall, with their eyes open and their sensory mechanism functioning normally. There is light around and a certain brain state is induced in them in accordance with certain partially known mechanisms, and they have the experience of seeing the table against the wall. Now suppose that their brain is fixed, in the relevant areas, in this state, and the table and wall hidden from them. Such a

Howard Robinson, *Perception*, London: Routledge (1994). Reprinted by permission.

fixing of brain state is conceivable, not only in the sense that it is logically possible; it is empirically possible, in the sense that we may conceive of ways of doing it which involved no breach of natural law. This is compatible with its not being practicable and even with our having reasons for thinking that it might never be practical. It might even happen by a remarkably improbable coincidence (given quantum theory) or there might be a drug which held constant the relevant areas of the brain. Proposition (1) asserts that if such fixing took place the subject would continue to have an experience exactly similar to that of seeing the table and wall—they would "see" a brown table-shape against a green background—even though the table and wall were covered and removed, so that they no longer acted on them.

Because there is fairly general agreement that our mental life is strongly tied to what happens in the brain, there is little inclination to deny proposition (1). Even those who are externalists about perceptual content tend, I think, to accept the sufficiency of the brain for the production of experience, phenomenally conceived. They might argue that what that experience is like depends on what is *standardly in fact* the brain state's external cause, but they would still accept that the brain state would sustain an experience of that kind in the deviant instance when the standard cause is missing. But even if this is not so, it does not matter, for we have already seen [in chapter V of *Perception*] that externalism about phenomenal content is false.

There seems, furthermore, to be a reasonable amount of empirical evidence for (1), and it also explains why veridical-seeming hallucinations should occur.[2] If it were not for the fact that perceptual processes, however stimulated, were sufficient to generate experience, it would be a mystery why such hallucinations should occur.

Nevertheless, (1) can be attacked, if rather desperately. Because this is a desperate strategy, and because, therefore, attacks on (2) are more common, I shall return to (1) after considering the rather popular objections to (2).

## 2   The Attack on (2): The Disjunctive Analysis

In order to reject (2) and defend naive realism it is necessary to deny that the relevant brain process produces more than a bare act of awareness in the case of normal perception, whilst allowing that the same process produces an internal object or content when artificial stimulation produces an hallucination. "I agree," the direct realist might say, "that being in a certain brain state is a sufficient internal causal condition for experiencing certain sense-contents, in this case a table and a wall, but I believe that we must give a separate account of hallucinatory or artificial experiences from those that we give of normal experiences. When the objects are removed and the brain state frozen, this is hallucination, and the subject 'sees' or 'has' images of the table and wall, but when the objects are the cause of the brain state, the subject sees them themselves, directly."

Don Locke adopts an argument rather like this in his attack on those who argue for sense-data on the ground that perception and hallucination are qualitatively indistinguishable. He calls their argument "the argument from qualitative similarity," and says that this presents us with a choice:

We can either allow that things that are, or at any rate could be, qualitatively alike are nevertheless ontologically distinct, or agree that we never perceive external objects. There seems no good reason for accepting the second alternative.[3]

In so far as Locke is merely pointing out that qualitative similarity does not entail ontological similarity, he is only using the same argument as was used in Chapter III [of *Perception*] against the argument from hallucination. The principle that qualitative similarity does not entail ontological similarity is accepted by most sense-datum theorists, for representative realists assert that data and physical objects share some properties. (Berkeley, of course, dissents, on the grounds that "an idea can be like nothing but an idea.")[4] It might also be true that we ought to give a different account of hallucinations as they in fact occur (for example, to schizophrenics, drunkards and drug-takers) than we give of perception, but those who suggest that such hallucinations need separate treatment presumably do so because they believe that normal hallucinations are very different from perceptions in their immediate causes—that is, that they involve the activation of different brain mechanisms. But in the present argument just the same brain state as is the immediate cause of the perception is the immediate antecedent of the corresponding hallucination. If the mechanism or brain state is a sufficient causal condition for the production of an image, or otherwise characterised subjective sense-content, when the table and wall are not there, why is it not so sufficient when they are present? Does the brain state mysteriously know how it is being produced; does it, by some extra sense, discern whether the table is really there or not and act accordingly, or does the table, when present, inhibit the production of an image by some sort of action at a distance? That such *ad hoc* hypotheses are implausible is the rationale of (2). Surely, difference of ontological status cannot plausibly be attributed to the sense-contents in question if they are the upshot of the same proximate causes. This conviction, however, is not universal. Dretske in *Seeing and Knowing* actually considers a case like the one I hypothesise in which the hallucination is caused by precisely the same brain process as causes the normal perception, yet treats it as just another form of the argument from hallucination: he therefore deals with it as Locke deals with hallucination:

> The pattern of this argument, the Argument from Hallucination, is obviously fallacious. I may not be able to distinguish between S's handing me a genuine one-dollar bill ... and S's handing me a counterfeit one-dollar bill.... If the counterfeit is good then these events may be indistinguishable. Surely, however, we cannot conclude that because I am being handed a counterfeit bill in the one case I must be receiving a counterfeit bill in the other case?[5]

Dretske shows no recognition that it might make any difference whether the immediate causes are the same.

I am aware of only two philosophers who face the case where hallucination and perception operate through precisely the same brain process and see the need to defend the view that nevertheless the products of that process are different in the two cases. The philosophers are Hinton and Pitcher.[6]

The general principle lying behind (2) in the original argument could be expressed in the slogan "same proximate cause, same immediate effect." Call this slogan "S." Pitcher accepts S, but in a form that would not sustain (2). He says:

> This principle S although it may be true for every cause-and-effect pair, is not true for them *under every description*.[7]

The idea is that though the immediate effect of a certain brain state may be always "seeming to see something red," and thus, in that respect, always be of the same type, they may also be of different types, in that, sometimes, the immediate effect will fall under the description "hallucinating something red" and, sometimes, under the description "seeing something red."

The general principle that immediate effects of the same type of proximate cause need not be of identical type under all descriptions is quite sound: indeed, no two *different* events could be of identical types under all descriptions true of them, unless they were corresponding events in mirror universes. More concretely, if someone strikes identical nails into identical walls with identical hammers with identical force, the effect in one case might be described as "the picture's being hung" and in the other as "the gas pipe's being severed," each description applying to only one of the effects. The description common to both effects will concern a nail moving a certain distance into a wall. It is plainly not arbitrary, however, what the common description is. If it were sufficient for the satisfaction of S simply that there be *some* common description then it would become vacuous. Suppose that, despite the qualitative identity of hammers, nails, walls and force of blows, in one case the nail penetrated one inch and, in the other, two inches. Intuitively, this would involve an infringement of S, for the same cause would have had relevantly different effects. Nevertheless, the effects are similar under some descriptions; for example, the description "a nail penetrating a wall." Even if in one case the nail had burst into flames the effects would have been identical under the description "something's happening to a nail." It is often said that any two things are similar in some respect: if this is true then any effects of some one type of cause will be identical under some description or other.

To save S from vacuity it is, therefore, essential to say something about the descriptions under which the events must be similar: some restrictions must be imposed. Intuitively, it is not difficult to do this. The different descriptions which applied to the nail applied in virtue of features of the situation which were more remote from the immediate cause—the hammer blow—than was its immediate effect, the nail's movement. They refer either to context—the presence of the picture—or to a further effect—the piercing of the pipe. Intuitively, S applies to the most specific and immediate characterisation of the effect. Thus the communality of a generic description such as "entering the wall" will not satisfy S if one nail entered by one inch and the other by two. One requires the kind of exactness that might answer to, or follow from, a natural law, and be susceptible to quantification. The difference between the nails penetrating one inch and two parallels what Pitcher says about the mental state caused by the brain process. He says that the same brain state will always cause a "seeming to see something red" but that sometimes it will do this by causing a genuine seeing and sometimes by causing an hallucination, where these two states are essentially different. We do not have a genuine case of S where the effects brought under the same description are analysed as having radically different structures or component elements. A sense-datum theorist has no problem with this, for they say that the same brain state causes one kind of effect—the having of a particular kind of sense-datum—by doing which it causes either a seeing or an hallucinating, depending on the further causes and circumstances. But for Pitcher seeing and hallucinating are not to be analysed into a truly common element plus differing extra features.

It seems, therefore, that when one realises the need to apply S to certain sorts of descriptions, Pitcher's argument will not work. Hinton does what is required and simply denies S. He says that it rests on "dubious and arbitrary ... metaphysical beliefs ... about effects of causes."[8] He presents an explicitly disjunctive analysis of such generic concepts as "experience" and "seeming to see." Such expressions are taken not as referring to something common to both perception and hallucination but generically to a disjunction of them both. Thus he deals with the final outcome of the process as follows:

The impulse reaches certain specified structures, and then what? My continuation was "and then one perceives a flash of light or has the illusion of doing so, as the case may be, according to the nature of the initial stimulus."[9]

He is quite aware of the motives that give rise to belief in S.

But it is natural to make some such retort as this, that what happens cannot depend on the initial stimulus; what happens next must be the same, whether the initial stimulus was light striking the retina, or an electric current passing through the retina, or whatever it was.[10]

But he rejects this "natural retort" on the grounds cited above, namely that it rests on arbitrary and dubious metaphysical beliefs. Hinton holds that S is a sound principle when applied to causal laws that relate physical or public events, but that it is mere prejudice to extend it to psycho-physical connections (or, for that matter, to mental-mental ones). His argument is that we know that S applies to physical laws because we can in those cases identify the effect independently of identifying the causes—this is part of the publicity of physical events—and have thereby been able to establish empirically the truth of S in these contexts. But we cannot do this for mental effects; for example, it follows *ex hypothesi* that one cannot tell the type of hallucination that we are considering from a perception without knowing the causal ancestry of the experience: the experience itself does not reveal which it is. Therefore we are not compelled to apply S in the mental case, for we have not identified the nature of the effect independently of the causal context and verified that S applies.[11] However, this is an adequate argument only if there are no general considerations in favour of S—only if, that is, S relies on empirical proof in each type of context.

First, we can concede that one is under no compulsion to accept S, if by compulsion one means logical necessity. Second, we can concede that S is more incontrovertibly established in purely physical contexts. It seems, however, that there are good reasons for extending it to psycho-physical contexts and, indeed, for adopting it as a perfectly general principle. One of the reasons for applying it in psycho-physical contexts has already been alluded to: how would the brain state know when it is required to produce an image to act as understudy for a genuine perception, and why should it bother to do so, as the hallucination serves no purpose except to deceive? If direct realism were correct for perception, then one would not expect (1) to be true; that is, the same process should not be suited to producing an hallucination. The second reason is a variant on this. Unless S applies in the psycho-physical case, the existence of the hallucinations becomes a mystery. Given that Hinton is conceding that hallucinations could be produced by stimulating just those brain states involved in perception, how are we to make sense of why this should be so if it is not by thinking of hallucinations as cases in which the state is activated and performs its normal function—that is, has its normal causal upshot—in an abnormal context? Otherwise the production of hallucinations in this way would seem to cast the brain in a role something like that of a Cartesian demon, producing an effect specialised solely to the context of deception. In order to make sense of why hallucinations should be generable from perceptual processes, I suggest that we have to be able to make sense of "what the brain state does in both cases"—that is, of a common element not analysable into Hinton's disjunction. Thus we face a choice between accepting the radical unintelligibility of why there should be hallucinations in these contexts or of accepting that S is applicable here.

It seems, therefore, that S is sound (contra Hinton) and sound in a strict enough sense (contra Pitcher) to justify (2).

## 3   Anti-Realist Intuitions

It might be argued that this response to Hinton is excessively *realist* about experience. I talk as if it is some sort of entirely objective matter of fact that the mental state produced by the brain state is thus and so, whereas, it might be argued, psychological states are a matter of interpretation and construction. Davidson's and Dennett's theories of belief-desire psychology are instances of the rejection of a hard-core realism about mental states and its replacement by a theory according to which the mental is constructed by our interpretative practices.[12] It would be wholly bizarre to suggest that the very *existence* of sensation depended on such practices, but perhaps less so to claim that its exact structure and logical features depend on what we make of it. It would not, therefore, be some independent question of fact whether the psychological state that was our perceiving something were identical in kind with the corresponding hallucination, but a matter of how our language or theorising about perception and hallucination structured them.

We are now onto a theme that we have met before, when discussing colour in chapter III [of *Perception*], and will meet again when discussing intentionality, namely the dependence of mind on language or "grammar." There seem to me to be at least two objections to its present application. First, the hybrid mixture of realism and interpretationism about sensations is not plausible in this case. It is not that the idea that brute sensations which exist independently of thought might be given structure by thought is, on reflection, implausible. Rather it is that, in this case, the direct interpretations of perception and veridical hallucination do not seem to be different. In both cases, we structure the experience as being as of an external reality; it is only at a second level that they are distinguished, when the hallucinatory experience is discounted. This defeasibility seems too remote a feature to make any difference to how we characterise the direct product of the brain process.[13]

The second objection is like one we found when discussing the "grammatico-dispositional" approach to colour. There we found that it does not show a way of coping with the facts of "illusion." When a white object looks red, for example, the direct realist has a problem in explaining how red fits into the story. This is just as much a problem if one's realism comes from the "grammar" of language as it is if it is taken to be simply an expression of common belief. This brings out a general limitation with the disjunctive theory. It is natural to think of the disjunctive theory as constituting an attempted account of the difference between veridical and non-veridical perception. In fact, it can only apply to the contrast between perception and hallucination. In other words, it leaves untouched all those phenomena categorised as *illusions*, which are non-veridical *perceptions*. If one were to apply the disjunctive approach to illusions one would play straight into the hands of the argument from illusion. The disjunctive analysis allows that hallucinations involve awareness of something subjective, but that perceptions do not. If all non-veridical perceptions were treated in the same way as hallucinations, then every case of something not looking exactly as it is would be a case in which one was aware of some kind of subjective content. Only perfectly veridical perceptions would be free of such subjective contents. This is exactly the situation to which the argument from illusion leads, and we have already seen how this naturally collapses into the view that there always is subjective content and never direct awareness of the external object.[14]

The conclusion is that the disjunctive analysis is radically implausible, both in realist and not-so-realist versions; and that even if it were not, and could cope with the causal-hallucinatory argument, it is seriously incomplete, focusing our attention back onto the argument from illusion.

## 4 Defence of Premise (1)

Given the failure of the attacks on (2), we must return and see whether (1) is more vulnerable than it initially seemed.

One approach would be to challenge the straightforward realism about sensation that seems to be implicit in (1): it seems to be taken as a brute fact that brain states cause sensations or experiences, on a par with the fact that they cause further brain states. The discussion at the end of the previous section effectively covers this option. An anti-realism that makes sense-contents entirely dependent upon interpretation, denying any "brute" element, is wholly implausible; and a hybrid version has already been discussed.

Proposition (1) asserts that the relevant brain process always gives rise to a qualitatively similar experience, whether or not there is an ontologically common element. Hinton, as well as denying that there is an ontologically common element, also denies that there is any strict qualitative similarity. Hinton does not deny that perceiving and hallucinating may be qualitatively indistinguishable. He does deny that it follows from their indistinguishability that they are exactly similar. He thinks that by distinguishing inference on the basis of perception from the given nature of perception itself, he can avoid saying that the event of perceiving and that of hallucinating have an exact qualitative similarity, for it is only that we are inclined to judge that they have.[15]

The first thing to say about this claim is that it has a point only as a prolegomenon to the disjunctive analysis: only if the brain process is followed by different effects in the two cases will it be relevant to deny qualitative similarity between the effects. The second is that it is *per se* implausible. One might judge qualitatively different experiences to be similar if one were hurried or slapdash, but if they appeared similar however closely they were introspected, then the suggestion that they were really different seems implausible and arbitrary, if not vacuous. Is Hinton suggesting that a close enough inspection would always show up a difference? This could be so only if S were denied, and S has been adequately defended already.

Given a sensible realism about experience, there is only one way that I can see in which proposition (1) can be denied. The defence of (2) shows that one is obliged to accept that the relevant brain state produces the same effect in both hallucination and perception. If this is not to involve something like a sense-datum in the case of perception, neither must it in hallucination. For the naive realist, the proper contents in perception are provided by the sensible features of external objects, and in hallucination these are missing, so the hallucination cannot seem like the corresponding perception. Under these constraints, what could be said about the factor common to both hallucination and perception?

The best that can be done is to say that hallucination consists of a kind of imaging which is phenomenally distinct from perceiving, and that this is the factor common to both. This imaging could be thought of as being like the imaging one does when one tries to conjure up what something looks or sounds like. As its connection with such thinking suggests, imaging of this kind is a kind of thinking—a sort of image-conceptualisation. This explains its role in perceiving. Perceiving will have two facets. First, there is the direct consciousness of external things, second there is imaging by which this is appropriated or grasped, and this second depends entirely on the brain: in so far as a feature of a perception is not imaged one has no reflective awareness of it. Thus one is only aware of perceiving some feature of the world if, in addition to consciousness falling upon it, it is also imaged. This would explain misperception of certain kinds. If I remove my glasses, my imaging becomes blurred and I am only able to assimilate confusedly what is in my bare perceptual consciousness.

I think this is the best theory that the naive realist can put forward whilst allowing a univocal role to the perceptual mechanism and brain. There are, however, several serious difficulties.

(1) The imagist approach to the common element denies that direct stimulation of the parts of the brain involved in perception will give perceptual-seeming experiences. It would be enough for the causal argument if stimulation of the rods and cones in the eye, and, hence, of the process up to and including the brain, caused a veridical-seeming experience. That this should not be the case seems both very implausible and, in so far as there is evidence, empirically false.

(2) On this theory, when a white wall looks red one is only imaging red, in a sense of "imaging" in which an image is introspectively distinguishable from perception. But, whatever the situation may be for hallucinations, ordinary misperceptions can often seem to be totally veridical.

(3) If the physical process is responsible only for the imaging, there appears to be no principled account of the relation of bare perceptual awareness to any physical process. This seems odd in itself, but the situation is worse when one takes on board the fact that it is the imaging that determines the exactness of the final experience. The bare perceptual consciousness could possess an acuity far beyond what we are ever fully conscious of; we simply do not notice because we cannot image appropriately. Deterioration of vision could be deterioration of our imaging capacity—no

bare perceptual change need be invoked. The theory is now reminiscent of the claim that the brain does not cause experience, but only edits most of it out—without a brain the mind would be overwhelmed, and would see the universe in every grain of sand—or, at least, in all its microscopic detail. There may be an important truth about the role of embodiment in this theory, but it is not helpful here, because the direct perception of the fullness of things would not correspond to the bare perceptual element in naive realism.

## 5  Conclusion

If this chapter is correct, then there is a subjective element in all perception, for which a brain state is a sufficient cause, and which contains all those phenomenal features that we are familiar with in perception. What is now to be discussed is whether this conclusion can be accepted without also accepting a version of the sense-datum theory. The conclusion does, indeed, appear to be nothing other than the sense-datum theory, but there are ways of construing these subjective contents which are meant to weaken this conclusion, and these must now be considered.

### Notes

1. This argument is used by Broad to refute naive realism in "Some elementary reflexions on sense-perception." He does not take it as proving a full sense-datum theory, however, because he prefers an adverbial account of content....

I claim that this argument is not clearly in the empiricists, nor, so far as I know, is it common currency before Broad. It has recently come to my notice that it is in the first of Malebranche's *Dialogues on Metaphysics*:

Now on the supposition that the world was annihilated and that God nevertheless produced the same traces in our brains, or, rather, presented the same ideas to our minds which are produced in the presence of objects, we should see the same beauties....

But what I see when I look at your room ... will still be visible even should your room have been destroyed and even, I may add, if it had never been built! I maintain that a Chinese who had never been in the room can, in his own country, see everything I see when I look at your room provided—which is by no means impossible—his brain is moved in the same way mine is when I now consider it.

Malebranche's conclusion, however, is not a normal version of the sense-datum theory, for he holds that "The dimensions I see are immutable, eternal, necessary." His eccentric platonising of ideas, even as they constitute the contents of perception, and the absolute (though inadequately explained) distinction he makes between ideas and sensations, makes it difficult to categorise his theory.

2. A classical source for the sufficiency of brain stimulation for experience is Penfield's *The Excitable Cortex in Conscious Man*.

3. Don Locke, *Perception and Our Knowledge of the External World*, 111–112.

4. *Principles of Human Knowledge*, sec. 8.

5. *Seeing and Knowing*, 71.

6. J. M. Hinton, *Experiences*, 75–93 [excerpted in this volume, chapter 2, pp. 28–30]; G. Pitcher, *A Theory of Perception*, 54–57. The disjunctive theory is also discussed by Paul Snowdon in "Perception, vision and causation" [this volume, chapter 3] and by John McDowell in "Criteria, defeasibility and knowledge" [excerpted in this volume, chapter 5]. McDowell is advocating the theory, but shows no sign of recognising that the functioning of the same proximate cause might constitute a problem for the theory. Snowdon, however, claims only to be analysing our ordinary concept and is, therefore, committed to no particular view about what to say on the basis of scientific hypotheses such as ours concerning the causal powers of the brain.

7. *Theory of Perception*, 56–57.

8. *Experiences*, 75 [this volume, p. 28].

9. Ibid.

10. Ibid.

11. Ibid., 77–82 [this volume, pp. 29–30].

12. See, for example, Davidson's approach to the role of interpretation in the construction of our cognitive states, and Dennett's instrumentalist construal of intentional systems in his early and middle writings.

13. When discussing phenomenalism in chapter IX [of *Perception*] we shall see that the disjunctive theory can be given a role in that kind of non-realistic theory, for we can use it to guide our account of the relation of the mental to the physical in that context. This is because, within a phenomenalistically constructed physical world, there is no fact of how the mental and the physical are related, it is a matter of how it is convenient to construct that relation. This is quite different from making the nature of the mental a matter for choice or convention within a physical realist framework.

14. Once again, the phenomenalist can be more flexible here, as we shall see in chapter IX, pp. 136–138 [of *Perception*].

15. This view is defended by Hinton in "Visual experiences" [this volume, chapter 1].

## Bibliography

Berkeley, G. *Philosophical Works*. Ed. M. R. Ayers. London, Dent, 1975.

Broad, C. D. Some elementary reflexions on sense-perception. *Philosophy*, 27: 3–17, 1952.

Dretske, F. *Seeing and Knowing*. London, Routledge and Kegan Paul, 1969.

Hinton, J. *Experiences*. Oxford, Clarendon Press, 1973.

Hinton, J. Visual experiences. *Mind*, 76: 217–227, 1967.

Locke, D. *Perception and our Knowledge of the External World*. New York, George Allen and Unwin, 1967.

McDowell, J. Criteria, defeasibility and knowledge. *Proceedings of the British Academy*, 1982, 455–479. London, Oxford University Press, 1983.

Malebranche, N. *Philosophical Selections*. Ed. S. Nadler. Indianapolis, Hackett.

Penfield, W. *The Excitable Cortex in Conscious Man*. Liverpool, Liverpool University Press, 1958.

Pitcher, G. *A Theory of Perception*. Princeton, Princeton University Press, 1970.

Snowdon, P. Perception, vision and causation. *Proceedings of the Aristotelian Society* 81, 175–192, 1981.

# 10 Selections from *The Problem of Perception*

## A. D. Smith

[A] denial that hallucination and genuine perception have a common nature is central to an increasingly influential account of perception, deriving
from the work of J. M. Hinton—one that is commonly known as the
"disjunctive" account of perception. This view denies that subjective
indiscernibility—which only means sameness as far as the subject can
tell—is a true guide to the actual nature of experiences, to the "what-it-is"
of such experiences, as Hinton puts it.[1] On the disjunctive account of these
matters, although the subject may definitely know something about the
character of his conscious state while yet being unsure whether he is hallucinating or genuinely perceiving, it is denied that such knowledge indicates
that there is an identifiable component in such experiences that is a "common core"—one that, if it were to occur in isolation, would be a hallucination, but is, or is a constituent of, a genuine perception when it is
supplemented by various extraneous, primarily causal, factors relating that
experience to the physical environment. That is to say, it is regarded as a
temptation to jump to the conclusion that it is just such a sensory state
that our subject definitely knows to obtain. The target of the disjunctive
theory is, as Hinton puts it, "the doctrine of the 'experience' as the common element in a given perception and its perfect illusion," "a sort of as-
it-were-picture-seeing [that] occurs as a common constituent of illusion
and true perception."[2] (Given our present concerns, for "illusion" read
"hallucination.") To use John McDowell's often echoed phrase, what is
rejected is a "highest common factor" account of experience.[3] Perhaps it is
true that a certain subject cannot tell whether he is genuinely perceiving
something or merely hallucinating, and yet know that he is at least having

Reprinted by permission of the publisher from "The Argument (from Hallucination)"
in *The Problem of Perception* by A. D. Smith, pp. 197–208, Cambridge, Mass.: Harvard
University Press. Copyright © 2002 by the President and Fellows of Harvard College.

an experience of a certain character; nevertheless, such epistemological facts should not lead us to infer that the subject is aware of enjoying a kind of experience of a determinate nature that is independent of whether he is genuinely perceiving or hallucinating. To underline the falsity of such an inference, the disjunctive theory proposes that we best express what our subject definitely does know in such a situation as his knowing *either* that he is perceiving something of such and such a sort *or* that he is hallucinating such a thing.[4] This is, to be sure, something that our subject definitely does know; and yet there is no suggestion that what he knows is that he is enjoying an experience with a determinate nature. Indeed, the nature of the state is precisely what is left open by such a construal of the situation. Such an either/or statement is, it is claimed, the bottom line in specifying *what is occurring*—something that is not further decomposable into an inner state (common to perception and hallucination) and extra conditions, the holding or not of which determines whether the case is that of perception or hallucination. In short, we should not follow Taine's famous characterization of perception as a "true hallucination"—an intrinsically world-independent sensory state plus various other conditions (though no doubt ones involving causality as well as "truth").[5] So even the most initially compelling employment of subjective indiscernibility—the switch from a hallucination to a genuine perception without any noticeable change at all—is simply rejected by the disjunctivists: despite the lack of any subjectively registered change, the subject in such a situation would indeed be aware of two different objects—one hallucinatory, and one real—that he cannot tell apart from one another. If the disjunctive account of experience is accepted, the generalizing move of our Argument [from Hallucination] will, of course, have no plausibility, since there will be no common nature to hallucinations and genuine perceptions to warrant the generalization of the introduction of non-normal objects of awareness from hallucinations to all perceptual situations.

A number of writers have argued that the generalizing step can be forced through, and hence the "disjunctivist" proposal refuted, by appeal to the principle that the same kind of total, proximate cause gives rise to the same kind of effect.[6] The idea is perhaps best explained by reference to a well-known passage in Russell: "Science holds that, when we 'see the sun,' there is a process, starting from the sun, traversing the space between the sun and the eye, changing its character when it reaches the eye, changing its character again in the optic nerve and the brain, and finally producing the event which we call 'seeing the sun.'"[7] If we replicate just the last events in the optic nerve and brain, shall we not generate exactly the same kind of visual experience as we have when we really see the sun—one that because of its unusual aetiology cannot be regarded as a genuine seeing of the sun, but must count as a hallucination? The suggestion is that since any hallucination involves awareness of a non-normal object, and since, moreover, such a hallucination may be generated in a subject by precisely replicating the proximate afferent inputs to the brain that occur during any veridical perception—so that any such veridical perception has the very same kind of total immediate cause as some possible hallucination—such veridical perceptions, too, must, by the causal principle, also involve awareness of a non-normal object.[8]

In fact, however, a blanket application of such a causal principle to the psychological domain is not something that can be uncontroversially relied upon these days. Hinton, for example, writes that "there is the feeling that if not everything, then at any rate every effect, must be what you might call 'narrowly identifiable'; meaning that one can state the what-it-is of it, to a degree of exactitude which satisfies normal human interest in the matter, without having to know what its proximate, let alone more remote, cause is."[9] He clearly means this to be a diagnosis of an error. And Paul Snowdon explicitly claims that perceptual experience is "essentially tied to a certain sort of cause."[10] Indeed, a position commonly known as "externalism" is widely accepted by philosophers today. The central tenet of externalism is that what cognitive state you are in is not a matter that can be specified independently of your relationship to an environment: that, as far as the cognitive domain is concerned, "methodological solipsism"—the claim that one can fully determine the nature of one's mental states by reflexion or apperception—is false. Externalists admit that there will indeed be *something* inner that is common to those in subjectively identical states, but insist that what can be thus identified as common is not identifiable as something *cognitive*. As McDowell says of such supposed inner contents, "These 'contents' could not yield answers to the question what it is that someone thinks; there is really no reason to recognize them as contents at all."[11] They are at best content "bearers" or "vehicles."[12] Applied to the topic of perception, the externalist claim is that the notion of *being aware of an object* is, though no doubt distinct in various ways from thinking, at least cognitive in the relevant sense, and so escapes the application of the causal principle.

It should not be thought that the following argument, due to C. D. Broad, suffices to rule out the viability of externalism, at least with respect to perception: "Suppose it could be shown that the occurrence of a certain disturbance in a certain part of a person's brain at a certain time is the immediate *sufficient* condition of his then having an experience which he would naturally describe as seeing or hearing or feeling a foreign object of a certain kind in a certain place. Then it would follow at once that the actual presence of such an object at that place at that time *cannot* be a *necessary* condition of the occurrence of the experience. From this it would follow at once that the experience *cannot* be, as it appears to be to the person, a prehension [a direct awareness] of the object in question."[13] This is not adequate to rule out the possibility in question because, for one thing, the logical principle on which Broad seems to rely here—that if $X$ is sufficient for $Y$, then nothing else is necessary for $Y$—is unsound. The correct principle is that if $X$ is sufficient for $Y$, then nothing else is necessary for $Y$ except what is necessary for $X$ itself. In the case in question, Broad's argument leaves it open that the "foreign object" may itself be necessary for the cerebral disturbance in question. Doubtless Broad assumed that no such necessary dependence would be present, but whether such an assumption is warranted depends upon precisely how we are to understand what it is for which such a brain disturbance would suffice. Broad characterizes it as "an experience which [the subject] would naturally describe as. . . ." One way of reading this is as saying that a certain type of brain event is sufficient to give rise to some experience or other with a certain phenomenal character. So read, the claim is doubtless true; and given that no *type* of brain event is necessarily the result of the presence of any "foreign object" at all, Broad's assumption would also be justified, and we should be warranted in concluding that no subjectively specified type of experience requires the presence of any such object. This, however, falls short of the conclusion Broad intends to secure: that no such object can be necessary to any *individual* experience with a given subjective character. In order to reach *this* conclusion, Broad will have to defend both of the following two possibilities: first, that a particular brain disturbance that was caused by a certain object could have been caused by another object (or none)—that is to say, a certain thesis about individual essences; and second, that neurological facts suffice to determine not only the phenomenal, but also the cognitive, character of an experience—to determine, for example, whether it is a case of direct awareness of a normal object or not. Failing to address these issues is simply to beg the question against "externalism," which claims, in relation to perception, that two subjectively identical experiences may differ in that one is, and one is not, the direct awareness of a normal object—with the implication that the latter, *that very experience*, could not exist without its normal object. No possible development of neurology or psychophysics could have any bearing on these issues. Although the causal principle in question may perhaps be acceptable at a purely scientific or naturalistic level of description, the currently widespread acceptance of externalism in the philosophy of mind and cognition shows that it would be at least strategically weak to rely on the principle in cognitive contexts. Because of this, I propose not to rely on any such blanket appeal to the causal principle, but to attempt to push through the generalizing step, *given that the earlier stages of the Argument have been accepted,* on a different, though related, basis. The qualification here is important. What I hope to demonstrate in the rest of this chapter is strictly conditional in nature: that *if* non-normal objects are accepted as objects of immediate awareness for cases of hallucination, the generalizing step goes through, and Direct Realism is shown to be false.[14]

What both genuine perceptions and possible hallucinations have in common, experientially, is that they are both *sensory* in character. In other words, the very same sensory qualities, or qualia, that are actually present to consciousness when we genuinely perceive may be present in a merely hallucinatory state. The first step to take in order to push through the generalizing move is simply to claim that such a hallucinatory realization of sensory qualities is metaphysically possible, and to interpret the initial premise of the Argument—that hallucinations are possible—in this sense.

A number of writers have, however, denied even this weak claim. R. J. Hirst, for example, writes that "Naive Realism can escape ... by denying that having an hallucination is perceiving or perceptual consciousness.... [D]espite subjective similarity the mode and objects of consciousness in hallucination differ in kind from those in genuine perception.... The Argument from Hallucination is thus answered by the suggestion that hallucinations are vivid, and especially eidetic, mental imagery; and where the subject is deceived by this imagery it is being confused with genuine perception owing to various disposing factors."[15] More recently, Brian O'Shaughnessy has written, in relation to vision, that "neither [hallucinatory nor dream] experience is a visual experience, being instead episodes in the visual imagination that are of such a kind that necessarily and delusorily they seem at the time to their owner indistinguishable from visual experience"; later he claims that "all hallucinations necessarily are caused by a diminution in the sense of reality."[16] And even more recently John Hyman has contended that, far from being qualitatively indistinguishable, genuine perception and hallucination sustain only "a non-symmetric doxastic relation"—that is, hallucinating subjects at best merely believe that they are experiencing the way a genuine perceiver does—so that hallucination is but "a *pseudo* experience."[17] The drawing of some such distinction has, indeed, an ancient pedigree: the Stoics, for example, distinguished between *phantasia* and *phantasma*, the latter being a "fancy of the mind [*dokēsis dianoias*] such as occurs while asleep," whereas the former is an "impression [*typōsis*] in the soul."[18] If hallucinations are intrinsically of a different character from genuinely perceptual experiences, and if it is only confusion in the subject that leads him to mistake a non-sensory state for a sensory one, then there is little prospect of convincing anyone of the plausibility of the Argument's generalizing step.

Now, I believe it would be unwise to dispute the claim that most, and perhaps all, actual cases of hallucination are instances of the kind of vivid imagery suggested. Nevertheless, the Argument can proceed even if this is true. Indeed, it is possible for the Argument to proceed even if we were to accept, for reasons deriving from the work of Hilary Putnam and Saul Kripke on reference and essence, that if this is true, hallucinations are *necessarily* such vivid imaginings, and essentially not sensory states. (The occurrence of the term "necessarily" in the previous quotation from O'Shaughnessy seems to indicate that he holds such a position.) For it would be a mistake to infer from this concession that the kind of state required by the Argument is not possible, and that it can therefore be blocked at its very first stage. This would be a mistake because, as with the Argument from Illusion, all that the present Argument requires is that there *could possibly be* genuine sensory experiences of the same intrinsic, qualitative character as veridical perceptions, but which are not veridical, nor even merely illusory: subjectively perceptual states that are not the perception of any normal object—a claim that O'Shaughnessy, for one, accepts.[19] Whether such states are properly to be called "hallucinations" is a question of little moment. This being so, I shall continue, in the absence of any handy term, to refer to the possibility in question as one concerning hallucination. Perhaps perceptual experiences of the same subjective character as genuine perceptions never actually occur in the absence of a normal object. Perhaps it would be fiendishly difficult, or practically impossible, for a neurophysiologist to replicate precisely the conditions for perceptual experience. Is it, though, *absolutely impossible* that such a thing should occur? If not, the Argument is up and running.

Although the assertion of the mere possibility in principle of truly sensory states of consciousness that are not genuine perceptions is so extraordinarily weak that I believe it would be absurd to deny it, in case any reader should have doubts on this score, the assertion is supported by both of the following considerations. First, I believe that in Part I [of *The Problem of Perception*] we have seen beyond a shadow of a doubt that no sensation, of whatever kind, is necessarily intentional in character. Now, hallucinatory states are certainly not a matter of merely enjoying "meaningless" sensations. They are genuinely perceptual in phenomenological character, being at least ostensibly directed intentionally to objects in the physical environment. But in virtue of such an extra phenomenological richness they can hardly be thought necessarily to *lose* the sensuous character that even sheer sensation possesses! Secondly, although it is debatable whether the previously discussed causal principle applies unrestrictedly to the psychological domain, it is surely not open to serious question that it does apply with respect to the merely sensory character of conscious states. If the activity of your optic nerve when you are genuinely perceiving something green is precisely replicated artificially, you will, other things about you being normal, seem to see something green *in a genuinely sensory manner*. Doubt has recently been cast by several writers on whether intentional states are truly attributable to a "brain in a vat"—a subject who would indeed fall within the class of hallucinators here in question. (Indeed, a suitably stimulated brain in a vat is perhaps the simplest case to have in mind when thinking about the Argument: a case of total hallucination in all sense modalities.) But a denial that such an envatted subject could possibly enjoy sensory experiences at all would be, as they say, heroic. A brain in a vat may perhaps wholly lack cognition of its environment; but it cannot, if it is otherwise functioning normally, seriously be supposed to be wholly nonconscious, like a stone. If such a brain were before you, would you happily excite it in a way that is known to give rise to excruciating pain in a normal embodied subject? McDowell sometimes characterizes a subject isolated from interaction with a physical environment in terms of inner darkness.[20] Now, perhaps McDowell does not wish to deny all sentience to such a subject;[21] perhaps he means merely to express in a dramatic way the fact that such a subject radically lacks any cognition of the outside world, and that opposition to the disjunctive account of experience works with a picture of inner subjectivity which entails that the "world has to be conceived as letting in no light from outside."[22] But the metaphor is wholly misleading. It is possible for the subject of a disembodied, but suitably stimulated, brain to be conscious; it is possible that it be with this subject experientially as though he were ordinarily perceiving a world. Indeed, by direct stimulation of the brain we can already induce flashes of light in the visual experience of embodied subjects. Such phosphenes are incompatible with everything being "dark within" in any straightforward sense of these words. To deny all of this is to deny that there is such a thing as psychophysics at all.

So, the initial premise of our Argument is that it is a metaphysical possibility that a conscious state with the same sensory character as any veridical perception should obtain even though that state is not the perception of any physical object or phenomenon: a state that is neither a mere belief, nor a dream, nor a vivid mental image, nor a state analogous to post-hypnotic suggestion, hunch, or premonition, but one that is truly sensory. Even the sheer metaphysical possibility of such states occurring is supposed to motivate acceptance of the generalizing step of the Argument, because we now have a common nature shared by genuine perceptions and possible hallucinations. In virtue of this common nature, it may be thought, what *would* be true of such a hallucination—namely, that the subject would be aware of a non-normal object—*is* true of any genuine perception.

In fact, however, our newly formulated premise, even though it now explicitly contains the claim that genuine perceptions and hallucinations can have at least a common sensory nature, does not by itself clearly warrant the generalizing step. That is because accepting such a premise is compatible with accepting the disjunctive account of perceptual experience. For although at least some disjunctive theorists, such as McDowell, do seem to deny the premise, the essential target of the disjunctivists is independent of any issue concerning the possibly sensory character of hallucination. For their primary claim is that the content of a veridical perceptual state cannot be adequately specified without mentioning the particular real-world objects of which the subject is (directly) aware in virtue of so perceiving.[23] What is being opposed here is the conception of perceptual experiences as "amongst the events, the intrinsic natures of which are independent of anything outside the subject," a "tract of reality whose layout would be exactly as it is however things stood outside it," so that "worldly circumstances are only externally related to experiences."[24] On the contrary, when a subject perceives a normal physical object, that very object, as John McDowell puts it, "figures in" perceptual consciousness.[25] As another recent disjunctivist has put it, "To think of conscious experience as a highest common factor of vision and hallucination is to think of experiences as states of a type whose intrinsic features are world-independent; an intrinsic, or basic, characterization of a state of awareness will make no reference to anything external to the subject."[26] The central disjunctivist claim is, therefore, that phenomenology cannot deliver the final answer concerning the intrinsic nature of our experiences, even qua experiences. Phenomenology does not tell us the "what-it-is" of at least some states of consciousness.

Now, this central contention of the disjunctive theory is surely nothing but Direct Realism itself. For, as McDowell puts it, what is being opposed is the view that, even in cases of genuine perception, "one's experiential intake must ... fall short of the fact itself"—that is, of the worldly fact that is perceived to obtain.[27] There can, for the Direct Realist, be no adequate characterization of a genuine state of perception as an experience, as a form of awareness, that leaves out the worldly object of which one is aware. For if one attempted such a characterization, either one would have to postulate an object of awareness more immediate than the worldly object, which simply denies Direct Realism, or one would have to suppose that the perception in itself is wholly objectless, which is absurd. Hence, McDowell can characterize the non-disjunctivist conception of even genuine perceptions as being "blank or blind."[28] By itself, however, such a claim is not inconsistent with the simple recognition that hallucinations are genuinely sensory in nature—or, more precisely, with the claim that non-veridical and not merely illusory sensory states of perceptual consciousness are possible—and if it were, that would only show that the disjunctive account, and, hence, Direct Realism itself, is false. For it is still open to a disjunctivist to claim that two states that are sensorily identical in nature can yet differ in cognitive status, in that one is, and the other is not, an immediate awareness of some normal physical object.

So we need one more consideration if we are to motivate the generalizing step of the Argument. The relevant consideration involves highlighting the importance of the *second* step in the Argument: the claim that the subject of a hallucination, in the sense now explained, is aware of a non-normal object. This second step is not supposed to be a second premise in the Argument: it is supposed to be *entailed* by the initial premise—entailed, that is to say, by the very nature of hallucination as it is being understood here. And for the moment we are accepting this entailment. Now, although the problem posed for Direct Realism by the possibility of hallucination is usually seen as that of how merely changing the causal antecedents of a type of sensory state, by plugging it into an environment, can make it the case that the immediate object of awareness is changed—so that we become immediately aware of a physical object in public space, rather than merely hallucinating—a much more challenging question is not how another object, a normal physical object, can intrude itself upon consciousness in virtue of our installing certain causal links, but *how the original non-normal object can thereby cease to be an object of awareness*. The impossibility of answering this question satisfactorily arises from the precise reason why a non-normal object is allocated to hallucination in the first place. Hallucinatory consciousness is sensory in nature. It is not like merely thinking or imagining an object. Rather, an object seems, as Husserl put it, to be *bodily present*. We do not speak of being "aware" of an object when we merely imagine one before us, however concretely we do it. It is precisely the sensory character of hallucination that leads us to speak of an *awareness* of objects here. In short, if we believe that a hallucinating subject is aware of a non-normal object, it is *only* because hallucination is, or involves, a sensory state. It is specifically the sensory character of such experiences that means that we are being genuinely *confronted by* a qualitatively characterized, non-normal object. Since genuine perception differs from such hallucination only in that more is present, any perception includes awareness of such a non-normal object.

Once again, we can bring in causal considerations to make the foregoing line of thought yet more compelling. When we suitably stimulate a subject's brain or afferent nerves, we *generate* a sensory experience in the subject. Now, to be sure, not any sensory experience is phenomenologically perceptual, as we saw in Part I [of *The Problem of Perception*]. If, however, the subject is otherwise suitably constituted, such a stimulus will, other things being equal, generate an experience that *is* perceptual in character: sensory and at least apparently intentionally directed to a normal object. After all, given that I am the way I now am, *all* that is required for me to seem to see as I now do is that my retinas be stimulated as they now are being. So, although we cannot uncontroversially assume that the same proximal physical cause necessarily gives rise to the same effect cognitively construed, it would be heroic to deny that it may give rise, even in the absence of a normal distal cause, to the same effect phenomenally, or sensorily, construed. In short, it is possible to generate a hallucination in the sense operative here. Let us consider such a possible hallucination and the veridical perception that it perfectly matches from the subjective viewpoint. Although the latter is a case of genuine perception, the ultimate stages of the causal chain leading from the environment to the subject's perception may be identical in character to that of the matching hallucination. This final stage alone suffices to generate a state characterized with respect to its phenomenal character. Therefore, given stage two of the Argument, a non-normal object is generated, as in hallucination. There is no getting round this fact. By virtue of having, in genuine perception, a more extended causal chain that goes right out into the environment, in a way that reliably carries information to the subject about the layout of that environment, we may, perhaps, find something *more* in the resulting perceptual state than is to be found in any proximately excited hallucination; but we cannot find any *less*. In particular, we cannot suppose the non-normal object to be absent. If any further cognitive function in relation to the environment is achieved in virtue of the hooking-up of a subject with an environment, it is one that must go through the non-normal object of which we are directly aware. If we are aware of a physical world, realistically conceived, in such perception at all, our awareness of it is indirect. Once you introduce immediate, non-normal objects as real constituents of any state of perceptual consciousness, they will be ineliminable from the analysis of any such state, genuine or not. Once you accept stage two of the Argument, you must accept the Argument as a whole and deny Direct Realism.

At this point, however, it may be suggested that the idea of being sensory should itself be subjected to a disjunctive analysis, since there are two radically different ways in which a state can be correctly so described. In a hallucination the sensory aspect of the experience is entirely a characteristic of a conscious state generated in the subject: sensation is generated by the operation of the sensory centres of the brain. In genuine perception, on the other hand, the sensuousness that is present in consciousness is a qualitative feature of a normal object in the physical world, a feature of which we are transparently aware. This particular disjunctive manoeuvre is, however, opposed by two facts. First, the suggestion conflicts with an earlier finding of ours. For it relies upon the truth of Naive Realism with respect to sensible qualities; and the falsity of this view was, I believe, demonstrated in Chapter 1 [of *The Problem of Perception*]. For I argued there that in order to escape the Argument from Illusion, sensory qualia had to be regarded as going toward constituting sensory experience itself, in such a way that the realization of such qualia entails that a sensory experience is occurring. No such quale can therefore characterize an insentient, merely physical object. In short, the suggestion conflicts with the primary/secondary quality distinction, which, I have argued, a Direct Realist must accept if he is to withstand the Argument from Illusion. Secondly, although the suggestion does not conflict with the pure form of the Argument from Hallucination as I have presented it in the present chapter, as one that relies for its first premise on the sheer possibility of genuinely sensory hallucinatory states of consciousness, it does conflict with the causal considerations that I have introduced to lend extra plausibility to that premise, should it be needed. For if it is accepted, as I think it must be, that the proximate causes of a hallucination suffice for the generation of a sensory state, a state whose sensuous character is *internal* to that state, then such a state is also generated when that causal chain is part of the more extended chain that we find in the case of genuine perceptions. At least the purely sensory nature of that state cannot, therefore, depend on the character of the more distant states of the causal chain involved in genuine perception, as the present proposal suggests.

As with the Argument from Illusion, therefore, once non-normal objects are introduced to account for certain perceptual phenomena, the generalizing step is unavoidable, and we are led to acknowledge the falsity of Direct Realism. Once again, if our Argument is to be blocked at all, it must be at the second stage, where non-normal objects are first introduced. Once these objects get into your philosophy, Direct Realism is sunk.

**Notes**

1. J. M. Hinton, *Experiences* (Oxford: Clarendon Press, 1973), p. 80.

2. Ibid., p. 71, and J. M. Hinton "Experiences," *Philosophical Quarterly* 17 (1967): 10.

3. John McDowell, "Criteria, Defeasibility, and Knowledge," *Proceedings of the British Academy* (1982): §3 [this volume, pp. 79–85].

4. There is some dispute among disjunctive theorists over how exactly to specify the relevant disjunction. Paul Snowdon, for example, has criticized Hinton's specific proposal—which employs the notion of *being under a perfect illusion*—and employs instead the disjunction "(there is something which looks to S to be *F*) v (it is to S as if there is something which looks to him (S) to be *F*)": "Perception, Vision and Causation," *Proceedings of the Aristotelian Society* 81 (1980–1981): 185 [this volume, pp. 41]. A weakness with this suggestion, of course, is that it applies only to visual experience (as Snowdon recognizes). We need not, however, enter into the niceties of this debate, since the general idea, in which alone we are interested here, is clear enough.

5. Hippolyte Adolphe Taine, *De L'Intelligence*, 2 vols. (Paris: Hachette, 1870), vol. 1, p. 408, vol. 2, pp. 5–6.

6. For a recent example, see Howard Robinson, *Perception* (London: Routledge, 1994), ch. 6 [this volume, chapter 9].

7. Bertrand Russell, *The Analysis of Matter* (London: George Allen and Unwin, 1927), p. 197.

8. Paul Snowdon, one of the leading disjunctive theorists, in effect accepts this argument, or at least does not reject it. Because of this, he retreats to the claim that a disjunctive analysis of experience is not a priori false. See "The Objects of Perceptual Experience I," *Proceedings of the Aristotelian Society*, supp. vol. 64 (1990): 130–131 [this volume, p. 57]. Although this may suffice for Snowdon's limited concern with conceptual analysis, in the present context such a response would, of course, be wholly inadequate.

9. Hinton, *Experiences*, p. 80.

10. Snowdon, "The Objects of Perceptual Experience I," p. 125 [this volume, p. 52].

11. McDowell, "Singular Thought and Inner Space," in *Subject, Thought, and Context*, ed. Philip Pettit and John McDowell (Oxford: Clarendon Press, 1986), p. 165, n. 54.

12. John McDowell, "*De Re* Senses," in *Frege: Tradition and Influence*, ed. Crispin Wright (Oxford: Blackwell, 1984), p. 103, n. 13.

13. C. D. Broad, "Some Elementary Reflexions on Sense-Perception," *Philosophy* 27 (1952); repr. in Swartz, *Perceiving, Sensing, and Knowing*, p. 39.

14. Many disjunctivists will, in fact, be happy to accept this conditional conclusion, since they deny that a hallucinator is aware of anything at all. This initially preposterous claim is the topic of Chapter 8 [of *The Problem of Perception*].

15. R. J. Hirst, *The Problems of Perception* (London: George Allen and Unwin, 1959), pp. 40–44.

16. Brian O'Shaughnessy, *The Will*, 2 vols. (Cambridge: Cambridge University Press, 1980), vol. 1, pp. xvii and 174.

17. John Hyman, "The Causal Theory of Perception," *Philosophical Quarterly* 42 (1992): 286 and 290.

18. Diogenes Laertius, *Lives of Eminent Philosophers*, tr. R. D. Hicks, 2 vols. (Cambridge, Mass.: Harvard University Press, 1995), VII.50.

19. Hence, as mentioned above, his turning to after-images in order to mount a parallel to the Argument from Hallucination against Direct Realism.

20. See, for example, McDowell, "Singular Thought and Inner Space," §8.

21. This is a big "perhaps." Speaking of the brain of a normal embodied subject that is then disembodied and envatted, McDowell says that "perhaps memory can give subjectivity a tenuous foothold here": John McDowell, "The Content of Perceptual Experience," *Philosophical Quarterly* 44 (1994): 201. Greg McCulloch, a follower of McDowell's, is even less concessionary: see his *The Mind and Its World* (Routledge: London, 1995), VIII.5.

22. McDowell, "Singular Thought and Inner Space," p. 160.

23. Disjunctivism also has another target. Hinton, for example, can characterize the target of his criticism as the idea of a visual experience as "'inner' independently of the extent to which it is given meaning by the subject's experience of life"; or as the idea that there is "a gap between one's report of such an experience and any proposition as to how some external object, event, or process looks; a gap exactly as wide as the gap between such an experience-report and *any* sort of proposition about the 'external world'": Hinton, *Experiences*, pp. 60 and 61 [this volume, pp. 23 and 24].

What seems to emerge from such passages as the real target of the disjunctive theory, at least for Hinton, is a traditional view according to which we are first aware of bare sensations, which we have then to interpret in some objective way, and according to which we can always return to such a bare reporting of experience uncontaminated by objective interpretation. Now, this may indeed be a wholly mistaken account of perceptual consciousness. Perhaps the most authentic way of expressing either a perception or a hallucination is saying *how things appear to you*. Perhaps an at least apparent presentation of an "external world" is indissociable from perceptual consciousness as such. But the Argument requires the denial of none of this. The Argument from Hallucination does not need, any more than the Argument from Illusion, to be based upon poor phenomenology.

24. Snowdon, "The Objects of Perceptual Experience I," p. 123 [this volume, p. 51], and McDowell, "Singular Thought and Inner Space," pp. 151 and 157.

25. McDowell, "Singular Thought and Inner Space," p. 146.

26. William Child, "Vision and Experience: The Causal Theory and the Disjunctive Conception," *Philosophical Quarterly* 42 (1992): 300–301.

27. McDowell, "Criteria, Defeasibility, and Knowledge," p. 471 [this volume, p. 80].

28. McDowell, "Singular Thought and Inner Space," p. 152.

# 11  The Theory of Appearing Defended

Harold Langsam

## 1  Introduction

In this paper, I explicate and defend a particular theory as to the ontological nature of experiences, a theory that may initially be summarized in the following preliminary formula: experiences are *relations* between material objects and minds.[1] The attractiveness of the theory is that it can reconcile what, to paraphrase Wilfrid Sellars, we might call the Manifest and Scientific Images of experience (Sellars 1963, pp. 1–40). In sections 2–4, I defend the theory against various well-known objections, and in so doing show how the theory is compatible with the accepted scientific picture of the world (the Scientific Image). In section 5, I argue that the theory is part of our commonsense thinking about the world (the Manifest Image). In this introductory section, I describe the theory and contrast it to its principal rivals.

My preliminary formulation of the theory is clearly inadequate, for surely almost all philosophers would agree that there is some sense of the word "experience" according to which it is true to say that experiences are relations between material objects and minds. For example, who would deny that for a subject to have an experience of an apple is for her to be related in some way to that apple? What I need to do is carefully describe a particular notion of experience, a notion pursuant to which my theory will be both nontrivial and controversial. This characterization of experience should also allow perspicuous formulations of rival theories; in other words, the characterization should be neutral as between competing theories of the ontological nature of experience.

Harold Langsam, "The Theory of Appearing Defended," *Philosophical Studies* 120: 33–59. © 1997 Kluwer Academic Publishers. Reprinted with kind permission from Springer Science and Business Media.

One helpful way to capture the relevant notion of experience is to contrast experiences with conscious (nonimagistic) thoughts. In other words, let us contrast two kinds of conscious states: experiences and thoughts. Thomas Nagel (1974) has famously tried to capture the elusive notions of consciousness and subjectivity by talking of "what it is like" for a subject to be in conscious states. In other words, conscious states are states such that there is something it is like for a subject to be in them. As a subject myself, I wish to suggest that what it is like to have a thought is very different from what it is like to have an experience. Colin McGinn goes even further, acknowledging that "thoughts are conscious," but that they are "mental states for which the notion of what it is like to have them seems strained at best" (1991, p. 25, fn. 4). I think McGinn goes too far, but his remark does at least point to how thoughts and experiences differ with regard to what it is like to have them. If the notion of what it is like to have a thought seems strained, it is perhaps because we have so little to say about what it is like to have thoughts. And perhaps we have so little to say here because what it is like to have one thought differs very little, if anything at all, from what it is like to have another thought. Moreover, even if there are slight differences between what it is like to have different thoughts, these differences do not seem to depend on, or reflect, or vary systematically with, differences in the contents of the thoughts. My mother is very different from H. Ross Perot, in her personal qualities, life history, how she looks, etc. But it is not clear that what it is like to think about my mother is at all different from what it is like to think about H. Ross Perot. And even if there are slight differences here, these differences do not seem to reflect the differences between my mother and H. Ross Perot. In general, regardless of what the subject is thinking, what it is like for the subject to be thinking will be pretty much the same.

Experiences are very different from thoughts in this respect. For what it is like to have an experience of something is generally very different from what it is like to have an experience of some different thing, and these differences do depend on, reflect, and vary systematically with (among other things) differences in the things experienced. What it is like for me to have a visual experience of my mother is very different from what it is like for me to have a visual experience of H. Ross Perot; we note this difference by saying that when I see them, they *look* very different to me. Similarly, we could talk about how they sound different, feel different to the touch, and smell different to me. More generally, they *appear* different to me. But nothing analogous can be said to mark the differences, if any, between what it is like to think about my mother and what it is like to think about H. Ross Perot.

This difference I have been describing between what it is like to have experiences and what it is like to have thoughts is often expressed by saying that experience has a phenomenal character,[2] whereas thought does not. Alternatively, experience is sensory, or sensuous; thought, again, is not. But not only can we talk in general of the phenomenal character of experiences, we can also talk of specific aspects of phenomenal character, what I call phenomenal features. Thus contrast a visual experience of something red, a red apple, say, with a mere conscious thought of the red apple. As with all thoughts, the thought of the red apple has no phenomenal character; nothing *appears* to me, neither the red apple nor anything else, when I think of it. But not only does the red apple appear to me when I have a visual experience of it, we can say something specific about how it appears to me: assuming conditions are normal, it appears red to me. Such appearances of red are referred to by philosophers in various ways; they talk of instantiations of apparent redness, phenomenal redness, or perceived redness, or they simply talk of red sensations. They refer to appearances of red in these ways in order to distinguish them from instantiations of redness *simpliciter*, where redness is considered as an intrinsic property of material objects. I will say that these appearances of red are instantiations of the *phenomenal feature* of redness,[3] and I will talk more generally of phenomenal features as the particular aspects of phenomenal character. So we can say that what distinguishes experiences from thoughts is the instantiation in experiences of phenomenal features. And the theory of experiences I wish to defend can now be more precisely formulated as the view that phenomenal features such as redness are relations between material objects and minds. The claim in the first paragraph of this paper that *experiences* are relations between material objects and minds should henceforth be understood as the claim that *phenomenal features* are relations between material objects and minds.

The main alternative to this theory is the view that phenomenal features are intrinsic properties. Views of this kind take different forms, depending on what kinds of objects the phenomenal features are taken to be intrinsic properties of. Thus we have the view that phenomenal features are intrinsic properties of mental objects (the "sense-data" theory—see Jackson 1977; Robinson 1985 and 1990), the view that they are intrinsic properties of brain states (Hardin 1988; Loar 1990; Flanagan 1992), and even the view that they are intrinsic properties of material objects (Strawson 1979; Harding 1991).[4]

Some philosophers seem to want to make the claim that the *phenomenology* of perception somehow supports the view that phenomenal features are intrinsic properties.[5] I shall simply note that I find this claim totally without merit. What phenomenology reveals to us are the specific ways that things appear to us; it reveals nothing to us about the ontological category to which these appearances belong.

The view that phenomenal features are relations between material objects and minds is sometimes called "the Theory of Appearing" (Price 1950, p. 61) or "the Multiple Relation Theory of Appearing" (Jackson 1977, pp. 89–90).[6] What does talk of appearing have to do with the claim that phenomenal features are relations? The idea is supposed to be that we describe the phenomenal features of our experiences by talking of how material objects appear to us, and therefore our appearance talk supports the claim that phenomenal features are relations between material objects and minds. For example, we speak of the apple as appearing red to me. "Appearing red" is a two-place predicate; it refers, I claim, to the phenomenal feature of redness, which is being referred to as a relation, a relation being instantiated by a material object (the apple) with respect to a mind (myself).

Note that those who oppose the Theory of Appearing must give an alternative account of appearance talk. For both sides to this dispute will presumably agree that to say that the apple appears red to me is to state that a certain kind of relation obtains between the apple and myself. I claim that the relation in question is the phenomenal feature of redness. Those who deny that phenomenal features are relations must give an alternative account of what this relation consists in. The "widely accepted" (Jackson 1977, p. 98, fn. 4) alternative account is that the relation in question is a certain kind of causal relation. Specifically, to say that the apple appears red to me is to say that the apple causally acts on me in a certain way to produce in me a certain kind of experiential state, an experiential state in which the phenomenal feature of redness is instantiated.[7] Thus, in defending the Theory of Appearing, I am also opposing the *causal* theory of appearing, or, as it is more familiarly known, the causal theory of perception. Although the causal theory may be, in Frank Jackson's words, "widely accepted," recent philosophical work (Snowdon 1981 [this volume, chapter 3] and 1990 [this volume, chapter 4]; Hyman 1992) has, I believe, seriously undermined the standard Gricean arguments in favor of it.

But my concern here is not with the causal theory of perception; it is with the Theory of Appearing, the claim that phenomenal features are relations that hold between material objects and minds. In this paper, I respond to various traditional arguments against this claim. I begin with the familiar Argument from Hallucination.

## 2  The Argument from Hallucination[8]

The Theory of Appearing claims that phenomenal features are relations between material objects and minds. But we can be more specific as to *which* material objects are supposed to enter into these relations. Let us focus on *visual* phenomenal features, phenomenal features instantiated in visual experiences. According to the Theory of Appearing, *which* material objects appear to us via visual phenomenal features? The objects we see, of course. If the apple is appearing red to me, for example, then I must be seeing it. More generally, phenomenal features relate objects of perception with the subjects that are perceiving them. These objects of perception are the objects we see, hear, smell, feel, and taste.

But now it may be thought that the existence of hallucinations poses a problem for the claim that phenomenal features are relations that hold between material objects and minds. For phenomenal features are sometimes instantiated even when *no* material object is being perceived. I will say that such (instantiations of) phenomenal features are phenomenal features of *hallucinatory* experiences.[9] (And similarly, I will talk of phenomenal features of perceptual experiences.) The phenomenal features of hallucinatory experiences cannot be instantiations of relations between material objects and minds, for the only material objects that can enter into these relations are objects of perception, and when a subject is hallucinating, he is not perceiving any material object.

Clearly, the view that I am defending, that phenomenal features are relations between material objects and minds, must not be interpreted as saying that *all* instantiations of phenomenal features are instantiations of relations between material objects and minds. It is the phenomenal features of *perceptual* experiences, not the phenomenal features of hallucinatory experiences, that are supposed to be instantiations of such relations. But the thrust of the Argument from Hallucination is that *no* phenomenal features are instantiations of relations between material objects and minds. According to this argument, if phenomenal features of hallucinatory experiences are not instantiations of relations between material objects and minds, then the phenomenal features of perceptual experiences cannot instantiate such relations, either. For perceptual experiences and their corresponding hallucinations are "indistinguishable from the subject's point of view" (Hyman 1992, p. 284), and therefore either the phenomenal features of both kinds of experience instantiate relations between material objects and minds (which clearly cannot be the case), or no phenomenal features instantiate relations between material objects and minds.

Why is the *indistinguishability* of perceptual experiences and their corresponding hallucinations supposed to exclude the possibility of the phenomenal features of perceptual experiences being instantiations of relations between material objects and minds, and the phenomenal features of hallucinations being instantiations of some other kind of universal? Perceptual experiences and hallucinations are indistinguishable in the sense that, for any sensory event, subjects are unable to tell, solely on the basis of experiencing that event, whether the event is a perceptual experience or an hallucination. A perceptual experience and an hallucination are indistinguishable to a subject when they seem to the subject to be the same, and a perceptual experience and an hallucination seem to a subject to be the same when they present the same *appearances* to the subject. But as we saw in section 1, according to the Theory of Appearing, talking about appearances is our way of describing the phenomenal features of our experiences. So if perceptual experiences and their corresponding hallucinations are indistinguishable, it must be because they instantiate the same phenomenal features. But if the phenomenal features of perceptual experiences and hallucinations are the same, then both kinds of phenomenal features must share all the same (intrinsic) properties. As we have seen, one of the properties of the phenomenal features of hallucinations is that they are *not* instantiations of relations between material objects and minds. So the phenomenal features of perceptual experiences cannot be instantiations of relations between material objects and minds, either, contrary to the claims of the Theory of Appearing.

I respond to the Argument from Hallucination by adopting a version of what is referred to in the literature as the Disjunctive Conception of Experience.[10] In brief, I deny what the Argument from Hallucination assumes: that the indistinguishability of perceptual experiences and their corresponding hallucinations can be explained only in terms of their instantiating the same phenomenal features. On the contrary, I will show that it is sufficient if they instantiate *similar* phenomenal features, phenomenal features that are the same in some respects but different in others. If we are to explain the indistinguishability of perceptual experiences and hallucinations, then we need only assume that the phenomenal features of perceptual experiences and hallucinatory experiences share the same "appearances," for as we just noted, it is sameness in appearance that is relevant to indistinguishability. But they need not share the same ontological character; in particular, the phenomenal features of perceptual experiences can be instantiations of relations between material objects and minds even though the phenomenal features of hallucinations are not. There is no reason to think that two phenomenal features cannot share the same appearance yet differ in ontological character. So the conclusion of the Argument from Hallucination that the phenomenal features of perceptual experience are not relations between material objects and minds is avoided.

Let me support these claims by means of an example. Consider some particular perceptual experience and its corresponding hallucination, the hallucination from which it is indistinguishable. The Argument from Hallucination says that this indistinguishability must be explained in terms of the two experiences instantiating exactly the same phenomenal features. So, for example, if both experiences present an appearance of redness, then they must both instantiate the phenomenal feature of redness. Whereas I respond that the indistinguishability can be explained even if we assume that the two experiences instantiate different phenomenal features. Instead of talking of a phenomenal feature of redness that is instantiated by both perceptual experiences and hallucinations, let us suppose that a perceptual experience that presents an appearance of redness instantiates a phenomenal feature that I shall refer to as the *phenomenal feature of redness*$_1$, whereas an hallucinatory experience that presents an appearance of red instantiates a different phenomenal feature, a feature I shall refer to as the *phenomenal feature of redness*$_2$. Consider again our two indistinguishable experiences that both present an appearance of redness. According to the Theory of Appearing that I wish to defend, the perceptual experience presents an appearance of redness in virtue of instantiating the phenomenal feature of redness$_1$, whereas the hallucination presents an appearance of redness in virtue of instantiating a different phenomenal feature, the phenomenal feature of redness$_2$. But if they instantiate different phenomenal features, how can they present the same appearance? Because although the phenomenal features are distinct, they are similar in certain respects; in particular, instantiations of both these phenomenal features constitute an appearance of redness. Just as red and yellow are different colors, yet are similar in that they are both colors, similarly, the phenomenal features of redness$_1$ and redness$_2$ are different phenomenal features, yet they are similar in that instantiations of both these phenomenal features constitute appearances of red. We might say that the phenomenal features of redness$_1$ and redness$_2$ are determinate properties of a determinable to which only they belong. In other words, there are two distinct phenomenal features of redness. The Theory of Appearing is committed to positing such pairs of phenomenal features for each distinctive way things can appear in experience, pairs of phenomenal features that present the same appearance but differ in ontological character. The similarity in appearance is needed to account for the indistinguishability of perceptual experiences and hallucinations; the difference in ontological character is needed so as to be able to maintain the defining thesis of the Theory of Appearing, the thesis that the phenomenal features of perceptual experiences (but not the phenomenal features of hallucinatory experiences) are relations between material objects and minds.

I described my response to the Argument from Hallucination as a version of the Disjunctive Conception of Experience; the sense in which the response commits the Theory of Appearing to a *disjunctive* view of experience should now be clear. Contrast it with a nondisjunctive conception of experience such as the sense-data theory. According to the sense-data theory, all phenomenal features are the same kind of thing, in the sense that they have the same ontological character. Specifically, they are all intrinsic properties, intrinsic properties of sense-data. But according to the Disjunctive Conception that I am defending, a phenomenal feature is *either* a relation between a material object and a mind (if it is the kind of phenomenal feature that is instantiated in perceptual experiences) *or* it is something else (if it is the kind of phenomenal feature that is instantiated in hallucinatory experiences). Or as I shall henceforth put the point, experiences themselves are either relations between material objects and minds (if they are perceptual experiences) or something else (if they are hallucinatory experiences).

The Disjunctive Conception of Experience defends the Theory of Appearing from the Argument from Hallucination by modifying the theory and restricting its application. Whereas the Theory of Appearing as originally presented says simply that phenomenal features are relations between material objects and minds, the Theory of Appearing as modified by the Disjunctive Conception of Experience says, more precisely, that it is only phenomenal features of perceptual experiences that are relations between material objects and minds. The modified Theory of Appearing (henceforth referred to simply as the Theory of Appearing) has nothing to fear from the Argument from Hallucination, but it is vulnerable to arguments of other kinds. In the next section, I defend the modified Theory of Appearing against one of these other arguments—the Causal Argument.

## 3   The Causal Argument[11]

The basic idea of the Causal Argument is as follows. Consider, for example, some perceptual experience and its corresponding hallucination, the hallucination from which it is indistinguishable. As we shall see, our best theories of how experiences are caused suggest that the "perception and hallucination might have the same immediate cause" (Robinson 1985, p. 174). But according to the Theory of Appearing, the perceptual experience and its corresponding hallucination are *different*, in the sense that the former is a relation between a material object and a mind, and the latter is not. So the Theory of Appearing is committed to the possibility of causes that are the same producing different effects. But causes that are the same do *not* produce different effects, they produce the *same* effects. Therefore, the Theory of Appearing must be mistaken in its claim that perceptual experiences and hallucinatory experiences are different.

Let us begin by justifying the claim that a perceptual and hallucinatory experience can have the same cause. I shall focus on the case of visual experience. Visual perceptual experiences occur at the end of a long chain of causal events, a causal chain that begins, in the case of opaque material objects, with light being reflected from the object seen. Thus suppose I am seeing an apple; what are the causal antecedents of my visual experience of the apple? The causal chain begins with light being reflected from the apple; it continues with the reflected light entering my eyes, stimulating various receptor neurons in the retinas, such stimulation giving rise to the transmission of electrochemical impulses to my brain, and especially to that part of the brain known as the visual cortex. The transmission of these electrochemical impulses results in the stimulation of various cells in the visual cortex, such stimulation giving rise to my visual experience of the apple. For present purposes, we may say that the immediate cause of a visual perceptual experience is the stimulation of some region of the visual cortex.

As we have noted, causes that are the same produce effects that are the same. Since it is only immediate causes that are relevant to the determination of subsequent effects, the stimulation of some particular region of the visual cortex should always result in the *same* kind of visual experience, regardless of what the causal antecedents of that stimulation are. In the case of my seeing the apple, the stimulation of the relevant region of my visual cortex results from a series of events beginning with light being reflected from the apple. But now suppose that the stimulation of this region of my visual cortex has a different set of causal antecedents. Suppose there are no apples in the visual field, or even anything that looks like an apple; in fact, my eyes are closed so I am unable to see anything. Nevertheless, we succeed in stimulating the relevant region of my visual cortex, perhaps through direct electrical stimulation. We know that direct stimulation of the visual cortex does produce visual experiences; such visual experiences are called *phosphenes* (Hardin 1988, p. 94). Supposing we could succeed in directly stimulating the same region of the visual cortex that was stimulated when I saw the apple, we would expect that I would have the *same* visual experience that I had when I saw the apple. But what is the force of "same" here? Presumably we would have a pair of indistinguishable experiences, experiences that present the same appearances. The former experience would be a perceptual experience of an apple. The latter experience would not be, for there is no apple to be seen; rather, it would be an hallucinatory experience of an apple. But the Theory of Appearing holds that perceptual and hallucinatory experiences are two different kinds of things: the former are relations between material objects and minds; the latter are not. So according to the Theory of Appearing, we have identical causes (two stimulations of an identical region of my visual cortex) giving rise to different effects. In one case the stimulation of my visual cortex gives rise to phenomenal features that instantiate relations between an apple and myself (the perceptual experience); in the second case the stimulation of exactly the same region of my visual cortex gives rise to phenomenal features of a different kind, phenomenal features that do *not* instantiate relations between an apple and myself (the hallucinatory experience). The defender of the Theory of Appearing must account for this apparent violation of the "same cause, same effect" principle.

I respond to the Causal Argument as follows. First, I argue that the "same cause, same effect" principle applies only to *intrinsic* changes: only intrinsic changes that result from the operation of identical causes must be the same. Intrinsic changes include changes in intrinsic properties of objects,[12] and changes in relations obtaining between objects whose intrinsic properties have changed. Second, I argue that although perceptual and hallucinatory experiences have different ontological characters (according to the Theory of Appearing), it is consistent with the Theory of Appearing that the *intrinsic* changes that accompany the occurrence of a perceptual experience, and the intrinsic changes that accompany the occurrence of the corresponding hallucination, are the same. I conclude that the Theory of Appearing need not be committed to the possibility of causes of the same kind producing different effects.

Why do I suppose that the "same cause, same effect" principle applies only to effects that are intrinsic changes? Consider the following situation. A worm is in the center of an otherwise empty ten foot long table. It crawls to the left edge of the table. Now consider an identical worm in the center of an identical table; the only difference is that there is now an empty soda can on the right edge of the table. The worm proceeds to do the same thing that it did previously: it crawls to the left edge of the table. We have the same causal process in the two cases: the worm crawling to the left edge of the table. Do we have the same effects? Clearly there is a sense of "effects" in which it can be said that the effects are different. In the second case, it is an effect of the worm crawling to the edge of the table that it is ten feet away from the soda can; in the first case, there is no soda can, and so it is not an effect of the worm's crawling that it is ten feet away from a soda can. Does this difference in "effect" show that we have a violation of the "same cause, same effect" principle here? Of course not. The soda can was not *affected* by the causal process at issue, and therefore its change in position with respect to the worm (or the worm's change in position with respect to it) does not count as an effect for purposes of the "same cause, same effect" principle. But why does its change in position not show that the soda can *was* affected by the causal process at issue? When we ask whether the soda can was affected, we are asking whether it underwent any *intrinsic* changes, that is, we are asking whether any of its intrinsic properties changed as the result of the worm crawling to the left edge of the table. Since none of its intrinsic properties did change, we say that the soda can was not affected, and therefore any resulting changes in the *relations* obtaining between the worm and the soda can do not count as effects for purposes of the "same cause, same effect" principle.

Let us apply these considerations to respond to the Causal Argument. We saw that, according to the Theory of Appearing, the stimulation of some portion of my visual cortex could in one case give rise to a relation obtaining between an apple and myself (a perceptual experience of an apple), and in a second case give rise to something different (an hallucinatory experience of an apple). The thrust of the Causal Argument is that this difference in "effect" is a violation of the "same cause, same effect" principle. But the analysis I gave of the worm cases also applies here to show that in fact this difference in "effect" does *not* count as a violation of the "same cause, same effect" principle (even according to the Theory of Appearing). In the worm cases, the crawling of the worm resulted in one case in a certain relation coming to obtain between the worm and the soda can: the worm and the soda can being ten feet apart; in the second case, the crawling of the worm did not have this result. Similarly, in the experience cases, the stimulation of my visual cortex results in one case in a certain relation coming to obtain between the apple and myself: the apple appearing to me (the perceptual experience); in the other case, the stimulation of my visual cortex does not have this result (the hallucinatory experience). In the worm cases, we concluded that the above described difference in "effect" does not count

as a difference in effect for purposes of the "same cause, same effect" principle. The change in spatial relation between the worm and the soda can
does not count as an effect, because none of the intrinsic properties of the
soda can were changed as the result of the worm crawling to the left edge
of the table, and therefore any changes in the relations that obtain between
the worm and the soda can do not count as effects for purposes of the
"same cause, same effect" principle. Similarly, in the experience cases, I
claim that the above described difference in "effect" is not a difference in
effect for purposes of the "same cause, same effect" principle. That the
apple comes to stand in the "appearing to" relation with respect to myself
does not count as an effect, because the apple, like the soda can, was not
affected by the causal process at issue. The stimulation of the relevant portion of my visual cortex did not cause any changes in the intrinsic properties of the apple, and therefore any resulting changes in the relations that
obtain between the apple and myself do not count as effects for purposes of
the "same cause, same effect" principle. Just as the spatial relations between
the soda can and the worm can change without any changes taking place
in the intrinsic properties of the soda can, so, too, it is consistent with the
Theory of Appearing that the apple can appear to me without any changes
taking place in its intrinsic properties.

What I have shown is that the mere claim that perceptual experiences
and hallucinations are *different*, in the sense that perceptual experiences
are relations between material objects and minds whereas hallucinations
are not, does not by itself commit the Theory of Appearing to possible violations of the "same cause, same effect" principle. This is because the
instantiation of such relations does not count as an effect for purposes of
the "same cause, same effect" principle (because it is not an intrinsic
change). More generally, I have argued that there are no intrinsic changes
that accompany the occurrence of a perceptual experience that do not also
accompany the occurrence of the corresponding hallucination.

I have *not* yet shown that there are no intrinsic changes that accompany
the occurrence of an hallucination that do not also accompany the occurrence of the corresponding perceptual experience. For with regard to the
phenomenal features of hallucinations, I have so far focused only on their
being different from the phenomenal features of perceptual experiences, in
that they are *not* relations between material objects and minds; I have not
described their ontological character in any positive way. Whether there
are intrinsic changes that accompany the occurrence of an hallucination
that do not also accompany the occurrence of the corresponding perceptual experience will presumably depend on what the correct account of

the ontological character of the phenomenal features of hallucinations turns out to be. Of course, if there are such intrinsic changes, then the Theory of Appearing is committed to possible violations of the "same cause, same effect" principle after all.

Let us recall that the Theory of Appearing is, in the first instance, a theory about the nature of perceptual experiences; although it must acknowledge that hallucinations are different from perceptual experiences with regard to their ontological character (section 2), it need not commit itself to any particular account of the ontological character of hallucinations. So long as there is some positive account of the nature of hallucinations which, when conjoined with the Theory of Appearing, does not have the consequence that the occurrence of an hallucinatory experience results in intrinsic changes that do not also result from the occurrence of the corresponding perceptual experience, then the Theory of Appearing is not committed to possible violations of the "same cause, same effect" principle. And there is no reason to think that no such positive account exists. Consider, for example, a view according to which the phenomenal features of hallucinations are relations between regions of physical space and minds, the regions of physical space in which the hallucinated objects seem to be. Now consider the conjunction of this view with the Theory of Appearing: according to this combined view, the stimulation of some portion of my visual cortex can in one case give rise to a certain relation coming to obtain between an apple and myself (a perceptual experience of the apple), and in another case give rise to a certain relation coming to obtain between a region of physical space and myself (an hallucinatory experience of an apple). In the case of the perceptual experience, I argued that the instantiation of a relation between the apple and myself does not count as an effect for purposes of the "same cause, same effect" principle, because the apple is not affected by the causal process at issue (the stimulation of my visual cortex). Similarly, in the case of the hallucinatory experience, the instantiation of a relation between a region of physical space and myself (the region of physical space where there seems to me to be an apple) also does not count as an effect for purposes of the "same cause, same effect" principle, for the region of physical space in question is not affected by the stimulation of my visual cortex. So the Theory of Appearing conjoined with this positive view as to the nature of the phenomenal features of hallucinations is not committed to possible violations of the "same cause, same effect" principle. Of course, much more would need to be said in order to defend this view of hallucinations; my purpose here has just been to say enough to show that there is no *prima facie* reason to think that the Theory of Appearing, when conjoined with a positive account of the nature of hallucinations, must be committed to the possibility of the same cause giving rise to different effects.

I have argued that the "same cause, same effect" principle applies only to effects that are intrinsic changes. In fact, the limitation of effects to intrinsic changes applies not only to the "same cause, same effect" principle, but to a variety of other contexts in which we are concerned with the nature of causal processes. For instance, it is often held that causal processes cannot operate at a spatial distance; more familiarly, "action at a distance" is impossible. In other words, the cause must be spatially *contiguous* to its immediate effect. Now it might be thought that the Theory of Appearing is committed to there being action at a distance. To return to our previous example, the immediate cause of my perceptual experience of the apple is the stimulation of some portion of my visual cortex. According to the Theory of Appearing, the phenomenal features of that experience instantiate relations between the apple and myself. So the effect of the stimulation of my visual cortex is that relations obtain between the apple and myself. The apple, as one of the relata, may be considered to be an *element* of the effect. And presumably the prohibition on action at a distance applies to elements of effects as well as effects. But the apple I see is not spatially contiguous to the stimulated region of my visual cortex. In other words, an element of the effect is not spatially contiguous to its cause. We apparently have a case of action at a distance.

In fact, we do not have a genuine case of action at a distance here. Action at a distance occurs only when the effect concerns the intrinsic properties of an object that is spatially separated from its immediate cause. As we have seen, the stimulation of my visual cortex results in relations obtaining between the apple and myself, but it does not affect the intrinsic properties of the apple, and consequently we have no action at a distance.

## 4   The Time-Gap Argument[13]

According to the Theory of Appearing, phenomenal features of perceptual experiences instantiate relations between material objects and minds. Let us attempt to describe the objects that stand in these relations in somewhat greater detail. Material objects have different properties at different times, and they *appear* differently at different times. Therefore, a visual perceptual experience, say, is not simply a relation between a material object and a mind, it is (at least) a relation that obtains between a material object *as it is at a particular time* and a mind. *Which* particular time is involved here?

It is natural to respond in the following manner. Experiences themselves occur at particular times, that is, the phenomenal features of experiences are instantiated at particular times. A perceptual experience is a relation between a material object and a mind, so to say that the perceptual experience occurs at some particular time is to say that the relevant relation obtains at some particular time. If a relation obtains at some particular time, then presumably the relation must obtain between objects as they are at that particular time. So, for instance, if right now Chelsea Clinton is five feet away from Roger Clinton, this simply means that Chelsea Clinton at the present time is five feet away from Roger Clinton at the present time. Similarly, if I have a perceptual visual experience of an apple and the experience occurs at time t, the experience is a relation that obtains between the apple as it is at time t and myself as I am at time t.

What the Time-Gap Argument claims is that this natural response is incorrect. Let us recall that visual perceptual experiences occur at the end of a long chain of causal events, a causal chain that begins with light being reflected from the object seen (if the object seen is opaque). The causal events in this chain do not occur simultaneously; some finite period of time (a "time-gap") must pass from the time light is reflected from the object seen to the occurrence of the visual experience. In order for a visual experience to occur, the light reflected from the object must first travel to the perceiver's eyes, and as light travels at only a finite speed, it cannot traverse the distance from the object seen to the eyes instantaneously.

As we shall see, the existence of this time-gap has some surprising consequences. Suppose my visual experience of the apple occurs at time t, and the light is reflected from the apple at time t–a, with "a" standing for some finite period of time. The character of the phenomenal features of a visual perceptual experience depends upon the composition and intensity of the light that is reflected from the object seen and subsequently reaches the eye. And the composition and intensity of the light that is reflected from the object seen is in part dependent upon the properties of the object's surface: its shape, orientation, molecular structure, etc. Of course, the nature of an object's surface may be different at different times. The character of my visual experience of the apple at time t is dependent upon the state of the apple's surface at time t–a, for it is at time t–a that the light is reflected from the apple's surface. Moreover, the character of my visual experience does *not* depend upon the state of the apple at any other time. For the character of my visual experience is affected by the apple *only* insofar as light is reflected from its surface at time t–a.

According to the Theory of Appearing, my visual experience of the apple, which occurs at time t, is a relation that obtains between the apple at some particular time and myself. *Which* particular time is involved here? Earlier I suggested that it is natural to suppose that if a relation obtains at some particular time, then the relation must obtain between objects as they are at that particular time. Applying this suggestion to the case at hand, we respond that my visual perceptual experience of the apple, which occurs at time t, is a relation that obtains between the apple *at time t* and myself at time t; in other words, the apple at time t visually appears to myself at time t. But we are now in a position to see that the existence of the time-gap has the consequence that this natural response is incorrect (the Time-Gap Argument). For the character of my visual experience depends not upon the state of the apple at time t, but upon the state of the apple at time t–a. Therefore, my visual experience of the apple, despite its occurrence at time t, cannot be a relation that obtains between the apple at time t and myself at time t. It cannot be the apple as it is at time t that is appearing to me, for the character of my visual experience depends not upon the apple as it is at time t, but upon the apple as it is at time t–a.

The proper response to the Time-Gap Argument should be apparent: the Theory of Appearing must reject the natural suggestion that if a relation obtains at some particular time, then the relation must obtain between objects as they are at that particular time. Although my visual experience occurs at time t, that is, although the "visually appearing to" relation between the apple and myself obtains at time t, the relation that obtains is between myself at time t and the apple at time t–a. This is the traditional response to the Time-Gap Argument, and, I believe, the correct one, but more needs to be said to make the response plausible. The natural suggestion I am rejecting is, in fact, a *natural* suggestion, and its negation might be thought to be puzzling. To say that my visual experience of the apple occurs at time t is to say that the phenomenal features of the experience are exemplified at time t; how can these phenomenal features be exemplified at time t and yet also instantiate a relation that obtains between myself at time t and an apple at some earlier time?

We need to be very careful in trying to express what exactly is supposed to be puzzling here. Certainly there is nothing puzzling in relations obtaining between objects as they are at different times. For instance, Abraham Lincoln in 1860 is taller than Ruth Westheimer in 1995. So if there is anything puzzling about my response to the Time-Gap Argument, it is not the positing of relations between perceivers at particular times and material objects at earlier times. Rather, what might appear puzzling is my claim that the relations themselves obtain at only one of these times, the later time. Here we have a clear contrast with the relation that obtains between Abraham Lincoln and Ruth Westheimer. Although we say that Abraham Lincoln in 1860 is taller than Ruth Westheimer in 1995, we do not say that the "is taller" relation that obtains between them obtains at any particular time. Certainly, we do not say that it obtains in 1860 as opposed to 1995, or vice versa; given that the relation obtains between an object as it is in 1860 and an object as it is in 1995, it would be absurd to say that the relation holds in one of these years as opposed to the other. And yet the Theory of Appearing does seem committed to this absurdity with respect to the "visually appearing to" relation. My visual experience of the apple is a relation that obtains between the apple at time t–a and myself at time t. And yet the relation itself obtains at only one of these times—at time t. For it is at time t that the phenomenal features of the experience are instantiated.

I proceed to show that what would be absurd when said about an instantiation of the "is taller than" relation is not absurd when said about an instantiation of the "appearing to" relation. There is a relevant difference between the two relations: the "is taller than" relation is an internal relation, whereas the "appearing to" relation is not. In David Lewis's words, "an internal relation is one that supervenes on the intrinsic nature of its relata: if X1 and Y1 stand in the relation but X2 and Y2 do not, then there must be a difference in intrinsic nature either between the Xs or else between the Ys" (1986, p. 62). The "is taller than" relation is internal, for it supervenes on the heights of its relata, and the height of a person is one of her intrinsic properties. That some person is taller than some other person is nothing over and above the following facts: the taller person is some particular height and the other person is some other particular height, the latter height being smaller than the former height. In other words, that the "is taller" relation obtains between two people is nothing over and above the instantiation by these people of certain intrinsic properties (being particular heights). In the example being considered, to say that Lincoln in 1860 is taller than Westheimer in 1995 is just to say that Lincoln's height in 1860 is greater than Westheimer's height in 1995. But then we should not be surprised that it would be absurd to say that this relation obtains in 1995 as opposed to 1860, or vice versa. For all there is to this relation obtaining is Lincoln being a certain height in 1860 and Westheimer being a certain smaller height in 1995.

But the "appearing to" relation is not an internal relation; that the "appearing to" relation obtains is something over and above the instantiation of certain intrinsic properties by its relata. This extra something is the instantiation of phenomenal features, features that, according to the Theory of Appearing, are not intrinsic properties of any of the relata. According to the Theory of Appearing, my perceptual visual experience of the apple is a relation that obtains between the apple at time t–a and myself at time t (the "appearing to" relation). But since the obtaining of this relation is something over and above the instantiation of intrinsic properties by the apple at time t–a and myself at time t, there is no reason why this relation cannot obtain at some particular time, say, at t, as opposed to t–a or some other time. On the contrary, the relation *must* obtain at some particular time, for the relation obtains when the phenomenal features of the experience are instantiated, and these features are instantiated at a particular time, in this case, at time t. The "appearing to" relation is similar to the "being thought about by" relation in this respect. Suppose I am thinking about my mother as she was ten years ago. The "being thought about by" relation obtains between my mother in 1985 and myself in 1995. But the relation itself obtains in 1995, not 1985, for the thinking itself, which is the instantiation of the relation, is going on in 1995. Similarly, my perceptual visual experience of the apple is the instantiation of the "appearing to" relation between the apple at time t–a and myself at time t, but the experience itself occurs at time t, not at time t–a. As the "appearing to" and "being thought about by" relations are not internal relations, we should not find these facts problematic. And therefore we should not find my response to the Time-Gap Argument at all puzzling.

Finally, it should be clear that my response to the Time-Gap Argument does not commit the Theory of Appearing to the existence of backward causation. Backward causation is causation in which the effect occurs prior in time to its cause. Many of us are inclined to believe that backward causation cannot occur. But it might be argued that if my experience of the apple, occurring at time t, is a relation between myself at time t and the apple at time t–a, then my experience must have been the result of backward causation. Recall that the immediate cause of my experience of the apple is the stimulation of my visual cortex. My visual cortex is stimulated after light has been reflected from the apple, so it is stimulated at some time after t–a. The effect of my visual cortex being stimulated is that a relation comes to obtain between the apple at time t–a and myself at time t. The apple at time t–a may be considered to be an element of the effect. But then we appear to have a case of backward causation here: the cause, the stimulation of my visual cortex, occurs at some time *after* t–a, and it produces an effect that includes as an element an apple as it is *at* time t–a.

In fact we do not have a genuine case of backward causation here. Although my visual experience is a relation between the apple at time t–a and myself at time t, the experience itself occurs at time t, *after* the stimulation of my visual cortex. It is true that an element of this experience is the apple as it is at time t–a. But the stimulation of my visual cortex does not affect the *intrinsic* properties of the apple as they are at time t–a or at any other time (section 3). And so we do not have a case of backward causation.

## 5  Naive Realism

The Theory of Appearing may be regarded as a form of naive realism.[14] I define naive realism as the view that phenomenal features are *properties* of material objects. Or, more precisely, it is the view that instantiations of phenomenal features are instantiations of properties of material objects. So far, I have characterized the Theory of Appearing as the view that phenomenal features (of perceptual experiences) are *relations* between material objects and minds. But whenever relations are instantiated, corresponding extrinsic properties are also instantiated, for objects instantiate extrinsic properties in virtue of standing in relations to other objects.[15] So, for example, if Sally is taller than Andrew, Sally instantiates the extrinsic property of being taller than Andrew and Andrew instantiates the extrinsic property of being shorter than Sally. Similarly, according to the Theory of Appearing, if, for example, an apple appears red to me, then the phenomenal feature of redness$_1$ is exemplified (section 2), the "appearing red" relation is thereby instantiated by the apple with respect to myself, and in virtue of standing in this relation, the apple also instantiates the extrinsic property of appearing red to me. More generally, according to the Theory of Appearing, instantiations of phenomenal features, in virtue of being instantiations of relations between material objects and minds, are also instantiations of extrinsic properties of material objects. So the Theory of Appearing can also be described as the view that instantiations of phenomenal features are instantiations of extrinsic properties of material objects (or, more simply, as the view that phenomenal features are extrinsic properties of material objects), and can therefore be regarded as a form of naive realism.[16]

Why do I wish to assimilate the Theory of Appearing to naive realism, to a theory whose very lack of credibility is made manifest in its name? Certainly naive realism was named by its detractors, in an attempt to suggest that only the naive could hold such a theory. But the detractors of naive realism do "protest too much." For it is not only the naive who subscribe to naive realism; we all implicitly hold this doctrine: it is part of our commonsense thinking about the world. More precisely, it is the Theory of Appearing that is part of our commonsense ("naive") thinking about the world, and I have assimilated the Theory of Appearing to naive realism precisely to highlight this "naive" aspect of the Theory of Appearing.

I find indirect support for my claim that the Theory of Appearing is part of our commonsense thinking about the world from the fact that many philosophers who reject the Theory of Appearing (and naive realism generally) are in effect forced to concede that naive realism is not simply the theory of the naive, it is the theory to which we all naturally commit ourselves. And insofar as they reject the Theory of Appearing, these philosophers are forced to concede that it is not only the naive who are misled; rather, we are all under an illusion as to the nature of our experiences and their relations to material objects. Thus C. L. Hardin, for example, notes that "[phenomenal] colors present themselves as properties of objects beyond the eyes, but this has proved to be an illusion, albeit a most durable one" (1988, p. 95).[17] It is an illusion according to Hardin because he holds that "colors are ... states of ourselves" (p. 82); "chromatic perceptual states ... are neural states" (p. 111). Similarly, Frank Jackson acknowledges that "colors appear to qualify objects distinct from us" (1977, p. 129), but as Jackson holds that colors are intrinsic properties of sense-data (which are not objects distinct from us), he must concede that this "appear[ance]" is an illusion.

What exactly do Hardin and Jackson mean when they talk of colors "appear[ing]" and "present[ing] themselves" as properties of external objects? What they mean (or what they should mean) is that we naturally take these colors, these visual phenomenal features,[18] to be properties of material objects. The visual phenomenal features do not force us to believe them to be properties of material objects by "appear[ing]" to us and "present[ing] themselves" to us in certain ways; rather, it is simply the case that we believe these visual phenomenal features to be properties of material objects (naive realism). According to my own account, we refer to these phenomenal features with two-place predicates (e.g., "appear red") and thereby think of them as extrinsic properties of material objects; in other words, we are committed to the Theory of Appearing. But the philosophers just cited hold that the Theory of Appearing is false, and therefore they are forced to characterize our belief in the Theory of Appearing as an illusion.

Surely it is an objection to those who reject the Theory of Appearing that they are forced to conclude that our commonsense thinking about the world is infected by a pervasive illusion. Why, then, do so many philosophers reject the Theory of Appearing? I suspect it is because they believe that the Theory of Appearing is unable to respond to the Argument from Hallucination, the Causal Argument, and the Time-Gap Argument. (I am not suggesting that Jackson and Hardin in particular reject the Theory of Appearing for this reason.) But as I have shown (sections 2–4), the Theory of Appearing can adequately respond to each of these arguments. And so we may justifiably continue to believe in it, and to endorse our common-sense, "naive" thinking about the nature of our experiences and their relations to material objects.[19]

**Notes**

1. By "material objects," I mean perceptible physical objects such as medium-sized bodies.

2. In claiming that experience has a phenomenal character, I remain neutral on the question of whether this phenomenal character is determined by intentional features of experience or by intrinsic, nonintentional features of experience ("qualia"). In general, the theory I defend in this paper takes no position on the question of whether qualia exist.

3. In fact, my talk of *the* phenomenal feature of redness is somewhat imprecise, for as I explain in section 2, the theory that I am defending must posit *two* distinct phenomenal features of redness, one that is instantiated in perceptual experiences, and one that is instantiated in hallucinations. Nevertheless, I shall continue to speak in this introductory section of *the* phenomenal feature of redness, so as not to complicate matters unduly at this early stage of the discussion.

4. It should be clear that I am using the word "feature," as in "phenomenal feature," in such a way that a feature can belong to *any* ontological category: a feature can be a property, or a relation, or can belong to some other ontological category. In other words, the word "feature" is meant to be neutral with respect to the ontological category or categories to which the feature belongs. There is perhaps a different use of the word "feature" according to which it is just a synonym for "property"; I am *not* using the word in this latter sense.

5. See, for example, Jackson (1977, p. 129) and McGinn (1983, p. 132).

6. See Chisholm (1971) for a general discussion of the Theory of Appearing. An early discussion of the Theory of Appearing can be found in Moore (1922, pp. 244–246).

7. Jackson (1977, pp. 96–99) argues against the Theory of Appearing by claiming that its analysis of "looks-statements" (e.g., "The apple looks red to me") is inferior to that provided by the causal theory. I do not find his arguments persuasive. The *locus classicus* of the causal theory is Grice (1961). An even earlier discussion of the theory can be found in Price (1950). Specific versions of the causal theory can be

found in Chisholm (1957), Jackson (1977, chapter 7), Goldman (1977), and Tye (1982).

8. For discussions of the Argument from Hallucination, see, for example, Price (1950, chapter II), Ayer (1956, pp. 87–95), Pitcher (1971, pp. 13–20), and Snowdon (1992). I do not discuss the Argument from Illusion, for as Price acknowledges (1950, p. 62), the Theory of Appearing has an obvious and adequate response to the Argument from Illusion. Similarly, Moore recommended the Theory of Appearing on the basis of its ability to provide a response to the Argument from Illusion (1922, pp. 244–246).

9. So sometimes I will use the term "phenomenal features" to refer to universals of a certain kind, and at other times I will use the term to refer to instantiations of such universals in experiences of certain kinds (e.g., "phenomenal features of hallucinatory experiences"). The sense in which the term is being used will always be clear from the context.

10. The Disjunctive Conception of Experience is defended by Hinton (1973) [excerpted in this volume, chapter 2], McDowell (1982) [excerpted in this volume, chapter 5], and Hyman (1992). See especially McDowell's use of the theory to respond to the Argument from Illusion (1982). Further discussions of the Disjunctive Conception can be found in Snowdon (1981, 1990) [this volume, chapters 3, 4], McDowell (1986) and Child (1992). Although Hinton is generally credited with the formulation of the Disjunctive Conception of Experience, the basic idea is also considered, but ultimately rejected, by Price (1950, pp. 31–32). See also Austin (1962, p. 52).

11. A particularly fine presentation of the Causal Argument can be found in Robinson (1985, section IV). As far as I am aware, defenders and expositors of the Disjunctive Conception of Experience have not, for the most part, attempted to respond to the Causal Argument. As Robinson observes, the "two most recent exponents [of the Disjunctive Conception of Experience], Snowdon and McDowell, ignore the difficulties posed for the theory by allowing that perception and hallucination might have the same immediate cause" (p. 174). Hinton is the one defender of the Disjunctive Conception of Experience who does attempt to respond to the Causal Argument (1973, pp. 75–93) [excerpted in this volume, pp. 28–30]; unfortunately, I do not understand Hinton's response and thus cannot evaluate it. Robinson discusses and criticizes Hinton's response at pp. 175–177.

12. I am using the word "objects" in a narrow sense, according to which such entities as events, states, and processes are not objects.

13. Probably the most careful discussion of the Time-Gap Argument is Suchting (1969). Other recent discussions include Ayer (1956, pp. 93–95), Armstrong (1961, pp. 144–152), Dretske (1969, pp. 71–75), and Pitcher (1971, pp. 44–50). Note that the Time-Gap Argument is sometimes called the Time-*Lag* Argument.

14. Price characterizes the Theory of Appearing as a "modification" of naive realism (1950, p. 54). I define both the Theory of Appearing and naive realism slightly differently from the way Price does.

15. See Lewis (1986, p. 61): "We distinguish *intrinsic* properties, which things have in virtue of the way they themselves are, from *extrinsic* properties, which they have in virtue of their relations or lack of relations to other things."

16. A different form of naive realism is the view that phenomenal features are *intrinsic* properties of material objects. A discussion of this view is beyond the scope of this paper; I will simply note that I do not believe that this view can provide an adequate account of perceptual illusions.

17. Hardin goes so far as to say that "colored objects are illusions" (1988, p. 111). See also Hardin's discussion of the "externality of colors," that which makes colors "seem to be outside our bodies" (p. 82).

18. Both Jackson and Hardin hold the view that the visual phenomenal features *are* the colors. Note that the Theory of Appearing is not committed to this view; it is perfectly consistent with the Theory of Appearing to hold that whereas visual phenomenal features (i.e., color appearances) are relations between material objects and minds, colors are intrinsic properties of material objects. According to this latter view, color illusions occur when there is a lack of correspondence between an object's color and its color appearance.

19. I would like to thank Eric Hiddleston, Susanna Siegel, Todd Blanke, Gilbert Harman, Margaret Wilson, David Lewis, and Gideon Rosen for comments on earlier drafts of this paper. An earlier version of this paper was read at the University of Virginia; I would also like to thank Daniel Devereux, Mitchell Green, Paul Humphreys, and George Thomas for their comments on that occasion.

## References

Armstrong, D. M. 1961. *Perception and the Physical World*. London: Routledge and Kegan Paul.

Austin, J. L. 1962. *Sense and Sensibilia*. London: Oxford University Press.

Ayer, A. J. 1956. *The Problem of Knowledge*. Harmondsworth, England: Pelican Books.

Child, W. 1992. Vision and experience: The causal theory and the disjunctive conception. *Philosophical Quarterly* 42, 297–316.

Chisholm, R. J. 1957. *Perceiving*. Ithaca: Cornell University Press.

Chisholm, R. J. 1971. The theory of appearing. In M. Black (ed.), *Philosophical Analysis*, pp. 97–112. New York: Books for Libraries.

Dretske, F. 1969. *Seeing and Knowing*. Chicago: University of Chicago Press.

Flanagan, O. 1992. *Consciousness Reconsidered*. Cambridge: MIT Press.

Goldman, A. 1977. Perceptual objects. *Synthese* 35, 257–284.

Grice, P. 1961. The causal theory of perception. In his *Studies in the Ways of Words*, pp. 224–247. Cambridge: Harvard University Press, 1989.

Hardin, C. L. 1988. *Color for Philosophers*. Indianapolis: Hackett Publishing Co.

Harding, G. 1991. Color and the mind-body problem. *Review of Metaphysics* 45, 289–307.

Hinton, J. M. 1973. *Experiences*. Oxford: Clarendon Press.

Hyman, J. 1992. The causal theory of perception. *Philosophical Quarterly* 42, 277–296.

Jackson, F. 1977. *Perception*. Cambridge: Cambridge University Press.

Lewis, D. 1986. *On the Plurality of Worlds*. Oxford: Basil Blackwell.

Loar, B. 1990. Phenomenal states. In J. Tomberlin (ed.), *Philosophical Perspectives* 4, *Action Theory and Philosophy of Mind*, pp. 81–108. Atascadero, California: Ridgeview Publishing Co.

McDowell, J. 1982. Criteria, defeasibility and knowledge. *Proceedings of the British Academy* 68, 455–479.

McDowell, J. 1986. Singular thought and the extent of inner space. In P. Pettit and J. McDowell (eds.), *Subject, Thought and Context*, pp. 137–168. Oxford: Clarendon Press.

McGinn, C. 1983. *The Subjective View*. Oxford: Clarendon Press.

McGinn, C. 1991. *The Problem of Consciousness*. Oxford: Basil Blackwell.

Moore, G. E. 1922. *Philosophical Studies*. London: Routledge and Kegan Paul.

Nagel, T. 1974. What is it like to be a bat? *Philosophical Review* 83, 435–450.

Pitcher, G. 1971. *A Theory of Perception*. Princeton: Princeton University Press.

Price, H. H. 1950. *Perception*. 2d ed. London: Methuen and Co.

Robinson, H. 1985. The general form of the argument for Berkeleian idealism. In J. Foster and H. Robinson (eds.), *Essays on Berkeley*, pp. 163–186. Oxford: Clarendon Press.

Robinson, H. 1990. The objects of perceptual experience II. *Proceedings of the Aristotelian Society*, Supplementary Volume 64, 151–166.

Sellars, W. 1963. *Science, Perception and Reality*. London: Routledge and Kegan Paul.

Snowdon, P. 1981. Perception, vision, and causation. In J. Dancy (ed.), *Perceptual Knowledge*, pp. 192–208. Oxford: Oxford University Press.

Snowdon, P. 1990. The objects of perceptual experience I. *Proceedings of the Aristotelian Society*, Supplementary Volume 64, 121–150.

Snowdon, P. 1992. How to interpret "direct perception." In T. Crane (ed.), *The Contents of Experience*, pp. 48–78. Cambridge: Cambridge University Press.

Strawson, P. 1979. Perception and its objects. In G. McDonald (ed.), *Perception and Identity*, pp. 41–60. Ithaca: Cornell University Press.

Suchting, W. A. 1969. Perception and the time-gap argument. *Philosophical Quarterly* 19, 46–56.

Tye, M. 1982. A causal analysis of seeing. *Philosophy and Phenomenological Research* 42, 311–325.

# 12   The Obscure Object of Hallucination

Mark Johnston

Like dreaming, hallucination has been a formative trope for modern philosophy. The vivid, often tragic, breakdown in the mind's apparent capacity to disclose reality has long served to support a paradoxical philosophical picture of sensory experience. This picture, which of late has shaped the paradigmatic empirical understanding of the senses, displays sensory acts as already complete without the external world; complete in that the direct objects even of veridical sensory acts do not transcend what we could anyway hallucinate. Hallucination is thus the mother of Representationalism, which insists that it is mental intermediaries that make other things and other people available to the subject of experience. When stimulated the senses produce representations or images, and it is only by grace of appropriate causal origin that these count as of or about external objects. Consequently, all the senses directly reveal about external objects is how they affect us; they show us nothing of how such objects are in themselves.

However paradigmatic this picture has become, it must be swept aside in order to command a clear view of the matter. But the picture is grounded in a battery of arguments with a considerable lineage and much to be said for them.

The argument from hallucination begins from the disputed, but not ultimately deniable, fact that there could be cases in which delusive and veridical sensings really are indistinguishable from the point of view of the one enjoying them. It attempts to confound so-called Direct Realism by concluding that quite generally objects of the same category exhaust all that is directly present in delusive and veridical sensings. Yet this conclusion seems at odds with the evident fact that veridical sensing is an *original*

Mark Johnston, "The Obscure Object of Hallucination," *Philosophical Studies* 120: 113–183. © 2004 Kluwer Academic Publishers. Reprinted with kind permission from Springer Science and Business Media.

source of knowledge of *external particulars*. Sensing continually expands the topics of our thought and talk. By contrast, hallucination is in this respect *derivative*, in a quite precise sense, which I shall attempt to explain. It thus appears that the objects present in veridical sensing are not exhausted by those that could be given to a mere hallucinator.

Many who take that view have attempted to diagnose definitively the error in the argument from hallucination. Success has proved elusive.[1] There are a variety of arguments from hallucination. One such argument seems to me to contain no error at all; namely the explanatory appeal to a common factor in veridical sensing and hallucination in order to account for (i) subjectively seamless transitions between certain cases of sensing and hallucination, and (ii) the distinctive features of hallucination itself.

Yet I am a "Direct" Realist, and a radical one at that.

If this combination of Direct Realism and acceptance of an argument from hallucination seems puzzling, I suggest that this is because many of the currently dominant options in the philosophy of perception are ill-posed.[2] This is particularly true when it comes to the controversy between so-called Conjunctivists and Disjunctivists over the nature of hallucination and veridical sensing.

Throughout, I mainly shall concentrate on seeing. The central points can be straightforwardly adapted to sensing in general.

1. The Conjunctive Analysis of seeing has it that when a subject is seeing

(i)   the direct object of her visual awareness is not some particular in the external environment, but something that she could be aware of even if she were hallucinating,

and—the crucial conjunction—

(ii)   by contrast with the hallucinatory case, her visual awareness is appropriately caused by some external particular in the scene before the eyes. Thanks to this causal connection the material particular counts as an indirect object of experience.[3]

Any Sense Datum Theory that treats sense data as the only objects of immediate awareness, and treats the distinction between hallucination and seeing along the lines of (ii), is obviously a version of the Conjunctive Analysis. But other models, sometimes offered as real alternatives to such Sense Datum Theories, such as the Adverbial Theory and various Intentionalist accounts of visual experience, can also take a Conjunctive form.[4] Central to the Conjunctive Analysis, as I am understanding it, is the deployment of the idea of a direct object of experience and the implication that the only direct objects of experience are those that could be presented in hallucination.

2. There is an influential argument for the Conjunctive Analysis, an argument from observations about hallucination and a very plausible principle governing causation. The argument also serves to introduce the contrast between direct and indirect objects of experience. It will be instructive to see just what is wrong with this argument, and whether it nonetheless serves to provide some constraints on an account of hallucination.

The argument for the Conjunctive Analysis begins with and depends on a distinction; a distinction between the fact that someone is hallucinating, which entails that he is not seeing, and the fact that he is enjoying an act of awareness of a certain kind, a mental act with a certain character and directed at certain objects, namely *the act of awareness that happens to be involved in hallucination*. The point of the distinction is to suggest that this second is a kind of act that might happen to occur in non-hallucinatory cases as well. The subsequent argument aims to have us accept that the kind of act of awareness involved in hallucination supervenes just on the state of the subject's brain, in the sense that an occurrence of an act of such a kind requires no more than the subject's brain being in a certain state.

To that end, the next observation is hard to resist: Whatever the relevant state of the subject's brain might be, the subject can get into the relevant state in two relevantly different ways. In the standard case—the case of seeing—that state is the last effect of a causal chain beginning with light coming from the object, then continuing with the stimulation of the retina and the optic nerve, then involving the activation of the visual cortex. In the non-standard case—the case of hallucinating—the earlier parts of the causal chain involving the external object, light (and perhaps the optic nerve) are bypassed. The same kind of state of the visual system, indeed the same kind of total brain state, can be produced either way.

Now we have a crucial step. If in the case of hallucination such a total brain state is sufficient for the act of awareness involved in hallucination, how could it cease to be sufficient for that kind of act of awareness when the very same kind of total brain state is caused by a longer, more involved causal process, say the causal process characteristic of seeing? The act of awareness involved in hallucination has a certain character, and is an awareness of whatever object it is an awareness of, just thanks to the occurrence of that total brain state.

In defense of the step, the following sort of thing can be said. If we were to hold that a different kind of act of awareness—say, one with different kinds of objects—was caused or constituted by the same kind of brain state when that brain state was itself caused in the standard way then we would be committed to something extremely odd. We should have to suppose something akin to action at a distance. For the brain state would have to "look back" and inspect its causal antecedents in order to see what mental act to cause or constitute. Otherwise, how could brain state "know" that it should cause or constitute direct awareness of things in the environment when it was preceded by a normal causal chain going all the way out through the visual system to an external object? How could the brain state "know" to instead cause or constitute the kind of visual awareness involved in hallucination, awareness which is not of any object there in the scene before one's eyes, in the case where there was no such normal external connection? Obviously there is no such action at a distance or "looking back." The brain state does not know such things. Irrespective of how it is caused, the brain state causes or constitutes an act of awareness with a certain character and directed at certain objects, the very type of act of awareness that occurs in the hallucinatory case.

We have no choice then, so the argument goes, but to suppose that in the pair of cases at hand the same type of proximate physical cause produces or constitutes the same type of immediate mental effect, i.e. the type of act of awareness that is present in the case of hallucination. That is to say that the same type of act of awareness is present in a case of seeing and a case of hallucination. Since types of acts of awareness are plausibly individuated by the types of objects that they present to the subject, this common type of act of awareness is not an awareness of objects of different types or categories. It is an awareness of the kind of thing that one could be aware of even if one were hallucinating.

Although that is a substantial result (if it is a result), as yet the argument has not delivered the Conjunctive Analysis. For all the argument has shown so far, it remains an open possibility that in the case of seeing as well as the common act of awareness there is another act of awareness, to wit, the act of being directly aware of external objects and their visible features. Since acts of awareness are plausibly individuated by their direct objects, this would be an act of awareness not identical with any act of awareness common to seeing and hallucination.

The second part of the argument for the Conjunctive Analysis mops up. It examines versions of this last possibility and aims to rule out those inconsistent with the Conjunctive Analysis.

To proceed in just this way: One option is that this further act of awareness that is seeing is wholly distinct from the common act of awareness, i.e. does not overlap with it or include it as a proper part. But this is difficult to accept. For it would follow that in the case of seeing there are two wholly distinct acts of visual awareness, the one awareness of external objects and the other awareness of what one could be aware of even if one were hallucinating. Now consider the qualitative aspect of what a subject is aware of in the two allegedly distinct mental acts. Surely it would have to be the same or at least subjectively indistinguishable for the subject. Otherwise a subject who has been seeing lights on in a ceiling and who has his seeing "short-circuited" by direct stimulation of the relevantly active parts of his brain would be in a position to notice that the change has taken place. And we know that this need not be so. (The reasons for granting this premise are set out in detail below.) Thus we are involved in supposing that whenever a subject is seeing there are two wholly distinct—as it were parallel—acts of visual awareness, each of the same or indistinguishable qualities. And that is not a comfortable resting place. Accordingly, we should reject the first option.

The remaining options are that the two acts of awareness have a part in common or that the one wholly contains the other. But it is puzzling how to model this. What is it for one act of awareness to overlap another or include another as a proper part? One act of awareness might be directed at a second and so have the second as its object, but this is not at all relevant here. For neither seeing nor the common act of awareness is an act of awareness whose *object* is an act of awareness.

The friend of the Conjunctive Analysis offers what he supposes is the only tenable model. The act of awareness involved in seeing must simply be the common act of awareness "augmented" in a certain way, namely by being causally connected to external particulars. The act of awareness involved in seeing must be no more than the common act of awareness, *an act of awareness that also happens to count as "of" external objects because it is appropriately caused by those objects.* In seeing there is no second act of awareness with a different direct object. In seeing there is a single act of awareness whose direct objects are exhausted by what one could be aware of even if one were hallucinating. But that act of awareness has external particulars as its "indirect" objects in just this sense: It is appropriately caused by those external particulars.[5]

This argument for the Conjunctive Analysis is an inference to an explanatory model that purports to best account for the consequences of the narrow supervenience of the act of awareness involved in hallucination.[6] The argument also has the advantage of explicating the otherwise obscure distinction between direct and indirect objects of awareness: something gets to be an *indirect* object by being the appropriate cause of an act of awareness already individuated in terms of other objects of awareness. The argument elaborates an old thought, which some find in Malebranche, who puts matters this way:

> Now on the supposition that the world was annihilated and that God nevertheless produced the same traces in our brains ... we should see the same beauties ... What I see when I look at your room will be visible even should your room have been destroyed and even I might add, if it had never been built.[7]

In modern jargon; having the kind of awareness involved in hallucination supervenes on states of one's brain. Those states could match the brain states of one who is seeing. So the one who is seeing must be having the same kind of awareness, albeit caused by appropriate objects.

Despite the venerable credentials of the argument, we should reject the Conjunctive Analysis of veridical sensory awareness, especially its maneuvering with the direct/indirect distinction. What is so odd about the analysis is that it entails that the objects of hallucination are present to us in a way that external particulars cannot be, *even when we are seeing external particulars*. We should instead hold out for a view to the effect that when we see, or more generally sense, external particulars those particulars are no less "directly" present to us than anything is in hallucination.

That is after all the best explanation of why the external particulars that are sensed can be immediately demonstrated, and so become topics for thought, talk and, in fact, even subsequent hallucination. Such immediate demonstration does not go by way of the conjectural hypothesis that there really are external objects which are the appropriate causes of the acts of sensory awareness that one is enjoying. Yet someone who accepted and lucidly understood the Conjunctive Analysis would be justified in regarding the presence of external particulars as at most a reliable conjecture concerning extrinsic connections between his visual experience and external causes. So even when he takes himself to be seeing and not hallucinating he might express his lucid understanding by picking external objects out as "the appropriate causes of this sensory experience." But as against this implication of the Conjunctive Analysis, our relation to the things we are seeing is not well captured in this way. We can successfully demonstrate them without relying explicitly or implicitly on such a conjectural causal description. When we see particular things, they are just presented as there to be attended to and demonstrated. They are the antecedent hinges to which we can attach descriptions that then serve to identify things not seen or sensed. Without external particulars immediately seen or sensed, the whole scheme of descriptive identification of particulars would be ungrounded.

In order to attend to and demonstrate what we see, we certainly need no more in the way of implicit auxiliary assumptions than we need to attend to and demonstrate the items that we hallucinate. This suggests that external particulars are as "directly" present to us as anything that is present to us in hallucination.

Moreover, the Conjunctivist's direct/indirect distinction has no phenomenological rationale. There is no good phenomenological sense in which, when I see the pattern in the Persian carpet, which pattern I could also hallucinate, I am more directly aware of the pattern than I am of the carpet. We should aim to do without this invidious distinction, which counts the particulars we see as derivative objects of awareness.

Nonetheless, the argument from the narrow supervenience of hallucination presents a challenging constraint. We must find a way to combine the common object of awareness that is arguably present in hallucination and seeing with the no less "direct" awareness of external objects that is definitive of seeing. We cannot treat the common object of awareness and the objects of the act of seeing as wholly distinct. Nor should we treat the distinctive objects that are seen as "indirect" objects of awareness in the fashion of the Conjunctive Analysis. We need to put the common object of awareness together with the distinctive objects which we see without merely *tacking on to* the common object of awareness the external objects which we see.

Before developing a positive account which does precisely this, let me deal first with the now widespread claim that no such account is really needed, thanks to the viability of so-called "Disjunctivism."

3. One way to avoid saying that items are present to us in hallucination in a way that external particulars could never be present to us, even when we are seeing, is to avoid saying much at all about hallucination. In the contemporary debate, the Conjunctive Analysis is often opposed by self-styled "Disjunctivists," who pursue this strategy in a principled way. They hold that there is nothing more to be said about pairs of indistinguishable veridical and delusive sensings of say, a dagger hanging in the air, than the following. In the veridical case one *is* seeing a dagger hanging in the air, while in the delusive case one *merely seems* to be seeing a dagger hanging in the air. On this view, there is no neutral condition—the appearing of a

dagger—common to indistinguishable cases of seeing and hallucination. There is only a neutral disjunctive description that applies to both cases. You are either seeing a dagger or you just merely or falsely seem to be seeing a dagger. Call it "the appearing of a dagger" if you like, but remember that that is just shorthand for a disjunctive report, not the description of a kind of mental act common to hallucination and seeing.[8]

The Disjunctivist has a quick way with the argument from the narrow supervenience of the act of awareness involved in hallucination. What narrowly supervening act of awareness? According to the Disjunctivist, all we need is to recognize the fact that people hallucinate. And it is agreed on all sides that the fact that someone is hallucinating does not narrowly supervene on his brain state. For there could be neural duplicates, one of whom is seeing while the other is hallucinating. The Disjunctivist just denies that there is an interesting type of mental act that supervenes just on one's brain state. Seeing a dagger does not, and merely seeming to see a dagger does not. The first step in the argument for the Conjunctive Analysis—the crucial motivating distinction—is rejected.

4. It is worth noting that Disjunctivism is self-consciously a strategy for resisting Conjunctivism, not the mere negation of Conjunctivism. So both could be false. Disjunctivism is a disjunctive account of the neutral notion of sensing, or more specifically, of having a visual experience. Its central claim is that there is no act of awareness common to cases of hallucination and seeing. On the other hand, the Conjunctive Analysis is an analysis of seeing by *genus* and *differentia*; an analysis that first demarcates the genus of visual experience in terms of a conjunct that could be satisfied whether or not one was seeing or hallucinating, and then attempts to differentiate seeing by way of a second conjunct that requires a certain kind of causal connection between the subject's experience and an external object. And it is crucial to the Conjunctive Analysis, as I am understanding it, that it makes the invidious distinction between direct and indirect objects of awareness. Accordingly, as against both Disjunctivism and Conjunctivism there could be a common factor—an act of awareness common to hallucination and seeing—but no good sense in which the objects of hallucination are more direct objects of awareness than the objects seen.

Thus, rejecting the Conjunctive Analysis is one thing, accepting the Disjunctive View is quite another. In fact, the Disjunctive View is deeply unexplanatory when it comes to accounting for (i) certain phenomenologically seamless transitions from hallucination to seeing, and (ii) the distinctive nature of hallucination itself.

5. Here is an example that will serve as our stalking horse. You are undergoing an operation for an aneurysm in your occipital lobe. The surgeon wants feedback during the operation as to the effects of the procedure on the functioning of your visual cortex. He reduces all significant discomfort with local anaesthetic while he opens your skull. He then darkens the operating theater, takes off your blindfold, and applies electrical stimulation to a well-chosen point on your visual cortex. As a result, you hallucinate dimly illuminated spotlights in a ceiling. (You hallucinate lights on in *a* ceiling. As yet, you are not at all aware of *the* lights or *the* ceiling of the operating theater.) As it happens, there really are spotlights in the ceiling at precisely the places where you hallucinate lights. However, these real lights are turned off, so that the operating theater is too dark to really see anything. (Well, all right, the surgeon has a small light to see into the back of your skull.)

While maintaining the level of electrical stimulation required to make you hallucinate lights on in a ceiling, the surgeon goes on to do something a little perverse. He turns on the spotlights in the ceiling, leaving them dim enough so that you notice no difference. You are now having what some call a "veridical hallucination." You are still having a hallucination for you are not yet seeing the lights on in the ceiling, the explanation being that they still play no causal role in the generation of your experience. Yet your hallucination is veridical or in a certain way true to the scene before you; there are indeed dim lights on in a ceiling in front of you.

In the third stage of the experiment the surgeon stops stimulating your brain. You now genuinely see the dimly lit spotlights in the ceiling. From your vantage point there on the operating table these dim lights are indistinguishable from the dim lights you were hallucinating. The transition from the first stage of simple hallucination through the second stage of veridical hallucination to the third stage of veridical perception could be experientially seamless. Try as you might, you would not notice any difference, however closely you attend to your visual experience.

Of course, at the level of brain states, there will be some causal explanation for this experiential seamlessness. Whether one's brain is stimulated by the scene before one's eyes or by the direct application of electrical impulses, the effects on one's brain will be very similar in respects relevant to the causation of experience. This explanation in terms of brain states raises another explanatory question, which is our real concern. When we say that either way the effects on the brain are very similar in respects relevant to the causation of experience, we rely upon a picture according to which the differences at the level of brain states make no discernible difference at the level of experience. It is very likely that there are some intrinsic differences between the brain processes in the two cases. The idea of such differences not making a discernible difference at the level of experience begs for a characterization of what is taking place at the level of experience. Accordingly, our question is: What kinds of things can visual experience be a relation to so that in a case of hallucination and a case of seeing there need be no difference which the subject can discern? In itself, appeal to ever so slightly different brain states cannot answer that question.

It is a question that the Sense Datum Theory is designed to answer. According to that theory, in indiscernible cases of hallucination and veridical perception one is directly aware of mental items, that is, items which would not exist but for the experiences in question. Because of the similar or identical mental qualia they instantiate, these mental items are indiscernible, or at least not discernible by the subject in the circumstances. The difference between hallucination and veridical sensing is then this: in the veridical case the mental item is appropriately causally related to nonmental items, e.g. the lights on in the ceiling, that the mental item represents. In virtue of that relation holding in the veridical case one is aware of non-mental items *by* being aware of a mental item. The Sense Datum Theory can thus naturally endorse the Conjunctive Analysis of experience. For in its Non-Phenomenalist forms, the Sense Datum Theory treats veridical experience as the enjoying of an interior mental state that happens to be appropriately caused by an external non-mental item. The experiential element in seeing, the visual awareness involved in seeing, is something that could occur whether or not there are external objects.

But, once again, this is to provide a bad candidate for seeing. Of all of our mental acts, sensing in general, and seeing in particular, is the best candidate for direct acquaintance with the thing sensed or seen, and not just with something that could be present to us whether we are genuinely sensing or hallucinating. Hence the lack of appeal of any view which has it that items could be present to us in hallucination in a way that external particulars could never be present to us, even when we are seeing.

That is the insight properly emphasized by the Disjunctive View. But the Disjunctive View is not the best vehicle for developing the insight. The Disjunctive View has nothing satisfactory to say in answer to the pressing question: What kinds of things can visual experience be a relation to so that in a transition from a case of visual hallucination to a case of seeing there need be no difference which the subject can discern? Once the resources are found to address this question, the Disjunctive View will fall to the wayside.

In order to answer the pressing question, some friends of Disjunctivism have resorted to higher-order attitudes or acts to try to provide an account of delusive experience.[9] On this view, you are hallucinating lights on in a ceiling when it falsely seems to you that you are seeing lights on in a ceiling. Visually hallucinating a dagger is falsely seeming to oneself to be seeing a dagger.[10]

As against this, being susceptible to visual hallucination is a liability which just comes with having a visual system, i.e., comes with being able to see, and does not require the operation of the ability to think or believe or reflectively grasp the fact that you are seeing, any more than seeing requires this. It is not a higher-order mental act than the act of seeing itself. Consider, to vary an example of David Armstrong's, a dazed truck driver, who in the middle of the night negotiates the entrance to the Nullaboor Highway. Being on the verge of falling asleep, the driver is not aware of what he is doing. But what he did required him to see the traffic lights. Yet since he was oblivious to what he did, it seems forced to say that he seemed to himself to be seeing the traffic lights. Likewise, by a happy coincidence, a dazed truck driver could have had a veridical hallucination of the lights, again without his seeming to himself to be seeing the lights. To hallucinate lights, it need not seem to you that you are seeing lights. Hallucinations need not be grand nor phantasmagoric. They need not even be noticed by the hallucinator. One might hallucinate without ever noticing it, just as one never notices most of the faint after-images that fill one's visual experience.

The same thought emerges from a natural construal of the simplest animal seeing and hallucination. A fully "mind-blind" animal, an animal without attitudes directed at its own sensory acts, say *a cane toad*, could see the lights moving in the highway and scurry away. Likewise by happy coincidence, the same cane toad could suffer a veridical hallucination of lights moving and scurry away. In neither case does it deploy the concept of itself seeing things. So there is nothing which corresponds to the cane toad's seeming to itself to be seeing lights on the road. Why should hallucination, a certain kind of failure to see, require a more complex mental operation than seeing itself?

Furthermore consider that on the higher-order view of hallucination, hallucinating some number n lights is, on a first pass, to be analyzed as falsely seeming to oneself to see n lights. Now take a mixed case; a case of seeing the eleven lights on the ceiling while at the same time hallucinating eleven lights one for one "alongside" the lights one is seeing. In such a mixed case it could seem to one that one is seeing more than twenty lights.

There is an explanation for this: one really is seeing eleven lights and is hallucinating another eleven lights. But now on pain of incoherence we cannot tolerate the view that one's hallucinating eleven lights is its falsely seeming to one that one is seeing eleven lights. For by hypothesis, one is seeing eleven lights, and one is falsely seeming to oneself to be seeing more than twenty lights.

So the account should be developed as follows: hallucinating n lights is just to be analyzed as falsely seeming to oneself to see n more lights than one is in fact seeing. But we can ask for an explanation of why one falsely seems to oneself to be seeing n more lights than one is in fact seeing. And the natural, appealing and correct explanation is that one is hallucinating n lights. By treating this *explanans* as analytically equivalent to the *explanadum*, the higher-order attitude account of hallucination leaves no room for a perfectly good explanation.

The same point can be made against the theory in its unrefined form: It is *because* you are hallucinating n lights that you seem to yourself to be seeing n lights. But the point is, if anything, more compelling when the theory takes on the needed refinement: It is *because* you are hallucinating n more lights than you are really seeing that it seems to you that you are seeing n more lights than you really are seeing. The higher-order attitude account makes nonsense of perfectly good explanations by identifying *explanans* and *explanandum*.[11]

On top of all that, the higher-order attitude proposal—that visually hallucinating an F (or some number n Fs) is falsely seeming to oneself to be seeing an F (or n Fs)—faces still another objection, the objection from blindness denial. One night in bed I am struck blind, but I am so traumatized that I still seem to myself to be seeing the gloomy room around me. Need I be enjoying *a visual hallucination* of the room around me for this to be true? Not at all; it could be that I have no visual presentation whatsoever, yet my denial of this consists precisely in my seeming to myself still to see the room around me. Of course, this may in some sense be less than the full-blooded "falsely seeming to oneself to see" that does crucially involve visual hallucinations. But allowing that very distinction between kinds of seeming to see just serves to highlight the need for a substantive account of visual hallucination. And furthermore, there is the intermediate case of blindness denial in which I mistake an eidetic memory of a recent visual experience for a present visual experience. Although I am falsely seeming to myself to see an F, I am not visually hallucinating an F. So not only is falsely seeming to oneself to see an F not necessary for visually hallucinating an F, it is not sufficient either.

Moreover, just considering the case of blindness denial helps to make vivid the explanatory import of such remarks as: It is *because* you are hallucinating eleven lights that you seem to yourself to be seeing eleven lights. For the case of blindness denial shows that the cited *explanans* is not the only case in which the *explanandum* might hold. It could be a genuinely empirical question whether one seems to oneself to be seeing eleven lights because one is hallucinating eleven lights *or because* of one or another form of blindness denial.

The moral of the foregoing is this: Instead of the higher-order attitude account of hallucination, we need a first-order account of the objects of seeing and of hallucination, an account that explains why one could be mistaken for another, even though in seeing one is aware of external objects while in hallucination one is not. We should reject the Conjunctive Analysis, while also rejecting odd suggestions such as that all subjectively indistinguishable cases of hallucination and seeing have in common on the side of experience is that they are disjuncts in a disjunction, or that hallucination is an act of a higher-order than seeing.

After all, hallucination is a distinctive kind of mental act, related in systematic ways to veridical perception and illusion. Once such relations are set out in some detail, Disjunctivism will appear in its true colors, namely as a defensive failure fully to engage with the philosophical terrain. Disjunctivism's methodology is backwards; it arises as an attempt to answer the argument from hallucination, and not from an investigation of the distinctive features of hallucination itself.

6. The first philosophical question to ask about hallucination is whether it really admits of an act/object analysis. Is the hallucinator really encountering a genuine item in some category or other?

To begin on this issue, there seems nothing incoherent about Macbeth's self-interrogation: "Is *this* a dagger, which I see before me … or a fatal vision proceeding from a heat oppressed brain?" That remains so even if his question is paraphrased as "Is *this*, which I see before me, a dagger or a fatal vision proceeding from a heat oppressed brain?"[12]

The paraphrase highlights the appeal of an act/object account of hallucination. For it is natural to construe the thought the paraphrase expresses as a truly demonstrative thought, the having of which involves the hallucinator demonstrating an item and wondering to which category it belongs. In this sense the hallucinator's thought has a character and demonstrative content analogous to, say, the thought naturally expressed by "Is this, which I see before me, a dagger or a hologram of a dagger proceeding from some clever technology?" In each case it seems that the subject has attended to, and gone on to demonstrate an item, which is then the topic of his thought. As a result, there is in each case a determinate correct answer to the demonstrative question that the subject poses. So we may suppose that the "this" in question in the first, Macbeth-like case is not a dagger but a fatal vision, whatever exactly that turns out to be. And we may suppose that the "this" in question in the second case is not a dagger but a dagger-hologram. In both cases an item in some category or other is presented to the subject and then demonstrated. The character of the items in question determine the character of the sensory consciousness enjoyed by the subjects. In this respect, hallucination is akin to visualizing, in that its character as a sensory experience seems determined by an item that occupies the subject's visual attention.

Compare another case, where a serious demonstrative construal seems quite forced. Suppose that Frederick seeks the Spear of Longinus, the spear that according to John's Gospel pierced the side of Jesus on the cross. Frederick then discovers Form Criticism, and realizes that it is somewhat likely that the author of this very late gospel interpolated such an event so that a certain prophesy of Isaiah would appear to be vindicated. So Frederick wonders "Is this which I am seeking a real spear, or merely a fiction from a pious legend?" Here it seems clear that the occurrence of "this" is not really a demonstrative occurrence. It is not that Frederick is in any sense presented with some item, which occupies his visual attention and which he then demonstratively identifies so as to consider what category of thing it is. Frederick's thought could be expressed, without loss, in this demonstrative-free way: "Is what I am seeking a real spear, or merely a fiction from a pious legend?" So although the object of Frederick's seeking is the Spear of Longinus, this does not force on us a serious act/object analysis of seeking. For to say that the object of Frederick's seeking is the Spear of Longinus is just to say, in a roundabout way, that Frederick seeks the Spear of Longinus. Yes, the verb "seeks" obviously takes a grammatical object, but this does not show that seeking is always a relation to some item or other.

Contrast hallucination, where the argument for the act/object analysis does not depend on the fact that the verb "hallucinates" often takes a grammatical object, but rather on the fact that hallucination seems to serve up distinctive items for demonstration; items from which, as we shall see, we can learn certain novel things.

So I shall take it as a point against any account of hallucination if it does not treat hallucination as a distinctive kind of mental act directed upon an item that can occupy the subject's visual attention. I do not say that this is anything like a full-dress defense of the act/object account of hallucination. Such a defense would have to engage with the subtleties of the Adverbial Theory.[13] I mean only to provide a preliminary constraint, which an adequate theory *might*, in the end, flout. Still, a theory which was as explanatory as the allegedly adequate theory while nonetheless treating hallucination as a distinctive kind of directedness toward an item would be the one to prefer. That, at any rate, is what we shall be aiming for.

If we accept the act/object model of hallucination, we then must investigate the objects of hallucination. They show at least three interesting features.

The first is that although we can hallucinate real things and real people, no such hallucination could be an original source of *de re* thought about those particular things or people. In this way, hallucination differs from veridical sensing, which characteristically provides new particulars as topics for thought and talk. I can hallucinate my mother talking to me on the phone, but I could not do this unless I already had an independent way of making singular reference to my mother. If I had been abandoned to the monks at birth and knew nothing of my mother or of mothers in general, then I could not hallucinate my mother talking to me. Even if I hallucinated a woman who happened to look just like my mother, there would be nothing that would make that hallucination *of* my mother, as opposed to my aunt, or any other woman who appeared like her. Hallucination does not *introduce* particular topics for thought and reference. Hallucination of a specific mother or a specific dagger is parasitic upon *antecedent* singular reference to that mother or that dagger.

The point may be thrown into sharper relief by way of a putative counterexample to the claim that hallucination could not be an original source of *de re* thought about particulars. Suppose that in the fashion of *The Manchurian Candidate*, our hero is subjected to deep brain washing, but in this case to the following effect: One year after the brain washing he will hallucinate a particular politician he has never heard of, but is about to meet. The content of the hallucination will compel our hero to passionately kiss the politician when he meets him on a public occasion, thereby causing the politician to lose a crucial part of his electoral support. Surely, so the objection goes, our hero's hallucination was *of* the politician he was about to meet for the first time. So wasn't that hallucination an original source of *de re* thought, thought about the very politician that he subsequently met and kissed?

My answer will be no surprise. To the extent that we take the hallucination to be of the very politician in question, and not simply of a template that the politician happens to satisfy, to that extent we are thinking of the hallucination as a sort of mental picture which counts as *of* the politician because of the referential intentions of the brainwashers. It is only in so far as they intended our hero's hallucination to be of the politician that it is of the politician rather than just of a template that he happens to satisfy. Again, it is antecedent singular referential intentions, antecedent *de re* thoughts, which give the hallucination its directedness towards a particular person.

The next observation about the objects of hallucination involves a direct contrast on just this point, a contrast between hallucinating particulars and hallucinating the qualities that are either common to the senses or peculiar to the sensory modality in which one is hallucinating. I can secure my *first* singular reference to the quality cherry red or to the structural property C major by way of hallucinating a scene or a tune. Frank Jackson's Mary could come to know what red is like by hallucinating a red thing or by having a red afterimage. Indeed, we shall later encounter a case which implies that, as a matter of empirical fact, the paradigm red—the reddest of the reds—can only be presented in delusive experience. One can come to know what "supersaturated" red is like only by afterimaging it. While one is afterimaging it, one could compare how much more saturated it is than the reds exhibited by the reddest of the standard Munsell color chips, there before one on the table. Likewise, a painter might discover in hallucination a strange, alluring color, which he then produces samples of by mixing paints in a novel way. Here we have all the signs of *de re* knowledge of quality. One comes to know what certain qualities are like, and so one is able to place them in a quality-space with other qualities of the same family.[14]

I know of no satisfactory Disjunctivist account of the fact that hallucination can provide us with original *de re* knowledge of quality but not original *de re* knowledge of particulars. And as we make more observations about hallucination as such, the irritating unhelpfulness of Disjunctivism will become more evident.

The fact that hallucination can provide us with original *de re* knowledge of quality reinforces the case for the act/object account of hallucination. If I acquire original *de re* knowledge doesn't there then have to be a *res* from which I acquire it? The Adverbial Theorist will insist that the only *res* in play is an experience of a certain type. But the *de re* knowledge which hallucination can provide seems to be *de re* knowledge of a quality, and not necessarily of any experience type. I need not focus on any experience type as such. Indeed, I need not conceptualize my hallucinatory experience in any way. I may not even recognize that it is an hallucination, or even raise the question for my own consideration. Still, I can learn from my hallucination what a certain shade of red is like. How can I do this unless my hallucination involves awareness *of* that shade, unless that shade is an object of my awareness?

Furthermore, the fact that hallucination can provide us with original knowledge of quality, but not original knowledge of particulars, suggests that the primary object of hallucination is somehow more qualitative than particularized, that it is individuated in terms of properties rather than in terms of particulars.

A third observation reinforces this suggestion, for it points to one way in which particular objects of hallucination get determined as such. Suppose Noddy's aunt has a voice that sounds exactly like the voice of Noddy's mother. On Mondays, Wednesdays and Fridays Noddy dwells on his mother and her many virtues. On the other days of the week Noddy dwells on his aunt and her many virtues. Noddy also has a tendency to hallucinate, especially when he gets maudlin. So on Mondays, Wednesdays and Fridays Noddy hallucinates his mother calling his name over and over on the phone. On the other days of the week, Noddy hallucinates his aunt calling his name over and over on the phone. All this could be true even if all the qualities of Noddy's auditory presentations are the same on each day of the week. If one hallucinates a certain sound and it immediately strikes one as one's mother talking on the phone then it just follows that one has hallucinated one's mother talking to one over the phone. *Mutatis mutandis* with one's aunt talking to one over the phone. In such cases there is a sense in which one cannot go wrong about just who it is that one is hallucinating. For in such cases who it is one is hallucinating is determined by whom one immediately takes it to be.[15] If I waver and ask myself—"Is it my mother or my aunt that I am hallucinating?"—no particular person will be determinately the object of my hallucination.

Contrast the case of actually hearing one's mother over the phone. As it turns out, Noddy's family is very close. Both his mother and his aunt are concerned about Noddy's mental state, and they call him regularly. They have an arrangement that divides the labor of calling. Noddy's mother calls on Mondays, Wednesdays and Fridays, and Noddy's aunt calls on the other days of the week. But one Friday, Noddy's aunt substitutes for Noddy's mother. When she calls Noddy immediately takes himself to be hearing his mother. It immediately strikes him as his mother talking to him on the phone. But he is wrong about who it is that he is hearing on the phone. It is his aunt and not his mother. The particulars that are the objects of hearing are not determined by how the qualitative auditory array strikes the subject, in contrast to the particular objects of auditory hallucination, which are often so determined. (Perhaps they are determined within qualitative limits—even if I crazily take the hallucinated sound of my name to be Abraham Lincoln giving the Gettysburg Address, I won't have hallucinated Lincoln giving the Gettysburg Address. But something close to this seems possible in dreams, in which, for example, a blowfish might immediately strike me as William Jefferson Clinton.)

This suggests that we should distinguish primary and secondary objects of hallucination, where the secondary object is determined by how the primary object immediately strikes the subject. If the primary object were not particular but rather qualitative, this would explain why, when it comes to particulars, hallucination cannot be an original source of *de re* thought. As a first pass, hallucination gets to be of or about particulars as a result as striking the subject as of or about those particulars. Its so striking the subject depends upon the subject's existing repertoire of singular reference.

This predicts that one might have hallucinations that one does not construe as of this or that particular thing but simply takes on their own qualitative terms. Suppose I become a connoisseur of my own drug-induced hallucinations and dwell on their qualities as such. When I simply contemplate my hallucination it need not strike me as of this or that particular thing. If, in my contemplative mood, my hallucination does not strike me as *of* this or that particular thing then it will not be of this or that particular thing. So even if I had a visual presentation that was in every way just like that enjoyed by a hallucinator of a dagger, I might be hallucinating nothing more than a dagger-like array of visible qualities. I would be enjoying this primary object of hallucination and there would be no secondary object.

My thesis will be that items suited to be the primary objects of hallucination are the factors in common between hallucinations and corresponding veridical sensings, common factors that explain the possibility of seamless transitions from cases of hallucination to cases of veridical perception.

But before we turn to a general account of the primary objects of hallucination we need to remove the implication that hallucination gets to be of or about particulars *only* as a result of striking the subject as of or about those particulars. This certainly does happen, but it also seems that hallucinations can come with singular reference to certain particulars somehow built in. Cathected thought about one's mother might not only cause a specific hallucination but may also anchor the reference of that very hallucination to one's mother. To the extent that this is possible—and I only want to allow it as a possibility—a subject may be wrong about the secondary object of his hallucination. His hallucination may immediately strike him as of his aunt, even though it is of his mother. Likewise, one might sensibly wonder among a group of similar particulars which it is one is hallucinating. This might serve to make some sense of the psychoanalytic idea of a purely latent particular object of hallucination, one that is not at all manifest to the hallucinator.

Even if cathected thought about one's mother or about a certain dagger anchors the singular reference of a hallucination to that mother or that dagger, there is no need to qualify our earlier claim that hallucination is wholly derivative when it comes to singular reference to particulars. The supposition of "anchoring" itself presupposes antecedent singular reference to the mother or the dagger by way of the cathected thought responsible for the hallucination.

What does need elaboration is just the account of the relation between the primary and secondary objects of hallucination. Let the primary object incorporate everything about which the hallucination could provide original *de re* knowledge. Then we should allow that the particulars that are the secondary objects of the hallucination might be determined by two different mechanisms—the mechanism of anchoring or the mechanism of the primary object striking the subject a certain way. So in the right circumstances, Noddy could have a hallucination that was *of* his mother and *of* his aunt. It could be anchored to cathected thoughts about his mother, yet it could immediately strike him as of his aunt.

How then should we conceive of the primary objects of hallucination so that they could play the roles just described *and* be the common factors that are also among the objects of awareness in the corresponding veridical cases?

7. Here is a proposal concerning the primary objects of hallucination that at least has the right shape to account, first, for subjectively seamless transitions, and second, for the distinctive features of hallucination itself.

Consider the sensed field or scene before your eyes. Now attend to the relational and qualitative structure that is visibly instantiated there in the scene. It consists of just the properties and relations of which you are visually aware, when you are seeing the scene. It is a scene type or *sensible profile*, a complex, partly qualitative and partly relational property, which exhausts the *way* the particular scene before your eyes is if your present experience is veridical. This *way* that things are if your present experience is veridical involves a *layout*. Whichever particulars are implicated they have to stand at certain times in certain positions in a three-dimensional space at certain directions and distances from your position now. Despite including such relations to a particular place and time, the layout is a relational type rather than a token, a universal rather than a particular. Different things could instantiate the same spatio-temporal layout.

The sensible profile or *way* the scene is involves more than the layout. For example, it includes the further condition that the relational layout be filled in with some particulars or other that have such and such qualities. But again, this *way* the scene is could be instantiated by many different groups of particulars. The way is not particular but universal, not a token but a type, albeit a complex of relational and qualitative universals or types. While the sensible profile itself can be instantiated in the scene before the eyes only if each quality and relation in the complex is instantiated there, some of the qualitative and relational parts of the complex could be instantiated in the scene before the eyes while the whole profile or complex itself is not instantiated there.

Your seeing the scene before your eyes is your being visually aware of a host of spatio-temporal particulars instantiating parts of such a profile or complex of sensible qualities and relations. The suggestion is that in the corresponding case of a subjectively indistinguishable hallucination you are simply aware of the partly qualitative, partly relational profile. This means that the objects of hallucination and the objects of seeing are in a certain way akin; the first are complexes of sensible qualities and relations while the second are spatio-temporal particulars instantiating such complexes. The visual system is adapted to put us in contact with the scenes or visible instantiations around us. When the visual system misfires, as in hallucination, it presents uninstantiated complexes of sensible qualities and relations, at least complexes not instantiated there in the scene before the eyes.[16]

A refinement is needed to capture the attractive idea that thanks to our conceptual sophistication we often non-inferentially see things as members of various kinds. As I wrote this, among the things that I was seeing out of the corner of my eye was an Italian greyhound, sitting under my desk. The Sony Corporation is now making dog-robots: they run, they bark and they wet the carpet. (Though that, I understand, is only available on the deluxe model.) I suppose that they can sit under desks. Perhaps Sony could make a dog-robot that out of the corner of my eye I might mistake for Lucca, the Italian greyhound. But if we are fully to capture what I was seeing when I wrote this, we would have to mention an Italian greyhound, seen *as such*. My visual awareness was not merely qualitative in a way that allowed for some other kind of thing, a mere simulacrum of an Italian greyhound, being under my desk. The sensible profile that had to be instantiated before me if my act of visual experience was to be veridical involves the kind Italian Greyhound, or so I suppose. After all, it was thanks to veridical experience and some modest conceptual sophistication that I first came pick out the breed Italian Greyhound by asking an owner on the street "What breed is THAT?"

Contrast a visual hallucination subjectively indistinguishable from what I saw when I wrote these words. Its primary object does not directly implicate any specific breed. It would be a "veridical" or accidentally correct hallucination if located in the right position under my desk there was Lucca the Italian greyhound, or a small whippet or an appropriately mocked up robot, or a Lucca-like hologram or whatever other simulacrum you like to mention. While a hallucination or an afterimage might allow for direct demonstrative reference to a novel quality, such as supersaturated red, thereby originally providing me with a new topic for thought or talk, no hallucination or afterimage could be the original source of demonstrative reference to a novel breed or "natural" kind. Suppose someone ignorant of Italian greyhounds hallucinated a plausible profile. Nothing would make it of an Italian greyhound as opposed to, say, a stunted whippet.[17]

So it is not exactly right to say that a case of seeing Lucca and a corresponding case of hallucination involve the very same sensible profile or complex of sensible qualities, sensible relations and sensible kinds.[18] The profile that is the object of the hallucination is less demanding, in that it could be exemplified by a variety of different things of different kinds. In being presented with this less demanding profile, I am not presented with a breed, but only with the qualitative aspects of the breed, aspects that could be exemplified by an appropriate hologram or mocked up dog robot. So the proposal is that such less demanding sensible profiles—complexes of certain structuring relations and qualities, but not of genuine kinds—are the primary objects of hallucination. The structure of qualities that one might hallucinate is in fact a proper part of the more demanding sensible profile that one is aware of in a corresponding case of seeing. In hallucinating an Italian greyhound a qualitative profile that could be satisfied by an Italian greyhound or a Sony dog-robot or a clever hologram is presented to me. When I see an Italian greyhound that qualitative profile is presented along with Italian Greyhoundhood. Which is to say that part of the *seen* profile involves the property of *being an Italian greyhound* qualified such and so, where "being qualified thus and so" involves having the structure of qualities that one could indeed hallucinate.

The sensible profile account can be understood as a philosophical gloss on the notion of "seeing as," one which simply draws out a certain ontological consequence of seeing some particular as of a kind, qualified thus and so, and standing in relations of proximity and distance to other particulars of various kinds and variously qualified. In seeing Lucca as an Italian greyhound sitting under the desk I am aware of Lucca instantiating a certain sensible profile. Structured and merely qualitative parts of that same sensible profile can also be given to me in hallucination, but there is no sense in which they are given to me more directly than Lucca is when I see her. Moreover, when I see Lucca as an Italian greyhound sitting under the desk, there is no sense in which the property of being an Italian Greyhound sitting under the desk is more directly given to me than Lucca herself. The objects seen—instantiations of sensible profiles—are not "indirect" objects of awareness in the fashion of the Conjunctive Analysis. When we see them, our awareness of them is not mediated by anything of which we are more directly aware.

We can now satisfy the constraint that emerged from our discussion of the argument from the narrow supervenience of hallucination. We have a way of "combining" the kind of awareness that is present in hallucination and seeing with the no less "direct" awareness of external objects that is definitive of seeing. When we see we are aware of instantiations of sensible profiles. When we hallucinate we are aware merely of the structured qualitative parts of such sensible profiles. Any case of hallucination is thus a case of "direct" visual awareness of less than one would be "directly" aware of in the corresponding case of seeing. In hallucination we are not aware of the visible instances which seeing presents, and we are not aware of the visible natural kinds which seeing presents. We are instead aware of a proper part of what we are aware of in the corresponding case of seeing, a sensible profile that is no more than a certain layout of qualities.

The claim that we are "directly" aware of more in a corresponding case of seeing may still seem at odds with a common picture of psychophysical causation, a picture on which light reflected from the object seen first stimulates the retina, which then activates the optic nerve and then the visual cortex and then, *finally, as a causal consequence of all this* the act of seeing the object occurs. If seeing the object is thus understood as the first mental event at the end of a chain of physical events then the Conjunctivist is vindicated after all. For consider that in subjectively indiscernible cases of hallucination and seeing the very same kind of final physical events—say instances of the very same pattern of neural firing in the visual cortex— could be involved. But then by some sound version of the "same kind of proximate cause, same kind of immediate effect" principle it will follow that the very same kind of acts of awareness is found in the two cases. That is to say that the same kind of act of awareness is present in a case of seeing and a case of hallucination. Since types of acts of awareness are plausibly individuated by the types of direct objects that they present to the subject, you can't in the two cases be *directly* aware of objects of different types or categories. The distinctive objects that we see are not the direct objects of any act of awareness that occurs at the end of a physical causal chain, they can only be assigned derivatively as the objects of that act because they were at some earlier relevant juncture in the physical causal chain. And this is precisely the sense of "indirect object" which the Conjunctivist had in mind all along.

Yet behind this supposed proof of the Conjunctive Analysis is a picture of the relationship between the brain and the mind familiar from newspaper cartoons, where thought and experience are depicted as a sort of mental bubble secreted from the head. That is, the decisive move in the conjuring game is to slide in the supposition that the connection between a physical processes and awareness is itself process causation, as if energy leaked from the external world into the mind via the brain.

As against this picture, the relation between seeing an object and the long physical process involving first the light coming from the object and then the operation of the visual system is *not* the relation between a first mental effect and a prior physical process that causes it. Seeing the object is not the next event *after the visual system operates*. Seeing the object is an event materially constituted by *the long physical process* connecting the object seen to the final state of the visual system. Seeing the object is an event that is (as it actually turns out) constituted by a physical process that goes all the way out to the object seen. There is accordingly no "looking back" required by the last brain state or pattern of neuronal firing in order to determine whether to cause veridical awareness of external objects as opposed to the type of awareness involved in hallucination. There is no such "last" brain state that then causes seeing.

Seeing is an environment-revealing mental act that is materially constituted by a physical process that subtends the revealed environment. In this way, seeing is more than the solitary work of the visual system or, indeed, of the whole brain. Seeing goes all the way out to the things seen, the things with which it acquaints the subject. Things seen are thus "closer" to the subject than any mere external cause of a mental or brain event could be. That is why they are available for immediate demonstration, and hence as new topics for thought and talk.

The failure to understand the relation between the underlying causal process and seeing as material constitution, rather than process causation, is one of the deepest sources of the Conjunctive Analysis.

The constitutional basis for the act of awareness involved in hallucination is the state of the hallucinator's visual system, while the constitutional basis for seeing is (as it actually turns out[19]) the state of the visual system plus the appropriate causal influence by external things. The right causal connection does not itself cause seeing. The right causal connection guarantees that the visual channel is open so that direct visual awareness of external things takes place. There are thus distinctively different acts of awareness involved in hallucinating and seeing, individuated by different objects of awareness.

Nevertheless, just as the constitutional basis for a hallucination can be a proper part of the constitutional basis of another, subjectively indiscernible, act of seeing *so also* the objects of a hallucination can be proper parts of the objects seen in another, subjectively indiscernible act of seeing. The sensible profile account models exactly this. When we see we are aware of instantiations of sensible profiles. When we hallucinate we are aware merely of sensible profiles which are structured qualitative parts of the sensible profiles whose instantiations we see. Because such hallucinated sensible profiles can mimic particularity, in a sense to be explained, we can undergo subjectively seamless transitions from hallucination to seeing and back again. The common awareness of qualitative sensible profiles is the common factor that Disjunctivists have missed.

8. This account of hallucination will not seem viable to those who hold that we can never be aware of uninstantiated complexes of qualities and relations. But it seems difficult to hold to this general principle. Concentrate again on the scene before you, and attend to the *way* the scene is. Here you are concentrating on a general manner of presentation of a scene that happens to be satisfied by *the* scene before your eyes. That manner of presentation is not given to you linguistically, for no words could exhaust the dense specificity of the way the scene looks to you. What is that non-linguistic manner of presentation if it is not a complex of sensible qualities and relations? What is it to attend to such a manner of presentation if it is not to be aware of it?

"Ah," the opponent will say, "but this is by hypothesis a complex of qualities and relations instantiated in the scene before the eyes—you want a complex that is *not instantiated there!*" But the opponent is here trying to hold to an unstable stopping point. For it is contingent that the scene before you is just the way it looks to you to be. You could be aware of the complex of sensible qualities and relations without that whole complex being instantiated. In the minimal case you could be suffering a local illusion, say a Müller-Lyer illusion to the effect that two lines before you are unequal. Then the complex of sensible qualities and relations will not itself be instantiated, even though many components in the complex will be instantiated. In the extreme case, in which you are enjoying a full-blown, phantasmagoric hallucination, none of the qualities or relations will be instantiated.

In this way, sensible profiles that happen not to be instantiated in the scene before the eyes raise no more ontological difficulties than items with which many philosophers are already quite comfortable, namely those manners of presentation that happen to have no referent. As we shall see below, the analogy between sensible profiles and manners of presentation is no accident. Sensible profiles are manners of presentation that are themselves presented in sensing. Indeed this is a distinctive aspect of sensory experience, one that marks it off from belief or thought. Sensory manners of presentation are themselves sensed.

When we survey cases, the idea of awareness of sensible profiles uninstantiated in the scene before the eyes can come to seem quite natural. When we close our eyes and look at the sun we are visually aware of some specific shade of orange. Nothing having the shade is presented or given in experience. Similarly, in the pitch dark, one is visually aware of a certain shade of black ("brain-greyness") and not of any black shaded (brain-grey) thing. It won't do to say that one is visually aware of nothing in the pitch dark; the question could obviously arise as to whether there is a tint of indigo in what one is aware of in the pitch dark. The case of visual awareness of a quality in the pitch dark must stand as a difficulty for those views which hold that in all cases in which you have visual experience some physical particular is appearing to you, even if it is the air or the space before your eyes.[20] In the pitch dark, you are not seeing the air or the space before your eyes. It's *too* dark to see such things.

So far we have awareness of simple qualities—colors, not in any way spatially bounded. Let's move to a complex qualitative and relational structure. There is a state that a subject can get into by being exposed to bright monochromatic unique green light (500 nanometers in wavelength) in an otherwise dark room for about twenty minutes. If we then turn the stimulus off, illuminate the room, and have the subject look at a small, not-too-bright achromatic surface, he will see a red afterimage. If the subject turns so that the afterimage is then superimposed on a small red background then something wonderful happens. The subject will then be after-imaging a *supersaturated* red, a red more saturated than any surface red one can see, a red purer than the purest spectral red light, light with a frequency of around 650 nanometers.[21]

Supersaturated red is a missing shade of red, which you can only after-image, i.e., can never see but only have presented to you as part of an uninstantiated complex of sensible qualities and relations. In the case just mentioned, the complex will be the property of being a supersaturated red round thing at a certain changing distance and direction from the present position, at the present time. The relational element—the spatio-temporal layout as I have called it—mimics spatial and temporal extent and thereby mimics particularity, so that although it seems as if an after-image is a moving particular, in fact there is just a complex of sensible qualities and relations.

Of course it will be said, and quite rightly, that no property moves, and no mere complex of properties moves; and so, no sensible profile moves. But just as we made a distinction between primary and secondary objects of hallucination we can distinguish the primary features of the sensible profile that is the primary object of hallucination and the secondary features of the secondary, or construal-dependent, object. The features of the primary object are its properties, the properties pertaining to a certain complex of universals, properties such as containing supersaturated red as a constituent. The secondary "features," the features of the secondary object, are given by *how* the primary object immediately strikes the subject as being. So thanks to containing certain properties in certain relations to continuous places and times, a primary object can immediately strike the subject as a moving particular, say as an evanescent supersaturated red patch sailing through the air. It isn't anything of the sort, but nonetheless one proper report of the hallucination or the after-imaging cites the secondary object and its secondary features, as in "He after-imaged a supersaturated red patch sailing through the air."

Likewise, it will be said that no sensible profile is supersaturated red.[22] Being supersaturated red is a secondary or construal-dependent feature of the secondary object of hallucination, a matter of how a profile that contains supersaturated red might immediately strike a subject.

These observations about construal-dependence suggest a solution to the so-called problem of intensional identity, a problem that arises in sharp form for the objects of hallucination. Macbeth could hallucinate very similar sensible profiles with a time gap in between. Macduff could also hallucinate very similar sensible profiles with the same time gap in between. The sensible profiles might strike Macbeth as the very same dagger, first appearing here and then there, whereas very similar sensible profiles might strike Macduff as a dagger appearing here and then a duplicate dagger appearing there. If so, the correct report of Macbeth's hallucination would be of the same dagger appearing here and then there, while the correct report of Macduff's hallucination would be of two different but similar daggers appearing, one after the other. This could be so even if all four dagger-simulating profiles were identical but for their constituent locations and times. The identity or difference of secondary "objects" of hallucination is a construal-dependent matter, a "secondary feature" determined by how primary objects strike the relevant subjects. A sign of this: Absent special cases such as those in which their respective hallucinations are anchored in thought about some actual dagger or daggers, no sense is to be made of Macbeth and Macduff hallucinating either the same or different daggers. The most vivid form of the puzzle of intensional identity asks how there could be items for which the issue of numerical sameness and difference does not even arise. And the solution to the puzzle is that there could not be such items.

Note well that appeal to construal-dependent objects is just a *façon de parler*. There are no genuine items whose numerical identity or difference is solely a matter of whether they strike a subject as numerically identical or different. When we talk of secondary objects of hallucination we are to be understood as talking of the objects that figure in certain correct reports of hallucination, the accusatives of the verb "hallucinates" and its cognates. When we talk of secondary features of these "objects," and specifically of their identity and difference, we are to be understood as talking of how certain genuine items, namely the primary objects, strike the relevant subjects. There is no need to suppose that there are further genuine, but somehow non-existent, items whose identity or difference is a construal-dependent matter. Our slogan should be that it is fine to talk of intensional objects of visual awareness, but there are neither merely possible nor inexistent intensional objects. (More on this below when we contrast Elizabeth Anscombe's account of intentional "objects" with Meinongian accounts.)

For another example of a complex sensible profile, consider the Waterfall Illusion. You look at a waterfall and then look away at a rope ladder hanging on the side of the cavern. The rope ladder is stationary and you see it as such. But you are also presented with upward movement of ladder rungs, somehow superimposed on what you see. You don't believe that the ladder is both stationary and moving upward. You see the stationary rungs over there and at the same time you are presented with a complex quality—

upward movement of the rungs over there—which if it were instantiated would be instantiated by the same rungs moving upward. But in the Waterfall Illusion, nothing is instantiating this quality; that is why it counts as an illusion.[23]

Thinking of sensible profiles as sensory manners of presentation helps explain why we can be taken in or deluded by certain hallucinations and illusions but not by others. In a convincing case of hallucination or illusion we are presented with a sensible profile which is typically presented only when it is instantiated. In the Waterfall Illusion something is presented that could not be instantiated and we are baffled and not taken in. The sensible profile or manner of presentation matches nothing we have seen before.

As a last example, in order to illustrate something of the range of qualities that might figure in sensible profiles, consider the case of the speckled hen. You hallucinate a speckled hen, one with a lot of speckles. Is there a reason to suppose that there is some definite number of speckles you hallucinated? Some insist on the completeness of the visual field, supposing that for each virtual point in the field there will be some determinate quality associated with that point. They then reason that since an apparent speckle will involve some pattern of discontinuity in determinate color, there must be a definite number of speckles that you hallucinated. Others deny that the visual field need be determinate in this way. This is presumably a substantive question about a matter of fact, albeit a matter of fact not easily ascertained. But notice that the sensible profile account can handle the possibility that experience is in some respects merely determinable. For one thing, merely determinable qualities like Having A Lot Of Speckles may figure in sensible profiles. For another, the constituent qualities may all be fully determinate, but a certain sensible profile could strike a subject as being a hen with a lot of speckles, without it being the case that there is some number n, such that the sensible profile strikes that subject as being a hen with exactly n speckles.

Taking the primary objects of hallucination to be profiles or complexes of qualities and relations is isomorphic in certain ways to a one-sided Sense Datum Theory. According to this view, which H. H. Price dubbed "The Selective Theory," in veridical experience one is aware of external physical particulars; while in hallucination one is aware of an internal mental object, which one can sometimes systematically mistake for an external physical particular.[24] However the Selective Theory carries extra baggage. It explains subjectively seamless transitions by postulating a category of mental objects—the sense data—and a category of mental qualia had by just these objects. Neither category is needed on the sensible profile account.

As opposed to the categories of mental events, acts and states understood as aspects of an embodied person or animal, the category of mental objects, i.e. the category of mental particulars that are not themselves events, acts or states, is not a happy category. How can a mental object, something whose existence is directly dependent on a subject's awareness of it, be at the same time complex and have the internal unity that makes for a complex particular as opposed to a complex of properties? The mental object or sense datum has no matter constituting it, and it has no capacity to maintain itself through change. So what unites its qualitative parts into a particular, re-identifiable over time? The absence of any good answer accounts for the silliness of questions concerning the numerical identity through change either of sense data or of mental objects quite generally. (The same point, I believe, applies to numerical identity of pains, and other bodily sensations, which suggests that the profile account might be adapted to bodily sensations.) The category of mental objects, a category that has wreaked so much confusion in our thinking about the mind, is the off-spring of a restricted range of options within which to locate the primary objects of hallucination, and of delusory experience more generally. A bad Nominalism has been the enabler of a bad Mentalism.

The sensible profile account jettisons mental objects such as sense data in favor of partly qualitative and partly relational complexes, which whenever they are instantiated are always instantiated by physical particulars. Furthermore, there is no need for a category of qualia or mental qualities over and above the ordinary category of qualities. Hallucination is a mental act directed at sensible qualities and relations, but these qualities and relations are the familiar ones, which if instantiated could only be instantiated by physical particulars. What Frank Jackson's Mary does not know is not what some mental quale is like. What she does not know is what redness is like.[25] In not yet seeing red she has had no experience which reveals its nature. The interesting thing is that a hallucination or an after-image could help her just as much as a veridical experience could.

Indeed sometimes, as in the case of supersaturated red, you can come to know what the relevant quality is like *only* by hallucination or after-imaging. This would be my further challenge to those Disjunctivists like Hilary Putnam (at least the Hilary Putnam of his second Dewey Lecture[26]) who see no force in the request to provide an explanation at the level of experience of subjectively seamless transitions. Do they also see no force in the request for an explanation of how hallucination and after-imaging can be a novel source of knowledge of quality, but not of particulars or of "natural" kinds like breeds?

So, the positive account of hallucination and of veridical sensing can be summarized as follows: In sensory hallucination one is aware of complexes of sensible qualities and relations. In veridical sensing one is aware of instantiations of complexes of sensible qualities, relations and sensible natural kinds. There are no qualia. It is ordinary qualities and complexes involving them that account for the so-called subjective character of experience.

9. Are there really complexes of qualities and relations of the sort I have been appealing to? Do they have a place in a serious ontology? Upon inspection, the general category of such complexes turns out to be a familiar one, and quite hard to do without. Consider the complex property of being an HCl molecule, i.e. the property of being a Hydrogen ion bonded to a Chlorine ion. For this property to be instantiated, it must be the case that two other properties are instantiated, and furthermore that the instantiations of those two properties stand in a certain relation. To be specific: it must be the case that the property of being a Hydrogen ion must be instantiated, and the property of being a Chlorine ion must be instantiated, and the instantiation of the first property stand in the relation of bonding to the instantiation of the second. What accounts for this necessary connection between the instantiation of the property of being an HCl molecule and the instantiation of the following three things: the property of being a Hydrogen ion, the property of being a Chlorine ion, and the relation of bonding? The best explanation is that the latter three things are not wholly distinct from the complex property of being an HCl molecule. They are components of that property. That property is structured out of them.

This is just what we need to explain the ontology of sensible profiles, such as the property of being a red round supersaturated patch at a certain distance and orientation from me now. Profiles are what ontologists call structural properties, properties structured out of properties, relations and perhaps particulars.[27] As emphasized in the remarks about the layout, a crucial relational element figuring in sensed complexes is really a structured relational property: the property of being at a certain distance and orientation from the observer's position at the time of observation. There is of course no special obstacle preventing such relational properties from being components of more complex properties.

But it should be noted that whereas properties and relations simply exist or, as some say, exist at all times, this need not be true of relational properties. Relational properties are formed by saturating with particulars some but not all of the positions in a given relation. So, arguably, relational properties exist only when the saturating particulars exist. If Louis Armstrong no longer exists, not only does no one now sing with Louis Armstrong, but the relational property of singing with Armstrong no longer exists. So if we took the passage of time very seriously, so as to deny that times exist at any time other than when they are present, it then would follow that the time-involving relational properties which are crucial components of the primary objects of hallucination exist only during the relevant hallucinatory episodes. So the primary object of a hallucination would exist only during the corresponding hallucinatory episode.

Even so, the complexes that are the primary objects of hallucinations have all the objectivity of Fregean senses. Contrary to the fundamental assumptions of the Mentalist treatment of hallucination, there is nothing essentially private about such objects. But for the medical impossibility of two people occupying the very same position at the same time, you and I could hallucinate the very same primary object. Of course, our hallucinations still would be different mental acts because we are different subjects. So you could not have my hallucination. But that is for the same reason that you could not have my vaccination.

The things that instantiate sensible profiles or complexes of sensible properties are the varieties of spatio-temporal particulars around us: objects, stuff of various sorts, events and states. These are the things that are seen *as*, or more generally sensed *as*, having the complex properties in question. Such complex properties or sensible profiles will also be the sort of things that are the primary objects of hallucination.

It is thus awareness of sensible profiles that provides the common factor. But notice that awareness of the sensible profiles that particulars have no more gets in the way of being aware of those particulars than my visual awareness of my fingers gets in the way of my awareness of my hand. Just as I see my hand *as* having five fingers, I more generally see particulars *as* having this or that sensible profile. (More on this below, when we focus upon the issue of indirection.)

Again, the common factor is merely a part of what I am aware of in the veridical case. It is of course the factor that is not in common, namely awareness of sensible particulars and sensible kinds, which makes all the difference.

10. There are really two differences here, the one having to do with acquaintance and the other having to do with propositional knowledge. With respect to the first difference, it is because we are aware of more than what we could ever hallucinate when we see or veridically sense that we can secure original reference to more by seeing or veridically sensing. The Disjunctivist's mistake was to go in for overkill. To respect the distinctive role of sensing we need to explain how an act of veridical sensing could acquaint us with *more* than the corresponding case of hallucination. But this is entirely compatible with recognizing a common factor in such corresponding cases. We need not insist, in the teeth of the phenomenology, that hallucination acquaints us with nothing.

To get a feel for the second difference, which concerns propositional knowledge, concentrate on the objects that the present account associates with veridical sensory acts. We sense what I have called instantiations of sensible profiles. These can be the stuff or continuants that are instantiations of kinds, and the states and events that are instantiations of properties and relations. So for example we see such things as gold or Lucca or Lucca chasing a cat or the sleekness of Lucca's coat. And we will typically be prompted to immediately or non-inferentially judge such things as that it's gold, or that it's Lucca or that Lucca is chasing a cat or that Lucca's coat is sleek. That is to say that on the present account our immediate perceptual judgements are formed as a result of awareness of their truthmakers. I think that this points to a new and promising combination of Reliabilism and Foundationalism, one on which what is sensed neither justifies nor merely causes immediate perceptual belief, but instead confers the kind of authority on immediate perceptual belief which allows it in its turn to justify the inferential beliefs based on it. But that, as they say, is another story.[28]

More to the present point, we have arrived at an account of what is distinctive about sensory manners of presentation of sensed particulars, and what makes sensing such particulars so different from discursive thought about them. *As sensible profiles, sensory manners of presentation are themselves objects of sensory awareness. Sensory awareness thus acquaints us with sensible profiles, which are sensory manners of presentation of particulars.*

Notice how this account bears on the question of whether and in what way sensory experience is conceptually demanding.[29] As the friends of non-conceptual content insist, there is something very distinctive about sensory manners of presentation. *Sensory manners of presentation are complexes of sensible properties, and they themselves are sensed.* But this is compatible with a conceptualist claim to the effect that almost all sensing of particulars is sensing those particulars *as thus and so*, where sensing them *as thus and so* is a deployment of a "conceptual" ability, an ability which is typically possessed only if one could go on to judge that they are thus and so.

By way of summary then, so long as we are clear about the distinctive character of sensory manners of presentation we can say that hallucination is a case of awareness of a sensory manner of presentation without awareness of anything which instantiates that sensory manner of presentation. Sensory manners of presentation are none other than (complexes of) the very sensible properties we see or more generally sense particulars as having.

Notice that our sensible profiles or sensory manners of presentation differ from Fregean senses in at least one important way. They do not determine reference. It is not the case that an experience involving a sensory manner of presentation counts as an experience of an external particular because that external particular happens to have a nature that matches the sensory manner of presentation. There is after all the possibility of veridical hallucination. One could have a veridical hallucination of a reddish glow around an artichoke, a hallucination produced in one by the artichoke in one's midst emitting a kind of radiation that acts directly on one's brain. The radiation could be of such intensity that the artichoke in one's midst actually does glow red. But despite the match between the artichoke and the hallucinated profile one would not as a result be seeing the artichoke glowing red.

Frege's view can still seem to leave the mind with the challenge of connecting with external particulars, a challenge that his view meets first by having mental acts of grasping senses and then having external particulars be the referents of those senses which they satisfy. But this is the wrong model for sensory consciousness. Sensing just takes in instantiations of sensible profiles, and not by way of an antecedent act directed toward a sense or a propositional content which external things may or may not satisfy. Propositional attitudes come in the wake of sensory acts directed at external particulars, and we get to conceive of the general conditions which external things may or may not satisfy thanks to our antecedent sensory awareness of instantiations of sensible profiles. The mind never faces the challenge of connecting to external particulars from the impoverished position of intercourse merely with items that one could anyway hallucinate. To the contrary, acts of sensing—seeing Lucca, hearing Lucca chase the cat and so on and so forth—are individuated in terms of the external particulars they are directed at.[30]

This should put to rest one sort of worry about indirection. The present account is not one on which we sense external particulars *by* sensing manners of presentation or sensible profiles that they happen to instantiate. The sensible profiles or sensed manners of presentation do not determine reference to external particulars. We do not get to external particulars by entertaining them and having them determine external particulars. So it is not in general true that it is *by* having an experience involving a certain sensible profile that one is aware of external particulars.

Hallucination is a degenerate state, a failure of the visual system to function properly. When the visual system functions properly and one sees the scene before one's eyes one has not overcome (thanks to causation or whatever) the challenge of connecting with external objects merely from a state common to hallucination and seeing. To the contrary, there is no such challenge; having external objects and their visible features disclosed to us is the default ability that comes with having a functioning visual system.

11. There is another source of the worry about indirection, namely the controlling influence of a thought that has wreaked havoc in modern philosophy. We could put that thought this way:

The Phenomenal Bottleneck Principle: If two acts of awareness are qualitatively indistinguishable for their subject then objects of the very same type are directly presented in each act of awareness.

This principle expresses the idea of a "phenomenal bottleneck" in the sense that objects can only really get through to a subject, can only really be directly present to a subject, by making a distinguishable qualitative difference to the subject's awareness. The principle also motivates the idea of sense data as direct objects of awareness, direct objects whose properties are determined by how things appear to the subject. It follows from the principle and the conception of sense data as direct objects of experience that there would have to be a distinguishable change in how things appear to a subject for different types of sense data to present successively to that subject.

To get a feel for the effect of the principle independently of commitment to sense data consider a pair of sensory experiences, the one veridical and the other hallucinatory, that are indistinguishable for their subject. According to the sensible profile account, the awareness of similar sensible profiles is what explains this indistinguishability from the subject's point of view. The Phenomenal Bottleneck Principle tells us that in each case the (direct) object of awareness is the same. Presumably it is the common manner of presentation or sensible profile. So to the extent that we are aware of external objects when we see, our awareness of them is indirect, mediated by awareness of a manner of presentation or a sensory profile.

The Phenomenal Bottleneck Principle thus forces us to look behind the most common external object-invoking reports of what we see or sense. Suppose I first see a dog, then I blink, and then I see a tricky dog-hologram that has replaced the dog before me. I don't notice the difference between the dog and the dog hologram. Yet I saw the dog and I saw the dog hologram. I was as directly aware of each of them as I ever am of anything. But the Principle says otherwise. Just because I mistook one for another, the Principle has it that the very same object was the only thing immediately present in these two cases, some object which is neither the dog or the hologram.

But now the Principle can be seen to be false. Suppose I am lying in bed as light gradually dawns in my room. Couldn't my experience be of a continuously increasing brightness, as the morning moves from gloom to full daylight? But then there will be small differences in brightness that I do not notice because they fall below the threshold of just noticeable differences. The Principle implies that there can be no such unnoticed or, on a plausible weakening, unnoticeable differences in what I am *directly* experiencing. But this means there must be discrete jumps in the brightness I directly experience, jumps that are at least as wide as just noticeable differences in brightness. But paradoxically, try as I might, I never am able to notice such jumps as I attend to my experience of the departing gloom. A simple logic gets me from the gloom to the brightness by differences that are not noticeable. The Bottleneck Principle delivers the consequence that the gloom and the brightness result in the very same type of immediate object of awareness. But how is it that the difference between the gloom and the brightness is clearly evident to me?

Something like the Phenomenal Bottleneck Principle helps motivate the false picture of the mind as facing a fundamental challenge of engaging with external objects, a challenge that even twenty years ago one might still have hoped to meet by having immediate experience match and be appropriately caused by external objects. (This combination of descriptive and appropriate causation is now looking increasingly hopeless, so if there were a real challenge it would be insurmountable.) The principle is also the source of many curious conceits in modern philosophy. One such conceit involves the search for a distinctive range of qualities laid bare in experience, qualities corresponding to the presentation of each thing that we ordinarily take ourselves to be aware of. David Hume looks into his soul and finds nothing but fleeting impressions and ideas, and thus concludes that the enduring self is a fiction. William James discovers a distinctive persistent sensation at the back of his throat, and absurdly takes *this* to be a presentation of himself enduring over time. Each is manifesting the conviction that for one to be present in one's own introspective reflection there must be a distinctive qualitative sign. Otherwise, nothing could get through the bottleneck of experience and be present. So also, Hume famously claims that there are no distinctive impressions that could count as our being aware of external causation or identity through time or the unity of qualities in a common substance. So he concludes that we are never really aware of these things.

Even if we suspend Hume's Mentalism, which has it that all we could be directly aware of are impressions and ideas, and suppose instead that we are aware of some external things, the tradition still menaces us with further applications of the Bottleneck Thesis.

Consider for example a worry which bamboozled G. E. Moore, and which Thompson Clarke did much to clarify. Put aside Hume's Mentalism and suppose instead that we at least see the facing surfaces of things around us. Even so, all of this is indistinguishable from a case in which the facing surfaces are just fronts, as in a movie set. By the Bottleneck Thesis it follows that what we are always aware of is never more than the facing surfaces of things. The Bottleneck Thesis is thus incompatible with the natural idea that our sensory experience is directly of full-blown external objects, albeit an essentially aspectual experience of these objects, an experience of them from a viewing position that reveals only part of their nature.

This suggests that any appeal to the Phenomenal Bottleneck Principle to establish that we can only directly sense sensible profiles or sensory manners of presentation should not be taken as probative. For the Bottleneck Principle is just a summary of one controversial response to the very issue at hand, namely how much of the world is "directly" open to view. It just encapsulates the idea that our awareness of external, non-phenomenal objects can be at most "indirect." It does not independently motivate that idea. In the end, it may simply represent an influential but unhappy stipulation about how to use the terms "direct" and "indirect." To which the response should be to simply avoid these terms, at least when they are intended in the stipulated sense.

Consider the case of seeing the facing surfaces of the particular things around me. Is it correct to say that I see the particular things that I do *by* seeing their facing surfaces? It is certainly true in most cases that if I *were not* seeing the facing surface I *would not* be seeing the thing. But does this entail that I see those particular things *by* seeing their facing surfaces, and entail this in the loaded sense that implies that my seeing of particular things is *indirect*?

Arguably, this last thing doesn't follow. Take a case in which I see a thing without seeing its facing surface, as when I see my house on the hill from some miles away and so see it as a dot on the hill. I can't make out the facing surface of the house, it's too far away for me to see that surface. So in this case I am not seeing my house *by* seeing its facing surface. Nor am I seeing my house *by* seeing a dot on the horizon. There is no dot there to see. But there is no reason to regard this case of seeing my house as a special, more *direct* and therefore *less mediated* way of seeing my house as compared to, say, looking at my house from the street. That would be absurd, and this suggests although I might often see my house by seeing its facing front this does not entail indirection in the relevant sense.

I see the particulars around me *as* having such and so facing surfaces. I also see those particulars *as* having backs. These are backs that I am not now seeing, but which would complete what I am seeing in certain ways, were I to move and view those particulars in the round. This adumbrative aspect of ordinary seeing—as the translations of Edmund Husserl put it—is not well described by saying that the backs of the things that I see are *indirect* objects of my visual awareness. They are not objects of my visual awareness at all. I see things *as* having backs, backs of which I am not yet visually aware. "Indirect visual awareness" makes no sense here.

There is little to be said for the claim that I have indirect visual awareness of the particulars that I am seeing. For I am aware—as directly as I am ever aware—of the facing fronts of these particulars, and I although I am aware of these as having backs, I am not, even indirectly, aware of the backs of those particulars. What kind of novel arithmetic makes this add up to *indirect* awareness of the particulars, which in the present context we can think of as aggregates of their fronts and their backs?

No, the "as"-structure of sensory awareness is not the loaded "by"-structure of the friend of indirection. Similarly, it is not that we see particulars *by* being visually aware of the sensible profiles that they have or instantiate. Instead, we see them *as* having certain sensible profiles, which are after all just certain complex sensible properties. We may have to be visually aware of those sensible profiles in order to see particulars as having them, but this implies no indirection. Seeing with mirrors or through TV or the like aside, there really is no place for "direct" and "indirect" visual awareness.

The extent of the "as"-structure of sensory awareness is dependent on the extent of the subject's conceptual sophistication. Given increasing conceptual sophistication, the range of states and conditions of external objects that one can be immediately aware of increases. And this means that one is presented with richer and richer truthmakers for one's immediate perceptual judgements. More and more of the world lies immediately open to view.[31]

12. We are now in a position to articulate just what is right, and what is wrong, in the so-called Intentional Object treatment of hallucination, and thereby explain the innocuous sense in which the secondary objects of hallucination are indeed "objects."[32]

The Intentional Object treatment attractively holds to the act/object account of hallucination, while noting that in many cases of hallucination the object does not exist. So I can hallucinate Nergal—the ancient Babylonian god of the netherworld; the cause of pestilence, fevers, and mephitic odors—even if Nergal does not, and perhaps could not, exist. So the friends of intentional objects conclude that in hallucination objects that do not exist, Nergal and his ilk, are sometimes presented to the subject.

Now whatever the charms of non-existent objects, this argument that they are sometimes the objects of hallucination is a bad one. It does not follow from the act/object account of hallucination and the fact that we sometimes hallucinate the non-existent that there are non-existent objects.

It doesn't follow because, as we have seen, "the object of the hallucination" is a rotten definite description. It call equally well pick out quite different things. We need to distinguish the primary objects of hallucination—the sensible profiles—from the "objects" they pick up from antecedent thoughts and the "objects" they sometimes strike subjects as being. The act/object account of hallucination is secured by treating hallucination as visual awareness of an uninstantiated sensible profile. If some such presented profile strikes a subject as Nergal, then the subject counts as hallucinating Nergal. But we need not think of this secondary "object" of hallucination as an object in the genuine sense required to secure the act/object account of hallucination. For that account is already secured by the existent primary object, the object that strikes the subject as Nergal.

We can proceed as follows. As a first pass at an account of hallucinating particulars, we can say that

X's visually hallucinating @

where "@" holds a place for a designator which putatively designates a particular, consists in this:

There is some sensible profile of which X is visually aware,
And X is not visually aware of instantiations of this profile in the scene before his eyes,
And either this profile strikes X as being @ or X's visual awareness of the profile is caused in the right way by an earlier perception of @ or by thought to the effect that @ is such and so.[33]

Notice that the context "strikes X as being ..." is intensional, in the bland sense that it does not follow from the fact that something, say a dutiful father, strikes X as being, say, Santa Claus that Santa Claus exists. It is a very heady doctrine that we need non-existent intentional objects to account for what appears to be intensionality in the bland sense. There may be some subtle semantical argument that shows that this is so. But it would have to be of great generality, and have nothing in particular to do with hallucination. So far as hallucination itself goes, we call secure the act/object account of hallucination by appealing to sensible profiles as primary objects and treating apparent reference to secondary "objects" as the upshot of the familiar fact that some contexts are intensional merely in the sense of not having existential import.

So also, the context "is caused in the right way by a thought to the effect that ... is such and so" is intensional, in the bland sense of lacking existential import. Suppose a child dwells on the thought that Santa Claus is not coming down the chimney this Christmas and this causes him to hallucinate Santa Claus. His thought that Santa Claus is not coming down the chimney is true, but it does not entail that Santa Claus exists. If this is a case where his hallucination's being of Santa Claus amounts to an act of awareness of a certain sensible profile being caused by and referentially anchored to the child's thought concerning Santa Claus, then we need not think of the child's hallucination as a genuine relation to a non-existent object called "Santa Claus." At least, we do not need to do this to respect the act/object account of hallucination. The primary object fills the bill, while the secondary "object" is just assigned by way of an intensional context. A semantic theorist might give some interesting argument that we cannot make sense of thoughts to the effect that Santa Claus is not coming down the chimney without recognizing a non-existent thing named "Santa Claus." But that argument would have nothing in particular to do with hallucination. Again, as far as hallucination itself goes, we can secure the act/object account of hallucination by appealing to sensible profiles as primary objects and treating apparent reference to non-existent secondary "objects" as the upshot of the familiar fact that some contexts are intensional merely in the sense of not having existential import. Of course some secondary objects of hallucination are ordinary existents, such as one's mother or the dentist. But there is also the case in which the primary object of hallucination strikes the subject as d, where "d" is an ostensible designator that in fact designates nothing. In this case we shall speak of *mere* (secondary) objects of hallucination. Clearly, mere objects of hallucination do not form a further category of items alongside ordinary existents. Such talk of mere objects of hallucination is just a way of recognizing that certain contexts are intensional and so can be filled in with ostensible designators which do not designate anything.

Against this background, it is something of an irony that two closest friends of non-existent objects, namely Terence Parsons and Edward Zalta, have served up entities almost exactly like our profiles as, or as surrogates for, non-existent objects.[34] Both Parsons and Zalta follow Alexis Meinong, who arrived at the startling conclusion that predication does not require existence. He thus took the view that there are objects, such as The Golden Mountain, which are such that although they do not exist nonetheless have properties, such as being golden and a mountain. Accordingly, a Meinongian treatment of hallucination will identify the object of hallucination with a non-existent object with just the properties that the hallucinating subject is inclined to predicate on the strength of his hallucination. So on this view Macbeth hallucinates a genuine item in an odd category, namely a non-existent thing which has the properties of being a dagger, being bloody and being before him.

If there were such non-existent objects they could be mapped onto sensible profiles and vice versa. But the fact is that as far as hallucination goes, we don't need the non-existent objects alongside the profiles. The profiles simply exist. They are complexes of properties and some of them are the primary objects of hallucination. Nor, as we shall see, can the Meinongian non-existent objects be comfortably taken to be the secondary objects of hallucination.

Gilbert Harman is tempted by the Meinongian treatment of objects of hallucination in his paper "The Intrinsic Quality of Experience." In order to illustrate his Intentional Object treatment of delusory experience, Harman uses the example of Ponce De Leon searching for the Fountain of Youth.[35] But the case of searching for the Fountain of Youth is actually very different from the case of hallucinating, say, a bloody dagger. The hallucination is an encounter with some item that can capture the subject's attention, an item that the subject can then go on to demonstrate. Searching is not like this. To search is not itself to encounter any item that captures one's attention. So, when it comes to searching, the natural thing to say is that the context "searches for ..." is intensional in the sense of not having existential import. This is, in effect, a way of denying the act/object analysis of searching for. And this seems the right response, since searching does not itself involve the presentation of an item.

Denying the act/object analysis of searching for is of course compatible with insisting that the expression "searching for" always takes a grammatical "object," an object which can be used in the answer to the question "What is he searching for?" The important thing to recognize is that this grammatical "object" is not an item which searching for is a relation to. The grammatical object is a word or a phrase. The descriptive title "The Fountain of Youth" is the grammatical object of "searched for," but this is no evidence that searching for is a relation which held between De Leon and a non-existent object named "the Fountain of Youth." Similarly, the descriptive phrase "a bloody dagger" is the grammatical object of "hallucinated" in the report "Macbeth hallucinated a bloody dagger." But this is no evidence at all that hallucinating is a relation which held between Macbeth and a non-existent bloody dagger.

Elizabeth Anscombe develops this negative point in her paper "The Intentionality of Sensation: A Grammatical Feature." Anscombe holds that intentional objects are no more than the direct objects of psychological verbs in correct reports of the thought and behavior of subjects.[36] She also says that she does not intend this characterization to make intentional objects linguistic items of a particular grammatical kind, i.e. accusatives of transitive verbs. Her explanation of this deserves repeating. Consider whom Jack is said to have hallucinated according to (1).

(1)   Jack hallucinated Jill.

That is the intentional object of Jack's hallucination. And Anscombe is of course right, the correct answer to the question "Whom according to (1) did Jack hallucinate?" is not "The word 'Jill.'" It is simply "Jill." Jill is thus, in Anscombe's sense, the intentional object of Jack's hallucination as reported in (1).

This relativization to a specific report remains undischarged on Anscombe's account of intentional objects. For on her account

(2)   Jack hallucinated a woman

also relates Jack to an intentional object, namely a woman. Now Anscombe offers us no way of making sense of non-trivial claims of identity of intentional objects across reports. The intentional object of a report is just what, according to that report, the subject is G-ing where "G" holds a place for the psychological verb figuring in the report. On Anscombe's account, no sense has been given to the notion of the intentional object of one's experience. Speaking strictly, one should refer to the intentional object of one's experience as reported by using such and so sentence. As Anscombe's own title implies, even if her intentional objects are not themselves grammatical objects, being related to one of her intentional objects remains a grammatical matter. It has to do with the grammar of a report of a mental state.

Anscombe's sense of intentional object is perfectly harmless, and it helps to explain what it is to be a secondary object of hallucination. They are intentional "objects" of experience in something like Anscombe's jejune sense. They are what is cited in answers to questions of the form "What did the subject immediately take himself to be hallucinating?" Of course, this is not any kind of move in the direction of Meinong, or of his contemporary followers Parsons and Zalta, who will always find what they regard as a genuine item, be it existent or non-existent, with just the properties any subject is inclined to predicate on the strength of his hallucination.

Notice that Anscombe's intentional objects do not themselves provide for an act/object account of the mental act of hallucination. For one thing they are report-relative in a way in which items that we immediately encounter in hallucination are not.

Nor does talk of report-relative intentional objects help explain the possibility of an experientially seamless transition from a case of hallucination to a case of veridical perception. When I hallucinate lights on in a ceiling certain sentences are made true by this event, e.g.,

(3)   MJ is hallucinating lights on in a ceiling.

When I see the lights on in the ceiling certain sentences are made true by that event, e.g.,

(4)   MJ sees the lights on in the ceiling.

What according to (4) does MJ see? Answer: the lights on in the ceiling. What according to (3) did MJ hallucinate? Answer: lights on in a ceiling. At the linguistic level the two answers exhibit a grammatical similarity between an indefinite description and a corresponding definite description. This mildly diverting grammatical similarity has no power to explain how the transition from the experience that (3) describes to the experience that (4) describes could be subjectively seamless. Only non-grammatical features, aspects of the experiences as such, could do that.

So as well as Anscombe's innocuous intentional objects we also need the primary objects of hallucination, the sensible profiles which truly secure the act/object account of hallucination and account for subjectively seamless transitions.

The obvious cautionary remark is that whenever someone uses the shibboleth "the intentional objects of experience" they should be interrogated as to whether they mean to be endorsing a substantial and controversial doctrine like those put forward by Meinongians such as Parsons and Zalta, or a minimalist doctrine of Anscombe's sort. Much loose talk about intentional objects hovers indecisively between the two. As we have seen, the doctrines of Parsons and Zalta, at least as applied to sensing and hallucination, are unnecessary, and the Anscombe-style doctrine is incomplete; on its own it neither secures a genuine act/object treatment of hallucination nor accounts for seamless transitions.

13. To clinch the case against Meinongian accounts of hallucination we would need to show that the appeal to non-existent objects is not only unnecessary but also insufficient to account for the facts of hallucination. It seems that this is indeed so, for however the Meinongian multiplies non-existent objects to correspond to arbitrary, hallucination-prompted patterns of predication he must, in the end, also invoke construal-dependent "objects" that are not to be found among his non-existent objects. One case that strongly suggests just this arises from the partly fictionalized biography of John Nash, as depicted in the film, *A Beautiful Mind*. (I choose the film rather than the book of the same name because it is in the film that we are confronted with the peculiar and philosophically engaging condition of Nash's roommate.)

As things are presented in the film, in the early fifties Nash comes to Princeton for graduate school and then meets his English roommate, whom he knows as Charles Herman. Charles appears to be pursuing an advanced degree in English Literature; he seems to be handsome, charming, funny, wise, supportive and a great drinking buddy. Indeed, he strikes the viewer as having all the virtues you might want in a friend. But Charles is wanting in one significant respect. He doesn't actually exist. Charles is a mere object of Nash's hallucinations. The interesting thing is that Charles nevertheless becomes a central figure in Nash's life. Nash talks to Charles and Charles counsels Nash, who is desperately determined to have an impact on mathematics. Nash immediately and unhesitatingly takes Charles to exist, at least he does so during the early days at Princeton. Then, when Nash moves to M.I.T. Charles seems to betray him into the hands of a psychiatrist, a certain Dr. Rosen. Rosen ultimately persuades Nash that Charles is hallucinatory. This is a transformative moment for Nash. He has discovered that his best friend never existed. Even after many years of suffering, failure and emerging mental discipline, Nash still "sees" Charles—as the film depicts it, *the very same Charles*—with all his charm, jokes and supportive advice. But finally Nash adjusts; he simply takes Charles to be unreal, a figment of his imagination. Still, Charles "returns" from time to time, and it takes Nash all his effort to ignore him.

One striking thing about the film is that it is able to visually present a secondary object of hallucination, namely Charles Herman, "who" at first is taken by Nash to be real and then to be unreal. The film makes an effective visual case that this is how it was for Nash over different parts of his life: first Nash took himself to be seeing and talking to a real person, Charles Herman; then he took the same object of hallucination, namely Charles, to be unreal, a mere figment of his imagination. This means that "Charles Herman" is therefore quite an odd name, comparable in some ways to "Vulcan" as used by the astronomer Jean Leverrier. Leverrier introduced the name "Vulcan" to denote a planet between Mercury and the Sun, but he eventually came to suspect that Vulcan was nothing more than a figment of his theory-driven imagination. The astronomer's last view was the correct one, Vulcan was a figment of his theory-driven imagination, even though the name "Vulcan" was introduced to name a real planet. The name "Charles Herman" like "Vulcan" is an empty name, it denotes nothing at all. But nonetheless Charles Herman is a mere object of hallucination, just as Vulcan is a figment of Leverrier's imagination. (This suggests the resolution to the problem of empty names like "Vulcan" will go by way of explaining such predicates as "is a figment of Leverrier's imagination" just as the problem of explaining empty names like "Charles Herman" is resolved by explaining predicates like "is a mere (secondary) object of hallucination." Nothing is achieved by treating the denotata of such names as items in the arcane category of the non-existent.)[37]

In any case, how does this episode in the film raise a difficulty for the Meinongian treatment of hallucination? The Meinongian strategy is to identify the object of hallucination with a non-existent object with just the properties that the hallucinating subject is inclined to predicate on the strength of his hallucination. When it comes to Charles we may fairly ask whether the property of being real or the property of being unreal is to be bundled into the property characterization definitive of Charles. Neither will do at the exclusion of the other; instead what we intuitively want when it comes to Charles is an "object" that is first real, and then unreal.

It should come as no surprise to learn that the Meinongian is so ontologically profligate that he happily admits such objects. They don't exist of course, but the Meinongian considers that to be no obstacle to their having such combinations of properties. However odd you might find that, this is not the special difficulty that the case of Nash's roommate raises.

The difficulty is that making the property of being real first and unreal later a definitive feature of Charles (along with, say, his English charm and wise concern) clearly misidentifies the object of Nash's *first* hallucinations of Charles, the ones Nash had upon entering graduate school. For Nash could have had those very same hallucinations with the very same object even if he continued to be taken in by his hallucinations throughout his whole life, even if he never came to regard Charles as unreal. In that case, if we follow the Meniongian rule of identifying the object of hallucination with an non-existent object with just the properties that the hallucinating subject is inclined to predicate on the strength of his hallucination then we would include reality, but not unreality, as a definitive feature of Charles. For the object of Nash's first hallucinations was such a Charles, a Charles with no tincture of unreality. Hence, even with an extraordinary range of objects to choose from, the Meinongian fails to capture the "identity" across hallucinations of Charles, who was first taken by Nash to be real and then taken to be unreal.

The failure is easily diagnosed by the present account, which emphasizes the construal-dependent secondary "objects" of hallucination and their secondary, construal-dependent features. The identity across hallucinations of Charles is not a matter of objective preservation of significant properties by a genuine item, but rather a matter of how it strikes the subject of the hallucinations. The film *A Beautiful Mind* visually conveys what it supposes was immediately presented to Nash at different parts of his life. We see depicted different but somewhat similar sensible profiles which Nash took to be the very same thing, namely Charles, something which Nash first regarded as a real person and then as a figment of his imagination. There is no issue, at the level of Meinongian or other objects, as to how something that is a real person can be truly identical with something which is a figment of someone's imagination. Talk of identity here, like talk of mere secondary objects, is a *façon de parler*, a way of conveying facts about how things strike the subject of the hallucinations.

Obviously, the case of Nash's roommate will also tell against those theorists who treat the objects of hallucination as this-worldly abstracta individuated by their constituent properties, where the constituent properties are those the subject is inclined to predicate on the strength of his hallucination.[38] Charles, who starts out as real and then is evidently unreal, (if I may put it that way) is not to be found among such this-worldly abstracta.

Once again, even an abstract entity that includes the property of being first real and then unreal will not do, since it would have also to be the object of Nash's earliest hallucinations of Charles. But Nash could have had those very hallucinations individuated by their objects without ever, as it were, "seeing through them" and coming to regard his roommate as a figment of his imagination.

Our account of hallucination gives the following diagnosis of the case of Nash's roommate. At various times throughout his life Nash is presented with a series of qualitatively related sensible profiles, which include visual, auditory and tactile qualities. These are the sort of sensible profiles that might be enjoyed by someone having veridical experience of a charming, supportive English roommate. At first, Nash takes the sensible profiles to be a certain Englishman, Charles Herman, whom he takes to be his roommate. Later, as he gains some control over his reactions to his hallucinations, Nash still takes certain sensible profiles to be Charles, but he regards Charles as a mere figment of his imagination. Hence the intensional "identity" of Charles through episodes in which "he" is regarded as real and unreal.

Perhaps some viewers of the film will see another, less subtle, possibility depicted there. First Nash takes the sensible profiles to be an English roommate. Later, as he gains control over his reactions to his hallucinations, Nash then takes similar sensible profiles to be mere figments of his imagination. Rather than rest anything on an interpretation of the film, it is enough to point out that the two interpretations represent two distinct psychological possibilities. The first interpretation but not the second captures the centrality of Charles, a mere object of hallucination, in Nash's mental life. The sensible profile account with its resort to secondary, construal-dependent "objects" of hallucination distinguishes and deals with both interpretations.

Another route to the insufficiency of the Meinongian approach to hallucination derives from the fact that the object of hallucination is not wholly immanent. Its whole nature is not necessarily exhausted by how it strikes the subject. For example, my hallucination of a deep red patch could fade continuously, so that the reds I am visually aware of might be less and less saturated. A combination of physiology and an appeal to supervenience might support this claim of continuous fading. But then, thanks to the difference in grain between visual experience and what attention can reveal, there could be times t, t′ and t* such that:

What I experience at t will strike me as indistinguishable from what I experience at t′.

What I experience at t′ will strike me as indistinguishable from what I experience at t*.
Yet, what I experience at t will strike me as distinguishable from what I experience at t*.

The best explanation of this fact of the non-transitivity of indistinguishability, is that even in the case of hallucination the hallucinator can miss some of the qualitative features of his hallucination. If this is so then there will be more to the object of hallucination than how it strikes the subject. That means that we will go wrong by applying the Meniongian rule of identifying the object of hallucination with a non-existent object with just the properties that the hallucinating subject is inclined to predicate on the strength of his hallucination. As well as the construal-dependent secondary object of hallucination, we also need the construal-independent primary object of hallucination.

14. Our account of hallucination helps to settle the vexed question of whether hallucination narrowly supervenes, i.e. supervenes on the subject's total brain state.[39] There are really two questions here. One is trivial. The other has different answers depending on whether we are concerned with just the primary or also with the secondary objects of hallucination. The trivial question is whether the fact that someone is hallucinating supervenes just on his total brain state. The answer has to be no, of course, for there could be neural duplicates one of which is seeing, while the other is hallucinating.

The more interesting question emerges when we distinguish the fact that someone is hallucinating from his enjoying awareness of the kind of things involved in hallucination. This is a genuine distinction on any theory that allows that awareness of such things might be enjoyed even if the subject is not hallucinating but seeing. The sensible profile account, as well as the Conjunctive Analysis, are just such theories. So we may ask whether enjoying the kind of awareness involved in hallucination supervenes on one's total brain state.

The answer depends on whether we are individuating that kind of awareness in terms of just the primary or also the secondary objects of hallucination. Focus first on the primary objects—the sensible profiles. None of the familiar models of Externalism seem at all apposite in the case of awareness of sensible profiles. It is one thing to admit that the *verbalized thoughts* of a brain in a vat might come to be of or about processes in the computer stimulating the brain's sensory inputs, quite another to allow the same for hallucinations, now understood as directed at complexes of sensible qualities and relations.

First of all, in many cases of hallucination there is no external causal connection to objects in the environment that is positively relevant to someone's hallucinating this or that sensible profile. One's brain could just go into a state that constitutes one's hallucinating. So the kind of consideration that Hilary Putnam used to argue for Externalism concerning the thoughts of brains in vats does not get an intuitive hold here. However regularly produced by brain states outside my visual system my hallucinations of sensible profiles happen to be, they are not *about* the very states of my brain that are reliably causing them. Suppose, for example, that as a result of a drug-crazed youth, I spend the last ten years of my life hallucinating Vasarelly-like patterns, in a manner that is reliably casually produced only by certain recurrent states of my brain. It seems entirely odd to suppose that I have come to be visually aware of those states of my brain.

In other cases of hallucination, such as the surgeon directly stimulating one's visual cortex, there is a relevant external cause but it is also clearly not what one's hallucination, e.g. of patterns of light, is of or about. So neither Putnam's thoughts about the brains in vats nor the familiar causal versions of Externalism apply in the case of hallucinating sensible profiles.

Secondly, in such primary hallucination there need not be any representational content whose reference is determined by the use of representations in the wider linguistic community. Neither the alleged externality of thoughts employing natural kind terms nor anything like Tyler Burge's example of thoughts about arthritis applies in the case of hallucinating profiles, even if the subject happens to go on to describe what he hallucinated in such natural kind or socially determined terms.

Thus, if we are thinking of hallucinations as individuated in terms of their primary objects then there seems to be no obstacle to supposing that the kind of awareness involved in hallucination narrowly supervenes, i.e. supervenes on the total brain state of the hallucinator.[40]

This in its turn decisively counts against the view that genuine nonexistent objects are the primary objects of hallucination. For consider that for anyone who is seeing, it is possible that there is someone who is hallucinating, even though he is a neural duplicate of the one who is seeing. If we then take the primary objects of hallucination to be non-existent objects it will follow from narrow supervenience that in each act of seeing the one who is seeing is aware of a non-existent object as well as the good old "existent" objects there in the scene before the eyes. A repugnant consequence, and one that also shows that the primary objects of hallucination are neither inexistent tropes nor inexistent colored patches, as Panyot Butchvarov, among others, suggests. For the same reason, the primary objects of hallucination cannot be mere possibilia, as David Lewis and William Lycan have suggested. For mere possibilia are not among my objects of visual awareness when I am genuinely seeing the things around me.[41] So the only position for the friend of possible or of non-existent objects to take is that such objects are the secondary objects of hallucination. But then the friend of possibilia or the non-existent will run afoul of the fact that such secondary objects often are construal-dependent. They often count as the correctly reported objects of hallucination just because the subjects construe the primary objects of their hallucinations in certain ways. And again, the resultant problem of intensional identity remains the ultimate stumbling block for both Possibilist and Meinongian accounts of secondary objects. For since the identity of secondary "objects" is construal-dependent, there just may be no answer to the question as to whether or not any of Macbeth's secondary objects are identical with Macduff's. That is the definitive sign that we are not here dealing with genuine items, not even genuine items in some special or arcane category such as the merely possible or the non-existent.

If we think of hallucinations as individuated in terms of their secondary "objects" as well as their primary objects then matters of supervenience come out quite differently. For if a case of X's visually hallucinating @ amounts to there being some uninstantiated profile of which X is visually aware, and this profile striking X as being @, then what X is hallucinating will depend on how things strike him as being. This in its turn will depend upon X's antecedent repertoire of singular reference. The same dependence on X's antecedent repertoire of singular reference is found in a case where X's hallucinating @ amounts to there being some uninstantiated profile of which X is visually aware and X's awareness of this profile being caused in the right way by a perception of @ or by a thought to the effect that @ is such and so. It is now a philosophical commonplace that two people who are neural duplicates could have different repertoires of singular reference thanks to their inhabiting different environments. Thus, in so far as we think of hallucinations as individuated by their secondary objects, hallucinations will not narrowly supervene, even on the total brain state of the subject.

15. Having provided a positive account of hallucination in the face of the denials of the Disjunctivists, it may now be helpful to assemble our difficulties with the Conjunctive Analysis. Recall that the Conjunctive Analysis is

an analysis of seeing by *genus* and *differentia*; an analysis that first demarcates the genus of visual experience in terms of a conjunct that could be satisfied whether or not one was seeing or hallucinating, and then attempts to differentiate seeing by way of a second conjunct that requires a certain kind of causal connection between the subject's experience and an external object. The Conjunctive Analysis counts external objects as objects of seeing just because they play a causal role in producing a visual state that the subject could enjoy even if he were hallucinating. And external objects are indirect objects of experience. What is directly given is what one could be aware of anyway, even if one were merely hallucinating.

A good deal has been said about why the direct/indirect distinction is bad phenomenology and bad epistemology. But the difficulties with the Conjunctive Analysis go further. There is a problem with attempting to *analyze* seeing by *genus* and *differentia*. One will only get an *analysis* if the analysans is not itself part of the analysis of the genus. So we may allow a disjunctive genus of "neutral" visual experience, the genus consisting of acts of seeing or hallucinating (or after-imaging). But one cannot then go on to analyse seeing as occurring when we have an instance of this disjunctive genus and a further condition which rules out hallucination (and after-imaging). That would be unilluminatingly circular. No light would be shed on what it is to be an act of seeing, beyond its being different from an act of hallucinating (or after-imaging). By way of all analogy, consider following pseudo-analysis of an *in-off* in snooker, a shot in which the striker hits the cue ball and it ends up in the pocket:

An in-off in snooker is a foul shot in snooker (genus) which is neither a push nor a mere failure to strike the object ball, nor the potting of a ball other than the object ball, nor the touching of a ball by the striker with anything other than the tip of the cue (differentia).[42]

It takes the genus of a foul shot in snooker and then proceeds to differentiate the in-offs within the genus by means of further conditions. Forget the fact that the differentiating condition is here disjunctive; the real problem is that the genus of being a foul shot in snooker is itself disjunctive, and being an in-off is included among the disjuncts. Roughly, the rules of snooker say that to be a foul shot in snooker is to be either an in-off or a push or a mere failure to strike the object ball or the potting of a ball other than the object ball or the touching of a ball with anything other than the tip of the cue. So the account of an in-off by genus and differentia provides a necessary, non-empirical equivalence, but no analysis of an in-off. It does not tell us what essentially and intrinsically it is to be an in-off.

Nevertheless, this perfectly correct observation about a merely disjunctive genus being unfit for analysis is seriously overstated by the Disjunctivist slogan that hallucination and seeing have nothing in common. The genus of acts of visual experience can be merely disjunctive even though the acts (seeing, hallucinating) have *something* in common. (As if in-offs, pushes and pottings in snooker did not have snooker tables and cues and balls in common!) The crucial point is that the something in common need not be an *act of awareness* of which seeing is a subspecies. There can be a common *element* in awareness, which explains seamless transitions and so forth, but which is not itself a common *act* of awareness.

Why isn't awareness of a sensible profile a common act of awareness as between seeing and hallucination? It may be held to be; and if so, we would part company with even the minimal Disjunctivist criticism of the Conjunctive Analysis. But it does seem that once we adopt the act/object treatment of visual experience it is more natural to individuate an act of awareness occurring at a time in terms of an object that includes all one is aware of in the relevant sensory modality at that time. Otherwise we would have the result that in an act of visual awareness of a red sphere we would also have acts of visual awareness of redness, sphericity, the sphere and the red sphere. To the extent this offends—and I do not say it must—it will be natural to say that there are acts of seeing and acts of hallucinating but no common acts of awareness of sensible profiles; that is, nothing to provide the non-disjunctive genus of acts of visual awareness.

Suppose instead that we can treat hallucination and seeing as subspecies of the genus of acts of awareness of sensible profiles, with seeing differentiated by also being awareness of instantiations of sensible profiles. Still, since we have to invoke the full characterization of seeing in order to state the condition that differentiates seeing within the genus of acts of awareness of sensible profiles, we hardly have an "analysis" of seeing, as opposed to just another way of stating that there is a common factor in seeing and hallucinating.

However the status of the genus of acts of awareness of sensible profiles turns out, there remains a seldom remarked upon problem with the differentiating condition invoked in the Conjunctive Analysis of seeing. Philosophers sometimes speak of a "Hume" world, a world which is as close to ours at the manifest level as it can be compatible with there being no causation in that world. It seems an epistemic possibility that our world is a Hume world, but this does not have to be the epistemic possibility in which we never see anything. Therefore being connected to the thing seen by an appropriate causal process originating with the thing seen cannot be an a priori and necessary condition on seeing that thing. (Indeed, something which first strikes many a student of the history of vision is that the now standard conception of vision as requiring something coming from the visible object was a relatively late discovery. A standard Medieval conception was that something went out from the eye to the things seen, and this was only refuted by the relatively arcane observation that the visible stars were too far away to be reached by any such subtle probe.)

The same point—that it is not a priori that seeing requires an appropriate causal process originating with the things seen—arises from the coherence of the supposition of seeing through walls (or seeing the future without benefit of backward causation, for that matter). Someone could coherently arrive at the conclusion that he is not merely hallucinating but actually sees through walls, even though he knows that no causal process transmits information through the wall. That he is seeing the objects on the other side of the wall might still remain the best explanation of why he knows so much about their features. The claim that he is veridically hallucinating the actual features that the objects happen to have would itself need further explanation. How in the absence of relevant causation does there continue to be an impressive accidental correlation between what he experiences and the features of objects on the other side of the wall? A better hypothesis is that he is seeing the things and their features, that is why there is an impressive correlation between what he experiences and the features of those objects. The things on the other side of the wall and their visible features are disclosed to him.

Seeing is just having things and the visible features of those things disclosed to one, whereas veridical visual hallucination is just awareness of the visible profiles that they actually happen to instantiate. There! We have just made the distinction without invoking causation. Which is a good thing, because it seems the distinction could be exemplified even in a Hume world, contrary to the Conjunctive Analysis. (Notice that this is consistent with the widely held view that every actual case of seeing is necessarily constituted by the causal process that actually constitutes it.)

The final bone of contention with the Conjunctive Analysis concerns whether seeing admits of *an analysis* at all. We can say that seeing is just having things and their visible features disclosed to one. But although this emphasizes the disclosure of particulars as necessary to seeing (as opposed to hallucination), it does not analyze seeing. For what it is to be visible is itself to be explained in terms of seeing. Seeing is a distinctive kind of awareness whose objects can be clarified. So also with visual hallucination. But this is not to say that we can analyze seeing, let alone analyze it as the kind of awareness found in visual hallucination *plus* appropriate causation. Finding a contrasting condition that demarcates the thing under analysis is not in general to provide an analysis. To be red is to be a color that is not pink or green or blue or yellow or brown or white or black. None would take that to be an analysis of red. To be an act of seeing is to be a visual experience (awareness of a visible profile) that is not an act of hallucination or afterimaging. True; and as far as I can tell genuinely necessary and a priori. But no analysis: it does not set out *what it is intrinsically and essentially to be* an act of seeing.

16. Having sketched a view of hallucination, I would like to conclude by showing how it can be extended to accommodate illusion.

I have been working with a rough, implicit distinction between hallucination and illusion, along the following lines. Hallucination involves no novel awareness of any particulars, whereas in illusion this need not be so. In illusion, one is seeing some particular, but one's experience somehow gets the particular wrong. So one sees the stick *as bent* when it is in fact straight, or one sees the curled rope as *a snake*, when it is just a rope. We can say that illusion is seeing a particular combined with non-veridical *seeing* of the particular *as thus and so*. By contrast, hallucination involves no relevant seeing of particulars at all. (While hallucinating a dagger, you might also genuinely see some particulars to the right, as it might be, of your hallucinated dagger. But when you see those particulars as say, next to a dagger, you will be having an illusion induced by a local hallucination. The local hallucination itself is not a non-veridical case of seeing *as*.)

Now the non-veridical *seeing as* which is definitive of illusion involves the same dual structure that we discerned in the case of hallucination. There is, as it were, primary and secondary *seeing as*. Consider for example the difference between the Necker Cube flip, where an apex which appeared behind now suddenly appears in front, and a Duck-Rabbit flip, where an unchanged visible array no longer looks like a drawing of a duck's head but instead like a drawing of a rabbit's head. In the Necker Cube flip there is a change in the presented array, a change in the profile that is presented to you. The apex that was furthest away is now closest.

Consider then a Necker Cube flip from a veridical presentation of a wire cube to an illusory presentation of the same wire cube. After the flip, one is seeing the wire cube, but one is seeing it as having a certain orientation, which it does not have. This is primary *seeing as* in the sense that how the thing is seen is a matter of a distinctive difference in the sensed profile. Illusion is seeing a particular combined with non-veridical seeing of the particular *as thus and so*. When the *seeing as* is primary in this way, one is aware of a particular and one is aware of a complex profile, only part of which is instantiated by the particular. One also sees the particular as instantiating parts of the profile, parts that it does not instantiate.

Then there are cases in which the illusory seeing as is not, in this sense, primary. I suppose that there are versions of the rope-as-snake illusion that are phenomenologically more or less as follows. So far as the presented profile goes, it may just be the profile of a coiled rope over there in the corner of the darkened hut. But because you are primed by your fear of snakes, it immediately strikes you as a snake. Here is the secondary object of your experience, determined by how things immediately strike you. Your having an illusion of a snake is your being presented with an instantiated profile and its immediately striking you as a snake.

Once again, a plausible act/object account of illusion, combined with the correct observation that we sometimes have illusions of things that do not or could not exist, does not imply that sometimes the objects of illusion are objects that do not exist. Suppose in a poorly lit room you see a Bouvier des Flanders with a harness on its back. Because you have been primed by your recent study of mythical beasts, you see the huge dog as a Pisan Chimera, a lion with an antelope head growing out of its back. There are no Pisan Chimeras, and perhaps there couldn't be. But once again, one need not postulate non-existent objects to respect the act-object account of illusion. Your having an illusion of a Pisan Chimera is your seeing a huge dog and the dog's striking you as a Pisan Chimera. As before, we simply have an intensional context, not a non-existent intentional object.[43]

What then of the remaining sub-category of delusory experience, namely afterimages? Although they do not proceed from a heat oppressed brain, but from fatigued retinas, I venture that afterimages raise no distinctive ontological issues that are not already present in the case of hallucination. To afterimage is to be aware of an uninstantiated sensible profile. Or more exactly, taking into account the special case of "veridical" after-imaging, to after-image is to be aware of a sensible profile without being aware of anything instantiating it in the scene before the eyes.[44]

Notice one last advantage of this Anti-Mentalist account of delusory experience. There has always been lurking a strong, if not explicitly stated, argument from mentalistic accounts of hallucination, illusion, and after-imaging to a Projectivist treatment of all sensory qualities. Consider a mixed case, an experience with both delusory and veridical elements. Say you convincingly hallucinate a red circular patch, as it were "alongside" the exactly isomorphic red circular patch that you are seeing. It seems to you that you are seeing *two* red, circular patches. Even if we allow only the Selective Theory, and hold that in hallucinating you are aware of a mental object that has both the red quale and the circular quale somehow in it, while in seeing you are aware of a real red circular patch, there remains a powerful observation which the Projectivist can turn to his advantage. Isn't it the case that the redness and the circularity of the real red patch look for all the world just to be the very same redness and circularity that are had by the mental object? And isn't the only viable explanation of this that even in the case of seeing things and their sensible features we are directly aware of features of mental objects, which we project onto the things seen? The result, which can be couched but not changed by treating sensible properties as dispositions to cause mental objects in us, is a dreadful kind of Kantian Relationalism about experience. All the senses directly reveal about external objects is how they affect us; they show us nothing of how such objects are in themselves.

Our Anti-Mentalistic account of delusory experience cuts off this line of argument. It admits the powerful observation, but explains it without invoking mental objects and mental qualia. It *is* the very same redness and circularity in the two cases, but these are not qualia had by mental objects. They are ordinary qualities instantiated in a real patch, which is being seen while the same qualities also figure in an uninstantiated profile, which is being hallucinated. The way is thus opened up for an account of sensed qualities as intrinsic, non-relational features of sensible particulars. The senses can make manifest how things are in themselves, at least how they sensibly are in themselves. The Projectivist would be thus exposed as the victim of an "*Intro*jective Error"; the error of drawing sensed qualities into the mind.[45] This is the radical "Direct" Realism mentioned at the beginning.

There is then nothing in *delusory* experience, be it hallucination, illusion or after-imaging, which threatens a "Direct" Realist account of *veridical* experience. In fact, in each of these cases, we are always and only directly aware—or better, just aware—of something real and entirely non-mental.[46]

## Notes

1. For some attempts see J. L. Austin, *Sense and Sensibilia* (London: Oxford University Press, 1962); John McDowell "Criteria, Defeasibility and Knowledge," *Proceedings of the British Academy* 68 (1982) [excerpted in this volume, chapter 5]; John Searle, *Intentionality* (New York: Cambridge, 1983); Hilary Putnam, "Sense, Nonsense and the Senses," The Dewey Lectures, printed in the *Journal of Philosophy* 91(9) (1994); and

Jonathan Dancy, "Arguments from Illusion," *Philosophical Quarterly* 45 (1995) [this volume, chapter 7].

2. For example; in what follows I shall suggest that both sides in the debate over "non-conceptual content" are essentially correct and that both sides in the Intensionalism versus Qualia debate are mistaken in that experience is neither propositional nor qualia-involving.

3. For a recent defense of the Conjunctive Analysis see Howard Robinson's *Perception* (London: Routledge, 1994) [excerpted in this volume, chapter 9]. Some Conjunctivists, like David Lewis in "Prosthetic Vision and Veridical Hallucination," *Australasian Journal of Philosophy* 58 (1980) substitute a condition of systematic counterfactual dependence for the causal condition. They also sometimes require that there be matching between the object seen and the content of the experience. This last condition seems to me to be at odds with a proper understanding of illusion as seeing something combined with non-veridical seeing of it as such and so. One can see one's house in the distance as a dot. There is no significant matching, but one is seeing one's house. More on this account of illusion below.

4. Intentionalism has it that enjoying a visual experience is a *sui generis* propositional attitude—visually entertaining a content—a relation between subjects and propositional contents concerning various possible scenes. In this way, experience "says" things about one's environment. In simple hallucination the content entertained (what experience "says") is false. In veridical perception the content entertained is true. On the Conjunctivist version of Intentionalism veridical perception differs from hallucination only in this respect: in hallucination one's coming to entertain a content is oddly or non-standardly caused.

On the Adverbial Theory, enjoying a visual experience is sensing in a certain manner, so that when hallucinating a red thing you are being appeared to redly. The adverb characterizes the manner of sensing so as to attach a character to the sensing without requiring that the sensing have an object, material or immaterial. In general then, something of the form

S enjoys an visual experience of an F

gets translated into something of the form

S is appeared to F-ly

which commits us to events of appearing along with manners or ways of appearing, but not to contents visually entertained nor to sense data-like mental arrays. On this view, being appeared to F-ly would be the common factor as between seeing an F and hallucinating an F.

5. If you like, the act of awareness that is seeing is the common act of awareness *qua* appropriately caused by certain external particulars. The causal gloss is to be understood as capturing a necessary feature of anything that counts as seeing. But the "basis" or the thing that is so glossed is just the common act of awareness, some-

thing you could have even when you are just hallucinating. Thanks to Kit Fine for this way of putting the Conjunctive Analysis.

6. For a variant on this argument see Chapter IV of Robinson's *Perception*, ibid. Michael Thau independently offered essentially the same argument in conversation. Harold Langsam accepts a version of it in his fine paper "The Theory of Appearing Defended," *Philosophical Studies* 87 (1997) [this volume, chapter 11]. Langsam appeals to what he calls the same cause/same effect principle, suitably qualified to require that the causes and the effects be specified in intrinsic terms.

7. *Dialogues on Metaphysics*, reprinted in S. Nadler (ed.), *Nicholas Malebranche: Philosophical Selections* (Indianapolis: Hackett).

8. A Disjunctive Theory of experience was first broached by J. M. Hinton in *Experiences* (Oxford: Clarendon Press, 1973) [excerpted in this volume, chapter 2]. In "Perception, Vision and Causation," *Proceedings of the Aristotelian Society* (1981) [this volume, chapter 3], P. F. Snowdon deployed it against the Conjunctive Analysis. John McDowell uses it to resist the Cartesian conception of the mental in "Criteria, Defeasibility and Knowledge," op. cit.

9. Alan Millar makes this suggestion on behalf of Disjunctivism in his "The Idea of Experience," *Proceedings of the Aristotelian Society* 96 (1996), 75–90 [this volume, chapter 8]. It is also central to the important, but as yet unpublished, work of Christoph Erlenkamp. On behalf of the Disjunctivist, Millar writes

There is available an alternative, and perhaps more readily comprehensible, formulation according to which the claim that it looks to you as if an F is there is made true either by your seeing something which looks to you to be an F or by its merely seeming to you that you see something which looks to you to be an F. (p. 76 [this volume, p. 138])

10. This needs further refinement to distinguish hallucination from mere illusion. For an account of that distinction see the last section of this paper.

11. Suppose the Disjunctive Theorist now insists that she is not treating hallucination as an act of a higher order than the act of seeing, but rather insisting that both acts are in a certain way second-order. Seeing always involves seeming to oneself to be seeing, the cane toad and the dazed truck driver notwithstanding. Hallucination is falsely seeming to oneself to be seeing.

Even so, our little missing explanation argument can be pressed. Hallucinating n lights is again to be analyzed as falsely seeming to oneself to see n more lights than one is in fact seeing. Once again we can ask for an explanation of why one falsely seems to oneself to be seeing n more lights than one is in fact seeing. Once again the natural, appealing and correct explanation is that one is hallucinating n lights— an explanation which the Disjunctive Theorist has rendered empty.

12. At least this is so, if we allow a use of "see" which covers both hallucination and veridical visual perception, as in "After the drug takes effect you will see things, some of which aren't really there." In the course of discussing G. E. Moore's use of the

expression "directly see," Richard Cartwright offers just this paraphrase of Macbeth's thought. Cartwright's "Macbeth's Dagger" is reprinted in his *Philosophical Essays* (Cambridge, MA: MIT Press, 1987).

13. But see below, for points about how (i) original *de re* knowledge of quality and (ii) the Waterfall Illusion raise difficulties for the Adverbial Theory. More generally, it seems that any development of the Adverbial Theory will be in a certain way conjunctive.

14. I note that in some quarters there is some skepticism about the idea of knowing what a quality is like on the grounds that qualities are the ways in which particulars can be alike or unalike. As against this we do make direct comparisons and contrasts among qualities themselves, and these comparisons and contrasts are what structure the relevant quality spaces. Nor is there an easy translation of such comparisons and contrast among qualities into remarks about particulars. When we say that orange is more similar to red than it is to blue, we are not even implying that every orange thing is more similar to any red thing than it is to any blue thing. Moreover the apparent existence of uninstantiated colors like supersaturated red renders hopeless the general program of translating comparative remarks about colors into comparative remarks about particulars.

15. "Whom one immediately takes it to be" admits of an ambiguity that tracks the distinction between speaker's reference and semantic reference. Suppose someone blissfully ignorant of American politics sees George W. Bush and believes that he is called "George Herbert Bush." He then hallucinates the man. Which man, the son or the father? I suppose that even if his hallucination immediately strikes him in such a way as to lead him to say "That is George Herbert Bush" his hallucination is of George W. Bush, the speaker referent of his use of "George Herbert Bush" and not the semantic referent. Similar points apply to a variety of other cases in which one is confused about who is who.

16. The special case of veridical hallucination requires a qualification. As in the surgery case, you can hallucinate lights when there are indeed lights there in the scene before your eyes. The more exact statement is that in hallucination you are aware of a complex of qualities but not aware of any instantiation of it in the scene before the eyes. "Before the eyes" is something of a term of art which has caught on in philosophical discussions of seeing; things over my shoulder can be "before my eyes" when I am looking in a mirror.

17. Which is not to say that one could not attempt to use descriptive devices such as "the kind of dog that looks like this, whatever kind that is." But once again one would run into the problem of small whippets, a mixed breed of terriers and English greyhounds. These mongrels can look just like large Italian greyhounds. In any case, the fact that thanks to a hallucination one would be, at best, in a position to pick out the breed by way of an attributive use of a definite description drives home the point that hallucination does not acquaint one with so-called "natural" kinds like breeds.

18. How can so-called "natural" kinds be sensible kinds? Part of the explanation of how that is so is given in "Manifest Kinds," *Journal of Philosophy* (1998), where it is argued that the manifest forms of many natural kinds partly individuate those kinds.

19. See below for a discussion of whether external causation is analytically necessary for seeing, as the Conjunctive Analysis entails.

20. For sympathy with the air, see William Alston, "Back to the Theory of Appearing," *Philosophical Perspectives* 15 (1999). Alston there refers to a view I once entertained to the effect that the object of hallucination was a brain state. Susanna Siegel also takes up my old unpublished view in her dissertation *Perception and Demonstrative Reference* (Cornell, 2000). My point in trying out the brain state view was to attempt to identify hallucination with a radical illusion of location and of kind, a case where one is visually aware of something, but nevertheless a case in which one gets the location and nature of the thing in question radically wrong. As against this I would now say that a brain *state* is too small-scale and abstract a thing to be an object of visual awareness. And in illusion, however radical, there is always something which the subject sees and wrongly sees as thus and so. Since a brain state cannot be seen, it cannot be the object of a radical illusion. At the very least, attempts to assimilate hallucination to illusion in this way leave us with the nagging question as to how a particular thing that would not be veridically seen could be nonetheless seen when one is enjoying an illusion.

21. See Leo M. Hurvich, *Color Vision* (Sinauer Associates Inc., 1982), pp. 187–188.

22. There is a view that items in the category of quality are autological, i.e. hold of themselves; so that supersaturated red is (predicatively) supersaturated red. It is an interesting view, but I don't think it can be made secure enough to rest anything upon it.

23. The Waterfall Illusion is a good test case for an account of visual experience: we need to recognize the direct experience of contraries, without our own account becoming contradictory. In having a property complex built up out of contrary properties we do not have a contradictory object, only one that could not be fully instantiated. A property complex consisting of the property of moving and its contrary is no more a contradictory object than is a set consisting of those two properties. By contrast, it would be a good question to ask the Adverbial Theorist just how it is possible to have a sensing that is a *rungs-moving-and-staying-still-ly* kind of sensing. The problem is not with the adverbial barbarism. It concerns how the barbarism can be understood without implying a contradiction in the supposed sensing itself, just as if there were supposed to be a kind of running which was running at the same time quickly and slowly, and by the very same standard of speed. I just throw this out as a challenge: What is the Adverbial Theorist's account of the Waterfall Illusion?

24. H. H. Price, *Perception* (London: Methuen, 1932).

25. Similarly, as against the whole approach that Thomas Nagel made so seductive in "What is it Like to be a Bat?," *Philosophical Review* 73 (1974), the first issue is not what it is like to be a bat, but what "sonic hardness" is like. The whole character of the bat's sensory consciousness is given by the qualities of which it can be aware.

26. In his second Dewey Lecture, Putnam rejects the Sense Datum theorist's explanation of subjective matching as between a dream and a veridical experience:

the explanation starts with a familiar fact, the fact that when I am dreaming it seems to me as if I were seeing this or that and offers an explanation in terms of utterly mysterious entities or processes—one which lacks all detail at the crucial points, and possesses no testability whatsoever. ("Sense, Nonsense and the Senses," op. cit. p. 475)

But these remarks represent a serious underestimation of what the Sense Datum View and other common factor views are in a position to explain.

27. David Lewis famously argued against such structural properties in "Against Structural Universals." But as David Armstrong immediately pointed out, the whole Lewis argument depends upon the assumption that the only mode of combination available for properties is mereological. And clearly there are non-mereological modes of combination. For example there is the relational state of Mary's loving of John, somehow made up of Mary, the relation of loving, and John. But this is not mereological combination. For if it were, the same would have to be said of the relational state of John's loving Mary. But since these two relational states involve the same constituents, the consequence of thinking of each as a mereological sum of those constitutents is that the relational states would co-exist in just the same circumstances. But it is an unfortunate fact that love need not be reciprocated. In short, given that there are non-symmetric relations and relational states involving them it follows that there are non-mereological modes of combination.

While ontology is at issue, it is worth dispelling a potential confusion. My one remark to the effect that supersaturated red might never be instantiated aside, nothing I say in the text is inconsistent with Armstrong's principle of instantiation, which has it that every universal or basic property is instantiated. Everyone should admit that you can take instantiated basic properties and construct from them a structural property which is uninstantiated. So the sensible profile account is fully consistent with the principle of instantiation. There is no extra ontological baggage carried by the sensible profile account, none that is beyond the rejection of Nominalism and the adoption of a genuinely constructive approach to complex properties. As far as I can see anyone who took senses or modes of presentation seriously would find it very hard to avoid doing the same.

You need not believe in "transcendent universals"—universals that exist even though nothing ever exemplifies them—in order to accept the sensible profile account.

28. Told in some detail in "The Authority of Affect," *Philosophy and Phenomenological Research* 103 (2001) and "Better Than Mere Knowledge? The Function of Sensory

Awareness," in T. Gendler and J. Hawthorne (eds.), *Perceptual Experience* (Oxford: Oxford University Press, 2006).

29. For contrasting views on this issue see Christopher Peacocke's "Non-Conceptual Content Defended" and John McDowell's "Reply to Commentators," *Philosophy and Phenomenological Research* 58 (1998).

30. Those like John Searle in his influential book *Intentionality*, op. cit. who would assimilate the case of veridical hallucination to the Fregean paradigm by including among sensory manners of presentation the requirement that the external particulars presented are the causes of the very experience of presentation thereby miss the radical openness to the real which sensing provides.

31. For more on this see "The Authority of Affect," op. cit.

32. Intentional Object treatments of experience can be found in John Searle, *Intentionality*, op. cit. and in Gilbert Harman, "The Intrinsic Quality of Experience," *Philosophical Perspectives* 4 (1990).

33. The case of anchoring a hallucination to a past perception is not immediately relevant since there is no such thing as *perceiving* the non-existent.

34. Parsons and Zalta exemplify the two basic approaches to the theory of non-existent objects.

On Parson's approach as it appeared in *Non-Existent Objects* (New Haven: Yale University Press, 1980) there is a general abstraction schema which implies that there are "non-existent" entities corresponding to non-denoting descriptive phrases such as "the golden mountain." These entities are then said to have two kinds of properties. There are the "nuclear" properties such as being golden and being a mountain. These allow us to say such things as that the golden mountain is golden and a mountain. The non-nuclear properties are just the straightforward properties of the entity in question. This distinction is roughly parallel to the distinction in the text between primary (non-nuclear) and secondary (nuclear) features. With respect to this approach as applied to the case of hallucination, the remark would be that once we understand the primary/secondary structure of hallucination, we do not need to invoke the non-existent objects that Parsons' abstraction schema would generate from reports of what is hallucinated. The primary objects exist and their primary features are just their features, whereas the secondary "objects" and the secondary "features" are just *façon de parler*, ways of talking about what and how the primary objects are taken to be.

Engaging more deeply with Parsons would involve a discussion of his arguments against a Fregean theory of fictional objects. The thing to do would be to show just why, thanks to the distinctive nature of sensory modes of presentation, the considerations he cites in the fictional case do not carry over to the objects of hallucination. See Terence Parsons, "Fregean Theories of Fictional Objects," *Topoi* 1 (1982).

Zalta makes a crucial distinction between non-existent objects encoding properties and their exemplifying properties. Here the remark should be that once we understand the primary/secondary structure of hallucination, we do not need to invoke *non-existent* objects encoding such properties as being lights on in a ceiling and being at a certain distance and direction from a vantage point. Sensible profiles exist and "encode" such properties by being complexes built out of them. The related non-existent objects do no extra work, at least when it comes to hallucination. See Edward Zalta, *Abstract Objects: An Introduction to Axiomatic Metaphysics* (Dordrecht: D. Reidel, 1983), and *Intensional Logic and the Metaphysics of Intentionality* (Cambridge, MA: The MIT Press/Bradford Books, 1988).

35. Harman, op. cit.

36. "The Intentionality of Sensation: A Grammatical Feature," in R. Butler (ed.), *Analytical Philosophy* (Oxford: Blackwell, 1962).

37. For those who like intricate puzzles we may now add the further fact that as far as John Nash's real life goes, Charles Herman is also a fictional object of hallucination, one invented by the screenwriters of *A Beautiful Mind*!

38. This view, often heard in conversation is, roughly, the counterpart for objects of hallucination of an account of fictional objects presented in Saul Kripke's unpublished Locke Lectures and in Peter Van Inwagen, "Creatures of Fiction," *American Philosophical Quarterly* 4 (1997).

39. See Martin Davies, "Perceptual Content and Local Supervenience," *Proceedings of the Aristotelian Society* 92 (1992), Fred Dretske, "Phenomenal Externalism," *Philosophical Issues* 7 (1996) and the discussions by Jaegwon Kim, Paul Horwich and John Biro which follow in that volume.

40. Christopher Peacocke urged on me the thought that awareness of (what I have called) the layout, at least when understood as a structure of actual distances, directions and orientations from the subject's vantage point, may not narrowly supervene on the subject's total brain state. I think we agree here. I hold that the natural kinds that are the actual spatio-temporal relations will not be present in the primary object of hallucination, but only qualitative surrogates of these. Compare the remarks in the body of the text about the kind Italian Greyhound.

The qualitative surrogates of the actual spatio-temporal relations might be thought of as the "a priori forms of sensible intuition," to borrow an old phrase. They are the aspects of spatial and temporal organization—being here, being there, being adjacent, being engulfed, being bounded (and thus being shaped thus and so), being now, being then, being after, overlapping, occluding etc.—with which hallucination could acquaint a subject.

41. See chapters 1 and 5 of Butchvarov's *Skepticism about the External World* (New York: Oxford University Press, 1998). Butchvarov's book does present very compelling considerations in favor of an act/object account of hallucination, particularly

by way of his attack on the Adverbial Theory. William Lycan's account of the objects of appearance is given in "Phenomenal Objects: A Back-handed Defense," in J. Tomberlin (ed.), *Philosophical Perspectives* 1 (1987). David Lewis invokes a cluster of possibilia unified by relations of acquaintance in "Individuation by Acquaintance and by Stipulation," *Philosophical Review* 92 (1983).

42. That is, an in-off in snooker is comparable to one kind of "scratch" in pool. Oddly the characterization of an in-off as hitting the cue ball and having it end up in the pocket allows for an in-off nothing, i.e. hitting the cue ball into the pocket without contacting another ball. But that is how I remember it from my misspent youth. Maybe there is always an inexistent ball that the cue ball goes *in* to the pocket *off.* (By the way, for those who are not familiar with the game, snooker stands to pool as golf stands to miniature golf—it's trivial but not ludicrous.)

43. Similar remarks could be made if we thought of the phenomenon of priming as involving what I have called the mechanism of anchoring reference to that of the priming thoughts. Then the account of your having an illusion of a Pisan Chimera would appeal not to how the primary object strikes you but to the contents of the priming and anchoring thoughts.

44. An example of veridical after-imaging might be the following. As a result of having a strong green light shone into my eyes I after-image a pink circular patch on the wall in front of me. As a matter of fact there is a pink circular patch painted on the wall in front of me. It just happens to be wholly obscured by my after-image.

45. A theme developed in detail in my "Are Manifest Qualities Response-Dependent?," *Monist* 81 (1998) and in "The Authority of Affect" op. cit.

46. Earlier versions of this paper were read at Reed College, CUNY Graduate School, Harvard, Cornell, U.C. Berkeley, the Chapel Hill Colloquium and the "Metaphysical Mayhem" conference at Syracuse. I thank the discussants at all those places and elsewhere, especially David Hilbert, Brian McLaughlin, Alex Byrne and Susanna Siegel, each of whom prepared written responses that changed my view of some of the terrain. Special thanks to William Eckhart for his detailed comments and to Kit Fine, Christopher Peacocke, Mark Greenberg and Sean Kelly.

# 13　The Limits of Self-Awareness

## M. G. F. Martin

The disjunctive theory of perception claims that we should understand statements about how things appear to a perceiver to be equivalent to statements of a disjunction that either one is perceiving such and such or one is suffering an illusion (or hallucination); and that such statements are not to be viewed as introducing a report of a distinctive mental event or state common to these various disjoint situations.

When Michael Hinton first introduced the idea, he suggested that the burden of proof or disproof lay with his opponent, that what was needed was to show that our talk of how things look or appear to one to be introduces more than what he later came to call perception-illusion disjunctions:

> I do not at present see how it can be, or could be, shown that there is such a thing as (Q) [a statement which reports the occurrence of a visual experience in contrast to expressing a perception-illusion disjunction]. Consequently I do not see how it can be shown that there is such a thing as my psi-ing for these and other statements to be about; and since one surely should not make statements without being able to show that they are about something, this means that as far as I can see no such statements should be made. Perhaps I just can't see far enough, but I should like to be shown that this is so. (Hinton, 1967, p. 220 [this volume, p. 4])

I suspect that many readers on encountering either Hinton's presentation of disjunctivism or the accounts of it available from Snowdon or McDowell, would find surprising this demand about the burden of proof for the existence of a non-disjunctive sensory experience. Surely we know what a sensory experience is in just the sense that Hinton is denying. What we don't know, the line of the thought may go, is quite what the

M. G. F. Martin, "The Limits of Self-Awareness," *Philosophical Studies* 120: 37–89. © 2004 Kluwer Academic Publishers. Reprinted with kind permission from Springer Science and Business Media.

disjunctivist is saying in its place. Doesn't the burden of proof lie, then, with the disjunctive theory of appearances: first to clarify further what it has to say, and then to offer some appropriate defence of these outlandish claims?

The aim of this paper is to offer some of that elaboration, but also in turn to explain the way in which Hinton was correct in his challenge. Properly understood, the disjunctive approach to perception is the appropriate starting point for any discussion of the nature of perceptual experience. The key to the approach is not in its appeal to paraphrasing claims about experience in disjunctive form, but is rather in an appeal to the idea of indiscriminability in explicating the claims we accept about experience. The core thought is that we grasp the idea of sense experience as such, in contrast to sense perception, through recognising that there are things that we cannot know about ourselves just through reflection on the situation we find ourselves in. As I aim to explain below, a suitable modesty about what one can know about one's experiential state is the proper starting point for theorising about sense experience in general. Any theory which moves beyond such modesty and makes substantive claims about the properties that sense experiences possess needs to justify this boldness.

In what follows, there are two morals that I wish to draw. The first concerns the question of the conception of sense experience in general; the second concerns the claims that the disjunctivist is committed to concerning a special sub-class of hallucinations, those brought about through the same proximate causal conditions as veridical perceptions. It is in relation to the latter that the most striking (and many will find most implausible) claim that the disjunctivist makes, that there may be sensory states whose mental nature is characterisable in nothing but epistemological terms, in terms of their unknowable difference from cases of veridical perception. But the significance of this commitment can be understood only in the light of the former claim about experience in general. Before addressing those matters, I want briefly to raise two others: the prime motivation for endorsing disjunctivism, and the question of how we are to understand its formulations as provided by Hinton, Snowdon and McDowell.

1. The prime reason for endorsing disjunctivism is to block the rejection of a view of perception I'll label *Naïve Realism*. The Naïve Realist thinks that some at least of our sensory episodes are presentations of an experience-independent reality. When I sit here writing this, I am conscious of the various elements that make up a North London street scene. The same objects and aspects of these objects which I can attend to as part of the environ-

ment beyond me are also aspects of what I can attend to when I pursue the question, "What is it like for me now to be staring out of the window rather than writing my paper?" Mind-independent reality can form the subject-matter of sensuous experience. In affirming this the Naïve Realist finds common ground with those views of perception which attribute to it a representational or intentional content and seek to explain its phenomenal character in terms of that content—*Intentional Theories of Perception*. For it is common to support such theories by pointing out that our sense experience is transparent—that experientially we are presented with a mind-independent realm and not simply some array of mind-dependent qualities or entities whose existence depends on this awareness.[1]

The Naïve Realist, however, claims that our sense experience of the world is, at least in part, non-representational. Some of the objects of perception—the concrete individuals, their properties, the events these partake in—are constituents of the experience. No experience like this, no experience of fundamentally the same kind, could have occurred had no appropriate candidate for awareness existed. In this, sense perception contrasts with imagining and thought. For one can certainly imagine objects in their absence, so the mind's direction on an object does not require that it actually exist when one imagines. The same is true, arguably, of thought—we think of objects which in fact do not exist as well as thinking of the existent. The Naïve Realist insists that sensing is not like this, and in that respect the Naïve Realist finds common ground with the Sense-Datum tradition, or what more broadly I will label *Subjectivism*. For Subjectivists have long insisted that what is distinctive of sensing as opposed to thinking is that one really cannot sense in the absence of an object of sensing.[2]

Whatever its other merits, Naïve Realism is inconsistent with two assumptions which are common to much of the philosophical discussion of perception. The first of these is *Experiential Naturalism*: our sense experiences, like other events or states within the natural world, are subject to the causal order, and in this case are thereby subject just to broadly physical causes (i.e. including neurophysiological causes and conditions) and psychological causes (if these are disjoint from physical causes). One can manipulate the world so as to induce an hallucination in someone, for example, by suitable stimulation of their sensory cortices and possible manipulation of their psychological condition. One does not, in addition, have to invoke any further influence over other super-luminary entities, something neither physical nor mental, in order to bring about the experience. The second assumption is *The Common Kind Assumption*: whatever kind of mental event occurs when one is veridically perceiving some scene, such as the street scene outside my window, that kind of event can occur whether or not one is perceiving. One may hold to this assumption for different reasons—it is tempting to suppose that it is obvious just because by "sensory experience" we mean to pick out that event for which there is something it is like for the subject when they perceive or hallucinate, or whatever. And we are, of course, aware that from the subject's point of view there may seem to be no difference at all between a case of hallucination and one of perception. So the event in question must be of the same phenomenal kind as the kind of veridical perception it matches. One may also eschew phenomenological evidence for the commitment in favour of an appeal to causal considerations—that reflection on how we can bring about perceptions and hallucinations should lead us to suppose that the immediate effects of appropriate brain stimulation, the experiences caused, must be the same whether or not a perception or an hallucination is brought about. Either way, the assumption is that when we are thinking of the mental or subjective aspect of perception we pick out a kind of event or state which is common to cases of perception and hallucination.

Naïve Realism together with these two assumptions leads to contradiction. For first, assume that we have some event which is as the Naïve Realist supposes a perception can be: it is an awareness of some lavender bush which exists independent of one's current awareness of it. By the Common Kind Assumption, whatever kind of experience that is, just such an experience could have occurred were one merely hallucinating. By Experiential Naturalism, we know that there are sufficient appropriate physical and psychological causes of it. If the hallucinatory experience were relational in the manner that the Naïve Realist supposes the perception of the bush to be, then the causes sufficient to bring about the hallucination must also have been sufficient for some appropriate object to be present in the experience. By our assumption about the causes, this is done without assuming any extra causal correlations between the causes of the experience and any nonphysical object of awareness. Hence the bringing about of the experience must have been sufficient for the existence of its object—that is, the experience is of a kind sufficient for the existence of its object. If the experience alone is constitutively sufficient for this object of awareness in the case of hallucination, then the object in this case is not merely non-physical but dependent for its existence on the occurrence of this experience.[3,4]

Since the experience which occurs when one is hallucinating is of just the sort that occurs when one is veridically perceiving, the experience one has when one is veridically perceiving is by itself sufficient to constitute the existence of its object of awareness. According to the Naïve Realist, the object of awareness is experience-independent, yet in this case we are to suppose that there is in addition an experience-dependent object sufficient to account for the nature of the experience. So, contrary to the Naïve Realist's starting assumption, if the hallucinatory experience is a relation to an object of awareness, it is to a mind-dependent one, and hence the perception is a relation to a mind-dependent object, not the mind-independent object that the Naïve Realist hypothesises.

What if one assumes instead that the hallucinatory experience is not the awareness of anything at all? From the subject's perspective it may seem as if there is a table there before him or her, but in reality there is nothing for them to be standing in such a relation of awareness. We have to describe the situation as if there is such an object—we say that the subject "sees" a bush, or it is "as if" there is an apparent bush. In doing so, though, we do not really indicate any acceptance of ontological commitment; rather we treat the experience as having an "intentional object."[5] To make this move is to assume that the experience of the kind that the subject has when hallucinating does not need to have any objects of awareness as constituents of the experience—some experiences we treat as if they are the presentations of such objects, but they don't need any such objects to exist in order for them to occur. This position may seem to have the ontological advantage of avoiding any commitment to mind-dependent entities, and for that reason has often been preferred. But despite this advantage, it offers no respite from the argument we are now considering. Since the experience in question, the hallucination, is of just the same kind as the veridical perception, then the same holds of the veridical perception as of the hallucination. That is, the veridical perception does not have the objects of perception as constituents, despite the Naïve Realist's claims to the contrary.

So, Experiential Naturalism imposes certain constraints on what can be true of hallucinatory experiences. Such experiences either can have only experience-dependent objects, or not be relations to objects at all. By the Common Kind Assumption, whatever is true of the kind of experience that one has when one is hallucinating, the same must be true of the kind of experience one has when perceiving. So either one's experience when veridically perceiving is of some mind-dependent object, or the experience is not essentially a relation to any object at all.

Hence, Naïve Realism is inconsistent with these two assumptions. One way of reading the history of philosophy of perception is to see it in terms of a conflict between Naïve Realism and the kind of commitments reflected in these two assumptions.[6] Sense-datum theories hold on to one aspect of Naïve Realism, that experience is a relation between the subject and some object of awareness, yet reject the thought that such objects can be the objects in the world around us. Intentional theories of perception are often moved by the thought that one should hold on to the other aspect of Naïve Realism, that one is related to the world around us through perceptual consciousness, but thereby give up the element of Naïve Realism, that such awareness is genuinely a relation to such objects.

The motivation for disjunctivism, I suggest, is a desire to hold on to Naïve Realism. For reasons expanded on elsewhere, I suggest that we should think of Naïve Realism as the best articulation of how our experiences strike us as being to introspective reflection on them.[7] It is common to complain against sense-datum theories that they deny that we have genuine awareness of objects in the world around us, to complain that they introduce a veil of perception. The best sense one can make of this complaint is really that sense-datum theories are forced to say that the real nature of our sensory experience is not how it strikes us as being. But if Naïve Realism is the correct description of how our sensory experience strikes us, then an intentional theory of perception is no less revisionary than a sense-datum account. To hold on to our Naïve view of experience, though, we need to reject one of the starting assumptions: either Experiential Naturalism or the Common Kind Assumption.

Experiential Naturalism was implicitly rejected by the early sense-datum theorists who were sceptical of the completeness or unity of the physical world and open to positing the existence of many strange items.[8] Such a rejection may not be *a priori* incoherent but it comes at high cost. So too does a rejection of this argument through embracing transcendental idealism, as Merleau-Ponty suggests, and as Jerry Valberg more recently has recommended.[9] If we do not think of our experience of the world as itself being a part of the world, then we need not conceive it as having causal antecedents within the world—we then need not think of how such events can otherwise be brought about.

The disjunctivist response, however, remains committed to the broad empirical assumptions and methodological presuppositions which lead one to endorse Experiential Naturalism and hence the conclusions drawn from it about the nature of our experiences. It seeks to resist the rejection of Naïve Realism, therefore, simply by denying the Common Kind Assumption. That is, we hold on to Naïve Realism by insisting that the fundamental kind of event that one's sensory experience which is a veridical perception of the table in front of one is is a kind of event which just could not occur were one hallucinating. Even if some matching hallucination would either have to be an awareness of some mind-dependent object or of no object at all, nothing follows from that alone about the status of one's veridical perception.

2. What does the denial of the Common Kind Assumption amount to? The three disjunctivists with which I started, Hinton together with Paul Snowdon and John McDowell, offer significantly different formulations of the view. Contrast Hinton in the first quotation, with Snowdon and then McDowell:

Even if few things are certain, it is certain that there are what I shall call perception-illusion disjunctions: sentences or statements like "Macbeth perceives a dagger or is having that illusion," which you can compose by adding words like "... or $x$ is having that illusion" to a sentence which says that a particular person, $x$, perceives a thing of some particular kind. (Hinton, 1973, p. 37 [this volume, p. 20])

It looks to $S$ as if there is an $F$: (there is something which looks to $S$ to be $F$) *or* (it is to $S$ as if there is something which looks to him ($S$) to be $F$). (Snowdon, 1980–1981 [this volume, p. 40])

... an appearance that such-and-such is the case can be *either* a mere appearance *or* the fact made manifest to someone ... the object of experience in the deceptive cases is a mere appearance. But we are not to accept that in the non-deceptive cases too the object of experience is a mere appearance, and hence something that falls short of the fact itself ... appearances are no longer conceived as ... intervening between the experiencing subject and the world. (McDowell, 1982 [this volume, p. xx])

In each case the disjunctive form is specified in significantly different ways. Hinton and Snowdon focus on locutions of object perception, "$S$ sees $o$," which are commonly taken to be transparent in the object position. Hinton contrasts on either side of his disjunction the seeing of a flash of light with the having of an illusion of a flash of light. Snowdon, in contrast, treats both veridical perception and illusion as belonging on the privileged side of the disjunction, since both involve perception of an object, and keeps only hallucination to the contrasted side. In contrast to both of these, McDowell is interested in locutions of factual perception: "$S$ sees/can see that $p$." Such locutions are typically opaque in the complement clause, and the relation between talk of object perception and fact perception is complex—not every object mentioned in a perceived fact need be an object of perception; even if some fact must be perceived concerning any object of perception, it is not clear that there is any specific fact which must have been perceived in perceiving an object. McDowell's contrast case, then, is simply that of merely apprehending the appearance of $p$, rather than properly grasping the fact.[10]

Perhaps, then, rather than speaking in terms of *the* disjunctive theory of appearances, we should recognise a cluster of approaches, all of which have in common just a negative thesis: the thesis that we should not think that perceptual experience is to be analysed as a common factor of perception and either illusion or hallucination.

However, if we characterise the approach just in this negative way, then we are also liable to be misled. For this seems to offer merely an incomplete sketch of an account which needs further supplementation. First, one needs some further gloss of the "privileged" disjunct—the reference to perception or veridical perception. That there is some idea at the back of these theories is often implicitly understood when one reads them—these accounts are supposed, somehow or other, to defend some form of direct realism. On the other hand, the negative construal as yet does not tell us what to say about the "underprivileged" disjunct, the one that fails the condition to be counted as perception. Surely we need to know what more to say about these cases before we know what these approaches are telling us about perceptual experience in general. Jonathan Dancy offers a clear expression of this line of thought when he suggests:

The disjunctive account of perception really says that there are two quite different sorts of oasis-experience, which may none the less be indistinguishable to their owner. The first is the genuine article, and the second, though it is indistinguishable, has nothing in common with the first other than the fact that they are both oasis-experiences. In the standard formulation of the account, misleadingly, this is explicitly the way in which the second disjunct is characterized: we characterize it solely by saying that it is like what it is not. Presumably, however, there may be available a more direct characterization of the second disjunct, and in a totally explicit version of the theory it would indeed be characterized in that better way. The current characterization is just a sort of place-holder, showing what has to be said about the relation between the first and second disjunct. (Dancy, 1995 [this volume, p. 132])

Yet if we take Dancy's concerns seriously and attempt to spell disjunctivism out in more detail, we encounter two further problems. According to Dancy, in the proper dress of the theory, we should surmise that the full account of perceptual experience offers a clause for the privileged case of perception and the underprivileged case of illusion or hallucination. Where other theories can hope to offer a common explanation of the phenomena that we look to perception and sensory experience to provide, the supplemented disjunctivism will need to offer two distinct accounts. As such the approach necessarily lacks the consilience of conjunctive accounts of sensory experience. Struck by this obvious thought, it is no surprise that opponents are liable to think that justification needs to be provided for the disjunctivist position rather than vice versa—Hinton's attitude is liable to seem mere complacence.

Behind this lies a deeper worry. Is there really a coherent supplementation to the disjunctive account? Suppose we do get a further specification of the kind of mental event that occurs in the non-privileged circumstances. If what marks these cases out in the first place is just that they involve the absence of perception, then one may worry that whatever fixes what they have in common with each other will apply equally to any case of perception. That is to say, the further specification of hallucination will be something which is present not only in all cases of illusion or hallucination but also in the case of perception. The disjunctivist will then be left in the unhappy position of conceding that there is a common element to all of the cases, while still insisting that there is something distinctive of perception. Now if the common element is sufficient to explain all the relevant phenomena in the various cases of illusion and hallucination, one may also worry that it must be sufficient in the case of perception as well. In that case, disjunctivism is threatened with viewing its favoured conception of perception as explanatorily redundant.

In what follows I will address both of these concerns. Hinton is right to say that the disjunctivist conception of perceptual experience in general should in fact be our default conception. And Dancy is wrong to think that the disjunctivist specification is incomplete, that we should supplement the account of experience with a non-relational gloss of what illusory or hallucinatory experiences are. Nonetheless, the remaining worry about explanatory redundancy does pose a serious challenge to disjunctivism, as we shall see, and in the end addressing this challenge brings out the most distinctive and surprising aspect of disjunctivism: the limits to the self-awareness we can have of our own sensory states.

Properly understood, disjunctivism offers us an epistemological perspective on how we should conceive the debate about sensory experience. It helps bring out how weighty one's epistemological assumptions about the mind must be, if one is to advance beyond this epistemological stance.

3. How then should we think about sense experience? What gives us a grip on the notion? Contrast two different ways of thinking about the Cartesian story of lucid dreaming. Few of us have any problem grasping the idea of perfect hallucinations. At present, I have good reason to suppose that I am seeing a London street pretty much as it is. So I have a veridical perception of the unkempt lavender bush at the end of my road that marks the advance of late summer. Nonetheless, as far as I can tell, it seems a genuine

possibility that I could have been in a situation which was not one of actually perceiving my environment for how it was but which I would not have been able to tell apart from this, my actual situation, just through introspection and reflection on my experience. Such a case would surely be a perfect hallucination of the kind of scene that I am perceiving, as things stand, for what it is.

On the first conception of experience, one that someone who endorses the Common Kind Assumption might endorse, this starting point is further elaborated so. A perceptual experience is a kind of event which has certain distinctive features $E_1 \ldots E_n$. Not only is the possession of these features necessary and sufficient for an event to be an experience, but, in addition, an event's possession of them is introspectible by the subject of the experience. When I come to recognise the possibility of perfect hallucination just like my current perception, what I do is both recognise the presence of these characteristics, $E_1 \ldots E_n$, in virtue of which this event is such an experience, and also recognise that an event's possessing these characteristics is independent of whether the event is a perception or not. So in accepting the Cartesian possibility I display a grasp of a positive piece of knowledge about the nature of certain mental events.

Note that to accept this much still leaves open what characteristics $E_1 \ldots E_n$ are. For all that has been said we should construe these as an experience's being the presentation of such and such mind-dependent qualities, as a sense-datum theory supposes. Or we might instead take them to be representational properties, as an intentional theory would press. For our present purposes here, we can remain neutral about this matter. All that matters for our current purposes is that such views will attribute to subjects who grasp the concept of perfect hallucination both the power to identify the marks of experience in having an experience and a recognition of their modal independence of the conditions of perceiving. To this extent, then, such theories are immodest in their attribution of epistemological powers that subjects have when they give an explanation of how we come to have a conception of sensory experience which can be employed from the first person perspective.

This is not the only way to elaborate the initial sketch. Instead one may insist that the original instructions to conceive of perfectly matching hallucinations are all that is needed to give one a conception of perceptual experience. This second way of thinking about the idea of sense experience, we might call a modest or minimal conception. We need not look for some further characteristics in virtue of which an event counts as an experience of a street scene, but rather take something to be such an experience simply in virtue of its being indiscriminable from a perception of a street scene. Nothing more is needed for something to be an experience, according to this conception, than that it satisfy this epistemological condition. Rather than appealing to a substantive condition which an event must meet to be an experience, and in addition ascribing to us cognitive powers to recognise the presence of this substantive condition, it instead emphasises the limits of our powers of discrimination and the limits of self-awareness: some event is an experience of a street scene just in case it couldn't be told apart through introspection from a veridical perception of the street as the street.

Does this second conception really capture what we need? Well a proponent of the immodest view cannot fault a modest account for failing to capture in its conception of what a sense experience is all those situations that the immodest account deems to be perceptual experiences of a street scene. After all, by immodest lights the kind of experience one has when seeing such a street scene is of just the same kind as any non-perceptual event which is not a perception but still an experience as of a street scene, namely an event with the properties $E_1 \ldots E_n$. Since nothing can be discriminated from itself, the immodest approach will hold that the modest one should agree that these events are indiscriminable from a veridical perception of a street scene and hence are perceptual experiences as of a street scene. (Of course, by modest lights this consequence might not follow, but that would only be because the particular version of the immodest account is inadequate and the properties $E_1 \ldots E_n$ it specifies are not after all sufficient for an event's being a perceptual experience as of a street scene even in the case of veridical perception.) So immodest views may complain that modest ones fail to capture what defines an event's being an experience but not that their conception of experience is too narrow.

On the other hand, it is difficult for an immodest account to avoid complaining that modest ones are far too catholic in their conception of what can be an experience as of a street scene. Given all we have said so far, nothing rules out as possible a situation in which $E_1 \ldots E_n$ are absent but in which a subject would be unable to discriminate through reflection this situation from one in which a street scene was really being seen. For the immodest view in question, this could not be a case of visual experience as of a street scene, while by modest lights that would be exactly what it is.

Now surely this result would be unfortunate for any immodest view, given our initial assumptions. For we supposed that reflection on experience offers support to a Naïve realist construal of sensory experience. When one reflects on one's experience it seems to one as if one is thereby presented with some experience-independent elements of the scene before one as constituents of one's experience and not merely as represented to one as in imagination. Even if the experience does also possess the characteristics $E_1 \ldots E_n$, it need not manifest to the perceiver that these are present as opposed to Naïve realist aspects of experience. And it is at least not manifest that the experience is the kind of experience it is in virtue of the presence of these properties as opposed to being Naïve realist—for were it, then clearly it would not even seem to us as if Naïve realism is true. When we turn to a case of perfect hallucination, we know that the Naïve phenomenal properties which seem to be present in the case of veridical perception certainly cannot be present in the case of hallucination. Of course they may still seem to be present, and in as much as the hallucination is indistinguishable from the perception they will seem to be so. So, if the presence of $E_1 \ldots E_n$ as opposed to the presence of Naïve phenomenal properties is not manifest to us in the case of veridical perception, and anyway is certainly not presented as definitive of that's being the experience it is, then it seems plausible that what links the case of hallucination to the veridical perception is the seeming presence of Naïve phenomenal properties and not $E_1 \ldots E_n$. In that case, common sense has no reason to discriminate against a case of perfect hallucination which lacks $E_1 \ldots E_n$ but yet which seems to possess the properties relevant to its being an experience as of a street scene in the first place, the seeming presence of Naïve phenomenal properties.

If a modest account is too catholic in its conception of experience, immodest views will seem from a common sense perspective to be too restrictive. Even if the presence of $E_1 \ldots E_n$ is sufficient to determine that one is having an experience as of a street scene, nothing has shown why it has to be necessary. Rather, if it really is possible to produce an experience lacking those features but otherwise being indiscriminable from a perception of a street scene, the account will offer just one way in which such an experience can occur. A proponent of an immodest view can only hope to offer necessary as well as sufficient conditions for having an experience— and hence to explain the having of experience in terms of its favoured conditions—if it can ensure that the modest approach and its favoured form of immodesty coincide in the extension they give the concept of experience.

In turn, this coincidence of extension can be guaranteed only if the proponent of the immodest account embraces a substantive epistemic principle. That will be achieved only if the situation sketched above turns out to be impossible: that there cannot be any situation which is indistinguishable for its subject from actually perceiving a street scene and yet which lacks the relevant properties. In turn, one must assume that a subject couldn't but be in a position to discriminate a situation which lacked $E_1 \ldots E_n$ from one which possessed them. Here I just assume that for one situation to be indiscriminable from another requires only that it not be possible to know that it is distinct in kind.[11] Therefore to deny it is possible that a situation which is distinct in kind from an event possessing $E_1 \ldots E_n$ is not possibly knowable as distinct in kind, is to claim that for any situation distinct in kind from an event possessing $E_1 \ldots E_n$ it is possible to know that it is distinct.

Adopting this position is to attribute a privileged epistemic position to the subject of experience. For, according to it, a responsible subject who wishes to determine how things are with him or herself through reflection must not only correctly identify phenomenal properties of a specific sort when they are present, but also they cannot be misled into judging them present when they are not. It is not merely that the properties which determine an event as an experience are held to be self-evident on this view—that the presence of such properties indicates to the subject that they are present when they are present. It must also be the case that the absence of such properties when they are absent is equally detectible by the subject, so that there is always some way that a subject could tell that he or she was not so experiencing when not doing so. It is to attribute to responsible subjects potential infallibility about the course of their experiences.

Of course, some philosophers have assumed that these epistemic properties are definitional of the mental, and so see nothing substantive in the additional assumption. But the doctrine of infallibilism about the mental is particularly problematic in relation to sensory states once we are forced to admit that appearances systematically appear to us other than they are. For if we can be misled with respect to some properties of sensory experiences, there is a question as to what can motivate the claim that we are infallible in other judgements about them. As I indicated above, part of the motivation for disjunctivism is precisely the thought that introspection of our sense experience supports Naïve Realism, and hence forces us to see both sense-datum and intentional theories as forms of error theory.

The assessment of this epistemological commitment I'll leave for elsewhere. For this discussion, the only point to note is that given the need to rely on this assumption, an immodest approach to perceptual experience carries more theoretical burdens than does a modest approach. The burden of proof is not on the disjunctivist to show that we should adopt a less than conjunctive theory of appearances, the burden is really on any common kind theorist, to show that the theory they propose is not really too restrictive; or that the added epistemological burdens which come with demonstrating that are ones that we should accept.

This points to where Dancy was misled. In fixing on the concept of perceptual experience in general we seem to have no more resources than that we need to pick out something indiscriminable from veridical perception. So the most inclusive conception we can have here is an implicitly relational one. Any of the non-relational specifications that Naïve realist, or sense-datum, or intentional theories or some other approach can give us would seem just to offer at best a sufficient condition for meeting the relational specification. That would offer simply an account of one particular variant of experience, rather than an account of what experience must be. What most Common Kind theories (i.e. theories which endorse the Common Kind Assumption) ignore is that in giving an account of experience they normally succeed, if at all, only in giving sufficient conditions for one's experience to be a certain way, and fail to show that the conditions they offer are necessary. Without the latter being fulfilled, no such theory can claim to give a fully general account of experience.

Hence we can see that as long as our focus is on the concept of sensory experience in general, intended to cover all possible cases of what we would count as a sensory experience of a lavender bush, then our default position should be that of the disjunctivist. What we mean by this is no more than this is a situation which is indiscriminable through reflection from a veridical perception of a lavender bush.

4. So far, we have been looking at what the disjunctivist should say about perceptual experience in general. Its account of this is entirely minimal. For all that has been said, the account is not inconsistent with the view that there are some experiences among the non-veridical ones which fit the characterisations offered by sense-datum or intentional theories. The disjunctivist's general conception of experience does not have the resources to say that no such experiences can occur—as long as those experiences meet the relational condition of being indiscriminable from a veridical perception, then the disjunctivist is happy to count them as being among the perceptual experiences.

However, this cannot exhaust the content of an account of sensory experience which rejects the Common Kind Assumption. For, further reflection on the causal argument reveals that there is a specific range of experiences about which the disjunctivist is forced to say somewhat more. If disjunctivism is motivated along the lines that we are concerned with, namely by the need to resist the problem of perception in a way that retains both Naïve Realism and Experiential Naturalism, then a variant of the causal argument presents the disjunctivist with a challenge. Experiences which share the proximate causal conditions as veridical perceptions but which lack the further conditions for being perceptions cannot have Naïve phenomenal properties. But, as we shall see, there is reason to think that whatever kind of event these experiences are, the very same kind of event occurs when one is perceiving. So the disjunctivist needs an account of these hallucinatory events, and one which remains consistent with the assertion of Naïve Realism concerning veridical perception.

The challenge develops in two steps. The first develops from the so-called causal argument for sense-data or against Naïve Realism. In that form causal considerations are appealed to in support of the Common Kind Assumption. Here however, we will be concerned with a variant of this argument with weaker assumptions to a conclusion that does not entail the Common Kind Assumption. Whether this conclusion is really consistent with disjunctivism is then the concern of the second step, which we shall reach below.

The argument we focus on here is based on the versions used by Howard Robinson.[12] It develops so:

(1) When $S$ sees a pine tree at $t$, call this situation $v$, there is in $S$'s body some complete causal condition just prior to $t$ which determined the chance of this event of seeing occurring in $v$, call this condition $N$;

(2) It is nomologically possible that $N$ should occur in $S$ even if no candidate object of perception is present and conditions necessary for the occurrence of a perception are not met, and an hallucinatory experience instead occurs; call one such situation $h$;

(3) Where two situations involve the same proximate causal conditions, *and* do not differ in any non-causal conditions for the occurrence of some kind of effect, then the chances for the occurrence of such an effect are the same in both situations;[13]

(4) No non-causal condition required for the occurrence of the effects of $N$ is present in $h$ but absent in $v$;

(5) Whatever kind of experience occurs in $h$, there is the same chance of such an experience occurring in $v$;

(6) Hence whatever kind of experience does occur in situations like $h$, it is possible that such a kind of experience occurs when one is veridically perceiving.

Our conclusion (6) is not equivalent to affirming the Common Kind Assumption, however (as Robinson sought to use the stronger initial version of this argument to establish). For (6) is consistent with claiming that for the fundamental kind of event which occurs when one is veridically perceiving, there is no echo in the case of the causally matching hallucination. But while the disjunctivist may be spared inconsistency in rejecting the assumption but embracing (6), the resulting position imposes quite severe constraints on what can be said about the nature of the kind of experiences which are common to hallucination and perception in these cases. Before reviewing that, the argument itself should be further elucidated and defended.

Premisses (1) and (2) I take to flow from the general methodological concerns which render unappetising the rejection of the assumption of Experiential Naturalism. We have broad empirical grounds for supposing that altering the pattern of activity in an agent's visual cortex has consequences for what they can or cannot see. So there does seem to be a causal dependency of our visual perceptions on the activity of parts of the brain, even if we do not yet know the full pattern of this dependency. One may find questionable the metaphysical assumptions behind the idea of a complete causal condition for some state or event; but however suspect the notion is, it is unlikely that a rejection of it would provide suitable refuge for a defender of disjunctivism. Likewise, premiss (2) depends on the thought that neuroscientific methodology in general looks to local neurological causes in order to explain a given pattern of neurological activity. It may well not be excluded entirely *a priori* that there should be action at a distance within the neurological realm, but few neuroscientists with the hope of serious funding would pursue the hypothesis seriously. Hence a disjunctivist would be dialectically in a weak position, if their other commitments forced them to claim that action at a distance for neurological causes does in fact occur.[14]

However, one might still claim that the other aspect of (2), regarding what causal conditions produce, does not follow from our general empirical assumptions. The fact that visual perceptions depend causally on states of the visual cortex does not in itself show that the reproduction of those local causes in the absence of objects of perception would still produce experiences. Some sort of room is left open for a philosopher to claim that in the absence of conditions sufficient for perception, the causal preconditions of perception fail to produce any psychological effect at all. No one is yet in a position to falsify this hypothesis. So the argument for (6) is not demonstrative. Nonetheless, this would be a weak position for the disjunctivist to end up in: for it would commit them to determinate empirical consequences which they have insufficient evidence to predict.

Premiss (3) on the other hand looks like it is a purely metaphysical principle about the nature of causation, and not to be grounded solely in methodological concerns or broad empirical assumptions. This is a severe weakening of a causal principle employed by Howard Robinson when attacking disjunctivism, namely the doctrine of "Same Cause, Same Effect." On that view, where any situations involve the same proximate causal conditions then the very same kind of effects will occur. There are two modifications to this idea in premiss (3). First, "Same Cause, Same Effect" is usually stated in a form which assumes causal determinism where causes are sufficient for their effects. So stated, one might think that one could escape the consequences of the principle by denying determinism—indeed, Robinson discusses the prospects of so doing. Yet is clear that in a world in which there are indeterministic causes, a form of "Same Cause, Same Effect" can pose problems for a disjunctivist. After all, the Naïve realist thinks that there is a zero chance of a veridical perception occurring in a situation where there is no appropriate candidate to be the object of perception. If there are causal conditions for veridical perception, then they must give the occurrence of the event of perceiving a non-zero chance, hence the chances in the perceptual and hallucinatory circumstances must be different. Allowing for indeterministic causation alone won't provide space for such a consequence. We may as well, then, frame (3) in terms which allow for the causal connections to be chancy.

The more significant weakening, however, relates to the clause in (3) concerning non-causal constitutive conditions. In employing "Same Cause, Same Effect" Robinson and Foster aim to show that disjunctivism is not consistent with our general thoughts about the nature of causation. They assume that effects must always be constrained by patterns of local causation, such that any difference in two effects must be reflected in a difference in their local causes. Given this, they plausibly argue that unless there is action at a distance, distal objects can play no essential role in the individuation of any psychological event. A parallel line of reasoning can be found in some discussions of singular thought and of externalism. Various authors have argued that where one can find no difference in the causal powers of two psychological states, no difference in their possible effects, then the two states ought to fall under all the same psychological kinds. Again no difference in distal conditions alone are allowed to make a difference in the nature of the psychological state itself.

If one is committed to this line of thought, then (3) reduces to an indeterministic version of "Same Cause, Same Effect" since one is thereby committed to the view that no psychological effects have any interesting non-causal constitutive conditions attached. Of course, a disjunctivist who is also a Naïve realist will be ill inclined to accept "Same Cause, Same Effect" when so formulated. On their conception of experience, when one is veridically perceiving the objects of perception are constituents of the experiential episode. The given event could not have occurred without these entities existing and being constituents of it; in turn, one could not have had such a kind of event without there being relevant candidate objects of perception to be apprehended. So, even if those objects are implicated in the causes of the experience, they also figure non-causally as essential constituents of it.

Indeed, setting the discussion within an indeterministic framework offers support to the idea that for the Naïve realist the object of perception must play a non-causal role in determining whether the experience is a perception or not, whatever causal role it has in addition. For when we think of objects or events as having causal powers, we conceive of them as having the capacity to raise the chance of an effect, and of inhibitors as lowering the chance that would otherwise be there for the effect. In this way, causal influence is conceivable as coming in degrees. But the only sense in which we can account for the role for the object of perception as a constituent of the sensory episode is acting as a necessary condition on the occurrence of the perceptual event. Mere presence of a candidate object will not be sufficient for the perceiving of it, that is true, but its absence is sufficient for the non-occurrence of such an event. The connection here is not one of degrees of influence but that of a constitutive or essential condition of a kind of event.

So such theorists will be unimpressed by "Same Cause, Same Effect" as pressed by Foster and Robinson, and they will seek to resist any ancillary reasoning designed to make one accept it. However, they do not have the same reason to reject premiss (3), since that allows for the possibility that there are such non-causal constitutive conditions for the occurrence of certain kinds of events. What (3) retains is one of the main motivations for "Same Cause, Same Effect" and that is to suppose that where there is genuine causation, then there is a pattern of causes and effects which has an implicit generality. If a given causal condition has produced a certain kind of effect in one context, then there will be some general condition which differs between the two. It seems that to deny this would be either to claim that in the case of psycho-physical causation there need be no such determinacy of cause to effect, or to embrace in general a radical singularism about causation according to which the fact that particular causes were related to the effects that they had implied nothing at all about the general patterns of causation.[15]

Premiss (3) only has bite in this argument given premiss (4). If the disjunctivist can claim that there is a non-causal difference between the hallucinatory situation and the veridical perceptual situation with respect to the hallucinatory experience, then one will not be able to generalise back from what is true about this effect in the one situation to the other. As we noted above, they certainly do have reason to claim that there is such a non-causal condition in the case of veridical perception, for there is a candidate object of perception present which is absent in the hallucinatory situation. That would block the use of (3) to generalise from whatever is true of the veridical perception situation to what must be true of the hallucinatory situation. In the context of this argument we need to know whether the converse move can be blocked as well.

Well, one might argue that given that the veridical perceptual experience could only occur were an object of perception present, then the absence of such an object is a necessary condition on the hallucinatory experience occurring, and hence is a non-causal condition on the occurrence of such a kind of event. Clearly, this condition isn't fulfilled when one perceives, and hence one could, consistently with (3), deny that what occurs when hallucinating occurs when perceiving. The problem with this response is that it relies on us conceiving of the psychological effects that the proximate causal conditions produce entirely in terms of their relation to other situations than the actual one: we specify the effect by saying it is not a perception. For of course it is true of any effect which is essentially not a perception that it requires the absence of conditions which are sufficient for perception. But one can surely demand that what is needed is a description of the effect produced relative just to the situation in which it is produced. In what sense can this simply be an effect which is not a perception? Surely there is some positive account of the kind of psychological effect it is. And it is for this that we need to ask whether any non-causal conditions must be met. Otherwise, one should have the suspicion that the non-causal conditions on the occurrence of a perception are somehow counting twice over: once in the situation where one does have a perception, and again in the situation where there is no perception and nothing at all to be perceived. Therefore I suggest that premiss (4) correctly reflects the thought that is expressed by saying that hallucinations are "inner experiences." We have the conception that the occurrence of such events imposes no additional condition on the world beyond the subject's putative state of awareness.[16]

But now with this conceded we end up with (5) and (6) and the question whether this result is really consistent with a disjunctive approach to perception. This takes us to the second step of the argument.

5. To deny that what is present in perception is present in hallucination is quite consistent with admitting that what is present in hallucination is also present in perception. Even if the disjunctivist must grant that he or she is committed to (6), they have not yet been forced to endorse inconsistent assumptions. But is the position a coherent resting place? For there is a lingering worry that once one admits that the hallucinatory experience is common to the two situations, one undermines the motivations for disjunctivism in the first place by making the non-common element redundant to the explanation of the phenomenal aspects of experience.

There are two ways of spelling out the situation described in (6). One might claim that, when one perceives, two events occur: there is the genuinely perceptual experiential event, and this has no analogue in hallucination; then there is the purely experiential event, which also occurs when one is hallucinating. Given this model it is both true that something occurs only when one perceives, the genuinely perceptual experience, and something occurs which can also occur when one hallucinates, the purely experiential event. But is this a plausible model?

To answer this we need also to ask how we are to count experiences. If I hear a loud bang and see a bright flash there is a sense in which I have one experience, the experience of these two perceived events, a sense in which I have two experiences, a hearing and a seeing, and a sense in which I have three: the hearing, seeing and the event hearing-together-with-seeing. However we count these events, there is an intimate connection among them; perhaps some are constituents of others. What then of the relation between the supposed genuinely perceptual experiential event and the purely experiential event? If we ask of what happened in the subject's life such that they could reflect on and report it as such, then there seems to be just one thing to talk about. If one introspects a perfect hallucination of seeing a lavender bush, what seems to be available to introspection is just whatever would be available to introspection in actually seeing one. In the former case, all that one could introspect would be the one event, the purely experiential event. In the latter case, there are supposedly two events to introspect: the purely experiential event and the genuinely perceptual one. So, although there seems to be some questions to be settled anyway about the ways in which to count experiences, this proposal seems to double for us the number with which we answer that question.

If we say that in fact one can introspect both events in the perceptual case, then we need to explain why it should seem as if one cannot selectively attend to the one experience as opposed to the other. If we respond to this problem by suggesting that one can only introspect the genuinely perceptual event when perceiving, then one needs to explain why the purely experiential event, which is otherwise introspectible, should be screened out by the genuinely perceptual one. If we respond instead by saying that it is only the purely experiential event which one can introspect in both cases, then we lose the sense that the genuinely perceptual event is the experience one has when perceiving, that is a part of one's conscious life. If it is extruded from that, then the disjunctivist's position begins to look like nothing more than a linguistic variant on some Common Kind view: there is an introspectible element in perceiving which can be present in perception and hallucination; and there is a non-introspectible element which is only present when one is perceiving in virtue of which one counts as perceiving.

But this is not the only way in which one can accommodate (6). As we initially set the problem up we saw a need to talk not only of particular events but also the kinds of events that occur. Clearly events can be of more than one kind just as they can satisfy more than one description. In some sense no one denies that the one event, the perception, is of a kind which the other, the hallucination, is not. What is distinctive of the rejection of the Common Kind Assumption is the thought that the most fundamental kind that the perceptual event is of, the kind in virtue of which the event has the nature that it does, is one which couldn't be instanced in the case of hallucination. So we can accommodate (6) while rejecting the Common Kind Assumption by claiming that while the perceptual event is of a fundamental kind which could not occur when hallucinating, nonetheless this very same event is also of some other psychological kind or kinds which a causally matching hallucinatory event (i.e. one brought about by the same proximate causal conditions) belongs to.

Now this proposal faces at least the following formal difficulty. Presumably the hallucinatory event is fundamentally of some psychological kind. Whatever kind that is, the perceptual event is also of that kind. However, the perceptual event is not fundamentally of that kind, since we know that fundamentally it is of some kind which does not occur when hallucinating. So the disjunctivist will need to explain how it can be that one thing can be fundamentally $F$, something else can be $F$ and yet not be fundamentally $F$. This is an issue to which we shall return below.

More pressing yet, the objector may question whether the disjunctivist has not still made the kind of episode which is unique to the perceptual situation redundant in an account of consciousness and the mind. In formulating the acceptance of (6) in terms of kinds of events rather than in terms of the number of unrepeatable occurrences, the worry about the absence of a detectable difference between one event and two can now simply be reformulated in terms of a worry about the explanatory role of properties: two properties being present in one case, one property being present in the other.

First, a concern is that hallucinations and veridical perceptions will have in common certain phenomena that we associate with experience. Notably, hallucinations no less than perceptions are liable to coerce our beliefs and move us to action, and from a subject's perspective the situation will seem to be one in which they are doing the right thing by judging that that is a lavender bush when hallucinating one, if they have no ancillary information that reveals this not to be a case of perception. Likewise, as we have stressed throughout, reflection on experience or introspection of it is liable to lead to much the same judgements about how things are with the subject: that it looks to him or her as if there is a lavender bush there.

Some of these phenomena we may see as causal (and possibly rational) consequences of experience: given the nature of experience, a rational agent would come to make those judgements or act in this way. Other aspects we might think are partly constituted by so having an experience: what it is for things to seem one way to a subject rather than another is for them to be in such an experiential state. In the case of hallucination, to the extent that these phenomena do have any explanation, that explanation will derive from appeal to the kind of experience the subject is then having. And now, the objector will point out, given (6) above, we must concede that the very same kind of experience occurs when one is veridically perceiving. The phenomena which are in common between the hallucination and the perception are accompanied by a common kind of occurrence in both situations. So, the objector suggests, those phenomena will have a common explanation in the two situations, namely the occurrence of a kind of experience common to both perception and hallucination and the kind of event which is unique to perceptual situations will be explanatorily redundant.[17]

Consider a parallel case. Suppose one has a machine for sorting pieces of coloured cloth. The input to the machine is a jumble of pieces of cloth which are either scarlet or some non-red shade of colour. All of the scarlet pieces are sorted by the machine into its left hopper, while all of the other pieces go into the right one. One might hypothesise that the machine works by discriminating scarlet samples from other shades, so the presence of a sample in the left hopper is explained by its being scarlet. However, now consider another machine of exactly the same model presented with a jumble of cloth samples some of which are red, not all scarlet, and some various shades of non-red colours. This machine sorts all of the red samples, whether scarlet or not into its left hopper and the other samples into its right hopper. Now the more plausible hypothesis is that both machines sort samples into their left hoppers because the samples are red. In the original situation I described, it is still right to say that the samples in the left hopper are there because they are scarlet. After all, being scarlet is a way of being red, so mentioning this shade of the samples does give some explanatory information. Nonetheless, it seems wrong to say that the samples are in the hopper because they are scarlet rather than because they are red. Being red is more highly correlated with being sorted into the left hopper than being scarlet. So the property of being red here seems to screen off the property of being scarlet from having an explanatory role.[18]

The objector's worry about perception and hallucination echoes these intuitions. We have the same resultant phenomena in introspectively matching cases of perception and hallucination, and we know from the conclusion (6) that where we have causally matching situations we have the same kinds of event in hallucination and in perception. So the common kind of event between hallucination and perception seems better correlated with these common phenomena than the kind of event unique to perception and so seems to screen off the purely perceptual kind of event from giving us an explanation.[19]

This concludes the second step in the argument. The disjunctivist is in a weak position to reject (6), even if the argument for it is not demonstrative. (6) as it stands is not inconsistent with the letter of disjunctivism, the rejection of the Common Kind Assumption, but this does not remove the worry that there is no way of accepting (6) while still insisting that there is a distinctive role for only veridical perceptual experiences to play. The disjunctivist cannot remain simply with the claim about the concept of sensory experience in general, therefore, but must address the problem that this subset of cases presents us with. It must find some account of hallucinatory experiences in cases of proximate causal matching with veridical perception which does not lead to the screening off of veridical perception. How are we to proceed?

6. One response to the challenge questions the commonality of phenomena among perception and hallucination. Just as one may be a disjunctivist about experience, so too one may be disjunctivist about the consequences of perception. There are at least two ways in which one might develop this. The first is to claim that some of the psychological consequences associated

with perception cannot occur if one is hallucinating. For example, if one endorses an object-dependent conception of singular thought, then perceptual demonstrative judgements will not be available for a subject to make when suffering an hallucination.[20] Veridical perceptions may give rise to judgements such as that that is an orange, but no perfectly matching hallucination could do the same. One may extend this by suggesting that some of our intentions in action may be object-dependent too. Perhaps a subject moved to pick up a visible object intends that they should grasp that thing over there. But then no such intention could be present in a case of hallucination. If actions are individuated not by gross physical movements but by the intentions with which they are immediately performed, no action will be in common between a veridical perceptual situation and an hallucination either.

This mode of response seeks to find something implicitly relational among the phenomena consequent on perception—where acts of thinking are object-dependent, a subject can engage in such acts only given the truth of certain relational facts, that appropriate objects exist and stand in a relevant relation to the subject to be thought about or acted on. A more direct response here would be to appeal explicitly to relational facts which perceptions can explain in a way that hallucinations can not. Why was John able to pick up the glass that was on the table? Because he could see it, and could see where it was. Both Christopher Peacocke and Timothy Williamson have insisted that the explanatory potential of such a relational explanans cannot necessarily be matched by a conjunction of a non-relational psychological fact and some non-psychological relational facts in addition.[21] So the kind of relational facts which obtain when one is genuinely perceiving and not merely hallucinating (even veridically) may have an explanatory potential for relational facts which then obtain because of one's actions which could not be matched by the experiential properties common to perception and hallucination.

With these two responses one can at least rebut the challenge that the disjunctivist's conception of sensory experience is guaranteed to be explanatorily redundant. But they are not sufficient to lay the worries raised here to rest. For the responses block the conclusion through finding some implicitly or explicitly relational facts which are not in common between the two situations. This strategy does not address the question whether there are any common properties to the two situations which are distinctive of the subject's conscious perspective on the world. Nor yet the question whether, if there are any, why they can only be explained by what is common to perception and hallucination rather than what is distinctive of perception.

It would be a severe limitation on the disjunctivist's commitment to Naïve Realism, if the Naïve realist aspects of perception could not themselves shape the contours of the subject's conscious experience. Yet this aim would be frustrated if we rested with the above responses, since so far no reason has been offered to show why we must think of the fabric of consciousness as relational, and as not common to perception and hallucination. If we are to settle the concerns here, we need to make clear what can be, and what need not be, in common among matching perceptions and hallucinations. Here the notion of sense experience in general, that of being indiscriminable from veridical perception, plays a central role. It provides an answer to this question, and in turn, as we shall see below, an answer to the problem we face about (6).

For, the concept of perceptual experience in general is that of situations indiscriminable from veridical perception and this imposes quite severe constraints on what properties an hallucinatory experience must possess, and what properties it must lack. In this way, the general condition of indiscriminability offers a guide to what properties we should expect perception and hallucination to share.

If the condition of indiscriminability is to be met, then a situation of experience must not lack any property necessary for veridical perception the absence of which is recognisable simply through reflection. Likewise no such situation may possess any property incompatible with veridical perception whose presence is recognisable through reflection. If the former condition were not met, the claim of not knowable difference from perception could not be met: a subject might recognise the absence of the property in question when possessing the background knowledge that the property in question is a necessary condition of veridical perception; such a subject could thereby know on the basis of reflection that this was not a case of veridical perception. In the second case, the recognisable presence of a property incompatible with perception would likewise stand witness to the fact that this situation is in fact discriminable from veridical perception.

It was claimed above that introspection of veridical perception provides evidence in favour of Naïve Realism. That is to say, when one introspects one's veridical perceptions one recognises that this is a situation in which some mind-independent object is present and is a constituent of the experiential episode. Not all matching perceptual experiences will possess this property. A case of hallucination brought about through suitable stimulation of the brain will either lack an object altogether or present a merely mind-dependent one. Given the conditions outlined above, the lack of this property is not recognisable in such a case of experience. This constraint might be met in either of two ways. First, one might claim that in the case of veridical perception, the presence of this property is not really recognisable, that one cannot, after all, introspect that mind-independent objects are constituents of the experiential situation. Taking this route would be to deny that there are after all any introspective grounds for endorsing Naïve Realism. But this conclusion is not forced on us by the constraint in question. For the second route is simply to accept that although the hallucinatory situation lacks the property in question, one cannot know that the property is absent simply by reflection on this situation and hence that it at least *seems* to be present.

Note that we must take care in interpreting the use of "seems" here. It is common for philosophers to remark that seems talk can be used in different ways, sometimes to introduce talk of sensory states or events and sometimes simply to indicate a subject's evidential position or inclinations to believe.[22] Certainly the former would be inappropriate here. The point of the claim is not that when the subject has the hallucination, they are in some sensory state of the seeming presence of a lavender bush. Though this would be true, it would not be an illuminating point to make. Rather, the aim is to explain the sense in which an hallucinatory state may match a perceptual state. In order for the claim to play this role, we need to understand "seems" in a purely epistemological sense: to say that it seems to the subject as if this is a situation in which a lavender bush is a constituent of the experiential situation is just to say that the subject would be unable to tell this situation apart from one in which the subject would correctly recognise the presence of such a constituent. Whether this epistemological reading is sufficient to the task at hand is an issue to which we shall return.

Going in the reverse direction, we can determine of some particular matching hallucination that even if it possesses some distinctive feature not present in any veridical perception, one will not be able to recognise this feature of it just through introspection. Suppose, then, that an hallucination of a lavender bush may be realised in a situation where a subject is presented with a mind-dependent array of coloured patches, impressionistically resembling the light and form presented on a North London street. If this is to be a genuinely matching experience, reflection on and introspection of the scene presented cannot reveal its status as a mind-dependent array.

So in general we can claim the following: if any property of a veridical perception is introspectible—i.e. is recognisably present in perception through reflection—then such a property will either be present in all matching experiences, or will at least seem to be present, i.e. will not be knowably absent. Likewise, no property of a matching experience which is not a perception will be recognisable as such through introspection. So the common properties of perception and all matching experiences, including hallucinations, will just be either introspectible properties which are shared, or properties which all the experiences seem to have (i.e. cannot be known to lack through introspection).

Correspondingly, we can determine which consequences of experiences will be co-present in cases of perception and matching hallucination through similar considerations. For example, if veridical perception gives rise to rational judgement about the environment, then an hallucinating subject will be equally inclined to judgement as a perceiving one. A propensity to make a judgement is one, one can normally detect through reflection on the situation. If an agent had no propensity to judge that a lavender bush is present when having the hallucination of one, then the absence of inclination here would be a detectable difference from the case of veridical perception and hence a ground for discriminating the two situations. In this way, we can say in the basic case it is not merely that an agent does not know that they are not perceiving when hallucinating, where this indicates something consistent with agnosticism on the matter. If an agent in the case of veridical perception can judge that there is a bush there, or that they are seeing a bush, then in a case of perfect hallucination they cannot be left with no inclination one way or the other to judge the presence of bushes or the sighting of bushes. Rather they must equally be inclined to judge that there is a bush there and that they see one. In this case then, positively it must seem to them as if a bush is there and the sighting of a bush is occurring. The matching of the rational consequences of perception and hallucination will thereby carry over to action and behaviour more generally.

Despite the minimal constraint that indiscriminability imposes on the match between perception and hallucination, it provides all we need to answer our question about the properties shared between perception and hallucination. Given an initial assumption that perception has certain detectable consequences, indiscriminability requires that either hallucinations possess the very same properties or at least that they have the property of seeming to reflection to have those properties. Likewise, whatever properties an hallucination actually possesses, we must suppose them undetectable unless some veridical perception can also possess them or seem to possess them. These two consequences together tell us what we can assume are in common between perceptions and hallucinations in general.

7. With the answer to this question, we are just a step away from solving our problem. For we can also see that the fact that a perfectly matching hallucination is indiscriminable from a veridical perception is a fact potentially explanatory of several of the features of a situation. Why did James shriek like that? He was in a situation indiscriminable from the veridical perception of a spider. Given James's fear of spiders, when confronted with one he is liable so to react; and with no detectable difference between this situation and such a perception, it must seem to him as if a spider is there, so he reacts in the same way.

Is being indiscriminable from veridical perception really explanatory in this way? I argued above that being indiscriminable from veridical perception is the most inclusive conception we have of what sensory experience is. At best an intentional account or sense-datum view offers us an account of some sufficient condition for so experiencing, but there is no reason as yet to think any such account exhaustive of our conception. On an immodest conception of sensory experience, it comes as no surprise that an hallucination should have many of the same consequences as a veridical perception, and a common explanation will be sought in terms of the defining characteristics of such experience, $E_1 \ldots E_n$, that both the perception and the hallucination are alleged to share. So for such a theorist, the idea that the property of being indiscriminable from a veridical perception should have an explanatory role would seem implausible—surely such a property would be screened off from being explanatorily useful since $E_1 \ldots E_n$ will be present in both cases and adequate to the task. Once we recognise, however, that there is no reason to suppose that all hallucinations need have $E_1 \ldots E_n$, we can see that even if in some cases the presence of $E_1 \ldots E_n$ may explain the consequences of a sensory experience, we have no reason to think that that could be the only such explanation. There may be situations which possess characteristics $E'_1 \ldots E'_n$ quite distinct from $E_1 \ldots E_n$ yet equally indiscriminable from the veridical perception of a tree. We might then think of each of these sets of properties as ways of realising the property of being indiscriminable from a veridical perception. And then in that case, while each has some claim to explanatory potential, nonetheless an appeal to the determinable property of being indiscriminable from veridical perception may nonetheless be more explanatory precisely because it is present in a wider range of cases. Witness again our example of the sorting machine—an object is red through being scarlet or crimson or some other such shade. Nonetheless a swatch of cloth being red may be more explanatory of the machine's behaviour than the swatch being scarlet.

Nonetheless, the thought that the property of being indiscriminable from a seeing of a tree can have an explanatory role and have such in virtue of its relation to the property of seeing a tree generates a surprising conclusion in the light of our problem to do with screening off. Recall that any veridical perception of a tree is indiscriminable from itself, so the property of being indiscriminable from a veridical perception of a tree will be common to a case of veridical perception of a tree and a perfectly matching hallucination of the same. The indiscriminability property is, therefore, a common property across the situations with the potential to explain common consequences, while the property of being a veridical perception is unique to the one case. If we should just apply the principle of screening off universally without restriction, then we should conclude that being indiscriminable from a veridical perception of a tree screens off the property of being a veridical perception of a tree. But if that is so, then the property of being a veridical perception of a tree never has an explanatory role, since it is never instantiated without the property of being indiscriminable from such a perception being instantiated as well. But if the property of being a veridical perception lacks any explanatory role, then we can no longer show that being indiscriminable from a veridical perception has the explanatory properties which would screen off the property of being a veridical perception.

This puzzling consequence suggests either that we were wrong to assume that veridical perceptions do have a distinctive explanatory role, or that there must be some limitation to the intuitive principle about cases of screening off. Surely the former option is not palatable: nothing about the structure of the case really exploits features special to the case of perception. For any property we like that has effects partly in virtue of being recognised to be what it is, we can consider the parallel property of being indiscriminable from that property and our above line of reasoning will go through. It is overwhelmingly more plausible to suppose that there are limitations to the range of application of the principle of screening off.

In fact, in relation to cases of causation, it is commonly noted that such tests provide the wrong result for what caused what when we have cases of pre-emption. If my bullet pierces the victim's heart before yours, then the victim is killed by me, even if in a parallel case without my bullet but still with yours, the victim would still have died. The fact that your bullet is present in both cases where the same effect occurs does not show that it must be the cause in both. Our present example indicates that there are parallel cases to pre-emption in the case of explanation. Moreover, one might tentatively suggest here why the limitation needs to imposed on the test for screening off. In our present example, what seems key is the thought that the explanatory properties of the common property are derivable *a priori* from the special property. We can tell that the common property must be correlated with the outcome just from knowing what the special property can otherwise explain. Hence, there is a reason to think that the property of being indiscriminable from an *F* has an explanatory potential which is dependent on the explanatory potential of being an *F*. The same was not so in the case of scarlet and red, for while red has an explanatory potential deriving just from being the determinable of scarlet, its explanatory potential is not exhausted by that. So we may conclude that, as with cases of pre-emption, cases of inherited or dependent explanatory potential offer us exceptions to the general model of common properties screening off special ones.

8. Over the last few pages we have been pursuing the question whether one can coherently reject the Common Kind Assumption yet accept (6), the conclusion of the causal argument. The discussion of the last few pages should bring out quite how hard it is for the disjunctivist to maintain this position. For, suppose we accept that causally matching hallucinations, those with the same proximate causes as veridical perceptions, have some positive characterisation in terms favoured by immodest approaches, then the disjunctivist will be forced to grant that they do not have a coherent position. For example, if we assume that the causally matching hallucination is an event which represents the presence of a tree—that is, its having such representational properties are taken to explain why the experience is as it is and has the consequences that it does—then the explanation we can give of the salient features of the hallucination, and of how it brings about its effects, should equally be applicable to the case of veridical perception. After all, the explanatory potential of such properties is surely independent of whether the veridical perception of a tree independently could provide an explanation of these phenomena. On this assumption, the problem of explanatory screening off would certainly be pressing, and so granting that the perception and the hallucination possess these representational properties would imply that the Naïve Realist aspects of the perception are explanatorily idle. The same conclusion should be drawn if we account for the causally matching hallucination in terms of being the presentation of some mind-dependent array of colour patches. So while the disjunctivist can be agnostic about the nature of many hallucinations—they may be representational or subjective as long as they meet the condition of indiscriminability—when it comes to causally matching experiences, they are forced to reject any such positive characterisation.

At the same time, we have seen a range of properties which causally matching hallucinations can share with veridical perceptions without threatening the explanatory role of being a veridical perception: namely properties of being indiscriminable from the veridical perception. So this suggests that the disjunctivist can coherently hold on to the denial of the Common Kind Assumption and the truth of (6) by insisting that for just such experiences: i.e. causally matching hallucinations, the only mental properties that such events possess are those of being indiscriminable from veridical perceptions and any properties which follow from their being so indiscriminable. For these events alone, there is nothing more to characterise them than what can be said about the concept of perceptual experience in general.

But what does this restriction amount to? At the very least, it leads us to deny Dancy's assumption when he writes, "there may be available a more direct characterization of the second disjunct." On the account proposed here, the disjunctivist is committed to saying that, at least when it comes to a mental characterisation of the hallucinatory experience, nothing more can be said than the relational and epistemological claim that it is indiscriminable from the perception. There is a sense, then, in which the disjunctivist insists that there is only a negative characterisation of causally matching hallucinatory experience: it is nothing but a situation which could not be told apart from veridical perception. This fact links with the formal concern mentioned at the start of our discussion of (6): how could it be that the veridical perception is fundamentally of one kind and yet also of some other kind which it shares with the hallucination, where the hallucination must fundamentally be of that kind. Clearly for a veridical perception, being a veridical perception of a tree is a better candidate for being its fundamental or essential kind than being indiscriminable from being such a veridical perception. When we turn to the case of the hallucinatory experience, there are no other candidates for the kind of mental event it is—at least according to the disjunctivist—other than its being indiscriminable from the veridical perception; *faute de mieux* this is then the fundamental mental character of the event.

The essentially negative and relational characterisation here bears also on a criticism Timothy Williamson has made of disjunctive theories of mental states.[23] Focusing on McDowell's account of knowledge, Williamson raises the question whether resistance to traditional analyses of knowledge as "justified true belief *plus*" should frame itself as a form of disjunctivism. In the case of knowledge, the disjunctivist would seem to be forced to analyse belief in terms of a disjunction of either knowledge or some other state, "mere opinion," as we might say. Williamson presses the disjunctivist to give an account of the other state, mere opinion, in a manner which will hold only of non-knowledge cases and not equally apply to the case of knowledge itself. The conclusion he reaches is that there is no good candidate for this: and that we should allow that the situation of knowledge and the contrast cases both satisfy conditions for the common presence of belief: the concept of belief is autonomous and not reducible to the idea of knowledge or failed knowledge. As a result, Williamson suggests that the heart of resistance should be a form of non-conjunctivism: even if belief is an independent notion always present with knowledge and non-knowledge, knowledge is not to be analysed as belief *plus* something else.

I don't want to comment here on the success of Williamson's discussion of knowledge but rather to emphasise the difference of situation in relation to perception and sensory appearances, at least according to the position we have been concerned with here. As we have seen, Williamson is right that the notion of sensory experience that we end up with is one we are happy to say is equally present in cases of veridical perception and hallucination. When we specify cases of hallucination we do not do so therefore in terms of something which is only present in cases of hallucination— the presence of a mere or inner experience which couldn't occur in a case of genuine veridical perception. While some hallucinations might have a nature incompatible with being a veridical perception—hallucinations for which a sense-datum or intentional account were directly appropriate—we have seen that there are some hallucinations whose nature would have to be consistent with that kind of event occurring when one perceives veridically as well. So the label "disjunctivism" would be misleading if it had to indicate that what occurs in the two kinds of case is necessarily incompatible. At the same time, though, there is still something appropriate about expressing the view in disjunctive form. For all that can be said about the hallucination at a mental level is by contrast with the case of veridical perception, and that is just to indicate how the event is not as the veridical perception is. The notion common to perception and hallucination, that of sensory experience, lacks explanatory autonomy from that of veridical perception. And isn't that just what we express by saying that either this is a case of veridical perception, in which case certain consequences follow, or it is merely one of being indiscriminable from such a perception, in virtue of which certain other consequences follow?

Still, this leaves us with a striking consequence of disjunctivism: there are certain mental events, at least those hallucinations brought about through causal conditions matching those of veridical perceptions, whose only positive mental characteristics are negative epistemological ones—that they cannot be told apart by the subject from veridical perception. I'll return briefly below to what one might identify as the core of resistance here, but in concluding I want finally to spell out just a few of the key features of indiscriminability that as we have seen, need to be relied on heavily by a disjunctive account.

9. It is a nice question how exactly the disjunctivist should articulate the way in which indiscriminability is employed in the positive account of the notion of perceptual experience in general. First, there seem to be some obvious counter-examples to the claim that indiscriminability provides sufficient conditions for an event's being a sensory experience. Second, there are some problem cases generated by the seeming non-transitivity of apparent sensory indiscriminability. Finally, endorsing indiscriminability as a criterion of sameness across sensory experiences itself imposes certain restrictions on how things can seem to one to be when one suffers an hallucinatory experience.

Suppose John is inclined to inattention, or hastiness in judgement. When presented with an elm he is liable to treat the situation as one of being presented with a beech. When presented with a sample of scarlet he treats it indifferently with being presented with a sample of vermillion. It is not inappropriate for us to describe John's situation by saying that he can't discriminate a beech from an elm, nor scarlet from vermillion. But saying that for John there is no discriminable difference between these things is surely not to say that he experiences them all the same. So here indiscriminability would seem to be insufficient for sameness of experience.

The point seems more acute when we consider animals other than humans. To discriminate two things is to judge them non-identical. If one is to judge two experiences as of different kinds, one needs a concept of experience with which to make this judgement. We are inclined to ascribe to many creatures sentience where we withhold the attribution of sufficient sapience for self-consciousness. In that case, these creatures lack concepts of experience, as with other mental states. They cannot therefore judge that one experience is of the same or of different kind from any other experience. Does this not mean that all of their experiences are indiscriminable from each other for them, since they cannot judge them to be distinct? In turn, does that then have the consequence according to the disjunctivist that all of their experiences are the same?[24]

In response, we need to note an important difference between ascribing capacities or incapacities to a particular individual, or group of individuals, and more impersonal ascriptions of such capacities or incapacities which are not relativised to individuals at all. For example, contrast the claim that the fretwork on the screen is invisible to Mary with the claim that the fretwork is invisible *simpliciter*. The former claim implicates to the audience that Mary's sight is in some way deficient—perhaps she is short sighted, or perhaps her sight is not good in low lighting. Quite consistently with this claim, one may insist that the fretwork is perfectly visible, that it is visible to John, Alan or the normally sighted viewer. In contrast to talk of something's being visible or invisible *per se* without relativising to a viewer indicates that it cannot be seen by normally sighted people, and in certain contexts the claim may indicate that it couldn't even be seen by a creature with abnormally acute vision.

In general, where we ascribe an incapacity to someone, we indicate not only that they have failed to do something, but also that there is some ground in virtue of which they so fail. When we think of an individual's incapacity in relation to the specific ground for his or her incapacity—a ground which explains not only why they do not do *F*, but would not even do *F* in similar circumstances—we can still recognise that this impossibility or incapacity is quite consistent with the possibility that others do do *F* or at least could do it. On the other hand, when we talk of an incapacity or inability without indicating a subject lacking the capacity or incapacity, then we need not think in terms of a ground relative to an agent in virtue of which the act cannot be carried out. To say that something is invisible is not to indicate some specific lack in certain viewers, but rather to indicate something about it, that it cannot be seen. In parallel, when we talk of two things being indiscriminable, we need not mean that there is something about a given agent in virtue of which they cannot be told apart, but simply that it is not possible to know that they are distinct.

When the disjunctivist appeals to the idea of two things being indiscriminable through reflection in explicating the concept of sensory experience, it is this impersonal form of an incapacity or inability ascription that must be intended. What is being claimed is that, *ex hypothesi*, in a circumstance of perfect hallucination, matters are such that it is just not possible to know through reflection alone that this is not a situation of veridically perceiving some scene. So, it is entirely consistent with this appeal to indiscriminability to grant that two experiences might be indiscriminable through reflection for some particular agent, John, without the two experiences thereby being of the same kind. For John may be unable to know the difference between them due to some specific incapacity on his part—the excess of alcohol or lack of interest in the matter—which would not generalise to other individuals. In contrast, the disjunctivist explains sameness of experience by appealing to the unrelativised or impersonal sense of incapacity. That we can conceive of situations in which two experiences are different but not such as to be noticed by a given individual, does not show that we have access to the idea of experiences which are genuinely different but not noticeably so impersonally.

Likewise, when we turn to the experiences of sentient but unself-conscious creatures, to the extent that we do have a positive grip on the kinds of experience that they can have, and which can differ one from the other, we also have a grip on how such experience would be discriminable through reflection or not. As self-conscious creatures, we cannot help but classify experiences as they would be available to reflection as the same or different. So that a dog might fail to discriminate one experience from another, making no judgement about them as identical or distinct at all, that is not to say that we cannot judge, in ascribing them such experience, that there is an event which would or would not be judgeably different from another experience.

A different kind of challenge to the sufficiency of indiscriminability for identity of kind of experience comes from the alleged non-transitivity of indiscriminability for some observable properties. Certainly, given observers on particular occasions may fail to detect the difference in shade between sample $A$ and sample $B$, and also fail to detect the difference between sample $B$ and sample $C$, and yet be able to detect the difference between sample $A$ and sample $C$. If this leads us to the conclusion that experiences of $A$ are indiscriminable from experiences of $B$, and experiences of $B$ are indiscriminable from experiences of $C$, then we face a problem supposing that there are kinds of event which are sensory experiences of colour shades on the disjunctivist proposal. The indiscriminability of experience of $A$ and experience of $B$ would require us to suppose that these are just the same kind of experience; likewise for the experience of $B$ and of $C$. By transitivity of identity, this requires that the kind of experience one has of $A$ is of the same kind as the experience one has of $C$, but this contradicts the observation that the experience of $C$ is discriminable from the experience of $A$ since kinds of experience are discriminable only where distinct.

There are broadly two responses the disjunctivist can make here. On the one hand, they can point out that the contradiction derives from assuming that we can indeed talk about kinds of perceptual experience as I have throughout this paper, indifferently among perceptions, illusions and hallucinations. But the examples of distinct but indiscriminable shades could be taken to show that since our notion of perceptual experience is just grounded in the unknowability of distinctness of perception and hallucination there is no well-founded notion of kind of perceptual experience. All the facts about experiences in general are to be stated just in terms of whether a subject could know the distinctness of these experiences through reflection on their circumstance. This pattern of facts is just not well enough behaved to ground the existence of kinds.

On the other hand, despite the appeal of apparent examples of indiscriminable but distinct shades, one can seek to resist the argument and hold on to the idea of perceptual experience as forming kinds. One might follow Graff's suggestion that there is simply no good reason to believe in the existence of phenomenal continua and hence insist that if two samples really do look alike then they share a look.[25] Even if a subject may on occasion fail to notice the difference in look between adjacent samples, and indeed may be bound to fail to notice such a difference, nonetheless there is a difference to be noticed and which could be noticed. Alternatively, one may follow Williamson's suggestion that while in a given context a subject may fail to discriminate two samples, this does not show that there is no context in which the samples are discriminable and hence one can hold on to the claim that distinct samples are discriminable in at least some context.[26] By suitable application of the idea of impersonal indiscriminability, we can then insist that the experiences of $A$ and of $B$ are in fact discriminable, even if in the given context a subject fails to discriminate $A$ from $B$ and consequently fails to discriminate the experience of $A$ from the experience of $B$.

In fact, the disjunctivist will need to avail themselves of the latter response in any event to deal with sensory margins for error where the dimensions of variation do not even appear to generate a continuum. If I can tell by looking that there are fifty people in the room, give or take five, then I can't discriminate just by looking fifty people from forty-five or from fifty-five, yet I can discriminate forty-five from fifty-five. If we gloss this by saying that the experience of forty-five people is indiscriminable from the experience of fifty people, and appeal to indiscriminability through reflection as the criterion of sameness of experience we end up with the same inconsistency as above—the experience of fifty-five will both be identical and not identical with the experience of forty-five. Here, the disjunctivist will need to emphasise the difference between the scene actually present on a given occasion, which may contain fifty people, from the kind of veridical experience this gives rise to. For if there are limited powers of visual discrimination here, then we need to recognise that the very same type of situation can give rise to different kinds of experience—a presentation of fifty people may give rise to the same kind of experience as a presentation of forty-five people, but it may also give rise to the same kind of experience as a presentation of fifty-five people. The perception of forty-five people never gives rise veridically to the same kind of experience as the veridical perception of fifty-five people, and these two distinct kinds of experience are discriminable, as indeed they are when occasioned by seeing forty-five people and then fifty-five people. But since someone who is seeing fifty people may have either one of these experiences, it need not be that in all circumstances an experience of the kind one has when viewing forty-five people will always be noted as different by one from one in which one views fifty-five people. For example, on repeated presentation of fifty people, it may be that one has the one kind of experience and then the other without being able to tell that there is any seeming difference in the number of people present to one.

We should note one more consequence of taking indiscriminability as the criterion of sameness: the importance of the contrast between perceptions as individual events of particular situations, and perceptions as kinds of event, experiences which the individual perceptions fall under. For a given perception of a scene, it makes perfect sense to suppose that that very experience, i.e. the individual event, is a presentation of some particular individual object or some particular unrepeatable event. If we are to ask about the kind of experience it is, where we include by this the experience that one could have were one hallucinating, then we appeal to the indiscriminability of one experience from another. But now identical twins can be perceptually indiscriminable, so presumably the experiences of them will be reflectively indiscriminable. By this criterion, such perceptions give rise to the same kind of experience. Hence as a kind of experience, the particular objects or events drop out of the individuation of the experience.

Now this conclusion may seem puzzling. For we can certainly make sense of the idea of suffering an hallucination of the presence of Winston Churchill in the room. So it might look as if the disjunctivist is forced to press a surprising and substantive claim about what one can or cannot have an hallucinatory experience of. However, what I think this really brings out is that we can contrast two ways in which a given individual or event can feature in relation to our experience of the world. In one way, a particular object can be a part of one's experience of the world just in virtue of being the thing that one is currently aware of as presenting the particular visible appearance one attends to. One need have in this case no recognitional capacity for just that individual in order to be able to experience just them. But we do also have recognitional capacities and we certainly talk as if our recognitional capacities reflect sameness and difference in how we experience the world. A given individual can look to me to be Winston Churchill, as long as I am both acquainted with Churchill (perhaps only through descriptions, photographs or other representations) and have an appropriate sensitivity to ways in which Winston Churchill can look. Now this latter way in which Winston Churchill can enter my experience is certainly something independent of the actual presence of Churchill: on some occasion I may see someone appropriately dressed such that in seeing them it looks to me as if Churchill is in the room. So, if I have such a capacity targeted on Churchill, it may yet be true that when I hallucinate, the experience I have is as of Churchill in that it brings to bear this recognitional capacity.

Now note, that in a case in which one really sees someone who one sees as Churchill, i.e. one sees an individual and experiences them as recognisably being Churchill, there are two dimensions to talk about the appropriateness of the experience. Is this really a case of looking like Churchill (or has one mistaken an appearance, say of De Gaulle for Churchill in haste)? And, is the person who looks this way really Churchill, or someone who just looks the way Churchill looks? The import of the disjunctivist view of hallucination is just this common sense thought. When we consider a case of hallucinating Churchill, although the first question can still be raised, is this really a case of something's having the look of Churchill, the second question cannot be raised at all. There is no distinction to be drawn between really hallucinating Churchill to be a certain way and hallucinating an individual with Churchill's look. And that there should be no answer to this latter question is hardly contrary to our common thoughts about perception and hallucination.

In closing this section, I need to mention a couple of limitations in our discussion which need to be removed before we have a complete account of the matter.[27] Throughout I have written as if we are concerned solely with cases of perfect hallucination in which the scene hallucinated matches a situation of veridically perceiving some scene for what it is. Now a first concern with this is that we may question whether every conceivable hallucination has a corresponding veridical perception for it to match. Consider an hallucination of an Escher-like scene with an impossible staircase, for example; or the non-perception of Mark Johnston's example of supersaturated red. How does the account so far offered deal with these? We need first to highlight another limitation. Few, if any hallucinations, are perfect hallucinations: rather a subject may perceive some aspects of a scene and hallucinate or misperceive other aspects. So how is the account to be extended to these cases? One move would be to discuss not experiences *per se* but rather the various aspects of an experience, the different entities which one can experience and the ways in which they can appear to one. On a given occasion, seeing a lavender bush may involve the occurrence of a state of awareness whose specific character involves the awareness of various of the leaves and branches of the bush, the steely light of a London sky, the intricate patterns of dirt that line a city street. But there are other ways to see a lavender bush, and such seeings need have nothing particular in common with this viewing, other than they are all the perceptions of a lavender bush. To generalise the account, we would need to fix on the various aspects of a state of perceptual awareness, the ways in which it may be the same or different from other such states of awareness. Focusing just on cases of veridical perception, we can say that these aspects will all involve the presentation of that entity as it is. In turn, a sensory experience of that sort is the occurrence of a situation which is indiscriminable in this particular respect from a perception of the element in question.

The beginning of an approach to partial hallucinations is then to explain those aspects of the experience which are not perceptual in terms of that aspect of experience's indiscriminability from the corresponding aspect of a perceptual awareness of that element. In turn, one may seek to explain certain impossible experiences not by direct appeal to the idea of a veridical perception of that scene, but rather by explaining how an experience with each of the constituent elements is indiscriminable in that respect from a perception of that element. More needs to be said here—not least to accommodate aspects of the phenomenal character of experience which arise from global properties of a scene, the combination of elements, rather than just atomic elements of the presentation of objects or colour points in a given scene. That detailed elaboration belongs elsewhere, here I aim only to sketch how one might set about developing such an account.

10. Over the course of this paper, I've tried to fill out in some more detail what disjunctivism about perception needs to be committed to. There is a common thought that disjunctivism is a counter-intuitive thesis about sensory experience and that such an approach has so far been only incompletely specified, since we need to know more about the case of illusory or hallucinatory experience than disjunctivists are wont to say. What I've argued here is that the focus of discussion should rest with opposing views about the relation between phenomenal character or properties of

experience and some of its epistemological properties, how it can be known to be the same or different from some other mental event simply through reflection on one's circumstance.

In the first part of the paper, I argued that there is good reason to think that the disjunctivist is right to suppose that our broadest conception of perceptual experience is simply that which the disjunctivist uses—namely that of being indiscriminable through reflection from veridical perceptions. However, as the latter part of the paper presses, this agnosticism is not where the disjunctivist can rest. At least when such a view is motivated in part by a concern to recognise the place of mental events within a natural causal order, it needs to take into account the possibility of hallucinations brought about through proximally causally matching circumstances to veridical perceptions. In such cases, I've argued, the disjunctivist really has no option other than to claim that such experiences have no positive mental characteristics other than their epistemological properties of not being knowably different from some veridical perception.

I take it that it is at this point that the resistance to the disjunctive approach will be at its most acute. Can it really be that in a case of perfect hallucination there is no more to how things are with me, than that I cannot and could not tell this situation apart from genuine veridical perception? Surely that epistemological property of the circumstance is simply grounded in the positive presence of the phenomenal properties which are manifest to me when I reflect on my situation. Press this intuition further. We will be most convinced of this idea if we suppose that we do have insight into what it takes for one to have a sensory experience, that we can identify the relevant non-epistemological mental features which act as a ground to the facts of indiscriminability that the disjunctivist appeals to.

The issue here touches on some yet deeper concerns. Most, I suspect, think the kind of subjectivity we have as finite beings requires the presence of phenomenal consciousness. Moreover, there is some temptation to think of phenomenal consciousness as something conceivable independently of our self-awareness or self-conscious reflection on our situation and as something prior to such self-consciousness which acts as the ground for it. So, one might think, the presence or absence of phenomenal consciousness can be determined independently of the presence of self-conscious awareness or reflection on it, and only given its presence do we have a subject with genuine subjectivity. From this perspective, the disjunctivist's conception of these cases seems to introduce a form of philosophical zombie: a subject who may have thoughts and possess the ability to make judgements about phenomenal consciousness but who lacks phenomenal consciousness proper. In that case, one's intuition will be that the subject so described is not properly conscious and lacks genuine subjectivity or point of view on the world.

Of course, given that we have the strong intuition that an unfortunate subject who is subject to a total hallucination must still be conscious (after all this is the force of the objection to the disjunctivist), this picture forces us to think of phenomenal consciousness as constitutively independent of any relation to the world. In somewhat overblown terms, one might then think of phenomenal consciousness as some special stuff which gets added to the thoughts and other mental elements in order to engender subjectivity. In contrast, the Naïve realist is moved by the thought that phenomenal consciousness, as we are initially inclined to think of it in first reflection, is not any such stuff, but instead simply the presence to us of the ordinary world around us. Such presence is, *ex hypothesi*, absent when a subject suffers a total hallucination. Holding on to this relational conception of phenomenal conscious requires us, therefore, to think of the hallucinatory case in a different way from the story told above.

And the disjunctivism we have spelled out here suggests a more complex link between phenomenal consciousness and self-conscious awareness than the story told immediately above. What we do, the disjunctivist suggests, is to exploit our own self-conscious awareness and memory of experience in conceiving of how it would be to be presented with a lavender bush or how it would be to be in a situation indiscriminable from this. In our conception of the situation we exploit elements of self-consciousness and self-awareness, and in this we can see being so self-conscious is quite sufficient for subjectivity. This is not to say that self-consciousness supports subjectivity independent of phenomenal consciousness, as if a philosophical zombie had a point of view on the world but lacked phenomenal feel. Rather in managing to conceive of how things are from the subject's perspective in the case of total hallucination in terms of its being indiscriminable from veridical perception, we thereby imagine phenomenal consciousness too. What we don't have, though, is a grasp of what phenomenal consciousness in general must be like in a way that is prior to and independent of epistemological concerns: what we can and cannot know of one's own position through introspective reflection.

At this point there are two morals from our discussion above that it is important to keep in mind. The first is that we really should be sceptical of having any grasp on a necessary condition for how an event should be in order to be sense experience, apart from the modest criterion of indiscriminability from perception through reflection. For, as was remarked earlier, that could be so only if we have such powers of introspection that we not only successfully detect the presence of certain self-intimating properties when they are instantiated, but are sensitive to their absence when they are not. Few are now prepared to endorse the existence of the kind of infallibility of judgements about the mind which this position requires. The point of our discussion is really to draw out how far reaching the consequences of that reluctance can be.

The second moral concerns the initial motivation for disjunctivism. I've suggested that we should be moved to this position in defence of a natural conception of how our veridical perceptual experience relates us to the world around us. That is what leads us to Naïve Realism. Hence, taking that view seriously forces one to acknowledge that both sense-datum and intentional theories of perception amount to error-theories of sense experience. For if ordinary reflection leads to the acceptance of Naïve Realism, then such ordinary reflection cannot disclose the real nature of sense experience according to these views. If one is convinced that reflection on appearances is misleading, on what basis can one insist that nevertheless one is bound to be accurate about the presence or absence of phonenal properties? If one cannot tell what it really takes for experience to be one way rather than another, why should we think that one can still always tell that some mental presentation or other must be responsible for things to seem the way that they are? So the epistemological commitments of Common Kind views seem to be in tension with the reasons for accepting them. If all views must concede that some sensory appearances seem other than they are, then the disjunctivist has the simplest account of how this can be.

Nonetheless, clearly there is still work to be done to explain why this stopping off point may seem so incredible to us. That is work for elsewhere. The aim in this paper has simply been to identify exactly where that stopping off point should be, and to delimit what disjunctivism need and need not be committed to.[28]

## Notes

1. Recent defenders of intentionalism include Harman (1990), Peacocke (1983, 1992), Searle (1983), Tye (1995). In the analytic tradition its popularity can be traced back to Firth's discussion of the percept theory in the mid-century (Firth 1965), on the one hand, and Anscombe's critique of both sense-datum theorists and their ordinary language opponents (Anscombe 1962), on the other. With some caveats, one can also see it as dominant within the phenomenological tradition.

2. To this purpose, the term "sense-datum" was introduced first by Moore in Moore (1910) and made public in Russell (1912). Though out of favour in recent years, one can find defences of sense-data in Jackson (1977), O'Shaughnessy (1980), Foster (1986), and Robinson (1994). Subjectivism as here conceived captures a broader range of theories than just this, though, and includes for example the appeal to sensational properties in Peacocke (1983).

3. William Alston has recently defended a theory of appearing while claiming of hallucinations that we can consider them to be awarenesses of mental images, see Alston (1999, pp. 191–192). He suggests that nothing positively shows that mental images are dependent on our awareness of them, and if one could maintain this conclusion, the argument of the text would be blocked. However he does not discuss what model of the causation of hallucination we would then need to adopt: can the local conditions for producing mental images be sensitive to the absence of an external object of perception? If not, which is the overwhelmingly plausible conclusion to draw, then if the veridical perception is the same kind of mental state, we will get the conclusion drawn in the text.

4. Harold Langsam, who endorses disjunctivism, seeks to block the argument from hallucination by suggesting that there are possible accounts of hallucination on which an hallucination is, for example, a relation to the region of physical space where an object appears to be (Langsam 1997, p. 47 [this volume, p. 193]). However, Langsam's agnostic stance about the nature of hallucinations is misleading about the force of the argument against the Naïve Realist. Of course there may be some hallucinations which are examples of awareness of the mere air around us. But the pressing question is whether there are any which take the form indicated in the text and which are of the same kind as veridical perceptions. Langsam does nothing to show that such experiences are impossible, nor does he discuss the consequences of the possibility of their existence.

5. Such talk of intentional objects can be traced at least to Anscombe (1962), who claims Medieval authority for it, and this way of expressing the view is echoed in Harman (1990). Nonetheless, critics tend to read the talk as involving a commitment to a special kind of entity, which unsurprisingly leads to a dismissal of mystery mongering. No such ontological profligacy need be, or was intended by those who chose to talk in this way.

6. As I propose at greater length in Martin (2001).

7. See in particular Martin (2002).

8. This is true of Moore and Russell, who insisted that the objects of sensing must be independent of our awareness of them (see Moore 1922; Russell 1912; Broad 1925; Price 1932). For an early criticism of precisely this aspect of the sense-datum tradition (Prichard 1950).

9. Merleau-Ponty (1942); Valberg (1992).

10. However, Hannah Ginsborg reminded me that Hinton does discuss fact perception in the later monograph, *Experiences*, see pp. 101–124; so the contrast is perhaps not as stark as I present it here.

11. Here I follow the approach to indiscriminability found in Williamson (1990); see below for further discussion of the relevant properties of indiscriminability.

12. See, Robinson (1985, 1994) and also Foster (1986), but note the recantation of this in Foster (2000, Pt. Two, p. 2). Other recent versions of the argument can also be found in O'Shaughnessy (1980, ch. 5) and Valberg (1992).

13. That is to say,

$$\forall e \forall s \forall s' \forall C \forall N[[[In(s,e) \ \& \ In(s,C) \ \& \ In(s,N) \ \& \ K(e)] \ \& \ [CausCond(C,e,s) \ \& \ NcausCond(N,e,s)] \ \& \ [In(s',C) \ \& \ In(s',N)]] \rightarrow [\exists e'[K(e') \ \& \ In(s',e')]]]],$$

taking quantification over the events to have widest scope. (Thanks to Susanna Siegel for pointing out the need to disambiguate.)

14. Nicholas Nathan in unpublished work has sought to challenge the causal argument in just this way.

15. Perhaps no one has ever really endorsed such singularism about causation which would be to suppose that the truth of some singular causal statements had no implications whatever for general truths about what general circumstances occur with what other general circumstances, yet Anscombe (1981) is often credited with such a position.

16. John Foster in his most recent discussion of these matters suggests that the causal argument can be blocked by claiming that the object of perception acts as a direct cause in addition to any role it has in producing intermediary causal steps which can be replicated in the case of hallucination. The principle of "Same Causes, Same Effects" would therefore not be violated by the Naïve Realist. In response to the arguments considered here, Foster in addition needs to claim that the hallucination has a cause which is not replicated in the case of veridical perception, and indeed this is what he does, see Foster (2000, p. 41). For all that, Foster's suggestion here does just seem to be of the form of double counting, allowing the absence of a specific causal factor itself to count as a distinctive causal factor.

17. Just such a worry seems to be moving Scott Sturgeon in Sturgeon (1998, 2000, ch. 1).

18. One of the classical discussions of this is Mill's principle of difference in *A System of Logic*, III, viii, 2. For an interesting discussion of the limits of this strategy of explanation see Gendler (2002).

19. Someone might object that the most determinate property has to explain and not any of its determinables, but for a convincing exposition of the opposing view see Yablo (1992, 1997).

20. This is a theme familiar from Evans (1982), and McDowell, see in particular McDowell (1986). It is not clear whether Evans himself would have endorsed disjunctivism about perception, unlike McDowell he certainly did not think the content of perceptual experience object-dependent.

21. See Peacocke (1993) and Williamson (1995, 2000).

22. See Chisholm (1959) and Jackson (1977) for two such discussions.

23. See Williamson (1995, 2000, ch. 1).

24. Just such worries are expressed by Williamson in Williamson (1995).

25. See Graff (2001).

26. See Williamson (1990).

27. In the version presented at Oberlin, these last few comments were omitted. The suggestions made here may address some of the concerns that Susanna Siegel raises in the first part of her paper [Siegel 2004].

28. This paper originated as a twenty minute talk at CREA in Paris and a written draft was produced during a visit at the RSSS of the ANU; versions of the paper have been read to audiences in Paris, Canberra, Dubrovnik, Edinburgh, London, Leeds, Helsinki and Oberlin. I am grateful in particular for comments on this material to Tim Crane, Alan Hájek, Jen Hornsby, Véronique Munoz-Dardé, Panu Raatikainen, Susanna Siegel, Paul Snowdon, Maja Spener, Charles Travis, and above all to Scott Sturgeon for provoking much of the second half of the paper.

### References

Alston, W. 1999. Back to the theory of appearing. *Philosophical Perspectives* (Epistemology) 13: 181–203.

Anscombe, G. E. M. 1962. The intentionality of sensation: A grammatical feature. In R. Butler (ed.), *Analytical Philosophy*, second series. Oxford: Blackwell.

Anscombe, G. E. M. 1981. Causality and determination. In *Metaphysics and the Philosophy of Mind: Collected Papers, Vol. II*. Oxford: Blackwell.

Broad, C. D. 1925. *The Mind and Its Place in Nature*. London: Kegan Paul.

Chisholm, R. 1959. *Perception*. Ithaca: Cornell University Press.

Dancy, J. 1995. Arguments from illusion. *Philosophical Quarterly* 45: 421–438.

Evans, G. 1982. *The Varieties of Reference*. J. McDowell (ed.). Oxford: Clarendon Press.

Firth, R. 1965. Sense-data and the percept theory. In R. Swartz (ed.), *Perceiving, Sensing and Knowing*. Los Angeles/Berkeley: University of California Press.

Foster, J. 1986. *A. J. Ayer*. London: Routledge.

Foster, J. 2000. *The Nature of Perception*. New York: Oxford University Press.

Gendler, T. S. 2002. Personal identity and thought experiments. *Philosophical Quarterly* 52(206): 34–54.

Graff, D. 2001. Phenomenal continua and the sorites. *Mind* 110(440): 905–935.

Harman, G. 1990. The intrinsic quality of experience. In J. Tomberlin (ed.), *Philosophical Perspectives* vol. 4. Ridgeview Publishing Co.

Hinton, J. M. 1967. Visual experiences. *Mind* 76: 217–227.

Hinton, J. M. 1973. *Experiences: An Inquiry into Some Ambiguities*. Oxford: Clarendon Press.

Jackson, F. 1977. *Perception: A Representative Theory*. Cambridge: Cambridge University Press.

Langsam, H. 1997. The theory of appearing defended. *Philosophical Studies* 87: 33–59.

Martin, M. G. F. 2001. Beyond dispute. In T. Crane and S. Patterson (eds.), *The History of the Mind-Body Problem*. London: Routledge.

Martin, M. G. F. 2002. The transparency of experience. *Mind and Language* 17(4): 376–425.

McDowell, J. 1982. Criteria, defeasibility and knowledge. *Proceedings of the British Academy*.

McDowell, J. 1986. Singular thought and the extent of inner space. In P. Pettit and J. McDowell (eds.), *Subject, Thought and Context*. Oxford: Clarendon Press.

Merleau-Ponty, M. 1942. *La Structure de Comportement*. A. Fisher (trans.). Paris: Presses Universitaires de France.

Moore, G. E. 1910. Sense-data. In T. Baldwin (ed.), *Selected Writings*. London: Routledge (1993).

Moore, G. E. 1922. The refutation of idealism. In *Philosophical Studies*. London: Routledge and Kegan Paul.

O'Shaughnessy, B. 1980. *The Will*, 2 vols. Cambridge: Cambridge University Press.

Peacocke, C. A. B. 1983. *Sense and Content*. Oxford: Clarendon Press.

Peacocke, C. A. B. 1992. *A Study of Concepts*. Cambridge, MA: MIT Press.

Peacocke, C. A. B. 1993. Externalist explanation. *Proceedings of the Aristotelian Society* 93: 203–230.

Price, H. H. 1932. *Perception*. London: Methuen.

Prichard, H. A. 1950. *Knowledge and Perception*. Oxford: Clarendon Press.

Robinson, H. 1985. The general form of the argument for Berkeleian idealism. In J. Foster and H. Robinson (eds.), *Essays on Berkeley: A Tercentennial Celebration*. Oxford: Clarendon Press.

Robinson, H. 1994. *Perception*. London: Routledge.

Russell, B. 1912. *The Problems of Philosophy*, 9th edn. Oxford: Oxford University Press.

Searle, J. 1983. *Intentionality*. Cambridge: Cambridge University Press.

Siegel, S. 2004. Indiscriminability and the phenomenal. *Philosophical Studies* 120: 90–112.

Snowdon, P. F. 1980–1981. Perception, vision and causation. *Proceedings of the Aristotelian Society* 81: 175–192.

Sturgeon, S. 1998. Visual experience. *Proceedings of the Aristotelian Society* 98: 179–200.

Sturgeon, S. 2000. *Matters of Mind: Consciousness, Reason and Nature*. New York: Routledge.

Tye, M. 1995. *Ten Problems of Consciousness*. Cambridge, MA: MIT Press.

Valberg, J. J. 1992. *The Puzzle of Experience*. Oxford: Clarendon Press.

Williamson, T. 1990. *Identity and Discrimination*. Oxford: Basil Blackwell.

Williamson, T. 1995. Is knowing a state of mind? *Mind* 104(415): 533–565.

Williamson, T. 2000. *Knowledge and Its Limits*. New York: Oxford University Press.

Yablo, S. 1992. Mental causation. *Philosophical Review* 101(2): 245–280.

Yablo, S. 1997. Wide causation. In J. Tomberlin (ed.), *Philosophical Perspectives* 11, *Mind, Causation, and World*. Boston: Blackwell.

# Bibliography

## A  Papers on Disjunctivism[†]

Blackburn, S. 2005. Paradise regained. *Proceedings of the Aristotelian Society Supp. Vol.* 79: 1–14.

Brewer, B. 2008. How to account for illusion. In *Disjunctivism: Perception, Action, Knowledge*, ed. A. Haddock and F. Macpherson. Oxford: Oxford University Press.

Burge, T. 2005. Disjunctivism and perceptual psychology. *Philosophical Topics* 33: 1–78.

Byrne, A., and H. Logue. 2008. Either/Or. In *Disjunctivism: Perception, Action, Knowledge*, ed. A. Haddock and F. Macpherson. Oxford: Oxford University Press.

Child, W. 1992. Vision and experience: The causal theory and the disjunctive conception. *Philosophical Quarterly* 42: 297–316.

Coates, P. 1998. Perception and metaphysical scepticism. *Proceedings of the Aristotelian Society Supp. Vol.* 72: 1–28.

Comesaña, J. 2005. Justified versus warranted perceptual belief: A case against disjunctivism. *Philosophy and Phenomenological Research* 71: 367–383.

Conee, E. Forthcoming. Disjunctivism and anti-skepticism. *Philosophical Issues*.

Crane, T. 2006. Is there a perceptual relation? In *Perceptual Experience*, ed. T. Gendler and J. Hawthorne. Oxford: Oxford University Press.

Dancy, J. 1995. Arguments from illusion. *Philosophical Quarterly* 45: 421–438.

Fish, W. 2005. Disjunctivism and non-disjunctivism: Making sense of the debate. *Proceedings of the Aristotelian Society* 105: 119–127.

Fish, W. 2008. Disjunctivism, indistinguishability, and the nature of hallucination. In *Disjunctivism: Perception, Action, Knowledge*, ed. A. Haddock and F. Macpherson. Oxford: Oxford University Press.

[†] Including epistemological disjunctivism. See the editors' introduction, xiv–xvi.

Glendinning, S. 1998. Perception and hallucination: A new approach to the disjunctive conception of experience. *Journal of the British Society for Phenomenology* 29: 314–319.

Glendinning, S., and M. De Gaynesford. 1998. John McDowell on experience: Open to the sceptic? *Metaphilosophy* 29: 20–34.

Haddock, A., and F. Macpherson. 2008. Introduction: Varieties of disjunctivism. In *Disjunctivism: Perception, Action, Knowledge*, ed. A. Haddock and F. Macpherson. Oxford: Oxford University Press.

Hawthorne, J. P., and K. Kovakovich. 2006. Disjunctivism. *Proceedings of the Aristotelian Society Supp. Vol.* 80: 145–183.

Hilbert, D. 2004. Hallucination, sense-data, and direct realism. *Philosophical Studies* 120: 185–191.

Hinckfuss, I. C. 1970. J. M. Hinton on visual experiences. *Mind* 79: 278–280.

Hinton, J. M. 1967a. Experiences. *Philosophical Quarterly* 17: 1–13.

Hinton, J. M. 1967b. Illusions and identity. *Analysis* 27: 65–76.

Hinton, J. M. 1967c. Visual experiences. *Mind* 76: 217–227.

Hinton, J. M. 1973a. *Experiences: An Inquiry into Some Ambiguities.* Oxford: Oxford University Press.

Hinton, J. M. 1973b. Visual experiences: A reply to I. C. Hinckfuss. *Mind* 82: 278–279.

Hinton, J. M. 1980. Phenomenological specimenism. *Analysis* 40: 37–41.

Hinton, J. M. 1996. Sense-experiences revisited. *Philosophical Investigations* 19: 211–236.

Johnston, M. 2004. The obscure object of hallucination. *Philosophical Studies* 120: 113–183.

Langsam, H. 1997. The theory of appearing defended. *Philosophical Studies* 120: 33–59.

Locke, D. 1975. Review of J. M. Hinton's *Experiences. Mind* 84: 466–468.

Lowe, E. J. 2008. Against disjunctivism. In *Disjunctivism: Perception, Action, Knowledge*, ed. A. Haddock and F. Macpherson. Oxford: Oxford University Press.

Macarthur, D. 2003. McDowell, scepticism, and the "veil of perception." *Australasian Journal of Philosophy* 81: 175–190.

Martin, M. G. F. 1997. The reality of appearances. In *Thought and Ontology*, ed. M. Sainsbury. Milan: FrancoAngeli.

Martin, M. G. F. 2002. The transparency of experience. *Mind and Language* 17: 376–425.

Martin, M. G. F. 2004. The limits of self-awareness. *Philosophical Studies* 120: 37–89.

Martin, M. G. F. 2006. On being alienated. In *Perceptual Experience*, ed. T. Gendler and J. Hawthorne. Oxford: Oxford University Press.

McDowell, J. 1982. Criteria, defeasibility, and knowledge. *Proceedings of the British Academy* 68: 455–479.

McDowell, J. 1986. Singular thought and the extent of inner space. In *Subject, Thought, and Context*, ed. J. McDowell and P. Pettit. Oxford: Oxford University Press.

McDowell, J. 1994. The content of perceptual experience. *Philosophical Quarterly* 44: 190–205.

McDowell, J. 1995. Knowledge and the internal. *Philosophy and Phenomenological Research* 55: 877–893.

McDowell, J. 1998. Having the world in view. *Journal of Philosophy* 95: 431–491.

McDowell, J. 2002. Knowledge and the internal revisited. *Philosophy and Phenomenological Research* 64: 22–30.

McDowell, J. 2008. The disjunctive conception of experience as material for a transcendental argument. In *Disjunctivism: Perception, Action, Knowledge*, ed. A. Haddock and F. Macpherson. Oxford: Oxford University Press.

Millar, A. 1996. The idea of experience. *Proceedings of the Aristotelian Society* 97: 75–90.

Millar, A. 2000. The scope of perceptual knowledge. *Philosophy* 75: 73–88.

Millar, A. 2005. Travis' sense of occasion. *Philosophical Quarterly* 55: 337–342.

Millar, A. 2007. What the disjunctivist is right about. *Philosophy and Phenomenological Research* 74: 176–198.

Millar, A. 2008. Perceptual-recognitional abilities and perceptual knowledge. In *Disjunctivism: Perception, Action, Knowledge*, ed. A. Haddock and F. Macpherson. Oxford: Oxford University Press.

Neta, R. 2008. In defense of disjunctivism. In *Disjunctivism: Perception, Action, Knowledge*, ed. A. Haddock and F. Macpherson. Oxford: Oxford University Press.

Neta, R., and D. Pritchard. Forthcoming. McDowell and the new evil genius. *Philosophy and Phenomenological Research*.

Noordhof, P. 2002. Imagining objects and imagining experiences. *Mind and Language* 17: 426–455.

Pritchard, D. 2003. McDowell on reasons, externalism, and scepticism. *European Journal of Philosophy* 11: 273–294.

Pritchard, D. 2008. McDowellian neo-Mooreanism. In *Disjunctivism: Perception, Action, Knowledge*, ed. A. Haddock and F. Macpherson. Oxford: Oxford University Press.

Robinson, H. 1990. The objects of perceptual experience. *Proceedings of the Aristotelian Society Supp. Vol.* 64: 151–166.

Robinson, H. 2005. Reply to Nathan: How to reconstruct the causal argument. *Acta Analytica* 20: 7–10.

Schantz, R. 2005. Direct realism, disjunctivism, and the common sensory content. *Schriftenreihe-Wittgenstein Gesellschaft* 34: 321.

Schwartz, R. 2004. To Austin or not to Austin, that's the disjunction. *Philosophical Studies* 120: 255–263.

Sedivy, S. 2008. Starting afresh disjunctively: Perceptual engagement with the world. In *Disjunctivism: Perception, Action, Knowledge*, ed. A. Haddock and F. Macpherson. Oxford: Oxford University Press.

Siegel, S. 2004. Indiscriminability and the phenomenal. *Philosophical Studies* 120: 91–112.

Siegel, S. 2008. The epistemic conception of hallucination. In *Disjunctivism: Perception, Action, Knowledge*, ed. A. Haddock and F. Macpherson. Oxford: Oxford University Press.

Smith, A. D. 2008. Disjunctivism and discriminability. In *Disjunctivism: Perception, Action, Knowledge*, ed. A. Haddock and F. Macpherson. Oxford: Oxford University Press.

Smith, P. 1991. On "The objects of perceptual experience." *Proceedings of the Aristotelian Society* 91: 191–196.

Snowdon, P. F. 1980–81. Perception, vision, and causation. *Proceedings of the Aristotelian Society* 81: 175–192.

Snowdon, P. F. 1990. The objects of perceptual experience. *Proceedings of the Aristotelian Society Supp. Vol.* 64: 121–150.

Snowdon, P. F. 2005. The formulation of disjunctivism: A response to Fish. *Proceedings of the Aristotelian Society* 105: 129–141.

Snowdon, P. F. 2008. Hinton and the origins of disjunctivism. In *Disjunctivism: Perception, Action, Knowledge*, ed. A. Haddock and F. Macpherson. Oxford: Oxford University Press.

Soteriou, M. 2005. The subjective view of experience and its objective commitments. *Proceedings of the Aristotelian Society* 105: 177–190.

Sturgeon, S. 2006. Reflective disjunctivism. *Proceedings of the Aristotelian Society Supp. Vol.* 80: 185–216.

Sturgeon, S. 2008. Disjunctivism about visual experience. In *Disjunctivism: Perception, Action, Knowledge*, ed. A. Haddock and F. Macpherson. Oxford: Oxford University Press.

Thau, M. 2004. What is disjunctivism? *Philosophical Studies* 120: 193–253.

Travis, C. 2005a. A sense of occasion. *Philosophical Quarterly* 55: 286–314.

Travis, C. 2005b. Frege, father of disjunctivism. *Philosophical Topics* 33: 307–334.

Van Cleve, J. 2006. Touch, sound, and things without the mind. *Metaphilosophy* 37: 162–182.

Wright, C. 2002. (Anti)-sceptics simple and subtle: G. E. Moore and John McDowell. *Philosophy and Phenomenological Research* 65: 330–348.

Wright, C. 2008. Comment on John McDowell's "The disjunctive conception of experience as material for a transcendental argument." In *Disjunctivism: Perception, Action, Knowledge*, ed. A. Haddock and F. Macpherson. Oxford: Oxford University Press.

**B   Books and Book Sections on Disjunctivism**

Brewer, B. 1999. *Perception and Reason*. Oxford: Oxford University Press. Pages 227–236.

Campbell, J. 2002. *Reference and Consciousness*. Oxford: Oxford University Press. Chapter 6.

Child, W. 1994. *Causality, Interpretation, and the Mind*. Oxford: Oxford University Press. Chapter 5.

Fish, W. Forthcoming. *Perception, Hallucination, and Illusion*. Oxford: Oxford University Press.

Foster, J. 2000. *The Nature of Perception*. Oxford: Oxford University Press. Part Two.

Haddock, A., and F. Macpherson (eds.) 2008. *Disjunctivism: Perception, Action, Knowledge*. Oxford: Oxford University Press.

McDowell, J. 1996. *Mind and World*. Cambridge, Mass.: Harvard University Press.

Putnam, H. 1999. *The Threefold Cord: Mind, Body, and World*. New York: Columbia University Press. Pages 128–133, 151–154.

Robinson, H. 1994. *Perception*. London: Routledge. Chapter 6.

Smith, A. D. 2002. *The Problem of Perception*. Cambridge, Mass.: Harvard University Press. Pages 197–208, 210–211.

Sturgeon, S. 2000. *Matters of Mind: Consciousness, Reason, and Nature*. London: Routledge. Pages 10–21.

Valberg, J. J. 1992. *The Puzzle of Experience*. Oxford: Oxford University Press. Pages 98–100.

Williamson, T. 2000. *Knowledge and Its Limits*. Oxford: Oxford University Press. Pages 44–48.

**C   Some Background Work on Indiscriminability**

Farkas, K. 2006. Indiscriminability and the sameness of appearance. *Proceedings of the Aristotelian Society* 106: 207–227.

Graff, D. 2001. Phenomenal continua and the sorites. *Mind* 110: 905–935.

Hellie, B. 2005. Noise and perceptual indiscriminability. *Mind* 114: 481–508.

Raffman, D. 2000. Is perceptual indiscriminability nontransitive? *Philosophical Topics* 28: 153–175.

Williamson, T. 1990. *Identity and Discrimination*. Oxford: Blackwell.

**D   Disjunctivism in the Philosophy of Action**

Dancy, J. 2000. *Practical Reality*. Oxford: Oxford University Press. Pages 138–145.

Dancy, J. 2008. On how to act—disjunctively. In *Disjunctivism: Perception, Action, Knowledge*, ed. A. Haddock and F. Macpherson. Oxford: Oxford University Press.

Dancy, J. Forthcoming. Reasons and rationality. In *Spheres of Reason*, ed. J. Skorupski, S. Robertson and J. Timmerman. Oxford: Oxford University Press.

Hornsby, J. 1997. *Simple Mindedness: Essays in Defense of Naive Naturalism in the Philosophy of Mind*. Cambridge, Mass.: Harvard University Press. Pages 102–110.

Hornsby, J. 2008. A disjunctivist conception of acting for reasons. In *Disjunctivism: Perception, Action, Knowledge*, ed. A. Haddock and F. Macpherson. Oxford: Oxford University Press.

Ruben, D. 2008. Disjunctive theories of perception and action. In *Disjunctivism: Perception, Action, Knowledge*, ed. A. Haddock and F. Macpherson. Oxford: Oxford University Press.

Stout, R. 2004. Internalising practical reason. *Proceedings of the Aristotelian Society* 104: 229–243.

## E   Selection of Recent Work Relevant to Disjunctivism

Alston, W. P. 1999. Back to the theory of appearing. *Philosophical Perspectives* 13: 181–203.

Brewer, B. 2006. Perception and content. *European Journal of Philosophy* 14: 165–181.

Chalmers, D. 2006. Perception and the fall from Eden. In *Perceptual Experience*, ed. T. Gendler and J. Hawthorne. Oxford: Oxford University Press.

Crane, T. 2006. The problem of perception. In *Stanford Encylopedia of Philosophy*, ed. E. Zalta, http://plato.stanford.edu/archives/win2006/entries/perception-problem.

Djukic, G., and V. Popescu. 2003. A critique of Langsam's "The theory of appearing defended." *Philosophical Studies* 112: 69–91.

García-Carpintero, M. 2001. Sense data: The sensible approach. *Grazer Philosophische Studien* 62: 17–63.

Gendler, T., and J. Hawthorne. Introduction: Perceptual experience. In *Perceptual Experience*, ed. T. Gendler and J. Hawthorne. Oxford: Oxford University Press.

Gupta, A. 2006a. Experience and knowledge. In *Perceptual Experience*, ed. T. Gendler and J. Hawthorne. Oxford: Oxford University Press.

Gupta, A. 2006b. *Empiricism and Experience*. Oxford: Oxford University Press.

Hellie, B. 2006. Beyond phenomenal naiveté. *Philosophers' Imprint* 6, http://www .philosophersimprint.org/006002.

Hellie, B. 2007. Factive phenomenal characters. *Philosophical Perspectives* 21: 259–306.

Johnston, M. 2006. Better than mere knowledge? The function of sensory awareness. In *Perceptual Experience*, ed. T. Gendler and J. Hawthorne. Oxford: Oxford University Press.

Martin, M. G. F. 2002. Particular thoughts and singular thought. In *Logic, Thought, and Language*, ed. A. O'Hear. Cambridge: Cambridge University Press.

Noë, A. 2005. Real presence. *Philosophical Topics* 33: 235–264.

Noë, A. 2006. Experience without the head. In *Perceptual Experience*, ed. T. Gendler and J. Hawthorne. Oxford: Oxford University Press.

Pautz, A. 2007. Intentionalism and perceptual presence. *Philosophical Perspectives* 21: 495–541.

Snowdon, P. F. 2005. Some reflections on an argument from hallucination. *Philosophical Topics* 33: 285–305.

Soteriou, M. 2000. The particularity of visual perception. *European Journal of Philosophy* 8: 173–189.

Travis, C. 2004. The silence of the senses. *Mind* 113: 57–94.

Tye, M. 2007. Intentionalism and the argument from no common content. *Philosophical Perspectives* 21: 589–613.

Warren, W. H. 2005. Direct perception: The view from here. *Philosophical Topics* 33: 335–361.

# Contributors

**Alex Byrne**   Massachusetts Institute of Technology

**Jonathan Dancy**   University of Reading and the University of Texas at Austin

**J. M. Hinton**[†]   Oxford University

**Mark Johnston**   Princeton University

**Harold Langsam**   University of Virginia

**Heather Logue**   Massachusetts Institute of Technology

**M. G. F. Martin**   University College London

**John McDowell**   University of Pittsburgh

**Alan Millar**   University of Stirling

**Howard Robinson**   Central European University

**A. D. Smith**   University of Warwick

**Paul Snowdon**   University College London

[†] Deceased

# Index

Action at a distance, 155, 194, 210, 286–287

Act/object conception of perceptual experience, 118, 219–222, 244–245, 247–249, 257, 260

Adverbialism. *See* Adverbial theory

Adverbial theory, 117–118, 208, 221–222, 265n23

Afterimages, 44–46, 179n19, 231–232, 260

Albritton, Rogers, 86n5

Alston, William, xvii, xxvn18, 265n20, 313n3

Anscombe, G. E. M., 111n7, 233, 247–249, 312n1, 313n5, 314n15

Anti-realism about perceptual experience, 159–161

Argument from hallucination. *See* Hallucination, argument from

Argument from illusion. *See* Illusion, argument from

Argument from science, 28–30. *See also* Causal argument; "Same cause, same effect" principle

Armstrong, David, 111n7, 202n13, 217, 266n27

Austin, J. L., xxvn30, 26, 92, 102–104, 128, 202n10, 261n1

Ayer, A. J., 128, 202n8, 202n13

Backward causation, 198–199, 258

Baker, Gordon, 85n1, 87n17

Barnes, W. H. F., xxivn4, xxivn11, xxvin29

Berkeley, George, 155

Biro, John, 268n39

Bogen, James, 85n3

Bonjour, Laurence, 87n18

Brain in a vat, 173, 253

Broad, C. D., 163n1, 169–170, 313n8

Burge, Tyler, 111n7, 113n30, 254

Butchvarov, Panyot, 255

Byrne, Alex, x–xi, xxiiin2, xxvin25, xxvin27, xxvin28, xxvin30, xxviin37

Campbell, John, xxivn8, xxvin33

Cartwright, Richard, 264n12

Causal argument, xxi–xxiii, 153, 168–169, 176, 188–193, 209–210, 284–287, 300. *See also* Argument from science; "Same cause, same effect" principle

Causal determinism, 287

Causal pre-emption, 299–300

Causal theory of perception, xiv–xv, 33, 97, 117–118, 141, 184. *See also* Causal theory of vision

Causal theory of vision, 33–42, 46–47, 50–53, 56, 59–66. *See also* Causal theory of perception

Child, William, 111n1, 139, 148n3, 148n5, 180n26, 202n10

Chisholm, Roderick, xxvin29, 201n6, 202n7, 315n22

Clarke, Thompson, 242
Common element, ix, 22–25, 59–60, 92–93, 95–98, 118, 142, 157, 167, 257, 279. *See also* Common factor
Common factor, xv, 80–85, 140, 167, 214, 278. *See also* Common element
Conceptual analysis, 49–50, 60, 74n13, 178n8
Conjunctive analysis of perceiving/ seeing, 121, 130, 208–214, 228–230, 255–258, 278
Conjunctivism. *See* Conjunctive analysis of perceiving/seeing
Conscious character. *See* Phenomenal character
Cook, John W., 86n7
Crane, Tim, vii, xxiiin3, 148n2
Criteria, 75–79, 81, 84, 85n2, 86n4, 86n8, 87n14, 87n17

Dancy, Jonathan, xiii, xiv, xx, xxivn12, xxvin27, 111n12, 112n14, 262n1, 278–279, 284, 301
Davidson, Donald, 47n1, 159
Davies, Martin, 70–72, 101–102, 268n39
Demonstrative judgment. *See* Thought, demonstrative
Demonstrative thought. *See* Thought, demonstrative
Dennett, Daniel, 159
*De re* thought. *See* Thought, singular
Descartes, René, 85, 107
Deutscher, Max, 47n1, 74n11
Direct realism, 171, 175, 177–178, 207–208, 261
Disjunctivism
  about action, xiv, 130, 132–133
  about belief, 96–97, 99, 124–125, 130, 133–134, 301–302
  and the causal theory of perception, xv, xxvn23, 47, 56–57, 97
  characterizations of, ix–xi, 41–43, 55–59, 87n13, 91, 95–96, 130–132, 137–

139, 158, 167–168, 174–175, 186–188, 213–214, 257, 271–272, 277–278, 291, 302
  epistemological, xiv–xvi, 58, 82–84, 141
  and hallucinations, 112n21, 132, 216–219, 222, 255, 278–279, 300–302, 308–309
  and illusions, xi–xii, 132, 160, 278–279, 309
  and intentionality of perceptual experience, 173–174
  about the objects of perceptual experience, xxvin30
Dretske, Fred, 111n2, 111n7, 112n16, 149n14, 156, 202n13, 268n39
Duck-rabbit, 259
Dummett, Michael, 48n4, 87n17

Erlenkamp, Christoph, 263n9
Evans, Gareth, 62, 64, 86n10, 112n18, 315n20
Externalism
  about justification, 125–126, 129
  about mental states/content, 154, 169–171, 253–254, 287

Firth, Roderick, 312n1
Flanagan, Owen, 183
Fodor, Jerry, 112n16
Føllesdal, Dagfinn, 148n8
Foster, John, xxviin38, 111n6, 287–288, 313n2, 314n12, 314n16
Foundationalism, 85n6, 238
Frege, Gottlob, 239
Fregean senses, 237, 239

Geach, P. T., 11
Gendler, Tamar, vii, 314n18
Goldman, Alvin, 47n1, 74n12, 87n16, 202n7
Goodman, Nelson, 58, 106, 108
Goodwin, William, 87n12
Graff, Delia, 306

Grice, H. P., xiv, xxvn23, 33, 35, 47n1,
   47n2, 48n5, 48n7, 52, 65, 74n16,
   148n1, 201n7
Gunther, York, vii

Hacker, P. M. S., 85n1, 85n2, 85n3
Haddock, Adrian, vii, xxvin27
Hallucination
   argument from, 142–143, 153, 155–
      156, 168, 171–178, 185–188, 201,
      207–208, 219, 313n4 (*see also*
      Indiscriminability, arguments from)
   primary/secondary objects of, 223–225,
      232–234, 244–246, 248, 250–255
   veridical, 37–38, 168, 215, 217, 227,
      239, 258, 264n16
Hardin, C. L., 183, 200–201
Harding, Gregory, 183
Harman, Gilbert, 111n7, 246, 267n32,
   312n1, 313n5
Hawthorne, John, vii, xxviin36,
   xxviin37
Highest common factor. *See* Common
   factor
Hinton, J. M., viii–ix, xii, xiv, xvi, xx,
   xxiii, xxiiin2, xxvn23, 41, 58, 74n8,
   87n13, 110n1, 111n9, 137, 156–159,
   161, 167, 169, 179n23, 202n10,
   202n11, 263n8, 271–272, 277, 279
Hirst, R. J., 171
Homunculus fallacy, 103
Hornsby, Jennifer, xxvn22
Horwich, Paul, 268n39
Hume, David, viii, 73n1, 110, 113n35,
   241–242
Hume world, 257–258
Husserl, Edmund, xxivn7, 148n8, 176,
   243
Hyman, John, 171, 184–185, 202n10

Illusion
   argument from, 77, 80, 92, 94, 117–
      134, 160, 172, 177–178, 202n8,

   202n10 (*see also* Indiscriminability,
      arguments from)
Müller-Lyer, 231
waterfall, 233–234, 264n13
Imagery, xvii, 61, 153, 155, 162, 171–
   172, 174, 207, 313n3. *See also*
   Afterimages
Imagination, 7, 59–61, 176, 273, 282
Impossible staircase, 308
Indiscernibility. *See* Indiscriminability
Indiscriminability
   arguments from, xix–xxi, 10, 30, 80,
      82, 91–93, 98–105, 108–110, 117–
      125, 134–135, 138–139, 155–156,
      161, 185–190, 207, 215–216 (*see also*
      Illusion, argument from; Hallucina-
      tion, argument from)
   and the concept of experience, xxi, 32,
      96–97, 272, 280–284, 295, 298, 303–
      305, 310–311
   explications of, xx–xxi, 32, 133, 186,
      283
   and the nature of nonveridical
      experience, xiii, 98, 112n21, 132, 284,
      297–301, 309
   non-transitivity of, 92, 253, 305–307
Indistinguishability. *See* Indiscriminability
Infallibilism about the mental, 104–105,
   141, 283, 312
Inner experience, xxvn16, xxvn23, 23–
   24, 51–52, 54–57, 105, 131, 179n23,
   289, 302. *See also* Inner states
Inner states, 75–77, 81, 83–84, 86n4,
   86n9, 168. *See also* Inner experience
Intensional contexts, 245–247
Intensional identity, 232–233, 252, 255
Intentionalism. *See* Intentional theory
Intentional theory, x, 94–95, 172–173,
   208, 262n2, 273, 276
Internalism, 83, 88n19, 88n20, 125–
   127, 129
Internal relations, 197–198

Jackson, Frank, 92, 111n2, 111n6, 112n22, 118, 183–184, 200–201, 201n5, 222, 235, 313n2, 315n22
James, William, 242
Johnston, Mark, vii, x–xi, xix–xxiii, xxivn12, xxvn19, xxvn30, 308

Kenny, Anthony, 85n1, 85n3
Kim, Jaegwon, 48n4, 268n39
Kovakovich, Karson, xxviin36, xxviin37
Kripke, Saul, 58, 65, 172, 268n38

Laertius, Diogenes, 179n18
Langsam, Harold, xii–xiii, xvii, xx, xxii–xxiii, xxvin31, 263n6, 313n4
Lewis, David, 197, 202n15, 255, 262n3, 266n27
Loar, Brian, 183
Locke, Don, 155–156
Logical space of reasons, 84
Logue, Heather, x–xi, xxiiin2, xxvin25, xxvin27, xxvin28, xxvin30, xxviin37
Lycan, W. G., 255

Mackie, J. L., 109
Macpherson, Fiona, vii, xxvin27
Malebranche, Nicolas, 163n1, 212
Manifest image, 181
Martin, C. B., 47n1, 74n11
Martin, M. G. F., ix–x, xii–xiii, xvi–xxi, xxiii, xxviin36, 113n29, 313n6, 313n7
McCulloch, Gregory, 149n13, 179n21
McDowell, John, xiv–xvi, 57–58, 95, 111n1, 111n7, 112n18, 112n25, 113n35, 124–125, 130, 134, 135n9, 138–144, 149n13, 164n6, 167, 169, 173–175, 180n24, 202n10, 202n11, 261n1, 263n8, 267n29, 271–272, 277, 301, 315n20
McGinn, Colin, 67, 101–102, 148n1, 182, 201n5
Meinong, Alexis, 246, 248

Memory, 59–61, 69–70
Mentalism, 235, 242, 260–261. *See also* Phenomenalism
Merleau-Ponty, Maurice, 276
Mill, J. S., 314n18
Millar, Alan, x, xix–xx, xxiii, xxvin27, 111n9, 148n1, 148n2, 148n9, 149n11, 149n14, 263n9
Moore, G. E., 201n6, 202n8, 242, 263n12, 313n2, 313n8
Moya, Carlos J., 120, 135n2

Nagel, Thomas, 182, 266n25
Naive realism
arguments against, 94–95, 98, 177, 284–289
arguments for, 108, 199–200, 276, 281–283, 295–296, 211–312
characterizations of, xvii–xviii, 93–94, 97–98, 161–163, 199, 272–273, 295
and disjunctivism, xviii–xix, 91, 95, 273–276
and knowledge of experience, 107–110
Nathan, Nicholas, 314n14
Necker cube, 259
Neta, Ram, xxvin27
Nominalism about properties, 235, 266n27
Non-conceptual content, 238, 262n2
Nozick, Robert, 88n19, 88n20

Objects
intentional, 5, 233, 244–249, 260, 275
non-existent, 244–255, 260
non-normal, xxii, 168–169, 171, 174–178 (*see also* Sense-datum theory)
O'Faolain, Sean, 15
O'Shaughnessy, Brian, 119–121, 124, 171–172, 313n2, 314n12

Pain, 145–147, 235
Parsons, Terence, 246, 248–249

Peacocke, Christopher, 33, 112n16,
113n29, 148n1, 148n2, 149n12,
267n29, 268n40, 294, 312n1, 313n2
Pears, David, 33, 53, 56, 148n1
Penfield, Wilder, 163n2
Perception
direct vs. indirect, 142, 208–214, 228–
229, 242–243, 256
-illusion disjunctions, xii, xvi, xxivn16,
20–24, 27, 31–32, 111n9, 271, 277
Perkins, Moreland, 111n6
Phenomenal character, 93–94, 97–103,
174, 182–184, 236, 266n25, 290, 309–
311
Phenomenal consciousness. See
Phenomenal character
Phenomenal continua, 306
Phenomenalism, 164n13, 164n14, 216.
See also Mentalism
Phenomenal properties. See Phenomenal
character
Phenomenological argument, 82, 92. See
also Indiscriminability, arguments
from
Phenomenology of experience. See
Phenomenal character
Phosphenes, 3, 9–10, 22, 173, 190
Pitcher, George, 156–157, 159, 202n8,
202n13
"Plainly" seeing, xxivn14, 19, 22, 32n3,
58
Plato, viii
Price, H. H., 92, 103, 184, 201n7, 202n8,
202n10, 203n14, 234, 313n8
Pritchard, Duncan, xxvin27
Projectivism about sensory qualities,
260–261
Putnam, Hilary, 65, 172, 235, 254,
261n1

Qualia, 106, 171, 201n2, 235–236,
261, 262n2. See also Phenomenal
character

Qualitative character of experience. See
Phenomenal character
Quine, W. V. O., 34

Recognitional capacities, 100, 307–308
Reid, Thomas, viii
Relational properties, 236–237
Reliabilism, 109, 125–126, 238
Representationalism. See Intentional
theory
Representative realism, 117–118, 155.
See also Sense-datum theory
Richardson, John T. E., 85n1
Robinson, Howard, viii, x, xiii, xix, xxiii,
57, 111n6, 143–145, 178n6, 183, 189,
202n11, 262n3, 263n6, 285, 287–288,
313n2
Rorty, Richard, 87n11
Russell, Bertrand, 168, 313n2, 313n8
Ryle, Gilbert, 18, 103

"Same cause, same effect" principle,
xxii–xxiii, 29, 156–158, 168–171, 173,
176, 190–194, 228–229, 263n6, 274,
287–288. See also Causal argument;
Argument from science
Scenario content, 149n12
Scientific image, 181
Searle, John, 111n7, 148n1, 261n1,
267n30, 267n32, 312n1
"Seeing as" phenomena, 227–228, 243–
244, 259–260
Seeming, epistemic vs. phenomenal, 92,
111n2, 296
Selective theory, xxvin30, 103, 234, 261
Sellars, Wilfrid, 84, 181
Sensational properties, 149n12, 313n2.
See also Qualia
Sense-datum fallacy, 103
Sense-datum theory
arguments against, viii–ix, 9–11, 276
arguments for, xxiii, 142–143, 153,
155, 163

Sense-datum theory (cont.)
  characterizations of, viii, 27, 94, 103,
    183, 208, 216, 240, 275–276
  and the "same cause, same effect"
    principle, 157
  and the theory of appearing, 188
Sensory character. *See* Phenomenal
  character
Siegel, Susanna, xxvin28, xxviin37,
  265n20, 315n27
Skepticism
  about the external world, xv, 85,
    87n11, 107, 109–110
  about other minds, xv, 77–79, 85
Smith, A. D., xxii, xxivn7
Smith, Peter, 146
Snowdon, Paul, ix, xi–xii, xiv–xv,
  xxivn13, xxivn14, xxvin27, 87n13,
  97, 110n1, 135n9, 138–139, 141–146,
  149n10, 164n6, 169, 178n4, 178n8,
  180n24, 184, 202n8, 202n10, 202n11,
  263n8, 271–272, 277
Stoics, 172
Strawson, P. F., 33, 35, 47n2, 48n5,
  48n7, 63–66, 69, 86n8, 88n21,
  112n18, 148n1, 169, 183
Stroud, Barry, 109
Sturgeon, Scott, xxviin36, xxviin37,
  314n17
Subjective character. *See* Phenomenal
  character
Subjectivism, 94–95, 99, 103, 108, 273.
  *See also* Sense-datum theory
Suchting, W. A., 202n13
Supersaturated red, 222, 227, 232, 235–
  236, 308
Swampman, 72

Taine, Hippolyte Aldophe, 178n5
Taylor, Charles, 88n25
Teichmann, Jenny, 48n4
Thau, Michael, xxvin27, xxvin30,
  263n6

Theory of appearing, xvii, 184–201,
  313n3
Thought
  demonstrative, 43–46, 67–70, 100, 144,
    212–213, 219–220, 227, 229, 294
  *de re* (*See* Thought, singular)
  knowledge of, 106–108
  phenomenal character of, 182–183,
    231
  singular, 221–222, 287, 294
Time-gap argument, 194–198, 201
Transparency of experience, 7, 62, 273
Travis, Charles, 148n3
Tye, Michael, 111n7, 202n7, 312n1

Valberg, J. J., viii, 143–145, 276, 314n12
van Inwagen, Peter, 268n38
Veil of ideas. *See* Veil of perception
Veil of perception, 87n11, 109–110, 276

White, A. R., 48n4
Wiggins, David, 47n2, 48n7, 135n8
Williams, Bernard, 135n5, 135n8
Williamson, Timothy, xxivn5, xxviin35,
  96–98, 106, 108, 112n15, 294, 301–
  302, 306, 314n11, 315n24
Wittgenstein, Ludwig, xv, 75–79, 81,
  85n2, 86n6, 86n7, 86n8, 88n21
Wright, Crispin, xxvin27, 85n3, 86n4,
  87n14, 87n17

Yablo, Stephen, 314n19

Zalta, Edward, 246, 248–249